Drama, Oratory and Thucydides in Fifth-Century Athens

This study centres on the rhetoric of the Athenian empire, Thucydides' account of the Peloponnesian War and the notable discrepancies between his assessment of Athens and that found in tragedy, funeral orations and public art.

Mills explores the contradiction between Athenian actions and their self-representation, arguing that Thucydides' highly critical, cynical approach to the Athenian empire does not reflect how the average Athenian saw his city's power. The popular education of the Athenians, as presented to them in funeral speeches, drama and public art told a very different story from that presented by Thucydides' history, and it was far more palatable to ordinary Athenians since it offered them a highly flattering portrayal of their city and, by extension, each individual who made up that city.

Drama, Oratory and Thucydides in Fifth-Century Athens: Teaching Imperial Lessons offers a fascinating insight into Athenian self-representation and will be of interest to anyone working on classical Athens, the Greek polis and classical historiography.

Sophie Mills is Professor of Classics at the University of North Carolina at Asheville, USA.

Routledge Monographs in Classical Studies

Titles include:

Underworld Gods in Ancient Greek Religion
Ellie Mackin Roberts

Bride of Hades to Bride of Christ
The Virgin and the Otherworldly Bridegroom in Ancient Greece and Early Christian Rome
Abbe Walker

Intertextuality in Seneca's Philosophical Writings
Edited by Myrto Garani, Andreas Michalopoulos, Sophia Papaioannou

Drama, Oratory and Thucydides in Fifth-Century Athens
Teaching Imperial Lessons
Sophie Mills

The Poetics in its Aristotelian Context
Edited by Pierre Destrée, Malcolm Heath and Dana L. Munteanu

Text and Intertext in Greek Epic and Drama
Essays in Honor of Margalit Finkelberg
Edited by Jonathan J. Price and Rachel Zelnick-Abramovitz

Frankness, Greek Culture, and the Roman Empire
Dana Fields

Robert E. Sherwood and the Classical Tradition
The Muses in America
Robert J. Rabel

For more information on this series, visit: https://www.routledge.com/classical studies/series/RMCS

Drama, Oratory and Thucydides in Fifth-Century Athens

Teaching Imperial Lessons

Sophie Mills

Routledge
Taylor & Francis Group
LONDON AND NEW YORK

First published 2020
by Routledge
4 Park Square, Milton Park, Abingdon, Oxon OX14 4RN

and by Routledge
605 Third Avenue, New York, NY 10017

First issued in paperback 2022

Routledge is an imprint of the Taylor & Francis Group, an informa business

© 2020 Sophie Mills

The right of Sophie Mills to be identified as author of this work has been asserted by her in accordance with sections 77 and 78 of the Copyright, Designs and Patents Act 1988.

All rights reserved. No part of this book may be reprinted or reproduced or utilised in any form or by any electronic, mechanical, or other means, now known or hereafter invented, including photocopying and recording, or in any information storage or retrieval system, without permission in writing from the publishers.

Trademark notice: Product or corporate names may be trademarks or registered trademarks, and are used only for identification and explanation without intent to infringe.

Publisher's Note
The publisher has gone to great lengths to ensure the quality of this reprint but points out that some imperfections in the original copies may be apparent.

British Library Cataloguing-in-Publication Data
A catalogue record for this book is available from the British Library

Library of Congress Cataloging-in-Publication Data
Names: Mills, Sophie, author.
Title: Drama, oratory and Thucydides in fifth-century athens : teaching imperial lessons / Sophie Mills.
Other titles: Routledge monographs in classical studies.
Description: New York : Routledge, 2020. | Series: Routledge monographs in classical studies | Includes bibliographical references and index.
Identifiers: LCCN 2019055054 | ISBN 9780815365921 (hardback) | ISBN 9780351260322 (ebook)
Subjects: LCSH: Thucydides—Criticism and interpretation. | Oratory, Ancient. | Greek drama—History and criticism.
Classification: LCC PA4461 .M47 2020 | DDC 938/.505—dc23
LC record available at https://lccn.loc.gov/2019055054

ISBN 13: 978-1-03-247473-1 (pbk)
ISBN 13: 978-0-8153-6592-1 (hbk)
ISBN 13: 978-0-351-26032-2 (ebk)

DOI: 10.4324/9780351260322

Typeset in Times New Roman
by Apex CoVantage, LLC

Contents

Acknowledgements vii

1 The Athenian ... empire? 1

1.1 Introduction 1
1.2 Empire and rhetoric 6
1.3 Source problems and Athenian imperial rhetoric 7
1.4 "I would annex the planets if I could" (Cecil Rhodes) 9
1.5 "An empire exempt from all natural causes of decay" (Lord Macaulay) 12
1.6 "Imperious, irrepressible necessities of life" 15
1.7 "We do our humble best to retain by justice what we may have won by the sword" 20
1.8 The seductions of empire 24

2 Tragedy and Athens: Aeschylus and Sophocles 45

2.1 Introduction: Athens in and out of disaster 45
2.2 Aeschylus' Persians 52
2.3 Aeschylus' Eumenides 59
2.4 Sophocles' Oedipus at Colonus 64

3 Euripides, empire and war 81

3.1 Introduction 81
3.2 Heraclidae 83
3.3 Suppliants 88
3.4 Heracles 91
3.5 Peirithous and Theseus 92
3.6 Ion 93
3.7 Erechtheus 95
3.8 Hippolytus 97
3.9 Trojan Women 98

4 Aristophanic *Archē* 107

4.1 Comedy, truth and Athens 107
4.2 Remnants of the ideal 110
4.3 Wasps 111
4.4 Acharnians 113
4.5 Knights 115
4.6 Peace 117
4.7 Birds 118

5 Thucydides: what was really said? 130

5.1 Introduction 130
5.2 Thucydides' methods 131
5.3 Thucydides and mythology 138
5.4 Believing Thucydides 140

6 Thucydides' Athens: Λόγῳ μέν ... Ἔργῳι δέ 147

6.1 Book one 147
6.2 Book two 152
6.3 Book three 155
6.4 Book five 157
6.5 Book six 159
6.6 Book seven 163

Bibliography 178
Index 208

Acknowledgements

Great thanks must go to the University of North Carolina at Asheville for appointing me as NEH Distinguished Professor of Humanities from 2012–2015 and for granting me leave in the spring of 2018, during which much of this book was written. I am also grateful to the Institute of Classical Studies in London and its library for access to its unparalleled collection of sources and two very happy summers spent there, and to Beatrice Diesk, my research assistant in summer 2014. Thanks also to Thomas Harrison, Rosanna Lauriola, Polly Low, Andreas Markantonatos, David Pritchard and Angeliki Tzanetou for professional encouragement of various kinds, and to multiple audience members and readers over the years, some of them anonymous, who have helped me sharpen some of the ideas presented here and simply discard others. On a personal level, I thank my mother, Mrs. Kate Mills, for her unstinting love and support and for helping me find a title, and also my father, Mr. Roger Mills, for all his love and encouragement, and Clare and David Murphy for half a century of care and kindness. Above all, I thank Amy Joy Lanou for everything, always, with my love: λύσω τὴν ἐμαυτῆς ὗν ἐγώ. . . .

1 The Athenian ... empire?

1.1 Introduction

> For where else in the world has a race gone forth and subdued ... a continent ... peopled, not by savage tribes, but by races with traditions and a civilisation older than our own ... subduing them not to the law of the sword, but to the rule of justice, bringing peace and order and good government to nearly one-fifth of the entire human race, and holding them with so mild a restraint that the rulers are the merest handful amongst the ruled, a tiny speck of white foam upon a dark and thunderous ocean?[1]

> Each great metropolitan center that aspired to global dominance has said, and alas done, many of the same things. There is always the appeal to power and national interest in running the affairs of lesser peoples ... there is the horrifically predictable disclaimer that "we" are exceptional, not imperial.[2]

> Our nation is the greatest force for good in history.[3]

But what do any of these stirring quotations have to do with the power of Athens in fifth-century Greece? After all, Athens' sphere of influence was tiny by later standards, lasted considerably less than a century, was governed not by an emperor but by a democracy, and in its relative racial and other homogeneity was very different from the European empires that succeeded it or the Middle Eastern empires that preceded it. Moreover, no universally accepted theoretical definition of empire exists, and the relationship between empire and the broader question of power – harder, softer, or a vaguer, more general influence? – is highly contested.[4] Empires are established and maintained in many different ways,[5] and it may arguably even be inappropriate to use any modern theories of imperialism to analyze ancient society because the types of evidence surviving from the ancient world are so different from those of the modern world.[6] If empire is defined by models based on European domination in the non-European world, through the influential definitions of empire based on Marxist theory, which entwine imperialism with capitalism as part of an economic system, or even through the comparisons between the Roman Empire and the United States that were popular during

George W. Bush's presidency,[7] Athens' imperial power may be indeed be found wanting. Some scholars are reluctant even to use the traditional term "Athenian Empire." Athens is a "hegemony"[8] or "the greater Athenian State,"[9] or the question can be avoided entirely by retaining the Greek word *archē*, through unease at the connotations, either inappropriate or unsavoury, of the term "empire."[10] Many books on modern imperialism consider Rome as ancestor and model for subsequent empires and typically do not even mention Athens in their indices, even when offering a broad definition of empire which would seem to suit Athens in many respects: for example, Colås states, "any single polity that successfully expands from a metropolitan centre across various territories in order to dominate diverse populations can usefully be called an empire,"[11] but Athens, unlike Rome, is entirely absent from his book.

But a different picture emerges when empire is considered not through practical issues of territory and populations ruled, longevity or organization, but as a concept shaping power-relations between stronger and weaker parties, especially when expressed through the narratives that the stronger party uses to explain those power-relations. It is possible to find some intriguing similarities between the rhetorics and ideologies of the Athenian *archē* and European empires, even in the midst of radical differences. To take a deliberately extreme example, the anthropologist Georges Balandier defines "the colonial situation" as

> the domination imposed by a foreign minority, 'racially' and culturally distinct, over a materially weaker autochthonous majority in the name of a dogmatically asserted racial (or ethnic) and cultural superiority. One culture is fast-moving, technologically advanced and economically powerful; the other slow-moving, without technology or an advanced economy. To maintain authority, the colonising society has to use force and pseudo-justifications.[12]

Ionian Athens ruled predominantly Ionian Greeks, making the first part of Balandier's definition entirely inapplicable, but the speed, advancement and economic power of Athens *were* all factors in its dominance, and part of the image through which it emphasized its superiority over other Greeks;[13] and Athens' authority over its subjects was, as this book will argue, maintained by multiple pseudo-justifications. Victor Davis Hanson claims that Athens and the United States are both marked by "military power and idealism about bringing perceived civilisation to others,"[14] while John Ma's Athens is a place of "coercion, centralisation, economic exploitation . . . the awareness of power as spectacle . . . violence,"[15] all attributes that sound decidedly imperial.

Perhaps an empire resembles Justice Potter Stewart's famous definition of pornography: technically undefinable but we know it when we see it, given that, whatever technical definition of imperialism we espouse, we are still generally content to dub the Assyrian, Roman or British periods of domination over others as "empires", in spite of significant differences between them. Theoretical definitions of empire are important in defining general questions but only go so far, and though Athens did not have an empire if certain conventional definitions of empire are applied to its power, I hope to show in this chapter, primarily from texts, but with an eye also to inscriptions, art and architecture, that the *way* the Athenians thought about, talked about and presented Athenian power is profoundly "imperial."

To try to sketch a picture of the relationship between the historical facts of Athens' power in the Aegean and more subjective, even imaginative ideas of how that power might have shaped the attitudes of individual Athenians, I propose to use an unusually expanded range of sources to supplement what is otherwise relatively limited evidence.[16] If the sentiments made by representatives of the Roman, British or other powers typically designated as empires are compared with what is said about Athens and its power during the fifth century, or in later sources which are likely to reflect fifth-century sentiment, and if significant and multiple parallels between them emerge, then these similarities might begin to bring us to a closer understanding of what Richardson[17] dubs "mental wallpaper" at Athens, the kinds of uncontroversially accepted views of Athens which helped to shape, consciously or unconsciously, the beliefs of individual Athenians about what it means to be Athenian, and the possible influences of those beliefs on Athenian policies and actions. By exploring what is said of Athens in this broader context, I hope to begin to approach a psychology of Athenian imperialism.

Not every citizen was marked by the psychology that I will sketch. Indeed, a central difficulty of exploring ordinary Athenians' attitude to Athenian power is that Thucydides is the only historian who focuses fully on it, and he is highly unusual. As a member of the Athenian elite, and even a general, he might have been expected to endorse the claims about Athenian power that, as I will argue, most Athenians accepted. Instead, for reasons discussed later,[18] he largely rejected mainstream Athenian beliefs and wrote instead a searing critique of Athens' attitudes and actions. Given the tendency of scholarship of recent decades, under the influence of post-colonial theory, to interrogate imperialism, ancient or modern, many classicists view traditional portraits of "golden-age" fifth-century Athens still found in many popular accounts with great scepticism, making us open to trusting Thucydides' claims. We do not typically claim that imperialism could ever be justified or beneficial.[19] But while it is morally right to condemn imperialism, and to view any of its justifications very sceptically, it is not necessarily historically right to let modern qualms blind us to the idea that imperialism could be, at the very least a natural state of affairs,[20] and at most extremely attractive,[21] at all levels of society, both economically and psychologically, and it is important to attempt to imagine the implications of this attraction as a framework for considering fifth-century Athens.

"Everyone in a competitive society is, to some degree, the victim of an inferiority complex, which may be expressed in a manly determination to make good, in a desire for perfection . . . in a tiresome aggressiveness."[22] For the Athenian people, so invested in the claim that all citizens were equal in the democracy – although, as even a cursory reading of Aristophanes shows, the inequalities were demonstrable – the idea that they ruled much of the Aegean had an obvious psychological attraction[23] and may also have helped to ease potential social tensions between rich and poor. Whether or not they are fully consciously understood, the psychological benefits of being "at the top of the heap" can strongly influence how even relatively low-status members of imperialist nations see themselves.[24] In the specific case of Athens, the events of the Persian Wars and Athens' relatively rapid rise to dominance in the Aegean were so exciting[25] that they were continually commemorated throughout the fifth century in literature, oratory, tragedy, history and art.[26] Even Pindar (fr. 77; cf. 76), whose fellow Boeotians yielded to the Persians, endorses Athenian achievements against Persia, though otherwise he maintains a telling silence about the empire.[27] Although Thucydides' Athenians sometimes regard commemoration of the Persian Wars as a tiresome cliché,[28] many Athenians growing up through the 470s–430s BCE would have repeatedly heard and seen accounts of the great "founding myth" of Athens' extraordinary courage, self-sacrifice and sheer good fortune in the Persian Wars that created their spectacular power. How could they not, to some degree, have believed in the truth of the stories told to and about them?[29] In 480 BCE, Athens took the lead in a remarkable resistance against an invading army many times greater than the Greek forces, as they never forgot. Immediately afterwards, Athens was essentially offered the Delian League by its allies, an action easily interpretable as an admission of unalterable Athenian superiority, and became the cultural centre of Greece, attracting many foreigners willing to live there in spite of the disadvantages of not being Athenian citizens. All these facts can easily be "spun", with careful selection of evidence, to imply a kind of consent from those ruled by Athens, to promote a belief among the Athenians that their domination was the natural and best order.[30] Authority is conferred on the powerful by the very fact that they control more or less obedient others, so as to make that authority seem entirely natural.[31] Ideological justification has a tendency to begin with an unarguable truth but then "metastasize", sliding into non-truth through a justificatory impulse which, as I argue later, is central to rhetoric dealing with power imbalances between peoples.[32] In an Athenian context, it was unarguable that the Persians did invade Greece and were defeated, with Athens as a major contributor to that defeat, and that Athens was then asked to lead the post-war campaign.[33] But at this point, more subjective questions of merit and self-flattery begin to frame these facts and to shape Athens' self-image and subsequent behaviour.

It is often claimed[34] that the Athenians were unusual among imperialists in putting little emphasis on divine sanction for their power, but Athens' success in the Persian Wars, on which the empire was founded, was often explained theologically, for example by the contrast between Xerxes' *hybris* (Hdt. 7.24.1, 35) and Greek righteousness,[35] and, *pace* Thucydides, many Athenians certainly did consider their city's power pleasing to, and sanctioned by, the gods.[36] In fact, even lurking underneath some of Thucydides' words, one can get some sense of Athenian disbelief and disillusionment when it appears that their luck, or divine favour, is running out. The speeches of Thucydides' Nicias to increasingly demoralized troops in Sicily (e.g. 7.69.2, 77.1–2, 4) reveal something of what it was like when all the comforting beliefs in Athens' superiority through its prime place in the gods' hearts seem to have run out.[37] The confidence that fuelled Athens' conduct during the fifth century, as seen, for example, in the claim that though Athens consistently makes bad decisions, the gods turn its mistakes to the good (Ar. *Nu.* 585–9),[38] now seems to have been based on false beliefs, as a once natural order is incomprehensibly destroyed.[39]

If I am right about any of this, then Thucydides, for all his brilliance, will not be an entirely reliable guide to what most Athenians thought and said about their imperial power. I am not the first to make this suggestion,[40] but it has typically been discussed only in individual articles or in specific comments in commentaries. One aim of this book is to use evidence from Thucydides himself, evidence contemporary with him, some later evidence likely to reflect fifth-century opinion, and some comparative material to try to imagine not Thucydides' cynical, self-interested Athenians but ordinary Athenians experiencing the remarkable 70 or so years when Athens' star shone so bright. Paradoxically, in spite of my claims that Thucydides does not convey what most Athenians thought of Athens' power, this book has turned out to be somewhat Thucydidean in spirit, both in its attempt to get under the apparent meaning of what people say, the *logos*, to find the reality, the *ergon* underneath it; and in the belief that it is possible to trace human constants across space and time, Thucydides' ἀνθρώπινον (1.22.4). Great theoretical difficulties are inherent in discussing imperialism as though it were a universal phenomenon across time and space, but following Thucydides, lucky in being able to invoke "human nature" less self-consciously than a modern historian can, it remains undeniable that certain Athenian *narratives* about their power do resemble those of the rhetoric of the Roman Empire, of the British Empire and even of the United States of the 20th and 21st centuries.[41] Even as early as the Neo-Assyrian empire, some tendencies appear that have analogies with certain examples used throughout this chapter. The rhetoric of Ashurnasirpal II uses language of universal dominion which is typical of most subsequent empires,[42] and the Assyrians considered that they had a divine commandment to subdue the whole world. Conquest and punishment therefore upheld divine justice and drove out evil-doers: anyone resisting clearly deserved punishment.[43] Assyrian imperial rhetoric and art are more overtly violent than those of later empires, but its linkage of sheer power with religious appeals to portray the Assyrians as the gods' representatives on earth, punishing evil as gods do, has multiple analogues in later imperial rhetoric, including that of Athens, if in a weaker form.

Several methodological difficulties in this approach must squarely be confronted. First, privileging analogies over distinctions is always problematic, especially when one empire, with its own highly complex and individual political structure, is shoehorned into a comparison with another.[44] Thus some of the deliberately extreme comparisons I make throughout this chapter[45] might seem questionable. This is a reasonable objection, but deliberately extreme comparisons can sometimes throw certain initially obscure elements into relief, illuminating their significance. The Athenian empire was small in size and brief in duration, but its contours do map well onto the much grander contours of larger, longer-lived empires, less in material conditions than in elements of its rhetorical claims *about itself*. Comparisons between what different empires *say* about themselves offer a more specific and potentially more useful focus than attempts to make broader political or material comparisons between empires.[46] While Rome, Britain and the United States could make some grand claims about themselves that Athens could not really make, the general rhetorical contours of Athens' claims do conform, if in miniature, to the larger contours of the rhetoric of Rome and the rest: "imperialism lite" is still imperialism. It might also be argued that I place too much emphasis on funeral speeches as evidence for popular beliefs about Athens' power, especially since most surviving examples post-date the Athenian empire. This is less of a difficulty than might be supposed. Dating problems will be discussed in detail later, but here it is enough to say that funeral speeches are a highly concentrated collection of claims about Athens that appear more sporadically in a wide range of Athenian texts and in a wide range of contexts: sometimes such texts casually mention as uncontroversial facts claims that we instantly see as "false", suggesting that the funeral speeches, which focus intensively on Athens' excellence, can indeed illuminate some of the unthinking "wallpaper" assumptions about their city's character and position that Athenian citizens would have made.

Connection across times and cultures is embedded in historiography, because historiography is inextricably connected with reception. We receive exceedingly fragmentary information about past events and can only attempt to understand them by reinterpreting stories through imagination or our own understanding of human behaviour: otherwise history is a mere collection of things that happened.[47] So I operate on the assumption that useful insights may arise from supplementing some gaps in ancient evidence with material from other times and places in order to approach imagining some of the mental make-up of a citizen of fifth-century Athens, whose status could be low or average within Athens but high as a "ruler" of the empire, and consistently reaffirmed as such through multiple modes of public discourse. This first chapter will attempt to sketch a possible psychology of Athenian imperialism informed by fifth- and fourth-century Athenian material and supplemented more speculatively with comparative material. Once this framework has been established, later chapters will discuss the relationship between Athenian imperial ideology and Athenian drama with briefer references to other literary forms before moving to Thucydides' complex relationship with Athenian power. Steeped in that power and everything it brought his city, he cannot entirely reject it, yet he is determined to reveal what he saw as the violence and self-deception that lay under all the patriotic fictions about Athenian natural superiority and the justice of their power.

1.2 Empire and rhetoric

Athenians dominated a relatively small territory but shared the desire for continuing expansion that is one of the most commonly cited characteristics of imperialism,[48] from Assyria to Britain and beyond.[49] Athens' drive for expansion is expressed even in fourth-century funeral speeches, long after the end of Athens' control of the Aegean, and it permeates Thucydides' narrative, notably book one's account of the Pentecontaetia, but also the speeches of representatives of Athens, especially Alcibiades (6.18.2–3), and even Pericles at certain times.[50] An empire that does not try to expand is moribund, and Athens follows a standard imperialistic path in this respect. Yet crucially, expansion for its own sake is generally not enough to justify imperialism. Good reasons for expansion must be articulated to everyone. Those within the expanding state will need to be persuaded of the value of the inevitable sacrifices that such expansion will necessitate, but even more important is the crafting of persuasive reasons for the rightness of the imperialist's domination.[51] At some level, even the most ardent imperialists must admit that the unequal balance of power and advantage between those they rule and themselves is *prima facie* unjust, and must find some objectively convincing reason for their more fortunate position.[52] Justifications may be untrue or misleading – arguably, there could be no genuine justification for the imperialist's actions – but the imperialist must set them in plausible terms of an appeal to a greater good.[53] If one element of empire is the assertion of power by one over another via some form of justification, rhetoric and empire become virtually inseparable.[54] Imperial rhetoric enables its users to idealize themselves in the name of civilization, humanity, progress and so forth. Repeated affirmation of such values enables and justifies the authority of those in control through continued expression of their superiority. Rhetoric serves imperialist ideology through justifications which lead to the naturalization of a status quo which benefits the imperialists.[55] If certain views are voiced or portrayed frequently enough, they will come to seem natural. Over time, the general public will come to believe that the current state of affairs has "always" been like this: what is reassuringly unchanging can easily be spun into what is unchangeable.[56]

1.3 Source problems and Athenian imperial rhetoric

One of the most important repositories of sentiments about Athenian power are the funeral speeches (*epitaphioi logoi*) which from around 470 BCE[57] were spoken annually over the military dead of that year's campaigns to console the bereaved and legitimize the rightness of death in the service of the greater good of maintaining or expanding Athenian power.[58] Most examples post-date fifth-century Athens:[59] only Gorgias' fragmentary funeral speech (82F6 DK) and the speech of Pericles reported by Thucydides 2.35–46[60] are actually contemporary with the empire. Strasburger,[61] however, has made a compelling argument for believing that later sources reflect many fifth-century sentiments, given that from 394 BCE to 150 CE both *epitaphioi* and other speeches discussing Athens make such consistent claims about Athens' power, long after it was gone,[62] and given the high degree of compatibility that later *epitaphoi* show both with the fifth-century specimens,[63] and more haphazardly-preserved statements in fifth-century tragedy and scattered statements in Herodotus (e.g. 5.82.2, 7.139.5, 161.3, 8.142.3, 144.)[64] In particular at Hdt. 9.27, the Athenians claim the right to lead the right wing of the army by citing Athens' mythological/historical glories comprising the citizens' services to Heracles' children, the burial of the Seven against Thebes (both dramatized by Euripides), and Athenian resistance to the Amazons, all three of which are central in later glorifications of Athenian action. Not everything in post-imperial speeches about Athens directly reflects fifth-century topoi, since all contain material only relevant to their particular historical context.[65] But since they must appeal to their audiences by persuading them that the sacrifice of Athenian lives is a price worth paying to strengthen a city that has given so much good to its citizens and to Greece, they are likely to contain substantial appeals to established, uncontroversial wisdom.[66] Many indications within individual speeches suggest that they are recounting material very familiar to their audiences, so that there may be a smaller gap between imperial and post-imperial *rhetoric* than is usually assumed from the *political* differences between fifth- and fourth-century Athens. In our only complete fifth-century example, Thucydides' Pericles states (2.36.4) that Athens' ancient achievements are too familiar to need discussion: as I will argue in later chapters, Thucydides tends to downplay popular wisdom, and Pericles' assertion may explain why this speech, alone of our other specimens, makes no reference to the four traditional mythical/historical deeds of Athens that feature in every other *epitaphios* and, apart from the attack of the Amazons, also in fifth-century drama.[67] Some of Thucydides' other speakers paradoxically help to confirm the pervasiveness of the topos of the connection of Athenian excellence with its power by characterizing all justifications of Athenian power that depend on Athens' role in the Persian Wars as mere clichés.[68]

The earliest post-Thucydidean funeral speech is attributed to Lysias and dated to 394,[69] only ten years after Sparta conquered Athens, and it seems unsafe to assume that he could have made a complete break with every topos featured in speeches delivered before 404. Given the gaps in our evidence for Greek history, ten years is not a long time. Indeed, as early as 403, Athens began to explore renewing connections with cities which previously belonged to its empire, suggesting that no one had forgotten what Athens had been.[70] Isocrates was born in 436 BCE: he would have heard *epitaphioi logoi* during Athens' imperial period and would surely have internalized some of the sentiments about Athens that they contained,[71] while his appeals to panhellenism, promoting the superiority of Greek civilization, probably reflect older traditions concerning the Persian Wars:[72] in fact, at 4.74, he states directly that his praise of Athens is epitaphic material. In Plato's *Menexenus*, Socrates mockingly describes how proud he feels on hearing the colossal praise of Athens in funeral speeches.[73] To be credible,[74] such praise will at least partly depend on established wisdom, what "everyone knows", older topoi whose origin is likely to be fifth-century.[75] Most importantly, not only is there substantial overlap between scattered fifth-century evidence and more focused portrayals of Athenian power in later speeches, but also fifth-century public, monumental art portrays many of the Athenian military actions which later literary sources commend, and from decade to decade, such portrayals were a continuous visual presence in Athens. Decades after the victory over Persia, which is essentially inseparable from all justifications of the empire,[76] monuments celebrating that victory were still being produced, since the need to celebrate permanent Athenian hegemony becomes ever-stronger over time, and such celebration must be rooted in clear justifications.[77] At the other end of the time scale, Aelius Aristides, writing nearly 600 years after the Athenian empire, offers a huge compendium of claims reprising what much earlier sources claim for Athenian power.[78] Indeed, at 128 he states, "these rewards *are* hers", as though Athens' dominance was contemporary. At 258, he states that the peace after 445 was a state of good fortune for all Greece thanks to Athens, and other Greeks' ingratitude caused the Peloponnesian War (261). He minimizes Athenian cruelty at Melos and Scione[79] and claims that Athens was humane in having spared Mytilene (289), reminding his audience of Sparta's cruelty to the Helots, in a "two wrongs make a right" gambit familiar from earlier sources.[80] Given the innate conservatism of the *epitaphios* genre and the remarkable consistency of sentiments over such a long period, it seems highly likely that post-imperial sources do overlap with fifth-century sources sufficiently to be used to explore fifth-century Athenian imperial rhetoric and its potential influence on popular Athenian psychology,[81] even if not every single element in them is traditional.

1.4 "I would annex the planets if I could" (Cecil Rhodes)

Because empire must continue expanding to avoid dying, or the alarming perception that it might be dying,[82] and to be considered as part of the natural[83] order, imperial rhetoric tends to present its empire as endless in space and time,[84] whatever the more limited reality.[85] Ovid contrasts the constrained bounds of other nations with the Roman exceptionalism by which city and world are the same space.[86] Isocrates' *Panegyricus* claims that Athens has been, is, and will always be supreme in Greece with no alternative history imaginable, as the oldest, largest, purest and most famous city which has given the most benefits to others (4.23–6; cf. 12.120), while its righteous hostility to barbarians is traced right back to the Trojan War (42–4).[87] Claims to transcend time are especially natural to the *epitaphioi*, part of whose function is to console the living for their loved ones' mortality: the superiority of the city is central to these speeches, to prove that a city whose greatness is eternal is worth dying for. Thus it can be claimed that Athens' dead are not really dead but have uniquely transcended others' common fate,[88] or at the very least that, though bodies have died, fame is eternal.[89] Pl. *Mx.* 243d takes things further: Athens was not conquered – rather, it conquered itself.[90]

The ideal empire of rhetoric (not reality) has mastery over unbounded territory and over its subjects.[91] There is no room for any other power. Virgil's Jupiter assures Venus that her descendants will acquire divinely sanctioned *imperium sine fine* (Verg. *Aen.*1.279); Pompey[92] and Caesar[93] are praised for making the Roman empire coterminous with the *orbis terrarum*,[94] while "*finis imperii propagavit*" was on the monuments of the great generals.[95] Famously, the sun never set on the British empire. But before all these, Herodotus' Xerxes (Hdt. 7.8) introduces to the Persian elders his plan to conquer Greece. From the Greek perspective of Herodotus and his readers, Xerxes' plans manifest the *hybris* that would be his undoing, but his words also justify imperial expansion through arguments resembling those used by many other imperialists, including Athens. Since Herodotus essentially invents this speech, even if it may reflect certain elements of Achaemenid cosmology,[96] perhaps some contemporary Athenian justifications for expansion may shape his arguments:[97]

> Men of Persia, I am not bringing in and establishing a new custom, but following one that I have inherited.[98] As I learn from our elders, we have never yet remained at peace ever since Cyrus deposed Astyages and we won this sovereignty from the Medes. It is the will of heaven; and we ourselves win advantage by our many enterprises.[99] No one needs to tell you, who already know them well, which nations Cyrus and Cambyses and Darius my father subdued and added to our realm.[100] Ever since I came to this throne, I have considered how I might not fall short of my predecessors in this honor, and not add less power to the Persians; and my considerations persuade me that we may win not only renown, but a land neither less nor worse, and more fertile, than that which we now possess; and we would also gain vengeance and requital.[101] For this cause I have now summoned you together, that I may impart to you what I intend to do. It is my intent to bridge the Hellespont and lead my army through Europe to Hellas, so I may punish the Athenians for what they have done to the Persians and to my father.... For these reasons I am resolved to send an army against them; and I reckon that we will find the following benefits among them: if we subdue those men, and their neighbors who dwell in the land of Pelops the Phrygian, we will make the borders of Persian territory and of the firmament of heaven be the same.[102]

That their *imperium* was indeed *sine fine* would not have been difficult for the average Roman to believe, given the economic and political possibilities arising from the vast territory which Rome acquired. Any similar claims to universal domination would have been demonstrably untrue for the Athenians,[103] and yet their relationship to the rest of the fifth-century Greek world and the rhetorical and symbolic ways in which they expressed it fit surprisingly well with many elements of the list of facets of imperial rule offered by Bang and Kolodziejczyk (2012): symbolism, ceremony, diplomacy; universal or cosmopolitan high cultures; imperial rule as an expression of cosmic order; and the celebration of mastery over a multiplicity of diverse populations required to pay tribute to the ruler. While universal imperial rule is not an expression of cosmic order at Athens (although images of Athens as upholder of law and order are commonplace in Athenian rhetoric),[104] all other imperial traits have clear analogies in Athens on a smaller scale, in particular at the Great Dionysia, which encompasses ceremony and symbolism, high culture in literary form, and the offering of tribute by subject nations to their Athenian master. Indeed, Bang and Kolodziejczyk consider immense annual or biennial gatherings with spectacle, art, feasting and so on important in reinforcing notions of belonging and loyalty to the king, or *mutatis mutandis*, Athens' *archē*.[105]

Athenian power cannot literally subdue the world, but that power brings the world to them. Pericles states (Thuc. 2.38.2): "All the good things of the world come in to Athens so that for us it seems as natural to enjoy them as to enjoy our own native produce."[106] This interestingly impersonal description of Athenian trade as though the good things just arrive of their own accord, as though it were an element of nature rather than one of human origin,[107] based on potential economic exploitation, is significant. Trade by its nature implies taking as well, but here, the products merely "come in".[108] Already in Homer (*Od.* 8.159–64), as notably in the Roman empire, trade is considered less honourable than some professions,[109] so that Pericles' neutral language here helps to cast Athenians more easily as disinterested civilizers who take less from others than they give.[110]

[Xen.] *Ath. Pol.*2.7 agrees with Pericles' assessment, though his tone is sourer: thanks to the thalassocracy, "the Athenians have mingled with various peoples and discovered types of luxury. Whatever the delicacy in Sicily, Italy, Cyprus, Egypt, Lydia, Pontus, the Peloponnese . . . all these have been brought together into one place" (trans. Bowersock (1968)). Fifth-century comedy is especially rich in such sentiments. Hermippus, fr.63 in *Phormophoroi (Porters)* datable c. 428–5, offers a comic list of mouth-watering, useful and exotic Athenian imports from all over the empire, in a literally Homeric[111] catalogue of delights. Eupolis fr.330 describes a people (surely the Athenians)[112] as living in a πόλιν . . . θεοφιλεστάτην . . . ἀφθονεστάτην χρήμασι ("a city most loved by the gods and most abundant in resources"). The chorus of Aristophanes' *Holkades* (*Merchant Ships*), produced in the late 420s,[113] consists of merchant ships that convey materials from all over the world to Athens, and fr.428–31 list their cargoes of grains (428) and fish (430).[114] In Aristophanes' *Horae* (*Seasons*) fr.581, an unknown speaker, possibly Athena,[115] in dialogue with a sceptical interlocutor, lauds the delights of Athens (l.15): in the middle of winter there are cucumbers, grapes and violet crowns,[116] and the same man sells a remarkable range of goods, from thrushes to olives to haggises. "Isn't it the greatest good to get whatever one wants at any time of the year" (l.8–9)? The interlocutor says that he or she would only grant such prosperity to a city for a short time, to which the telling response is that other cities' prosperity is limited, but at Athens, such benefits are constant *because they worship the gods*, neatly combining topoi of exceptionalism, abundance and virtue that underpin many expressions of idealized Athenian imperialism. Lists can be a potent expression of imperial prosperity, the verbal equivalent of surveying one's kingdom from on high.[117] Lists also imply the possibility of choice, and choice implies freedom and agency – valuable commodities, especially for people whose actual agency is limited:[118] in spite of the ideology of democratic equality at Athens, clearly some were more powerful than others. It is significant that comedy emphasizes the plenitude offered Athens by its imperial economic power.[119] As I will argue in Chapter 4, comic writers present a relatively unflattering portrayal of contemporary Athens, so that the enumeration in these fragments of the economic benefits to Athens of its power rather than the relentless self-sacrifice on behalf of the Greek world found in tragedy and oratory may not be surprising.

Isoc. 4.42 offers a later variant on Pericles' topos. Other places were not self-sufficient, but were either lacking or overproductive.[120] Athens brought them opportunities for trade at Piraeus, where there is such abundance that even articles difficult to obtain are all easily found.[121] Abundance in everything, even the noble deeds of the dead,[122] is important in imperial claims:[123] Pericles cites the unique abundance of festivals in Athens (Thuc. 2.38.1),[124] and Isoc. 4.45 extends the claim: Athenian spectacle is superior both in terms of money spent and in artistic merit. Roman authors also extol the vast abundance flowing to their capital, the centre of human civilization, and celebrate their power to command and consume all the world's delights.[125] The drive for comprehensive possession can have literary and artistic consequences; the mixture of dialects at Athens that [Xen.] 2.7 attributes to Athenian sea power, paralleled with the mixture of Dorian, Ionian and possibly even Persian elements on the Parthenon,[126] the influence of Persian architecture on Pericles' Odeion,[127] or the dazzling array of literary genres that run through Virgil's *Aeneid*, for example.[128]

1.5 "An empire exempt from all natural causes of decay" (Lord Macaulay)

Territorial expansion needs justification, but territory is just the beginning. Empire must also expand temporally and psychologically so that nothing stands in its way.[129] It must be the only natural possibility, eternal,[130] and, if not actually coterminous with the beginning of time and space, at least very long-lived, so that the contemporary imperialists are essentially the same as their distant ancestors. Lys. 2.26 claims that deeds performed long ago are "as though they were new" and still create envy among "all mankind". Alternatively, imperialists imagine a time preceding their empire but create a narrative of the path to it in which it is the only logical possibility, as every earlier event inevitably leads up to it.[131] Cicero claims that Rome is progressing along Nature's road and is reaching perfection, since its people has grown great by planning, discipline and Fortune.[132] Athenian rhetoric retrojects Athenian power to very early mythological deeds which exemplify the virtues that Athens claims for its present.[133] Aristotle (*Rhet.* 1368a 10–11) states that the mere fact of a person having done something first, or alone or with a few, or having been chiefly responsible for it makes that action noble by definition, and Athens is often claimed as the first or only city to perform some Greek practice or bring some benefit to the Greeks.[134] Isocrates claims (4.23) that the further one goes back in time, the more obvious it is that Athens deserves hegemony.[135] Athens' tradition of helping the oppressed – central to the idealized Athens of tragedy[136] and even cited by Thucydides' Alcibiades (6.18.2) – is claimed to begin even before the Trojan War (Isoc. 4.52, 54). When other Greeks were living in scattered dwellings, oppressed either by anarchy or tyranny, Athens helped them and was the first to establish laws and a state (4.39). The strong cultural pressure on sons to match and ideally surpass fathers, appearing as early as the *Iliad* and prevalent also in Roman imperial rhetoric, can serve imperial traditions by stretching the empire both backwards and forwards in time.[137]

A certain type of language promotes the naturalness and totality of empire, by emphasizing generalized, abstract notions such as "nature", "civilization" and so on. Language solidifies around a series of concepts whose substance is presented as obvious, common sense and therefore beyond argument.[138] Hence Lord Macaulay's lofty description of the British Empire: "It is an empire exempt from all natural causes of decay. These triumphs are the pacific triumphs of reason over barbarism; that empire is the imperishable empire of our arts and our morals, our literature and our laws."[139] Thucydides himself was aware of how dangerously seductive reliance on this sort of language could be, not only for Athens but also for cities like Melos, for whom following the siren calls of "freedom" and "honour" would prove disastrous.[140]

By excluding alternative visions of the world that might raise inconvenient questions about the present, emphasis on the past offers stability, continuity and legitimacy to imperial power.[141] Imperial symbols and images often focus on past glories, because appeals to a supposedly immutable past can inspire and encourage, and legitimize current conditions. European empires used symbolism from Rome's empire as a part of their own history.[142] When Queen Victoria became Empress of India, the banners presented were shaped like those in pictures of Roman triumphs, and her imperial proclamation was organized as a timeless medley of Roman, feudal and Indian symbolism.[143] In its turn, the Roman Empire continually legitimized itself through backwards glances, the Ottoman Empire and Genghis Khan recalled Alexander, while Saddam Hussain used imagery from Nebuchadnezzar's Babylon.[144] American exceptionalism depends on an unchanging past that runs to an unchangeable future, through the tenet that the US is exempt from the normal patterns of decay of empire.[145]

On a smaller scale, Athens is also the same from the beginning of time, and its eternal benefactions to Greece deserve eternal rewards. Its power is the natural order, and the catalogue of Athenian exploits in the *epitaphioi* is a "cosmogony of Athenian excellence, a tradition of origins that could explain and verify all present claims."[146] Athens' forefathers systematically increased Athenian territory: sons, grandsons and so on will continue to do so. This process is especially clear in the *epitaphioi* in which Athenians of the distant past, recent past, and present demonstrate an unchanging system of values that in their turn contribute to their unchanging and eternal character,[147] but it is also clear in tragedies which present Athens to Athenians as a city of eternal excellence. This blend of past and present can sometimes lead to blatant oddities, such as the constitutional situation in Euripides' *Suppliants* 349–53 in which Athens is ruled by both Theseus and a democracy.[148] But the contradictions must coexist to normalize the current order and reassure listeners: somehow, this is how it has always been and how it should be. The predilection of imperialists to project their empire's history and justification backwards and forwards in time may partly explain why it is difficult to determine the specific era at which Athenian leadership of a league of allies dedicated to noble resistance against a common enemy was consciously transformed into the will to dominate subject cities.[149] The institution of the funeral oration is generally dated to around 470, and every extant specimen explains and justifies

Athenian power with the claim that the city is an eternal force for good. Such claims are central to much other imperial rhetoric: *epitaphioi* had been delivered for some 40 years before the historical date of Pericles' funeral speech reported by Thucydides, and if the content of early funeral speeches was as conventional as it is in later specimens, then Athens' imperial ambitions might be datable earlier rather than later.

Empire's drive for totality in time and space for its legitimization and justification through rhetoric extends even to creating its own images of its opponents, imagining and coopting their sufferings through literary or visual means. Roman authors offer oratorical space to those oppressed by Rome,[150] even allowing them eloquent condemnation of the cruelties of the victorious power and virtues similar to those of their conqueror,[151] but as authors from the victorious power, it is they who retain ultimate agency, by ventriloquizing the oppressed and recreating them in the image they wish.[152] Caesar understands that the Gauls desire liberty, because all humans do (3.10), but Rome's refusal to grant it proves Rome's absolute power, which only Roman citizens deserve to enjoy.[153] The ventriloquized cries of the subjected may elicit feelings – not mutually exclusive[154] – of vindictive triumph, relief or pity, but the imperial nation's essential power is inescapable. Sympathy may be expressed, but in the bigger context of unequal power, it is an ultimately impotent expression which need not affect the imperialist's behaviour.[155] Horace can admire and even pity Cleopatra at the end of Ode 1.37, but she is safely vanquished; Virgil's Dido and Turnus are sympathetic, but their deaths do not counterbalance the rightness of Rome's foundation. Similarly, Aeschylus portrays the Persians' anguish sympathetically, but it is expressed to Athenians in the context of their victory, eight years after the war, just as the city begins to exert its own power to subject others, for example, compelling the Naxians to remain in the Delian League, c. 471. In general, Athenian tragedy is shaped by a similar mentality, so as, for example, to allow criticism of patriarchy, but only through patriarchal voices. Plays like *Medea* ventriloquize genuinely troublesome women's issues, but that is all: airing the problems need not inspire action from those who could alleviate them. Meanwhile the Athens of tragedy itself is always, as Heracles complains to Theseus (E. *HF* 1249), ἐκτὸς . . . συμφορᾶς, "outside the disaster", while other cities are ventriloquized by Athenian playwrights as different from Athens (cf. Isoc. 12.121–2), places which make mistakes and need Athenian help to regain a partial stability which will not challenge Athens. Cic. *Phil.* 6.19 states that only the powerful have the privilege of liberty, and Thucydides' Athenians (cynically) and those of tragedy and oratory (idealistically) would agree.

Not only do empires speak for their subjects, but they can even claim that they owe any excellences they may have to their masters.[156] Especially in epitaphic rhetoric, the ideal Athens takes all qualities, all benefits – wheat, olives, laws, even the gods – as innately Athenian and distributes them to the rest of the Greek world.[157] Whether cynical or altruistic, the opportunity to control others, whether in rhetoric or reality,[158] remains highly seductive, and it is an unusual nation that voluntarily renounces that power. It is simply too important, practically, economically and psychologically to retain it, as Thucydides' Athenians state at Corinth (1.75.3–76.3), because the alternative, seen in the reactions of his Athenians at the end of the Sicilian expedition, is terrifying.

1.6 "Imperious, irrepressible necessities of life"[159]

It is a central paradox of imperial rule that it depends on force and needs to conceal force by promoting peace, justice and civilization.[160] Justification of conquest frequently features in the rhetoric of many powers. One inscription of Darius at Susa characterizes Persia as a kind of noble policeman: "My law, of that they feel fear, so that the stronger does not smite or destroy the weak."[161] Such justifications proliferate in later colonial discourse. Frederick Lugard, British Governor General of Nigeria in the early 20th century, considered the European powers "trustees of civilization for the commerce of the world", while Albert Serrault, Governor General of French Indochina at a similar era, claims that *nature* [my emphasis] has given white Europe invention, progress and scientific advancement, and must intervene to offer to humanity all the natural wealth of the territories of the "backward" races incapable themselves of offering it to the world.[162]

In western thought, Rome is the paradigm of empire,[163] in its military power, territorial reach and general confidence. The Romans considered that their empire was deserved, the proof essentially being that empire,[164] and augmenting it was good for them and for others. But even for Roman thinkers, less self-conscious about empire than later imperialists, military brilliance or desire for power could not be the sole reason for success. Thus ever since Numa (Liv. 1.21.1–2), Rome has been a pious city, and enemies' respect for their piety has protected them. Rome is great through "arma *virtusque*" (Procilius 7.6.3; cf. Liv. 7.6.3–4). Its power must only be used justly, preferably only to secure peace, and joined to wise policy[165] and moral characteristics such as simplicity and above all *humanitas*.[166] Men like Aeneas "*pietate insignis et armis*" were paradigms for Rome's success. Rome was considered fortunate in being centrally placed in the world and in possessing excellent natural resources,[167] but its fortune ultimately depended on the gods' favour, which rewarded Rome for its virtue and wisdom.[168] While there were dissenting voices, Romans seem broadly comfortable with their city's power and any measures required to retain it (if they could be justified, which they generally could be), in some contrast to the general impression of Athens' power that Thucydides expresses. But as this chapter, and much of this book, will show, once we move beyond Thucydides, Athenian rhetoric resembles Roman and other paradigms more than is sometimes argued, even though the material conditions of Athenian power are very different.

Justification of empire can take many forms, whether by invoking grand and abstract concepts or appealing to apparently concrete facts, but the most powerful justifications join abstract and concrete factors. In later empires, differences in physical appearance and culture between colonizer and colonist offered an instant way to naturalize empire:[169] on them, pseudo-justifications of the natural superiority of the colonists could be built and aligned with their civilizing mission, to claim that the supposed inferiority or barbarity of subject populations, manifest in supposed physical facts, created the need for rule by a civilized power.[170] Those in power typically claim that their power results from their superior civilization and that their power is just,[171] because their civilization would otherwise not be superior,[172] in a self-perpetuating cycle.[173] Virgil's Anchises famously expresses the Roman mission in his epigrammatic *"parcere subiectis et debellare superbos"* (*Aen.* 6.853), but the identities of *subiecti* and *superbi* are in the eye of the beholder,[174] and Mussolini's conveniently grand and vague "imperious, irrepressible necessities of life" can always be invoked to justify actions which appear not to conform to the idealized image of the exercise of power. Thus Robert Clive's "standard disavowal of imperial conquest"[175] states,

> [Since 1757] we *were roused* to an offensive by the *unprovoked injuries* of the *Tyrant* Nabob Serajah Dowlah.... Perhaps it was not so much *our choice as necessity that drove us* progressively into the possessions we presently enjoy [all italics mine].

Racism and imperialism are entwined in European history, but there was no racism in Athenian imperialism,[176] because there were no differences between other Greeks and Athenians of the kind that the British used to assert supposed superiority over Indians.[177] However, ancient thinkers did believe that heredity or geography and physical and mental qualities were connected, and Athenians and Romans used such supposed "facts" to claim their own superiority. In these justifications, geography is rolled into morality to privilege the status of "the middle." The logic of Roman imperialism states that because the Romans have the best geographic position (in the middle) they should improve others' conditions by placing them under the civilizing mantle of Roman rule. Their climate explains the innate superiority of Romans and rationalizes Roman power.[178] The political middle is similarly important, since it connotes equality and justice:[179] Polybius famously ascribes Rome's success to a mixed constitution which could be said to lie in the middle of monarchy, oligarchy and democracy.[180]

The imperial power naturally places itself at the centre of its world, and in an extended claim to the middle position, its rhetoric can claim that the empire is uniquely able to contain all elements, even those apparently contradictory to one another,[181] such as the three constitutions in Polybius' Rome or Theseus' status as king and democrat,[182] balancing everything in an almost perfect[183] combination.[184] Powerful nations claim that they blend their predecessors' best features while avoiding their faults, sometimes granting others some virtues, but not all, and not the most important ones.[185] Cyrus' tomb at Pasargadae blends aspects from a number of the traditions of his subject peoples;[186] for Virgil, the greatest virtues of Troy and Italy are united in a Roman super-race; and British imperialists defined Englishness as a mingling of Britons, Romans, Anglo-Saxons and Danes.[187] Greece as a whole could claim the superiority of a middle position through occupying a healthy and moderate mean between the barbarians of the uncivilized north and the overcivilized east.[188] Athens claims the middle of the

Greek cities literally, metaphorically and morally, combining Dorian and Ionian elements,[189] and, uniquely among the Greek cities, all virtues,[190] even those in apparent opposition,[191] to make it uniquely perfect. The adjective μέτριος with its derivatives can have strongly positive ideological implications in describing Athenian conduct (Isoc. 12.56, 130–1), and the Athenian kings in tragedy who represent Athens to Athenians are consistently characterized with moderation and its concomitant attributes of pity and openness to persuasion.[192] Since, as Pericles states, "everything" is available at Athens, economic fact helps to support more generalized claims. If Athens also possesses every virtue, it cannot be excessive or deficient in anything, so that its superior position in the middle justifies the city's power.

The British appealed to race and culture to prove their superiority to their subjects; Athens had to justify Athenian rule by different methods,[193] notably their claims to be the place of complete excellence.[194] All Greeks are good and better than barbarians, but the Athenians are super-Greeks who uniquely exemplify all Greek traits *more* than other Greeks do.[195] The restriction of Athenian citizenship to those born of two Athenian parents combined with the willingness of foreigners to live in Athens in spite of the disadvantages of metic status might have offered apparently factual support for such assertions for those who wished to believe it. In effect, Athens *is* Greece, a claim already lurking in Aeschylus and Herodotus,[196] while in some post-imperial texts, Athens is the human race itself, or at least its benefactor[197] or teacher, as already Pericles claims.[198] Isoc. 4.27–8 and 48–9 assert that Athens honours *logoi*, which distinguish us from beasts,[199] while 15.293–4 states that Athens is superior not just in war or government or preserving ancestral law[200] but in the very qualities of nature which elevate men over animals and Greeks over barbarians (cf. 12.163). Hyperides (6.5) compares Athens to the sun which visits the whole world and controls the seasons according to what is right, promoting everything useful in life for moderate and reasonable (σ[ώφροσι καὶ ἐ]πιεικέσι) men.[201] As discussed earlier, appeals to nature are important in promoting imperialism, and Athens is no exception.[202] Athens was not the only city which claimed to be autochthonous, but the Athenians alone developed an intense emotional attachment to their autochthony,[203] a development which may date from the period of imperial expansion.[204] Funeral speeches, tragedy and other texts continually explore the Athenian character and constitution, and by claiming autochthony, Athenians define themselves as of purer, superior descent than other Greeks in a way that partly foreshadows some aspects of modern racism.[205] Racial purity easily shades into a general morality, notably in Athenian rhetoric that Athens is the most just city in Greece because it never expelled others from its land.[206]

Athenian texts which claim Athenian preeminence in Greece especially emphasize that Athens is unique or alone.[207] The claim is connected with Athens' (supposedly)[208] unique stand in the Persian Wars,[209] and features in a consistent and widely ranging set of claims, historical and mythological, true and invented, which reinforce each other. Herodotus' Darius (5.102.2; cf. 6.94) enjoins his servant, "Remember the Athenians" as his particular target for future revenge. Thucydides' version of Pericles' funeral oration frequently claims that Athens' way of life is unique among the Greek cities.[210] Theseus' heroic deeds were his unique achievement (Isoc. 10.31). Combining several topoi of Athens' unique excellence and the justice which ensures its victories and enables the city to punish those who deserve it, Demosthenes (60.11) claims that in the Persian Wars Athenians single-handedly repulsed a host assembled from an entire continent and inflicted punishment for wrong inflicted on the rest of the Greeks.[211] Similarly Lysias (2.4–6) states that the Amazons (who are often assimilated to the Persians in Athenian art and literature) attacked Athens because they heard of its fame, but failed in their attempts and *alone* failed to learn better counsel and were punished.[212] At Ithome, the Athenians *alone* were sent home:[213] indeed they were, and the literal truth of the historical facts helped to promote Athenian belief in Athens' uniqueness, since propaganda that aligns with existing beliefs is always effective.[214] "Few against many" is another common and related topos,[215] as is that of "making a common war their own,"[216] an interestingly altruistic form of imperial grab. The Athenian imperial drive acts even on shared Greek history, de-emphasizing the Trojan War in favour of the Persian Wars.[217] Athens equals Greece.[218]

"What was absent that should have been there? Or was present that should not have been?"[219] The combination of skills in war and peace, or general physical and intellectual prowess, is particularly striking in Isocrates' accounts of Athenian perfection, in which other cities have certain virtues,[220] but only Athens, or its representative Theseus (10.31), has all of them.[221] In fact, as late as Aristides (*Panathenaicus* 248) we are told that many cities have some signal virtue – Argive antiquity, Arcadian autochthony and so on – but only Athens has everything. This tendency unquestionably shapes fifth-century Athenian narratives about Athens. Already Gorgias' *epitaphios* (82F6 11) notes the city's combination of γνώμην <καὶ ῥώμην>, which (15) enables them, with their φρονίμῳ τῆς γνώμης to crush the ἄφρων τῆς ῥώμης ("through judgement of right foiling madness of might", in Andrew Scholtz's rendering). Thucydides' Pericles claims that "differently" from others, the Athenians combine daring and reflection, philosophy and toughness:[222] prowess in peace as well as war (or more generally, words as well as deeds) is obviously crucial for imperialists, given the necessity of concealing force with righteousness and justice.[223] The story of Athens' part in rescuing the dead of the Seven against Thebes battle, one of the standard stories of the *epitaphioi* and dramatized in tragedy, comes in two incompatible Athenian versions:[224] sometimes, Athens must use force against Thebes;[225] in Aeschylus' *Eleusinioi* and Isoc. 12.171, Athenian diplomacy enables a peaceful handover of the bodies; Dem. 60.8 leaves details unclear. Both versions are "true" because they express individual elements of Athens' complete virtue.

The Athenians did not provide their subject allies with the huge technological benefits that Rome or Britain (or arguably the United States) claimed to have offered subordinate peoples, but they did claim that they had given civilization of all kinds to other cities. Even in c. 125 BCE an Amphictyonic inscription at Delphi praises Athens for bringing good to the world,[226] leading men to tameness (ἡμερότης)[227] from a bestial life, instilling community through the mysteries, and making the gift of agriculture a *common* good for men, though *privately* received.²²⁸ These claims are centuries old and push the excellences of Athens right back to the beginning of time, excluding all other possibilities, so that Athens appropriates agriculture, the Eleusinian mysteries that celebrate agriculture, and every other element of basic civilization.²²⁹ Isoc. 4.28–9 describes Demeter's visit to Athens after the rape of Kore, at the dawn of mythology. Demeter, "moved to kindness towards our ancestors by services which may not be told save to her initiates, gave these two gifts, the greatest in the world", "the fruits of the earth, which have enabled us to rise above the life of the beasts,"²³⁰ and the Eleusinian mysteries, through which initiates have a blessed death. Plato (*Mx.* 237d) claims that when other lands were producing wild animals, Athens chose to bring forth humans, "who outrank all other animals in intelligence and uniquely among animals regard justice and the gods", futher pushing such themes to the limit (*Mx.* 238b) with the idea that Athens introduced the gods to humans.

The assertion that even olive trees are originally uniquely Athenian is demonstrably current in the fifth century: as Herodotus 5.82.2 states, "it is said that" in prehistoric times, olives grew in Athens alone.²³¹ The generosity of Athens knows no bounds.²³² Isoc. 4.47 even imperializes philosophy by saying that Athens gave it to the world to educate us for politics, making us gentle to each other and able to distinguish between misfortunes due to ignorance (ἀμαθία) and those from necessity (ἀνάγκη). Gorgias (82F6 6–7) claims that Athens always favours τὸ πρᾶον ἐπιεικές, and both πραότης and ἐπιείκεια are both considered quintessential Athenian traits.²³³ Athenian characters in fifth-century tragedy, especially Theseus in Euripides' *Suppliants* and *Heracles* and Sophocles' *Oedipus at Colonus*, can uniquely determine who deserves mercy and who deserves punishment. Such Athenian talents rather resemble those of Rome as described by Virgil's Anchises (*Aen.* 6.853). To claim the ability to spare the humble and war down the proud (*parcere subiectis et debellare superbos*), ascribes to the leading power the facility for right judgement through which its power to control the world is justified. Though the topos clusters in fourth-century literature, it already underlies Gorgias' linguistic games: 82F6 8–10 claims Athens' ability to follow the most divine and common law both to say and not say, do and not do what is necessary at the necessary moment (τὸ δέον ἐν τῶι δέοντι). In tragedy, it is central. Aeschylus' *Eumenides* ascribes the creation of the first homicide court to Athens, while Theseus in Euripides' *Suppliants* is a forceful moral arbiter, consciously upholding proper Greek mores that the Thebans violate, rightfully crushing their arrogant violence, and deciding when Adrastus should be forgiven.²³⁴ Lysias, too, when recounting the same story, grants the Athenians special agency: once they *decided* that Polynices' army had suffered enough by their death, they helped them.²³⁵

One prevailing topos in Athenian narratives, which combines the superiority of Athenian civilization with Athens' generosity to Greece, is that of the reception of suppliants. Athens' reception of Adrastus and Heracles' children are traditional components of the *epitaphioi*, while tragedy adds Orestes, along with more problematic visitors such as Medea and Oedipus.²³⁶ Athenians could also cite demonstrable historical facts, such as their help to the Ionians (Hdt. 5.99.1), and above all their record in the Persian Wars,²³⁷ to maintain their image as the city that helps others. Alcibiades (Thuc. 6.18.2) states that such a policy created the empire, and its prevalence in extant Athenian literature of different genres suggests that the Athenians received active pleasure from repeatedly hearing and seeing these stories about themselves, especially when such narratives generally include rewards for Athens from grateful suppliants, such as eternal alliances or future supernatural help from the suppliant who promises to champion Athenian interests from beyond the grave.[238] While it is culturally specific to Athens in this form, in the importance it lays on help to the oppressed and the political reward gained by it, this Athenian trope has partial analogies with the discourse of appropriation discussed by Spurr, in which the colonizer claims territory as its own while transforming its claims into the response to a supposed appeal on the part of the colonized people.[239]

The prevalence of such stories in tragedy is striking and also offers some partial parallels with another discourse of imperialism sketched by Spurr in his discussion of travel-writing.[240] In travel-writing, the suffering of others can be consumed through the medium of writing, which can aestheticize poor countries through distance as an endless supply of disaster and pathos for readers' consumption. Some tragedy may work somewhat similarly:[241] audiences appreciate a drama through their separation from the stage, where their "power, privilege and security" contrasts with the "suffering, vulnerability, and even humiliation" of those on stage,[242] through keeping some distance from suffering through a detachment connected with aesthetic judgement.[243] So in the Athenian/democratic/imperial genre of tragedy, images of suffering awaken pity through the audience's imagination: the Athenians safely experience others' sufferings through images, since to identify totally with others' agony is impossibly dangerous. Imagination and reflection both connect audiences to and protect them from pain, in the Athenian tragic gaze, which aligns in certain aspects with the imperialistic world-view sketched by Spurr.[244] Meanwhile when Athenians look upon Athens in tragedy, they see a predominantly positive image of the city, even as they enjoy the pleasure of pitying those less fortunate.

1.7 "We do our humble best to retain by justice what we may have won by the sword"[245]

Athenians and Romans believed both that it could be glorious for the strong to dominate the weak, and that wars were forced upon them or were fought to defend mistreated allies.[246] The impulse was especially strong at Rome,[247] where the importance of only waging just wars was frequently expressed, orally and also ritually in the reliance on the *ius fetiale* as justification for war-making in early Rome.[248] Cicero (*Rep.* 3.35) states that Rome has gained power over the whole world by defending its allies, and while elsewhere he allows that less altruistic reasons sometimes drove Roman war-making,[249] it remained important that war should be justifiable somehow.[250] The Aztecs and Persians among others expressed similar scrupulousness.[251] Victory is proof that the campaign was just.[252] Empire must be natural, justified and benign, even if its superficial appearance is less so.

Hence the "balance sheets" of empire which often have been used to calculate the total good or harm done to their colonies by imperial powers.[253] Such balance sheets are not easily detachable from generally appealing ideas of the civilizing mission,[254] with the result that when wrongdoing is admitted, it is often safely relegated to the past or minimized, compared with the benefits the conquered have received.[255]

Isocrates (12.63–5) sets up a post-imperial balance sheet for Athens, admitting crimes at Melos, Scione and Torone, but setting these against "all" the good that Athens did: even the gods are not guilt-free and Sparta's behaviour was worse (66–71). Funeral speeches focus on the good that Athens has done for the Greek world. Athens' contribution in the Persian Wars stands above all others in its demonstrable historicity and the ease with which mythological Athens and historical Athens can be seamlessly melded, transcending time, so that the Athens of the Amazonian invasion behaves in exactly the same way – justly, courageously, victoriously – as the Athens of the Persian invasion.[256] In Lysias' detailed narrative of the Persian Wars (2.20–57), 2.20–2 is especially full of imperial topoi, such as Athenian nature, surpassing ancestors for expansion "*sine fine*", claims to geographical universality, emphasis on risks taken, connected implicitly or explicitly with what Athens deserves as a reward, the uniqueness of the city and its equation with the whole of Greece:

> For indeed, being of noble stock and having minds as noble, the ancestors of those who lie here achieved many noble and admirable things; but ever memorable and mighty are the trophies that their descendants have everywhere left behind them owing to their valor.[257] For they alone risked their all in defending the whole of Greece against many myriads of the barbarians ... from the former actions of our city [the Persians] had conceived a particular opinion of her: they thought that if they attacked another city first, they would be at war with it and Athens as well, for she would be zealous in coming to succour her injured neighbours; but if they made their way here first, no Greeks elsewhere would dare attempt the deliverance of others.[258]

Sparta is consistently the loser in these narratives. Sparta's strength was famously on land, not sea, but Isoc. 12.49–50 spins this fact into a dereliction of duty – Sparta contributed a feeble ten triremes, but the homeless Athenians offered a contribution excelling those of all others, while 4.95–98 invokes *noblesse oblige*: weaker states may be forgiven for caving to the Persians, but surrender is unbecoming for Greece's leaders, and Sparta was eventually shamed by Athens' example into reluctantly joining the campaign against Persia.[259]

Modern balance sheets of empire often have an economic focus but can include more intangible aspects of imperialism, such as the supposed cultural benefits of belonging to a community, or a sense of identity shared between benign imperialists and their subjects.[260] Kipling's famous phrase "the white man's burden,"[261] with its connotations of altruistic effort, may be compared with the frequent use of the word *ponos* (πόνος) in Athenian narratives of Athenian power.[262] The term recalls Heracles' heroic efforts on behalf of humanity and has traditionally Greek and heroic associations.[263] In Athenian idealizing rhetoric it often denotes warfare justified by Athens' "mission" – *polypragmosynē*[264] according to its enemies – whose explicit goals are always justice and the restoration of Greek civilized behaviour.[265] Athenian *ponos* is central to the tragedy and funeral speeches that highlight Athens' efforts on behalf of helpless suppliants.[266] Lys. 2.11–16 states that the rest of the Greeks were ashamed at expelling Heracles' children but too frightened of Eurystheus to resist him.[267] The Athenians, however, respected Heracles' virtue more than their own danger,[268] preferring to fight for the weaker with justice over favouring the powerful, and championed them despite receiving no benefits from Heracles and not knowing whether the grown-up Heraclidae would be worth the effort they had expended on saving them.[269] Athens is highly competitive in its altruism, reducing other Greeks to passive bystanders:[270] in both Euripides' *Heracles* and *Heraclidae* Athenians save Heracles or his children, removing Heracles from his traditional position as Greece's greatest hero and substituting Athenian heroes as the saviours of the saviour (cf. Lys. 2.16).

To accept help from Athens or any other imperially minded nation is to accept a transaction requiring clear reciprocation, in spite of any claims to the contrary, for the profit of the imperialist.[271] Profit, defined as "the *just* reward due to those who exercised *valour and virtue and energy*",[272] is inextricably linked with the imperial control which is a just reward for the imperialists' virtuous expenditures. Equally, power has responsibilities and the powerful should use their power "properly".[273] Using that power properly proves their virtues and therefore emboldens the further use of power in a kind of echo chamber which maintains and augments their dominance.[274]

Some fourth-century texts directly confront aspects of Athenian abuses of power and typically try to justify or at least minimize them. While some of these must be post-imperial attempts to justify the unjustifiable, it is not certain that all of them must be. Isoc. 4.105 attributes every intervention in other cities' affairs to a desire to promote the rights of the poor, a claim which is certainly in harmony with fifth-century justifications of Athens' power.[275] Isoc. 4.108–9 minimizes the massacre of Scione[276] and (110) attacks Sparta for hypocrisy regarding Melos.[277] Isoc. 4.101 interprets the treatment of Melos and Scione through Athens' mission to punish the wicked, assuring his audience that no loyal subjects received such punishments and that other cities would have acted no differently. For Isoc. 12.53–4, Athens occasionally did behave badly, but it also established democracies for the benefit of all the people. By chapter 70, Melos and others have been downgraded to "islets" so small that many Greeks are unaware of their existence. Isoc. 7.6 admits to a degree of Athenian arrogance, but the next chapter charges Sparta with the same tendencies.[278] Isoc. 12.115–8 has a certain Thucydidean appeal: the thalassocracy was unjust in some ways, but who would not have chosen it?[279] At 8.82–91, Isocrates does offer a long repudiation of imperial *polypragmosynē*[280] in which the practice of exhibiting the tribute at the Dionysia is especially condemned: the "simple-minded" admired the wealth which "flowed into the city unjustly",[281] but such wealth caused Athens arrogantly to neglect its own possessions and covet others': (85) "So far did they outdo all mankind in recklessness that whereas misfortunes chasten others and render them more prudent our fathers learned no lessons even from this discipline." This is a mirror image of the idealized image of Athens whereby Athens' outstanding virtue punishes others' *hybris*. At 8.91, he characterizes Athens as a tyrant and condemns the corrupting nature of *archē* (94). More familiar tropes soon return, however:

> For our ancestors proving themselves to be men of this character, handed on the city to their descendants in a most prosperous condition and left behind them an imperishable memorial of their virtue. And from this we may easily learn a double lesson: that our soil is able to rear better men than the rest of the world.

But most Athenian literature repeatedly emphasizes an idealized Athenian virtue, benefitting Greece in war and peace alike, so that the city deserves its preeminent position.[282] In tragedy, Athens receives rewards from those the city saves: all of them eventually show their gratitude (voluntarily, without pestering from their saviours who remain detached altruists), by offering alliances, promises of heroic help for the future and so on.[283] A successful empire depends on power, but the best sort of power is ideally not used at all, and it is both morally problematic and deeply unpopular[284] to claim that power is its own justification.[285] Imperial discourse, including that of Athens, must therefore conceal power under a veneer of altruism, even if the veneer is not entirely opaque. Athena's velvet-gloved strong-arming of the Eumenides (A. *Eum.* 826–9) is paradigmatic: "I too trust in Zeus – what need is there to mention that? – and I alone of the gods know the keys to the house in which his thunderbolt is sealed. But there is no need of that." Athens' generosity is an outward sign of a virtue which conceals a power that, at a deeper level, is its own, irrefutable proof that the city deserves its privileges. One common Athenian trope proclaims and conceals power simultaneously: true power is demonstrated when the master chooses to stay his hand, being capable of using his power but choosing not to.[286] Imperial power brings the power of choice, and Athens' power enables the city to choose to be generous or not.[287]

The choice to help is generally right, however. Helping friends is a Greek moral norm,[288] and since intervention and empire-building are linked,[289] almost by definition, Athenian imperialism is made to seem natural and right. While there might in theory be a distinction between genuine help given to genuine friends and simple desire for expansion,[290] in practice, one blends imperceptibly into another, and all intervention becomes "helping friends."[291] In a culture which promoted doing good to others rather than receiving good, as Thucydides' Pericles claims is uniquely Athenian (2.40.4), the "myths" or powerful ideological justifications promoted by tragedy and speeches and other media were a useful filter through which to view and conveniently disavow the vast benefits that the empire brought to the Athenians.[292] Pl. *Mx.* 244e claims that the only just accusation against Athens is that the city has always been too compassionate and helped the weak excessively, and this proud boast is already spun as a pretended criticism of Athenian policy by the obnoxious Argive Herald in Euripides' *Heraclidae* (176–8).[293] But Athens is so strong, morally and militarily, that it can afford to make "bad" choices (Ar. *Nu*. 585–9) or choices which are morally good but do not benefit them materially (Lys. 2.12) without harming itself.[294] This shows an extraordinary level of self-confidence that has a partial analogue in the cult of amateurism in British imperialism:[295] the amateur is by nature good enough, and does not have to try too hard. Pericles' funeral speech continually contrasts the Spartans' relentless focus on military power with Athens' effortless military preeminence that also allows for pleasure in relaxation (Thuc. 2.38.1, 39.1).[296]

Idealized intervention is central both to the rhetoric of Athens and that of subsequent imperialists who viewed their achievements in the light of notions of ancient glory and even divine blessing as a reward for their qualities.[297] But it is also a fundamental Greek ideal,[298] reaching back to Homer, with Achilles' "hero's burden" of *Iliad* 9.323–5 in which he compares his labours for the Greeks to those of a selfless mother bird who exhausts herself feeding her chicks, in order to argue that such effort for others deserves concrete reward,[299] and he is aggrieved at what he sees as the Greek army's ingratitude. Similarly, from an imperial power's perspective, any resistance can be dubbed ingratitude.[300]

1.8 The seductions of empire

Much of what has been said so far suggests that imperial rhetoric promotes a spectacular form of self-deception,[301] and later chapters will argue that Thucydides desires to unmask such self-deception throughout his *History*. One may well wonder how anyone, imperialist or subject, could be taken in by such obvious sophistries. But something simultaneously insubstantial and potent arises from the supposed justifications of empire,[302] based on the irrational or emotional appeal of concepts such as prestige, fatherland or destiny, which are powerful because they reassure people about their place in the world. Being able to control others' affairs successfully proves, as few other circumstances can, one's own mastery in the world.[303] We want mastery[304] and often to be part of something greater than ourselves,[305] and imperial power is a result of such spectacular success that its beneficiaries can easily claim that they are exceptionally favoured by the gods.[306] Rome's rhetoric is steeped in these beliefs,[307] and while Thucydides' Athens appears to be entirely different, drama, the *epitaphioi* and visual representations tell a different story. But even parts of Thucydides, above all Nicias' last desperate speeches (e.g. Thuc. 7.69.2), are marked by these beliefs, even as they are trampled in mud and blood in the Assinarus river. These beliefs are not confined to the ruling power, if their subjects are amenable to sharing in reflected glory of imperial prestige.[308] The habit of empire among the subjects of the powerful can be interpreted by the powerful as acceptance, and even authorization, of the status quo.[309] Once this habit is taken for granted, it brings a confidence in the imperialists' sense of innate superiority, and its inevitability,[310] as victory derives from, and proves, their military and moral courage:[311] this confidence can sometimes seduce even their subjects.[312]

The Athenians justified their power with appeals to their services in the Persian Wars. Thucydides is sceptical, but multiple rhetorical parallels from other powerful nations suggest that his picture should not be entirely trusted as a portrayal of general Athenian sentiment. Thucydides' Athenians nakedly seek to retain power however they can for their own advantage, but the Athenians of tragedy and other literature carefully justify their power by appealing to the benefits showered on Greece by Athenian virtue rather than the manifold advantages given them by the military force they used on their subjects when deemed necessary. Imperialists frequently deny imperialism. J.R. Seeley imagined pleasantly absent-minded British imperialists,[313] and Victorian imperialists claimed that the British Empire was not an empire in the usual (ancient) sense of the term.[314] As discussed earlier, representatives of the Roman Empire tended to ascribe its existence to the need for secure boundaries, others' aggression, or the need to defend allies. Sometimes, imperialists even argue that empire actually hurts them, rejecting any idea that empire brings the imperialist benefits, in a version of the topos of empire as burden.[315] But there is plenty of evidence from the culture of the British Empire, for example, to suggest that people were far from absent-minded about their empire and that it underlay all sorts of texts, monuments and institutions, domestic[316] as well as official.[317]

Since the ancient world was generally less squeamish than we are about the realities of power and the necessity that the weak should and maybe even ought to yield to the strong, Rome's insistence on the morality of its possession of its empire and on its benefits for its subjects is striking. In contrast, our historian of the Athenian empire makes his imperialists relentlessly cynical, and even their more idealized claims are frequently undermined. Given Thucydides' own statement of his care to create a factually reliable account, historians have often taken his Athenians' attitude to their empire at face value.[318] Moreover, epigraphical evidence is often interpreted through Thucydides and used to confirm his account. Athenian imperial inscriptions have often been used to argue that the language of Athenian alliance gradually mutated into the language of domination, a progression which can be made to align with Thucydides' trajectory from Pericles to Cleon at Mytilene to Melos.[319] But given the twin impulses of imperialism, both to assert authority and power, yet simultaneously to disavow force in favour of claims to generous leadership,[320] it may well be, that as Polly Low has argued, that we should not assume from inscriptions a clearly diachronic increase in Athenian assertions of power,[321] but rather, inscriptions can reveal "the ways in which power is used, controlled and represented."[322] Language such as "the cities which the Athenians rule" is an assertion of power, and sometimes, particularly after a rebellion, Athens doubtless needed to convey such a message.[323] The requirement that allies participate in Athenian religious practices (*ML* 40, 46, 49, 73) has also been interpreted as coercive, and on one level, it is. And yet, if only through the self-deception inherent in imperialism, it is also analogous to the many assertions in idealizing rhetoric that Athens invents or upholds Greek customs and generously offers them to other Greeks.[324] The allies are forced to participate or offered the opportunity to do so, depending on one's perspective.[325] Perhaps some Athenians and allies were moved by Nicias' plea at Syracuse (Thuc. 7.63.3):

> Remember how worth preserving is the pleasure felt by those of you who through your knowledge of our language and imitation of our ways were always considered Athenians, though you were not in reality, and were admired throughout Greece and had your share of the benefits of our empire.

Notes

1. Lord Curzon in Raleigh (1906) 35.
2. Said (1993) xxiii.
3. George W. Bush in 2002 quoted in Johnson (2004).
4. Pomper (2005) 1–2; Vlassopoulos (2010) 29; Münkler (2007) 4–17; Eckstein (2009). Cox (2005) 21–6; Maier (2006) discuss the eternally vexed question of whether the United States is an empire, and for a useful historiographically oriented account of the question, see MacDonald (2009).
5. Richardson (2008) 2; Webster (1996).
6. Although Samuel (1998) 3–11 argues for some important resemblances between the civic and military structures of peoples in the ancient world and those of modern nations.
7. Harrison (2008); Kelly (2009) xii. On studying empire through a comparative lens, see also Vasunia (2011).
8. Perlman (1991) 280–1; Griffith (1978); Kubala (2013) 133–4; Scheidel (2006). For Bradley (2010) 21, hegemony is control of one group by another, usually with some consent from the subordinate, secured by the promotion, acceptance and adoption of the hegemonic group's political, social and moral and intellectual ideals and norms. But imperial powers themselves often describe their power in similarly benign terms: Johnson (2004) 30; Maier (2006) 62–4.
9. Morris (2005) 3–4, 18–21; cf. Morris (2009) 99–103, 128–32.
10. Scheidel (2006) 8; Morris (2009) 99, 128–9; Kallet (2009) 56–8; Harrison (2005). Starr (1987), however, compares Athens directly with other ancient imperialistic nations in its tendency to oppress and exploit its subjects.
11. Colás (2007) 28. Even in the avowedly comparative and broadly ranging collection of papers on empires by Alcock et al. (2001), Athens' *archē* is barely mentioned, even though on at least three out of five of the criteria for empire suggested by Barfield (2001) 29–33, it could qualify; Maier (2006) is a notable exception to the neglect of Athens in comparative imperial histories.
12. Balandier (1970) 52, cited by Spurr (1993) 5–6.
13. Thuc. 1.70.4–7, 2.38.2, 40.1, 40.3; cf. Ar. *Eq.* 565–8, A. *Eum.* 996–1000.
14. Sternberg (2005a) 1 equates ancient Athenians and modern Americans through their "moral discomfort with empire." I would frame the argument slightly differently, arguing instead that each nation needed multiple reasons for justifying their power.
15. Hanson (2005) 8–9; Ma (2009) 227–8. Münkler (2007) 13–14 sees "many" imperial elements in Athens, though he considers it only a limited empire for reasons of scope and duration.
16. On the validity of such a methodology, see Harrison (2008) 13; (2005) 30; similarly, Mattingly (2011) explores the Roman Empire with a broad range of comparative evidence.
17. Richardson (2008) 6–7; cf. Ober (1989) 38–40; Crane (1998) 8–9. A related phenomenon is the psychology of the Athenian democracy explored by Wohl (2002): see esp. ix–xii, 27–8 for methodological questions related to exploring the psychology of (ix) a "long-dead community."

18 See Chapters 5 and 6.
19 Woolf (1997) 340; Green (1972) 48, 75–93; Kallet (2009) 43; Porter (2004) viii. Nigel Biggar's recent Ethics and Empire project, which offers a more favourable account of British imperialism, has been roundly condemned by many academics.
20 Few Romans questioned the concept of ruling others, much less its acceptability. It was their duty to offer others the peace and order that benevolent Roman control brought, and since Rome put such effort into its civilizing mission, it should "naturally" reap rewards for its pains: Campbell (2012) 169–80. Some scholars argue that Rome had no civilizing mission as such and that this claim was a projection of the values of later European imperialists attempting to justify their own actions, but see Hingley (2005) 64–7.
21 Gregory (2004) 10–11 argues that its attractions are still current even today (if not among most classicists), citing a continued "nostalgia for the aggrandizing swagger of colonialism itself, its privileges and powers." While these are tempered by anxiety and guilt, "its triumphal show and its effortless ethnocentric assumption of Might and Right" lurk in phenomena such as the War on Terror with its simple dichotomies of good versus evil. For Tharoor (2017) 214, it is "preposterous" to believe the "twaddle" of anyone claiming that the British Empire benefitted its subjects: this seems naïve to me.
22 Mason (1964) 11.
23 De Romilly (1963) 79–82. Maier (2006) 47–8, 77 discusses the psychological pleasure of domination; cf. Balandier (1970) 49.
24 Langer (1935) 108–12. While many elements in his account are specific to European imperialism, some of what he says of its general appeal resonates with Thucydides, especially Thucydides' explanation (6.24.2–4) of the origins of the Sicilian expedition in the appeal of faraway conflict, and pride in the extension of Athenian territory. Economic and practical considerations may drive such impulses, but more atavistic considerations such as "honor, prestige, power, and even plain combativeness" (111) are also important.
25 Raaflaub (1994) and (1998) sketches popular pride in the privilege of citizenship in the greatest and freest city in Greece and its opportunities for experiencing direct participation in government and in ruling others. The all-consuming nature of the empire, demanding vast sums of money, and commitment from its citizens, whether through dying for it or living to service it administratively, must also have influenced popular belief that it was both necessary and right: Raaflaub (1998) 17–19, 22–6.
26 For Athenian public art, see Hölscher (1998); Castriota (1992).
27 Hornblower (2004) 143, 248: "To [a] limited but real extent [Pindar's] odes offer us a sort of allied view of the empire."
28 Thuc. 1.73.2, 73.4, 74.2: the repeated phrase "getting into the ships" recurs in Lys. 2.40.
29 Strasburger (2009) 196–7.
30 The tendency is connected with the notorious question of the "popularity" or otherwise of the Athenian empire. The story of the revolt of Mytilene is used by de Ste Croix (1954) to suggest that the allies were relatively content with Athens' power: Bradeen (1960) argues the opposite, and indeed the theory of power offered by Barnes (1988) 95–127, which explains how hated rulers can still retain power, would tend to support a less idealizing view than that of de Ste Croix. Both de Ste Croix and Bradeen are selective in the evidence they use for their claims (cf. Legon (1968) 223–5): doubtless, the Athenians were equally selective with the evidence they used to argue that their power was just, deserved and generally beneficial for Greece.
31 Spurr (1993) 7.
32 To cite a comparative example offered by David Spurr, it is a fact that there is disease in Africa (as in many regions of the world), but through an imperialist mindset, factual description can easily slide into theories of Africa as a helpless, dangerous place, that urgently needs Western intervention, thence domination: Spurr (1993) 91.

33 The orators are highly consistent in this account: Lys. 2.47, 54–7, Pl. *Mx.* 241d, Isoc. 4.100., Aristid. *Ath.* 23–5; cf. Thuc. 1.75.2, 95.1, 130.2, 3.10.2. Hdt. 8.3.2 gives an alternative tradition: Strasburger (2009) 200–2.
34 For example, Morris (2009) 99–103; cf. 128–32.
35 Garland (2017) 107–14. Compare also the omens that are clearly bad but ignored or misinterpreted (Hdt. 7.37.2–3, 57.1–2) and tales of divine intervention against the Persians: Hdt. 8.13.1, 37.3–38, 65.1–6, 84.2, 94.2; 9.65.2.
36 See later, pp. 10, 11, 19, 21, 24 and cf. Samons (2000) 247–8.
37 Compare Euripides' epitaph over the Sicilian dead (Plut. *Nic.*17.4): "eight times triumphant *while the gods favoured both causes alike.*"
38 Compare Eupolis frr. 219, 234 and 330; Isoc. 4.29; 8.8, 12.124–5, Pl. *Mx.* 237c; Lycurg. *Leocr.* 82.
39 Hanson (2005) 274–87 gives a stirring account of the last years of the Peloponnesian War and Athens' obstinate rejection of Spartan peace proposals. Did they believe that the gods would always save them? Plutarch (*Nic.* 30) recounts a revealing story about a foreigner who was tortured for a long time after his incoherent account of the Sicilian disaster because no one could believe that the expedition had failed.
40 "Thucydides was probably writing against the gross distortions of Athens' past that the official tradition encouraged": Thomas (1989) 237.
41 In taking such a broad approach, I am pleased to follow Spurr (1993) 4, who acknowledges a huge variety in colonial experience but includes multiple transcultural comparisons in his account of the rhetoric of empire. Similarly, Lebow (2008) makes encouraging connections between the insights of Plato and Aristotle on human motivation and those created by contemporary research in socio-political theory. For an interesting comparison of Athens and the US as leaders, see also Lebow (2003) 310–59.
42 Given the tiny size of the area it controlled, Athens is an exception to this rule, but only partially: pp. 10–11 later.
43 Cline and Graham (2011) 37–45.
44 Maier (2006) 3–5.
45 As with the Balandier or Assyrian examples earlier, pp. 2, 5.
46 Webster (1996) 8–9.
47 In including imagination as part of history, I follow Collingwood (1946); Dray (1999) 191–228; Ober (1991) 252; Hingley (2005) 4–13. The process goes both ways: themes of contemporary interest inspire ancient historians to look for analogues in the ancient world. The Roman Empire inspired considerable scholarly interest in the 19th century (Liddel (2009); Walbank (1951) 59–60). Sir Richard Livingstone described Pericles' funeral speech as "one of the supreme expressions of the national idea." Livingstone was editor and translator of a 1973 version of Thucydides, and in 1937–8 led summer schools for colonial administrators: Samuel (1998) 5–6, 17–18; cf. Abernethy (2000) 194–5. More recently, "realist" theories of international relations frequently invoke Thucydides: Crane (1998) 61–71.
48 Hammond (1948) 105–6. Schumpeter (1955) 7 defines imperialism as "the objectless disposition on the part of a state to unlimited forcible expansion:" see also Colás (2007) 6–9, 31–70; Tully (2009) 23–5. Calhoun et al. (2006) define empire as "a political unity that is large and expansionist (or with memories of an expansionist past) reproducing differentiation and inequality among people it incorporates." Hoyos (2012) 3 cites Robert Werner's definition: "an expansionist mode of action, prompted by various causes, not directed to a precise end, resting on the conscious and programmatic disposition of a state, or interested parties authorised or recognised by it, with the aim of establishing and stabilising an imperium or Reich and of directly, in practice, ruling conquered groups, peoples and territories together with their institutions." In the 20th and 21st centuries, expansionist yearning stretches even into space: Snyder (1991/2003) 1–20.

49 Assyrian kings were charged at their coronations to extend Assyria's borders under the auspices of Ashur, so that resistance to the Assyrian army was resistance to divinity: Bedford (2009) 48. For the process as it shaped 19th-century England, see Said (1993) 106–10.

50 Pericles' funeral oration extols the expansion of Athenian territory by generations of Athenians and though he recommends curbing expansion in book one, this is merely temporary in the exigencies of war: Balot (2001) 173–4; Monoson and Loriaux (1998) 426. The ephebic oath encourages its takers to hand on a bigger and better country: Lycurg. *Leocr.* 76; cf. Plut. *Alc.* 15.4: "They swear to regard wheat, barley, vines, and olives as Attica's boundaries, so that they are trained to consider as their own all the tamed and fruit-bearing earth." Elsewhere Plutarch states (*Nic.* 12.1–2 and *Alc.* 17.2–3) that the Sicilian expedition aimed at expanding Athenian rule all the way to Gibraltar. Schumpeter (1955) 25–7 characterizes imperialism as an outgrowth of the warrior society in which life is fully realized only in war, so that organisationally and psychologically, imperialism acquires its own momentum.

51 Münkler (2007) 84; Wander (1997) discusses the euphemisms and appeals to morality in US political rhetoric; cf. Lebow (2008) 122: "To build identities and mobilize public support, states construct and project characters and narratives of themselves to which many of their citizens become deeply attached."

52 *Pace* Thucydides, I agree with Brunt (1978) 162: since the Athenians liked to see themselves as champions of the oppressed, "it seems very doubtful if many of them acknowledged publicly or in their own hearts that their empire was a tyranny": cf. Raaflaub (2004) 177. For why some of Thucydides' characters explicitly make this claim, see p. 155.

53 Colås (2007) 178; Münkler (2007) 80–107; Maier (2006) 61 well describes imperial ideology as "an exercise in lofty denial."

54 Takacs (2009) xvii–xxiii. One narrative must be maintained to the exclusion of all others: Said (1993) xii–xiii. "Empires have a voracious appetite for self-celebration and they reward their talented wordsmiths": Maier (2006) 20.

55 Spurr (1993) 156–9; cf. Balandier (1970) 24–5. For an account of appeals to civilization in the 19th and even 20th century, after the British empire had technically ended – imperial habits die hard! – see Tully (2009). Hingley (2005) 14–48 explores the way that a concept of civilization shaped Rome's view of itself, then later European writers' view of Rome, and therefore of their own (supposed) civilizing mission. Although he does not mention Athens, its rhetoric has many commonalities with that of his Romans.

56 Maier (2006) 21; Münkler (2007) 85–8 states: "the imperial mission is more than just self-justification . . . even if it fulfils that function perfectly well . . . the imperial mission converts self-legitimation into self-sacralization. Its quasi-religious sense of purpose means that empire is no longer in thrall to the random decisions of the politically powerful and socially influential" but given a grandeur above ordinary politics.

57 Thomas (1989) 207; Loraux (1986) 58–62.

58 Walters (1980) 1–2, 16–17 discusses the importance of these speeches as "ritual", even "liturgy". For the importance of ritual commemoration in establishing a community's historical memory (and creating "fact") see Connerton (1989) 41–71.

59 The funeral orations ascribed to Lysias 2, Demosthenes 60, Plato *Menexenus* and Hyperides 6.

60 Plutarch *Per.* 8.6 also mentions a funeral speech of Pericles dated to 439 BCE.

61 Strasburger (2009), originally 1958; Walters (1980); Loraux (1986) 64–5, 221–3, 252, 289; Rood (1998) 246 n.81; Pritchard (2000) 13–26; Tzanetou (2005) 101. One might cite as a partial analogy the relative continuity in Athenian social attitudes from the late fifth to fourth centuries discussed by Dover (1974) esp. 30–2. For more scepticism, see Connor (1987) 13, n.22; Loraux (1986) 252–62; Hornblower (1991) 118, 295. There are admittedly dangers in synchronic elision of so many decades (cf.

30 The Athenian . . . empire?

62 Strasburger (2009) 195–6. As well as the actual funeral speeches listed in n.59, compare Andoc.1.106–7, Dem.2.10–12, 3.24; 15.30; cf. 15.4; Lycurg. *Leocr.* 42, 47–51, 70, 72–88, 98–100, 104–6, Isocrates *Panegyricus* (4) and *Panathenaicus* (12), the encomium of Theseus in *Helen* (10), and Aristides' *Panathenaicus*. Thomas (1989) 196–237 considers the content of the *epitaphioi* "official tradition" (200), which strongly influenced general Athenian historical tradition; cf. Raaflaub (2004) 89, 166–77.

Ober (1989) 36–8) and Hornblower is especially wary of assimilating post-empire and fifth-century sources, but even he acknowledges that Thucydides probably gave less space to conventional themes than did later orators, implying that significant thematic continuity between the fifth and fourth centuries is possible.

63 Walters (1981) 205. Ziolkowski (1981) 133–6, 163, 173 shows that there is substantial common ground between Thucydides' speech and later funeral speeches, which Thucydides' idiosyncratic presentation obscures.

64 Raaflaub (1987) demonstrates that Herodotus' historical narrative frequently reflects contemporary questions, concepts and even vocabulary (227) of the Athenian empire; cf. Moles (1996).

65 For the relationship between tradition and originality in the speeches, see Frangeskou (1999); Herrman (2009) 14–24.

66 Speakers often acknowledge their debt to tradition: Thuc. 2.35.1; Dem. 60.10; Ober (1978) 119, 129–30; Thomas (1989) 200–2. People enjoy listening to what pleases them (Isoc. 8.3–11), and whether or not an individual actively supported Athenian interventionism, it is hard to imagine that he would have been entirely immune to the charms of stirring, yet also comforting, stories of his city's great past: Thomas (1989) 206.

67 Euripides' *Suppliants* and Aeschylus' fragmentary *Eleusinioi* dramatize Athenian insistence on upholding the laws of Greece and forcing burial of the bodies of the Seven against Thebes; in Euripides' *Heraclidae,* Athens rescues Heracles' children from persecution by Eurystheus; Euripides' fragmentary *Erechtheus* dramatized Eumolpus' attack on Attica. Athens' resistance to the Amazons is only mentioned in tragedy but is frequently represented in public art.

68 Thuc. 1.73.2–3; cf. 5.89.1. Thomas (1989) 211–13 states (211): "Far from being merely empty rhetorical convention, the broad epitaphic tradition of Athens' past recurs wherever defence, praise or emulation of the ancestors was called for." She supports this claim with both fifth-century examples (Hdt. 9.27.4) and fourth-century sources (Xen. *Hell.* 6.5.38–48, esp. 46–8, *Mem.* 3.5.8–12, 5.12, Ar. *Rhet.* 2.22.4–6), concluding (213) that the *epitaphios logos* was central to official tradition and to Athenian oral traditions"; indeed, "its ideals cannot be overemphasized."

69 On this speech, see Todd (2007), especially his introduction, 149–57, on its relationship to others of the genre. The commonalities between Hdt. 9.27 and themes in Lysias 2, Isocrates 4 and Plato's *Menexenus* suggest to him that such topoi were part of the genre "at least" as early as 430 BCE.

70 Perlman (1968) 258–9, 266. On the strong continuity of rhetorical theory and practice from the fifth to fourth century, see Heath (1990) and (1997) 231–4.

71 Ober (1978) 129; for echoes of Thucydides in Isocrates, see Wilson (1966) 55–6.

72 Hammond (1948) 112.

73 For the relationship between parody and convention in this speech, see Thomas (1989) 210–11; Rowe (2007) 92–103; Henderson (1975). Loraux (1986) 304–27 argues that Plato was ridiculing the absurdly flattering epitaphic descriptions of Athens to expose his fellow-citizens' complacency.

74 As it was to most citizens: Steinbock (2013) 33–5.

75 Raaflaub (1998) 21 estimates that between 2000 and 6000 citizens spent at least half a day at least 30 times in the assembly, not to mention the thousands in the council, juries and so on. In this intensely collective environment, it is likely that certain

common narratives would gradually take shape and then be used as "historical" precedents for shaping contemporary Athenian policy: cf. Raaflaub (2004) 168–72.
76 Rood (1998) 246.
77 Hölscher (1998) 163–4; Boedeker (1998).
78 *Panath.* 4, 8–13, 17, 25, 33, 40, 45, 62, 66–7, 70, 72, 75.
79 Cf. Isoc. 4.110–14 and 12.53–107.
80 Cf. Isoc. 12.70–3, 89–94; 4.110–32; 12.98–107.
81 Strasburger (2009) 201–4; Missiou (1992) 67–76. A strong continuity also exists between the language of the inscriptions of the Delian League and of the Second Athenian League: Low (2005) 97–8 and (2007) 218–22. Empires can live on in the national imagination even when they are formally finished: Ludden (2011) 132–5. Such psychological continuity, persisting long after the historical conditions which created it have receded, has arguably shaped recent debates surrounding Brexit, in which it is assumed that Britain will receive major concessions from the European Union with little offered in return: www.bbc.co.uk/news/uk-politics-40571123.
82 The balance between pride in the empire and fear for its vulnerability is especially noticeable in Livy's preface to *Ab Urbe Condita*.
83 Μόνοι γὰρ ἔστε ὑμεῖς ἄρχοντες ὡς εἰπεῖν κατὰ φύσιν ("For you alone are rulers by nature, so to speak"): Aristid. *Rom.* 91.
84 "Empire . . . is a project to dominate time as well as space": Maier (2006) 286.
85 Cf. Aristid. *Rom.* 61. *Panath.* 4–5, which states that praising Athens fully is simply impossible for an individual: "as in a boundless sea which sets no limits to the eye, each admires as much as he beholds" (trans. Behr (1986)).
86 *Fasti* 2.683–4; cf. V. *Aen.* 1.278–9.
87 Cf. Willis (2007) 333.
88 Hyperid. 6.27, cf. Dem. 60.19; Isoc. 4.92; 8.94; Dem. 18.192, 207, 208.
89 Thuc. 2.43.2, Gorg. 82F6 5–6DK, Lys.2.79–81, Dem. 60.32: cf. Grethlein (2013) 111–7.
90 Henderson (1975) 43 suggests that "Plato is intent on exposing (by taking it to an extreme) the mind of chauvinist fiction which would deny Athens' enemies credit even for Athens' defeat." In another possibly epitaphic echo, Pericles prophesies that Athens, not its enemies, may destroy itself (1.144.1; cf. 2.65.12). For variations on the topos, see Gorg. 82F6 25–6; Lys. 2.79; Dem. 60.19, 21; Hyperid. 6.28, 42.
91 Bradley (2010) 21; cf. Hardie (1986) 68; Dirks (2006) 286; Woolf (2001) 317–19. Lincoln (2007) 13.
92 Cic. *Cat.* 3.26; *de Prov. Cons.* 33; *Sest.* 67; cf. D.S. 40.4.
93 Cic. *Balb.* 64.
94 Coins suggest that Rome was grasping at universal domination as early as c. 76 BCE: Nicolet (1991) 23–35. Woolf (2001) 317–19 suggests that as early as the second century BCE, inscriptions show traces of the belief that the Roman people had a "mandate from heaven: to rule the world, even though it is not until Caesar and Cicero that the belief that all wars fought by Rome were justified comes into full flowering."
95 Cic. *Re Pub.* 3.15.24; Brunt (1978) 163. On British imperialists' portrayal of an "imperialist" Virgil, see Vasunia (2013) 152–3. Mattingly (1997); Fincham (2001); Webster (1996) and Hingley (2000) discuss the problematic influence on the history of scholarship of the Roman empire of overly benign British attitudes towards the British empire.
96 Lincoln (2007) 69–70.
97 Raaflaub (1987) esp. 227–8; Fornara (1971) 88. At Hdt. 7.50.3, Xerxes attributes Persia's power to its willingness to incur dangers, a standard Athenian topos (cf. Thuc. 2.39.4.) On Herodotus, Persia and Athenian imperialism, see Balot (2001) 114–35, and on the resonances of Hdt. 7.8α1 with Thuc. 6.18.7, see Macleod (1983b) 149–51.
98 Already the imperial topos of expansion throughout time is evident: Xerxes is merely following a natural and eternal process, inherited from his predecessors, and as he will say, it would be shameful to fall short of them.

99 Justifications of imperial conquest and subsequent prosperity in ancient Athens and Rome are typically linked, whether explicitly, or more implicitly, with the divine. The gods would hardly allow dealings of which they disapprove to prosper, and prosperity is proof that the existing order is right and good. In 2003, Dick and Lynne Cheney sent out a Christmas card bearing Ben Franklin's words: "And if a sparrow cannot fall to the ground without His notice, is it probable that an Empire can rise without His aid?": Mann (2004) 632.
100 Note the appeal to conventional wisdom, echoing the tendencies of the funeral orations discussed earlier.
101 In Athenian tragedy, Athens must often punish the wicked, acting as humans are morally bound to act (Lys. 2.19), but in the service of the gods, and Zeus himself can be "the punisher" (A. *Pers.* 827). Gorgias (82F6, 12–13) describes the Athenians as θεράποντες τῶν ἀδίκως δυστυχούντων, κολασταὶ δὲ τῶν ἀδίκως εὐτυχούντων ("helpers of the undeserving unfortunate, punishers of the undeservedly fortunate"). Persia's defeat is viewed as a deserved punishment: Lys. 2.56–7; Dem. 60.11; Isoc. 4.89, 120; Pl. *Mx.* 240d. Similarly, the defeat of the Amazons, assimilated with the Persians in literature and art on the *Stoa Poikile* (Paus. 1.15.2) as part of Athens' timeless battle against disorder and barbarism, is punishment for their foolish greed: Lys. 2.6. The punishment topos (for disloyalty) is also invoked to justify Athens' actions at Melos and Scione (Isoc. 4.101) and even appeared in the rhetoric of G. W. Bush after the Iraq war: Lincoln (2007) 98. George Grote, an enthusiast for both Athenian and British empires, "explained the transformation of the Delian confederacy into an Athenian empire by reference to the failure of members to perform their duties in an appropriate fashion:" Liddel (2009) 18.
102 Translation by Godley (1922). Büchmann (1895) 157 suggests that this is the earliest expression of the idea of an empire on which the sun never sets. On this passage see also Harrison (2009) 386–7.
103 Although Isoc. 15.234 hopefully claims that visitors' admiration of Athens qualifies the city to rule not only the Greeks but the whole world. "World" is not necessarily literal. Rome and China claimed world domination while being aware of one another: Münkler (2007) 11–12 .
104 Thus Castriota (1992) 194: "There was no context within the Greek world that would permit the assimilation of the larger Achaemenid or oriental ideology of oriental rule under a central monarchy appointed and supported by the gods." In this formulation, Castriota is right, but general tendencies towards domination through appeals to its rightness (and ultimately to divine sanction) are a legitimate parallel between the two. Even though the language of Athens' power was often (though not always) couched in terms of alliance rather than active domination (Castriota (1992) 194–7), by claiming Athens' outright superiority over others, the *epitaphioi* and other texts do justify the city's claims to domination in Greece.
105 Bang and Kolodziejczyk (2012a) 27–8; Barjamovic (2012) 55–7.
106 Cf. Aristid. *Rom.* 11–14.
107 Joseph. *BJ* 7.134 describes precious metals and ivory "flowing like a river" at Vespasian's triumphs, while Abernethy (2000) 280 cites the claim of a minister for the British colonies that "Java pours riches upon the homeland as if by a magician's wand."
108 Ramamurthy (2003) 47 discusses a similar phenomenon in British imperial advertising.
109 Cf. Nisbet and Hubbard (1970) 10 discussing Hor. *Od.* 1.1.16.
110 On this vital imperial claim, see also later, pp. 15–19.
111 It is prefaced with the lines, ἔσπετε νῦν μοι Μοῦσαι Ὀλύμπια δώματ' ἔχουσαι ("Tell me, Muses who dwell on Olympus").
112 KA (1986) 487.
113 KA (1984) 227.
114 Plut. *Per.* 12.6 lists all the precious materials and specialist craftsmen requisitioned for Athens' public works, and *Per.* 12.3–5, though clearly anachronistic in places

(Andrewes (1978) 1–5), portrays imperial Athens' sense of justified entitlement: they owe the allies no account of how their money is spent as long as they continue to defend them from the barbarians (12.3).
115 KA (1984) 300.
116 V. *Geo.* 2.149 claims an eternal spring for Italy in a similar list of unique abundance.
117 Spurr (1993) 13–15; Wilkins (1997) 255. For the utopian presentation of imperial Athens through such means, see Constantokopoulou (2007) 164–73.
118 Braund (1994) 46–7.
119 On utopian plenitude in comedy, see especially Ruffell (2000). Pherecrates fr.113 and Teleclides fr.1 link lists of abundant goods with a golden age when the earth flowed with soup (Pherecrates 113.3) or wine, and fish even leapt out of the sea to roast themselves (Teleclides 1.4–7). The golden age was golden because those living then were exceptionally just (Hes. *WD* 225–37) and while these claims are comic, not factual, it is intriguing that the conditions of a golden age also feature notably in the writing and art of Augustan Rome: Zanker (1988) 167–92. Galinsky (1996) 90–120 cautions that their expression is highly complex, but they do share some thematic similarities with the topoi of the idealized Athens, such as abundance, the balance of successful wartime and peacetime pursuits and moral virtue.
120 Athens is neither of these because the middle is the perfect way: later, pp. 16–17.
121 Claims to self-sufficiency (e.g. Thuc. 2.41.1) are in some tension with claims to all the goods of the world.
122 Lys.2.2; Ath. 20B.
123 Bradley (2010) 19–20; Williams (1980) ix.
124 As [Xen.] *Ath. Pol.* 3.2, 8, though he considers the abundance undesirable; Ar. *Nu.* 306–13; *Eq.* 582 claims Athenian superiority in "war, poets and power": Aristid. *Rom.* 95–9 lauds Rome in much the same way.
125 Joseph. *BJ* 7.132–4 with Bang (2009) 103. Clarke (2008) 209–12 discusses Rome's expression of the totality of its imperial control through expressions of abundance. Lincoln (2007) 75–59 discusses imperial abundance in the Achaemenid empire, and for the British Empire, cf. Ramamurthy (2003) 73–4; Samuel (1998) 88–9.
126 Root (1985); see, however, Castriota (1992) 184–93.
127 Miller (1997) 218–42, 243–58 discusses the incorporation of elements of Persian artefacts more generally into Athenian life and art.
128 Hardie (1986) 24.
129 The phenomenon is especially prevalent in the pervasiveness of the Roman empire in coins, cult, architecture and so on: Woolf (2001) 320–2. Through rather different means, the emperors of China also sought to make their power seem natural, eternal, unchanging and cosmic: Yates (2001).
130 Anxiety about its eternal quality may itself be an eternal concern of empires: Vasunia (2013) 135, 145; Raleigh (1906) 46–7; Hingley (2000) 28–37; Münkler (2007) 31.
131 Hardie (1986) 252. Quint (1993) 45.
132 *Rep.* 2.30; *Har. Resp.* 19; *Phil.* 6.19.
133 E.g. Lys. 2.4–6; Lycurg. Leocr. 98–101.
134 Such claims are already strong in Herodotus: 1.60.3; 2.51.1, 4; 5.78; 6.109.6, 112.3; 7.161; 8.11.2.
135 Cf. Isoc. 5.34; 12.124, 138, 148, 204.
136 Reality shows a rather more pragmatic Athens: Christ (2012) 118–76, esp. 145–54.
137 Takacs (2009) 2–4, 22–4; Schumpeter (1955) 25–7; Hdt. 7.8α2; Dem. 60.27–31 links the deeds of the contemporary members of the tribes with their heroic namesakes: cf. Isoc. 4.51–60, 15.306–7, 12.124; Hyperid. 6.3, 38.
138 Spurr (1993) 31–2. For the use of such terms in the *epitaphioi* ("benefactors," "saviours" and so on) see Walters (1980) 9. The *epitaphioi* often conceal the effort required to achieve naval excellence: instead, Athenian achievement is imagined as a mere fact of inborn nature – a "big word" – contrasted with arduous Spartan training, for example at Thuc. 2.39.1: Loraux (1986) 151. At Rome, abstract ideas of *gloria*

and *virtus* all stimulated the desire for military domination: Harris (1985) 17–38; cf. 47. For similarly "big words" in post-Iraq US rhetoric, see Lincoln (2007) 97–9; Johnson (2004) 4.
139 Mantena (2010) 72. The sentence encapsulates several tropes of empire: transcendence of time, reliance on abstract nouns, and the justification of empire through appeals to superior civilization.
140 Bosworth (1993) 36–7; compare also Thucydides' famous comments on the distortion of language by war at Corcyra, 3.82.
141 Already in the late third millennium, Ur-Nammu justifies seizing control of Sumer and Akkad by invoking a distant past of unification: Cline and Graham (2011) 31–2; see also Said (1993) 3–5.
142 Thornton (1965) 31; Vasunia (2013) 119–56 discusses the relationship between the British and Roman Empires.
143 Bang and Kolodziejczyk (2012) 1–2; Cannadine (2001) 2.
144 Cline and Graham (2011) 85.
145 In 1845, John L. O'Sullivan coined the term "manifest destiny", claiming America to be exempt from the cycles of history, having achieved a divinely ordained culmination of the westward movement of civilization. The strongly Christian emphasis of this belief is peculiar to America, but it too results from the need to make empire reassuringly eternal, right and benign, unlike all previous empires: Malamud (2010) 257; Williams (1980) 87–8.
146 Castriota (1992) 6.
147 The topoi populate other texts as well: Xen. *Hell.* 6.5.45.; Dem. 2.24; 16.14–15; Andoc. 1.107; Aeschin. 3.134; Isoc. 4.34–40; Xen. *Mem.* 3.5.12.; Xen. *Hell.* 3.5.10; Lycurg. *Leocr.* 42.
148 Cf. Isoc. 10.32–7; 12.128–9, 139, 143, 153; Pl. *Mx.* 238c–d.
149 Meiggs (1972) and Rhodes (1992), esp. 60–1, suggest that the change was gradual. For Fornara and Samons (1991) and Samons (2000) 72–5, 94, 110, 170–200, 331–2, an imperial mindset is rooted in the growth of Athenian confidence after the expulsion of the tyrants and was essentially in existence by the late 460s. Thucydides' theory of human nature roots a drive to imperialism so deep within human nature that it shapes his account of the Archaeology as well: Foster (2010) 8–43.
150 Adler (2012); cf. Adler (2011). Examples include Calgacus' speech, Tac. *Ag.* 30–2, cf. *Ag.* 15; *Ann.* 13.55, 14.35; Sall. *Iug.* 81.1; Mithridates' letter in *Hist.* 4.69; Caes. *BG* 7.77. "They cannot represent themselves; they must be represented": Edward Said, using an epigraph from Marx to frame his critique of Orientalism.
151 Clarke (2001) 105–6.
152 Adler (2012) 299. For Syme (1958) 528–9, Calgacus' speech is a powerful denunciation of Roman imperial conquest, but Rutledge (2000) argues that Tacitus casts him as superficially sympathetic, but actually lesser than his conquerors, so as to promote the necessity and desirability of their conquest. More recently, the US wrongly imagined Iraq as a kind of empty screen onto which it could project its own image, with disastrous consequences: Gregory (2004) 217.
153 Brunt (1978) 183.
154 Dio *RH* 43.19–20. Visual media can convey especially complex messages: for example, Trajan's column combines graphic portrayals of the torture of Romans by Dacian women to justify the campaign with reassuring representations of the triumph of civilization over barbarity: Ferris (2000) 61–8, and in general, 6–12, 36–9, 55–60, 148–50, 163.
155 A frequent boast of the idealized Athens is that it is preeminently the city which feels pity (Mills (1997) 106, n.74), but pity has an imperial dimension when it expresses the superior status of the pitier over the pitied. Sternberg (2005a) 7 (cf. Tzanetou (2005)) argues that the development of images of Athens as the city which is preeminent in pity are contemporaneous with, and a product of, the emergence of Athenian power.
156 Bradley (2010a) 131.

157 Hdt. 5.82.2; S. *OC* 694; Dem. 60.5; Pl. *Mx.* 237d–e, 238a; Isoc. 4.33; 12.124, 206; and in general Mills (1997) 61–6. Reality is strikingly at odds with the imagined Athens: Moreno (2009), discussing Athens' exploitative use of cleruchies, comments (214) "whereas tribute was (at least in theory) intended to fund the operation of an alliance, the benefits of such territorial encroachment flowed wholly to an Athenian 'master race' (in Badian's words)." Cairns (1965) 147 cites the *Daily News* commenting on David Livingstone's exploits: "a thrill of exultation at the thought that literally, the whole earth is full of our labours – that there is no region in which our industrial enterprise, our skill in arms, our benevolent eagerness to diffuse the blessings of civilization and pure and true religion, have not been displayed."
158 As an unnamed White House official famously stated to the journalist Ron Suskind, "We're an empire now, and when we act we create our own reality": October 17, 2004, *The New York Times Magazine*.
159 "This is an empire of peace, because Italy wants peace for itself and for all and decides to go to war only when forced by imperious, irrepressible necessities of life": Benito Mussolini, quoted by Nelis (2000) 404.
160 Hardt and Negri (2000) xiv–xv. Their "Empire" is not territory "owned" by one nation, but a post-imperial conglomeration of national and transnational powers, such as the IMF or WTO, but the totalizing tendencies that they describe closely align with those of traditional imperialists. While it is easy to fault some of their argument for lack of precision (e.g. Maier (2006) 109–10), their work remains stimulating and has influenced this chapter more than the citations may suggest.
161 Harrison (2008) 16; Cline and Graham (2011) 3–5. Xerxes appropriates an inscription of Darius which proclaims his strength, moderation and virtues in war and peace: Bridges (2015) 81–3; cf. Said (1978) esp. 21, 56–7. "Chronic wrongdoing or an impotence which results in a general loosening of the ties of civilized society may ... force the United States, however reluctantly ... to the exercise of an international police power": Theodore Roosevelt, quoted by Williams (1980) 131.
162 Serrault admits that colonization initially requires force; fortunately, it soon develops into an admirable, lawful and uncontroversial system: Spurr (1993) 29–30. Williams (1980) 112–36, 175–81 discusses the self-image of the United States as a benevolent world policeman and potential psychological effects on its citizens of this image.
163 Mattingly (2011) 10.
164 Brunt (1978) 163–4; cf. Dion. Hal. *Ant. Rom.* 1.5.2. Cic. *Rosc. Am.* 50 states that the Romans cultivated their own lands diligently and did not desire those of others: *therefore*, they added territory to the Roman state and made Rome's people great.
165 Cic. *Off.* 1.35; *Rep.* 2.30, 3.34–5. Dion. Hal. *Ant. Rom.* 2.16–18 explains Rome's success through Romulus' policies of sparing the conquered and giving them citizenship, moderation and justice, allied with military strength.
166 For the connotations of this admired but multivalent "big word", and its help in suppressing "the violence and appropriation necessarily involved in Rome's expansion," see Gordon (1990) 235–8. In particular, "*humanitas* [is an ideological instrument] developed to contain possible threats to the basic assumption ... that those who were in any moment in control deserved to be where they were. It is this view, supported by a religious conception of the world, which Max Weber memorably termed a theodicy of good fortune": Gordon (1990) 238.
167 Liv. 5.5.44; Vitr. 6.1.10–11; Brunt (1978) 164. See also pp. 18–19.
168 Erskine (2010) 35–6.
169 Vasunia (2005) 51; Cairns (1965) 74–6; Ramamurthy (2003) 6–7.
170 Bradley (2010) 36–7, 134.
171 "The secret of power was order. And order, to be secure, must be *just*": Thornton (1965) 30; cf. Abernethy (2000) 381–4.
172 "Without us ... indigenous populations would still be abandoned to misery and abjection; epidemics, massive endemic diseases ... infant mortality would still wipe out

half their offspring, petty kings... would still sacrifice them to vicious caprice; their minds would still be degraded by the practice of base superstitions... they would perish from misery in the midst of unexploited wealth": Serrault, quoted by Spurr (1993) 76–7.
173 Thornton (1965) 161. Münkler (2007) viii: "Fear of chaos, and the self-appointed role of defender of order against disorder, good against evil through which the empire sees and legitimizes itself, are corollaries of the imperial mission."
174 Brunt (1978) 183; Mattingly (2011) 24–5. According to Liv. 33.12.7, Romans as early as Cato invoked ancient Roman customs of sparing the conquered, but only the Roman power decides who deserves being spared, as Augustus himself acknowledges: "externas gentes, *quibus tuto ignosci potuit*, conservare quam excidere malui" (*RG* 3.2).
175 Dirks (2006) 173–4; cf. Williams (2012) 194–5.
176 Though for Kennedy (2017), "dangerous visions of purity" are endemic in Athens' literature and laws.
177 Bryce (1914) 58–69; Hall and Rose (2006) 19–20, 22–3.
178 Vitr. 6.1.10–11, Strab. *Geog.* 6.4.1–2; 8.1.3: Colås (2007) 32–3; McCoskey (2012) 47.
179 Balot (2001) 84, 194; Detienne (1996) 89–106; Vernant (2006) 208–211.
180 Polyb. 6.11–18; Aristid. *Rom.* 90.
181 Relevant here is the claim of Engels, cited by Loraux (1986) 213, 426–7, that any philosophical system "springs from an imperishable desire of the human mind – the desire to overcome all contradictions."
182 Mills (1997) 97–103.
183 Isoc. 1.16: Athens is not perfect because not even the gods are blameless!
184 Bang and Kolodziejczyk (2012) 27–8.
185 Cairns (1965) 98–9. Aelius Aristides' *Roman Oration* (41) dubs wisdom and restraint Hellenic qualities, while barbarians have riches and might. Rome combines superior versions of both: Oliver (1953) 879.
186 Harrison (2008) 17–18; Haubold (2007) 50.
187 Hingley (2000) 3–4, 86–95.
188 Pl. *Rep.* 4.435e–436a; Ar. *Pol.* 1327b18–36: Isaac (2004) 60–74; Williams (2012) 59–65.
189 [Xen.] *Ath. Pol.* 2.7; Aristid. *Panath.* 8–17.
190 Mills (1997) 71–4. The Persians combine vices as the Athenians combine virtues: Isoc. 4.151–2. Even in pederasty, Athens claims the middle (Pl. *Symp.* 182a–d): slow, inarticulate Elis and Boeotia have no strictures about gratifying lovers, in tyrannically ruled Ionia, such love is forbidden, but in democratic Athens, they follow the right principles.
191 The pervasive contrast of μέν and δέ in Greek makes the ability to combine contrasting elements especially natural in Greek writing. On the topos of combined contraries in *epitaphioi*, see Loraux (1986) 153–4. "Only the people here have a good reputation through their contrarieties" (Aristid. *Panath.* 62, trans. Oliver (1968)), as both the most ancient of Greeks through their autochthony but also young like Dionysus. In Lys. 2.50 (cf. Thuc. 1.105.4), old and young are joined as a perfect army to resist enemies, the old with their experience, the young with their nature: Athens prevails and will always prevail, even when relying on soldiers too old or too young for an ordinary army. In Thucydides 6, Alcibiades, who articulates a cynical version of Athens' idealized portrayal of its vigorous attention to helping others, is Athenian imperial man gone astray in his ability to be everything to everyone (Plut. *Alc.* 23.2–6): Balot (2001) 167–8. Plut. *Alc.* 35.2 notes that Alcibiades' successes gave him such a reputation for limitless daring and intelligence that when he failed in anything, people assumed that he had done so deliberately, since no one would believe in his inability.

One may compare the limitless daring and intelligence of Athens itself and the claims that its defeats are self-defeats, not defeats imposed by others.
192 Mills (1997), esp. 105–6.
193 Thus Morris (2009) 132 considers "empire" an inappropriate term to denote Athenian power: "I believe that calling the Athenians' fifth-century *archē* an empire is a mistake because the sense of foreignness was, by the standards of . . . other ancient empires . . . very weak." I suggest, however, that Athens' *conception* of and justifications offered for its power do closely resemble those of "proper" empires.
194 For incomplete virtue in other cities, especially Sparta, see Thuc. 2.39.1, 40.2; Isoc. 4.92; 12.46, 208, 217; Pl. *Mx.* 240c4–d1. Isoc. 12.120–2 states (122) that cities other than Athens are full of matricide, incest, child-eating and other horrors of tragedy.
195 Gorg. 82F6; Thuc. 2.37.1, 40.2, 41.1; Pl. *Mx.*238c–d; Isoc. 4.64–5, 73; 12.124, 151, 164, 196–7, 208–9; Dem. 60.10–11; Hyperid. 6.35–6; Lycurg. *Leocr.*14; Aristid. *Panath.* 92–3.
196 A. *Pers.* 234; Hdt. 5.105.2; 7.5.2, 8β1–3, 11.2, 138.1, 139.1; 9.3.1; Lycurg. *Leocr.* 82; Dem. 60.23; Isoc. 4.48, 67, 71–2; 15.299; 16.27.
197 Lys. 2.18; Pl. *Mx.* 237e–238a.
198 Thuc. 2.41.1; cf. Isoc. 4.50.
199 Millender (2001) 149–51 discusses related Athenian assertions of cultural superiority over Sparta through greater literacy.
200 Isoc. 4.39 states that the Greeks once had no laws and dwelt in scattered regions (resembling the description of Sparta at Thuc. 1.10.2), so Athens took over some places and offered examples to others. Athens, unlike Sparta, supports the common laws of Greece: Isoc. 4.55–8, 12.213. Athens invented laws, but did not invent too many of them, unlike some states, and in the so-called "unwritten laws", again reigns supreme: Thuc. 2.37.3; Isoc. 7.40–2, 12.144; cf. Gorgias 82F6 20–4.
201 Further, Athens resembles the sun (but really, the sun resembles Athens) because it "continually punishes the wicked, [gives aid] to the just, [and dispenses] equality instead of injustice to all." Translation by Herrman (2009) 39.
202 Isoc. 12.124, 198; Pl. *Mx.* 238e–239a.
203 Mills (1997) 62–3: Hdt. 7.161.3; Thuc. 2.36.1 (somewhat obliquely); E. *Erechtheus* fr.360. 5–13; Ar. *Vesp.* 1075; Lys. 2.17–18, 43; Dem. 60.4; Isoc. 4.24, 12.124, 8.49; Pl. *Mx.* 237b, 254c–d; Lycurg. *Leocr.* 41, 83; Hyperid. 6.7. For the connection of authochthony and collective nobility, see Thomas (1989) 217–21; Rosivach (1987). Shapiro (1998) discusses the theme in art.
204 Isaac (2004) 131–2.
205 Isaac (2004) 33–41. Pl. *Mx.* 245d states that as pure-blooded Greeks, Athenians preeminently hate alien races.
206 Lys. 2.17; Isoc. 4.24; Aristid. *Panath.* 25–6. The tradition of Athenian autochthony was contested. Herodotus (1.57, 2.51) states that non-Greek Pelasgians once inhabited Attica and that the Athenians drove them out of Attica (6.137.1): Shapiro (1998) 130–1.
207 Rosenbloom (1995) 99 discusses the conjunction of the "Athenians alone" and "Athenians first" motif and its connection with Marathon.
208 Plataea's contribution at Marathon was well known: Hdt. 6.111.
209 Athens is alone in battle and alone among cities: Hdt. 7.10β1, 161.3; 8.140β4; 9.27.2, 5–6; E. *Hcld.* 306; S. *OC* 261; Thuc. 1.73.4; Lys. 2.20, Dem. 60.4,10, 11; Isoc. 4.25, 109; 16.27; Pl. *Mx.* 240a, Aristid. *Panath.* 222, 225. Spartan selfishness is often contrasted with Athenian altruism, explicitly or implicitly: Isoc. 4.93, 112; 5.42; 12.41, 45–6. Broader explorations of the attractions of being "the only" one lie outside the range of this book, but there is a striking similarity between Athens' images of itself and the description of the ideal figure of the Lone Ranger by Dorfman (1983) as combining the opposing traits of "ferocity of competition and gentleness

of compassion" (99), preferring persuasion to force but sometimes being compelled to use violence, and offering his services to all while gaining no benefits from his abilities (100).
210 Not strictly true, of course: see 2.40.3–4 with Mills (1997) 63–4.
211 Cf. Lys. 2.20. Cic. *De Or.* 1.196 makes similar claims for Rome and if we had more non-Athenian or Roman examples from the ancient world, we would doubtless read similar sentiments, as Isoc. 12.200–2 suggests. Even Gandhi was not immune: "I believe that the civilization India has evolved is not to be beaten in the world. . . . Rome went, Greece shared the same fate, the might of the Pharaohs was broken, Japan has become westernised, of China nothing can be said, but India is still, somehow or other, sound at the foundation": Vasunia (2013) 147.
212 Cf. Pl. *Mx.* 239b, Dem. 60.8. Athens has the power to punish every invader, mythical or historical: Isoc. 12.193–6.
213 Thuc. 1.107.3; Plut. *Cim.* 17.2.
214 Similarly, Athenian claims to having given all benefits to the Greek world are obviously untrue, but Athens was demonstrably culturally supreme in Greece.
215 Lys. 2.24; Pl. *Mx.* 241b; Andoc. 1.107, 3.5; Hyperid. 6.19, 35; Aristid. *Panath.*125, 167.
216 Isoc. 4.86; Lys.2.44; Dem. 60.10; Lyc. *Leocr.* 104; Hyperid. 6.5.
217 Thuc. 2.41.4; Hyperid. 6.19, 35; cf. Isoc. 4.83.
218 Lys. 2.42; Dem.18.202–3; Isoc. 4.68, 92–9; 16.27: Marincola (2007) 112. Gregory (2004) 23 cites a 2002 essay by Fareed Zakaria in the *New Yorker*, claiming that America "remains the universal nation, the country people across the world believe should speak for universal values." Others experience violence, but violence targeting the United States is an attack on humanity itself. So too, the *epitaphioi* sometimes equate Athens' disasters with Greece's: Lys. 2.21, Dem. 60.24 with Loraux (1986) 82, 144.
219 Gorgias 82F6 1–2.
220 British descriptions of Maori fighting allow that their enemy is courageous, chivalrous and talented at using terrain in their favour, but deny them the ability to think strategically, while the idea that they beat the British through simple military superiority was unthinkable: Belich (1986) 311–17.
221 Isoc. 4.26–7, 41–2, 51; 12.128, 165–6, 176, 197, 227; 15.77; Dem. 60.17; Pl. *Mx.* 238b; Aristid. *Panath.* 235–53.
222 Thuc. 2.40.1, 3; Lys. 2.42 (of Themistocles); Isoc. 6.15, 7.74: Parry (1981) 165. The combination of virtues is already an ideal in the *Iliad*: Loraux (1986) 153–4. The most famous expression of this is at *Il.* 9.443; cf. 6.78–9, 7.288–9, 9. 53–4, 12. 213–4, 13.727–8, 15.282–4.
223 The use of military power for morally beneficial intervention to help the oppressed is especially striking in Euripides' *Heraclidae* and *Suppliants*: cf. Isoc. 4.51–60, 79–81; Hyperid. 6.3. In 1914, Sigismund Goetze painted five pictures of Britannia on the Ambassadors' staircase of the Foreign Office, comprising Britannia Sponsa (Viking Bride), Colonorum Mater, Britannia Bellatrix (teaching its colonies the art of war), Nutrix (teaching them peace); and Pacificatrix, in which the colonies contribute to a Pax Britannica: Wilsdon (2000) 218.
224 The Thebans have a different story altogether: Pind. *Nem.* 9.22–4, *Ol.* 6.12–16; Paus. 1.39.2.
225 E. *Supp*; Lys. 2.7–10; Isoc. 4.58, 10.31, 14.53.
226 Oliver (1968) 18–19; Pliny (*Ep.* 24.1–4) attributes such claims to Greece more broadly.
227 Cf. A. *Eum.* 14.
228 Compare the texts cited in n.216 earlier. Isoc. 12.45–6 contrasts early Athens with early Sparta, selfish, aggressive and neglectful of farming and the arts, claiming also (153) that the great Spartan lawgiver Lycurgus learned his trade from Athens. Furthermore, 12.164–7 invents a history in which the time of the Ionian migration strongly

The Athenian . . . empire? 39

resembles fifth-century Athens, in bringing economic and political benefits to the colonized, and crushing barbarians.

229 Isoc. 4.34, 40; Dem. 60.5; Plut. *Cim.* 10.6. Athens takes credit for the Eleusinian mysteries and agriculture long before the days of supreme Athenian power: Mills (1997) 61, n.48.
230 All translations of Isocrates are by Norlin (1928–9).
231 Cf. E. *Tro.* 801–3; S. *OC* 694–706. For olives as emblematic of civilization, see Detienne (1970).
232 Thuc. 2.40.4; Isoc. 4.29–30 ("beloved of the gods . . . devoted to mankind", Athens shared the great blessings that she had acquired with everyone); 4.34–5, 52; 15.57; Aristid. *Panath.* 4 with Oliver (1953) 92–3. In Aristides' *Roman Oration* (98) which owes a considerable debt to Isocrates' *Panegyricus* (Oliver (1953) 879–80), Rome's generosity is similarly highlighted. Hyperid. 4.33; Isoc. *Letter to Philip* 1.17 claims Athens is the most useful city and (19) has often saved the Greeks.
233 Isoc.12.56; Dem. 24.51; Arist. *Ath. Pol.* 22.4; Plut. *Per.* 39.1, 4; Aristid. *Panath.* 271.
234 Theseus greatly appealed to the Victorians. Ruskin in *Fors Clavigera* letter 22 (1872) calls him a lawgiver and peacemaker, "exterminator of every bestial and savage element": Harrison (1976) 101–19 (109).
235 Lys. 2.7–10; cf. Isoc. 4.55–6.
236 Even Demeter is Athens' suppliant: Isoc. 4.28.
237 In Isoc.14.1, the Plataeans specifically cite Athens' reputation for rescuing victims of injustice. Historical examples blend with pre-imperial mythological stories (such as Theseus' liberation of Greece from Minos and his clearing of the way from Trozen to Athens) to affirm Athens' self-image as the city which helps the oppressed and in their turn shape Athens sense of its place in the Greek world: Mills (1997) 13–29.
238 See later, pp. 61, 68, 87–8, 90–1, 92.
239 Spurr (1993) 13–15. For Gregory (2004) 4, similar stories are key to the self-image of the colonial west: "myths of self-sufficiency in which 'the West' reaches out only to bring to others the fruits of progress that would otherwise be beyond their grasp."
240 Spurr (1993) 43ff.
241 See later, pp. 47–50, 53–4, 65–8.
242 Falkner (2005) 166–7.
243 Spurr (1993) 52–3; on the connection of pity with detachment, see Halliwell (2002) 215–7; Sternberg (2005a) 7.
244 Dougherty (1993) 91 quotes Hawkes (1973) 211, who compares drama and colonization as both "acts of civic construction", by imposing the shape of the dramatist's culture on the new world and making the world "recognisable, habitable, 'natural', redeeming untouched landscape by bringing a humanising art."
245 Raleigh (1906) 5.
246 "I think everyone would agree that war is right if you are being wronged yourselves or aiding another who is being wronged": Andoc. 3.13.
247 Diod. Sic. 32.5. Note, too, the Rhodians' reproach to the Romans at Liv. 45.22.5.
248 Livy 1.32; Cic. *Off.* 1.35–38; Dion. Hal. *Ant. Rom.*2.72; Harris (1985) 166–75; Drexler (1959), esp. 97–9.
249 *Off.*1.38: Harris (1985) 164–5. Harris' argument that Roman imperialism was fundamentally aggressive, not (as they claimed) defensive, has been hugely influential and is hard to refute: Rich (1993) 38–68, however, makes some important qualifications.
250 Harris (1985) 172–3; Griffin (2008) 88–90. On Roman expressions and practice of the just war and the justice of their domination, see Drexler (1959); Champion (2004) 162–213. The importance of actively justifying war, with appeal to the gods and heroes, is attested in Sparta (Thuc.2.74.2, 4.87.2), and Samons (2000) 247–8 argues that the transfer of a substantial sum of money to Athena's treasury in 432 BCE was a way of ensuring the goddess' protection and approval for the ensuing war.

251 Olko (2012) 263–5. From a Persian perspective, attacking Greece was quite justified because the Greeks had given Artaphrenes earth and water (Hdt. 5.73), creating a treaty that they then violated: Lincoln (2007) 30–2.
252 Harris (1985) 170; Mattern (2004) 189–91. For a fascinating account of the conflicting mixture of claims to moral superiority and cruelty inherent in 19th-century African colonialism, see Cairns (1965).
253 Harrison (2008) 7; for Athens, see Finley (1978); Meiggs (1972) 255–72.
254 Harrison (2008) 10.
255 Compare Albert Serrault's words, earlier n.172, or those of Lord Curzon (Raleigh (1906) 4–5): "our mission there is one of obligation and not of profit; and that we do our humble best to retain by justice that which we may have won by the sword."
256 Isoc. 4.68–72, 6.42, 12.193–5.
257 Cf. Thuc. 2.41.4.
258 Translation by Lamb (1930).
259 Cf. also Isoc. 12.112, 189–90.
260 Compare Nicias' appeals to the allies, Thuc. 7.63.3–4.
261 Mantena (2010) 71 discusses British portrayals of India as their burden; cf. Spurr (1993) 111–3. "Our frontiers are today on every continent ... only the United States ... bears this kind of burden": J.F. Kennedy, quoted by Williams (1980) 198–9.
262 Compare the claims (earlier n.216) that Athens undertakes individual dangers for the common good. Isoc. 8.39–40 claims that Athens' *polypragmosynē* brought it danger but kept it just and helped the wronged. To embrace *ponos* was honourable: in Isoc. 6.56, a Spartan speaker claims that the Spartans are the greatest lovers of *ponos* among the Greeks. Lord Curzon's speeches continually emphasize the altruistic effort that he and others have expended on the empire: Raleigh (1906).
263 Hdt. 9.27.4, S. *Phil.* 248, Pind. *Pyth.*1.54 with Loraux (1982) 172–6, 190. It can also be connected with the idea that Athens' imperial labours bring the city success because of the gods' favour: Rosenbloom (2006b) 253 n.31 cites Ps.-Epicharmus (ap. Xen. *Mem.* 2.1.20), "The gods sell all goods to us for *ponoi*."
264 On the term, see Ehrenberg (1947); Kleve (1979).
265 Mutschler and Mittag (2008) 109. Isoc. 4.106 remarkably claims that the 70 years of the Athenian empire saw universal peace. Livy 33.33.5–7, ventriloquizing the delight of the Greeks at being granted freedom (197 BCE), has them laud Rome in language resembling that of the *epitaphioi* as: "a people, which at its own expense, and through its own effort and danger (*labore ac periculo*) fights for others' freedom, not only for people in its vicinity or on the same continent, but crosses the seas so that there should be no unjust rule anywhere in the world and that human and divine right and law may be mighty everywhere." Compare similar sentiments in the praise of Augustus or Rome for excellence in war and peace and clemency applied at the proper times: most famously Verg. *Aen.* 6.853, but also Prop. 2.16.41, 3.22.21–2; Ov. *Am.*1.2.51–2, *Trist.*1.2.123; Vell. Pat. 2.86.2.
266 E. *Supp.* 574–7; cf. 189, 323. For πόνος and εὔκλεια in Euripides, cf. de Romilly (1963) 134–5, n.2. See also Boegehold (1982): Raaflaub (1994), esp. 103–11. In later tradition compare Isoc. 4.52 and Hyperid. 6.26. Tod (2007) 214 comments on Lysias' frequent use of *kindunos* ("danger"), like *ponos,* a word implying courageous self-sacrifice.
267 Cf. E. *Hcld.* 19–25. In Isoc. 4.54, 56 the children ignored the other states because they were simply too feeble to help them.
268 Tod (2007) 223 notes the "care taken not to use the language of personal benefit" here.
269 Cf. E. *Hcld.* 171–8; Isoc. 12.194, 10.31; Dem. 60.8.
270 Todd (2007) 225; Loraux (1986) 81–2.
271 Burton (2011) 161–2. On the complexities of reciprocity (self-interest concealed by a supposed altruism) in the Greek world, see the essays in Gill, Postlethwaite and

Seaford (1998), esp. Van Wees (1998) 13–15; Missiou (1998) 189–91, who argues that Athens focused less on traditional ideas of reciprocity than did Sparta, preferring instead to help the weak with no need for repayment. But at least in tragedy, Athens is always rewarded for its efforts: even if Athenians in real life disavowed reciprocation for their benefactions, were they sincere? See also Low (2007) 200–1.
272 Thornton (1965) 98 with my emphases.
273 Thornton (1965) 37; Williams (2012) 192.
274 Said (1993) 106; Raaflaub (1994) 135–6. The growth of the Delian league can fit this model: Isoc. 4.72 claims that Athens was so famous for justice that the Greeks voluntarily handed over the thalassocracy (cf. 7.17, 80; 9.56; 16.27.)
275 Compare [Xen.] *Ath. Pol.* 1.14 (who condemns the policy). In fact, the upper classes benefitted as much as the lower ones from empire through financial opportunities such as owning land in allied territory: Thuc. 8.48.6; [Xen.] *Ath. Pol.* 2.20; Hornblower (1987) 165, 174; Davies (1984) 55–9.
276 Melos is mentioned neutrally at 15.113.
277 The Athenians of Thuc. 5.105.3 warn the Melians that Sparta will not care about justice enough to save its colonists from their fate.
278 At Isoc. 12.46–7, the misdeeds of Athens and Sparta are again compared and those of Sparta are considered greater; at 5.46–7 Athenian offences are condemned but considered less important than their services. Aristid. *Panath.* 213–20 offers the lengthiest explanation of Athenian abuses of power, combining a number of earlier tropes, some defensive, some minimizing, some appealing to *Realpolitik* and some aggressively accusing Athens' accusers of hypocrisy.
279 Liddel (2009) 17 compares a parallel claim of the liberal apologist for empire, Edward Bulwer Lytton: "Once Athens was in the clutches of empire, she would never surrender it: who, he asked, could ask England to surrender her colonies?" Ober (1978) 126–8 discusses less favourable views of the Athenian *archē* in fourth-century oratory, arguing (128) that the orators "and probably the Athenian people as a whole" were ambivalent about the empire. But old habits and desires die hard: Isoc. 8.6, 64–5. Vasunia (2013) 134–5 cites the justifications of empire in Charles Dilke's *Greater Britain* (1868). Dilke admits to British misbehaviour but also claims, "No nation has . . . ever governed an alien empire more wisely or justly than we the Punjab," (509) and hints that any abuses are the fault of India's own flaws.
280 For the relationship of the speech to the contemporary Greek political context and Isocrates' purpose in condemning what is seen elsewhere as glorious and desirable, see Laistner (1927) 15–19.
281 Cf. Thuc. 2.38.4.
282 Lys. 2.43, 47, 57; Isoc. 4.21, 33. From the *Iliad* on, it is a standard claim that "those with more to contribute to a collective project deserve a larger share of the divisible 'good' that the group has to offer": Balot (2001) 112, cf. 18.
283 See Chapter 2 and 3 later.
284 Cox (2004) 605 considers this concealment one of the most basic laws of international relations.
285 Thornton (1965) 34. Thucydides' Athenians are remarkable for repeatedly daring to make this claim.
286 At E. *Supp.* 723–5, Theseus could have sacked Thebes but chooses not to; cf. S. *OC* 905–8; Pl. *Mx.* 242c–d. Such portrayals doubtless gave Athenians active pleasure in the knowledge of their collective virtue and restraint, since the conquered in the ancient world were considered the property of conquerors whose good will alone might save them: Balot (2001) 149–50, n.36. On the phenomenon at Rome, see Takacs (2009) 58–9; Burton (2011) 117–9. The "humbled and submissive enemy" is popular in Roman iconography: Mattern (2004) 186. For some British imperial examples, see Dirks (2006) 17. Subjects can appeal to morality and justice: the conqueror can always choose to be swayed by them or not, and clemency is never automatic.

42 The Athenian . . . empire?

As Lateiner (2005) 77 says, "He who can show mercy may well choose not to." In 58 BCE Caesar represented himself as the champion of the freedom of the Gallic peoples and promoted his clemency (*BG* 1.45, 8.3, 21–2): Brunt (1978) 178. But at *BG* 8.44 he cuts off prisoners' right hands as a supposedly necessary punishment.

287 Athenian self-love is given a nasty dose of reality when the news of Aegospotami reaches the city and they fear that what they did at Melos and elsewhere will be visited on them: Xen. *Hell.* 2.2.3–4. In a different context, but offering an illuminating perspective on the psychology of dominance, Fincham (2001) 29 comments: "lurking beneath every situation of colonial dominance is an underlying sense of the fragility of control."

288 Gill, Postlethwaite and Seaford (1998). In contrast to UN treaties, in the ancient world intervention portrayed as helping the wronged is a norm and even an obligation: Low (2007) 177–8.

289 Thuc. 6.18.2. Intervention will probably bring material reward to add to the glow of virtue, due to Greek norms of reciprocity (Arist. *Eth. Nic* 1167b17–1168a27): Low (2007) 200–1. On reciprocity and benefaction in relations between Greek cities, see also Karavites (1980) and (1982).

290 Isoc. 8.30 makes this distinction (cf. 8.26, 58, 108) but its essential vagueness makes it useful: Low (2007) 207.

291 Low (2007) 202. Isoc. 4.107 claims that Athens created cleruchies to protect the cities, not for Athenian aggrandizement, but see Plut. *Per.* 11.5: Morris (2005) 45–6.

292 Strauss (1986) 51–3 offers a concise summary of the economic benefits that the empire offered Athens.

293 Cf. Thuc. 6.13.2, Isoc. 4.53; Andoc. 3.28, cf. 31.

294 Tzanetou (2005) 104–6.

295 Cain and Hopkins (2002) 39: "The 'cult of the amateur', so familiar until recent times in every sphere of life from sport to politics, had its origins in this distinctive – because innate, hereditary and hence general – character of aristocratic power." Ober (1989) 177–8 notes the Athenians' dislike of orators who seemed to be trying too hard at writing speeches, preferring those who demonstrated easy superiority.

296 For Loraux (1986) 150–1, the funeral oration is the "privileged locus of the proclamation of Athenian 'nonprofessionalism.'"

297 Spurr (1993) 117.

298 Missiou (1992) 111–21 (cf. Low (2007) 183–5) argues that Athens moulds the Greek norm into a specifically Athenian pattern (112) "characterized *by the absence* of *an avowed, calculating expectation of reciprocity* [her emphases]", but cf. n.269 earlier.

299 Lebow (2008) 85. As Aristotle states (*Eth. Nic* 1124b9–18), conferring benefits is a mark of superiority and preferable to being their recipient.

300 Sparta's ingratitude for Athens' help to the Heraclidae, their ancestors, features in E. *Hcld.* 1034–6 (cf. 584–6), and Isoc. 4.61–2 (cf. 5.33–4), though Lys. 2.13–15 denies that Athens expected any reciprocation. For the Peloponnesian War as ingratitude to Athens, cf. Isoc. 4.107, 12.69; Pl. *Mx.* 242a, 243b, 244b–c. The words that Plutarch ascribes to Pericles (Plut. *Per.* 12.3–4) on the legitimacy of Athens' use of the tribute indicate a great sense of Athenian entitlement based on their services to the allies: Loraux (1986) 83. For later complaints of the powerful about ingratitude from the weaker, see Cairns (1965) 43–4 (colonizers' complaints of African ingratitude); Kagan (1998) 34 (America's complaints about hostility to their power). Ingratitude is a consistent theme of contemporary US rhetoric on Iraq and Afghanistan: Pillar (2013); compare Donald Trump's words, quoted in www.alaraby.co.uk/english/blog/2017/1/20/donald-trump-said-what-about-the-middle-east. After military operations that gassed more 9000 Iraqis, Winston Churchill complained about "pouring armies and treasure into these thankless deserts": Gregory (2004) 148; cf. also Robinson (2014).

301 Hingley (2000) 8.

302 Ideological power gains its influence by being unable to be fully tested by experience: Mann (1986) 22–4. From the perspective of those in power, "Men are very willing to look upwards rather than sideways, and to grant their respect to those whose vision they sense to be broader than their own": Thornton (1965) 29; Colås (2007) 9. And it is always possible to find confirmation of what one would like to believe: Vasunia (2013) 126–7 cites the pro-British writing of the Indian essayist Nobinchunder Dass; see also Mannoni (1964) 138–9; Colås (2007) 88–9.

303 Thucydides' Pericles was perhaps aware of this when he exhorted the Athenians to fall in love with their city's power (2.43.1); on later praise of Athens' power, especially its power to transform all situations and expectations, Lys.2.4–6; Isoc. 4.58–60, 12.190. Said (1993) 131 comments on European "self-forgetting delight in the use of power – the power to observe, rule, hold, and profit from distant territories and people."

304 As Charles Krauthammer stated, referring to a resurgent aggressive American foreign policy, "power is its own reward": Krauthammer (2001); Engel (2001). For the connection of imperial mastery with a specific Athenian concern with masculinity see Wohl (2002) 174–9.

305 Lebow (2008) 14–19, 61–72, argues (17) that "people who identify with nationalities or nations to some degree seek vicarious fulfillment and enhanced self-esteem through their victories." For Schumpeter (1955) 12, nationalism "satisfies the need to surrender to a concrete and familiar super-personal cause, the need for self-glorification and violent self-assertion. . . . At the time of the Boer War there was not a beggar in London who did not speak of 'our' rebellious subjects." How did news of the destruction of Melos strike the beggars of Athens?

306 Cairns (1965) 153–4.

307 Brunt (1978) 161–2.

308 On the Parthenon, "each member state of Athens' pan-Aegean symmachy was an essential part of a greater, prestigious entity": Castriota (1992) 226–9. Colås (2007) 3 considers some positive effects of empire for both sides: "prosperity, stability and sense of belonging which to this day can still muster support across the globe from both elites and subaltern populations."

309 Cross-cultural research suggests that people prefer to identify with high-status groups: Lebow (2008) 134. Nicias (Thuc. 7.63.3) appeals to the "pleasure" felt by allies whose knowledge of Athens' language and imitation of their ways led them to be honoured like Athenians with a share in the empire. On the complex relationship of colonized to European colonizers, see also Abernethy (2000) 254–73, 300–12, 374–5; Robinson (1972).

310 Thornton (1965) 51–2, 155; Dirks (2006) 139–40.

311 Thornton (1965) 48–9; Said (1993) 149.

312 Low (2005) 103–4 discusses IG1³ 101 (ML 89), an inscription recording honours paid to the Neapolitans, Athens' loyal allies, at the end of the Peloponnesian War. The Neapolitans must pay for this decree – an apparent expression of Athens' imperial control (e.g. Osborne (2000) 37) – but Low suggests that paying for the inscription might actually emphasize the importance of their relationship with Athens, and perhaps even offer the illusion of equal status between the two cities, since a fragmentary relief with the inscription appears to represent them shaking hands.

313 Harrison (2008) 11. The United States firmly denies that it is an imperial nation and thus that it is an exception to the cycles of history by which empires fall; cf. Cox (2005); Johnson (2004) 191.

314 Reisz (2010) 214–6.

315 Dirks (2006) 110. The related idea that imperial power corrupts is endemic in Thucydides.

316 Empire pudding combined items – sugar, spices, rum and so forth – from Britain's possessions: https://trove.nla.gov.au/newspaper/article/32060563. Cf. also Kriegel (2003).

317 MacKenzie (2005) 8, 20–3.
318 Thus Grant (1965) argues that fifth-century diplomacy is far from diplomatic in our terms (cf. de Ste Croix (1972) 16–28) and that Thucydides represents it accurately, but most of his evidence is Thucydidean, so that his argument is circular. But Meiggs (1972) 389 states: "If we compare the language of modern imperialism . . . it is very difficult to regard these Thucydidean speeches as genuine reports of public utterances."
319 Low (2005) 93–5.
320 On this process as it shapes the claims of the *epitaphioi* in particular, see Walters (1980) 5–12.
321 In any case, we do not have enough securely datable inscriptions to trace such a process.
322 Low (2005) 95.
323 Osborne (2000) 37.
324 Cf. Low (2005) 105–8: use of the Ionic alphabet on many fifth-century inscriptions expresses a power that is not simply coercive but "a more subtle, homogenizing approach to the construction of power, in which Athens is not so much the enforcer of an Athenian way of life as a facilitator of some wider, perhaps panhellenic relationship."
325 Parker (1996) 143 discusses potential allied ambivalence to such participation: cf. Smarczyk (1990) 549–69, 592–611.

2 Tragedy and Athens
Aeschylus and Sophocles

2.1 Introduction: Athens in and out of disaster[1]

For the past couple of decades, it has been orthodox to consider tragedy as an intellectual and didactic literary form, heavily marked by its origins in the Athenian democracy.[2] Many of the practices preceding tragic performance are unquestionably connected with the workings of the democracy,[3] and in conjunction with an appreciation of the complex questions which tragedy itself raises about democracy, ideology, morality, citizenship, justice, the family and so forth, a further claim easily arises, that tragedy promotes a kind of self-examination and even perhaps self-criticism among its citizen-spectators.[4] Additionally, it is argued that democracy encourages its citizens to question and criticize its own institutions in a manner unavailable to citizens of more authoritarian societies. For Pelling,[5] part of civic ideology was "to worry about [civic ideology] in the right place", and tragic theatre provided vital opportunities for such explorations. Goldhill[6] puts the argument especially strongly: tragedy and comedy "implicate the dominant ideology put forward in the preplay ceremonies in a far from straightforward manner; indeed the tragic texts seem to question, examine, and often subvert the language of the city's order."

Others modify this intellectualized portrait of tragedy. Heath emphasizes tragedy's emotional dimension, and Sourvinou-Inwood its religious aspects.[7] Jasper Griffin is generally sceptical of Goldhill's position, considering it an anachronistic product of the thought processes of liberal thinkers in modern democracy, arguing that it is not clear that ancient playwrights actually did wish their audiences to question their own values in ways that we consider desirable today.[8] Certainly, in his *Apology*, Plato represents Socrates as distinctly embattled in his efforts to jolt the Athenian populace out of self-satisfaction, and his eventual fate might suggest that clear-eyed self-examination was not entirely attractive to those who condemned him to death. Responding to Griffin,[9] Goldhill contends that the city of Gorgias, Thucydides, Plato, Socrates and the sophists would be amply capable of embracing the combination of irony, didacticism and questioning that he considers central to tragedy. But are such spectators representative?[10] Thucydides, Plato and Socrates were hardly convinced democrats, while questioning current orthodoxies was central to sophistic thought: by definition, therefore, the sophists may well not represent mainstream Athenian opinion. Athens' intellectual atmosphere certainly did allow more criticism of the city than was possible in Sparta, but the democracy itself may not always have been entirely tolerant,[11] and even if Plato, Socrates and the rest could comfortably negotiate a combination of irony, didacticism and questioning, the same might not necessarily be true for the majority of spectators. What sort of relationships should we imagine in the minds of spectators between spectacles of acute violence and suffering, and deliberation on and criticism of the contradictions inherent in the democratic polis? Are all, or mostly all, spectators expected to undergo a speedy psychological shift from visceral emotional reaction to questioning their own beliefs and actions, or is this just for a few?[12]

P.J. Rhodes has even questioned the idea that tragedy is an essentially democratic art form, suggesting instead that it explores issues important to the polis in general, rather than the democracy specifically. He cites multiple examples of slippage in earlier work between "civic" and "democratic", or between "polis", "democracy" and "Athens", arguing that the terms are not interchangeable.[13] The slippage may go even further than Rhodes argues – not only between "polis", "democracy" and "Athenian", but also between "questioning" or "criticism" and "self-questioning" or "self-criticism."[14] Tragedy asks penetrating questions about life in the polis, but dramatic performance contains no means of *forcing* spectators to apply such questions directly to themselves, and in fact its very form deliberately complicates the possibility that they might do so. I believe that the playwrights always left their audience some "escape routes" away from difficult self-examination and that some spectators probably took them, especially when Athens itself is portrayed in tragedy.

Tragedy is undoubtedly political in some sense, and the connections between democratic institutions, preperformance practices and tragic performance are indisputable. But some of the ceremony surrounding the Dionysia, such as its emphasis on war and military values, and especially the exhibition of the tribute of Athens' subjects,[15] is an affirmation of Athens' self-image and justification of Athenian power, whose affirmative tone recalls that other highly democratic institution, the *epitaphios logos*. Certain individual plays have even clearer connections with the *epitaphioi* because they bring to life before the eyes of spectators stories about Athens' ancient prowess that are central to the "historical" portions of these speeches.

Athenians were not the only spectators at the Dionysia, and if, as Goldhill suggests, those Athenians had a "heightened awareness" of the non-Athenians in their midst, so that the festival becomes "an area of public self-awareness and self-promotion for the city and the citizens,"[16] some Athenian audience members at least might be more disposed towards a view of Athens, and themselves as Athenian citizens, that was closer to the image of Athens outlined in Chapter 1 than to a critical image. Aristophanes (*Ach.* 600–7) comments on the Athenians' exceptional enjoyment of praise of Athens, while Plato's Socrates in *Menexenus* sarcastically comments that listening to a funeral speech makes him feel taller and better-looking, and its after-effects last for days.[17] The audience also contained a high proportion of the men who also made political decisions in the assembly. If they were to view certain events on stage in the light of decisions they had previously made, and some of those decisions themselves were shaped by the image of Athens imagined in Chapter 1, some might have preferred to feel reassured, not challenged, about those decisions.[18]

Kevin Lee argues that the process by which the archon chose the poets whose work would be performed at the Dionysia was probably "conservative, cautious and reliant on precedent", reflecting "not the confident opinion of an expert . . . but of a man who was, by definition, average." While more challenging visions of the city would not be censored, "any challenging material had to be presented in an acceptable way and within tolerable norms." Poets also had to appear at the *proagon* in front of interested parties, a ceremony which Lee considers was "something of an ordeal which forced the poets to confront their public responsibility in a direct way." While dramatists had many motivations for writing, victory at the competitions was highly desirable: since some "messages" would be more attractive to audiences and judges than others, dramatists might shape their plays accordingly.[19]

Inherent in the practices surrounding tragic performance as well as some actual tragedies, then, were powerful possibilities of affirmation and reassurance as well as self-examination. Additionally, the striking spatial and temporal indeterminacy of tragic drama complicates the assumption that it could stimulate an actively critical approach in spectators, both because no author can compel his audience to draw specific conclusions from his work, and because of the way that tragedy presents suffering to its audiences.

Tragedy appears to work most effectively where there is a gap between the circumstances of the play and of the audience: spectators must care about the suffering of the characters on stage but need distance to appreciate the play as a play.[20] If the gap is too great, they will be disengaged; if it is too small, they cannot focus properly on the play, as happened during a staging of the *Oresteia* in Berlin in 1945 against a huge photograph of the ruined city, which traumatized many of the audience.[21] On a different, but related, note, the simulations in the virtual reality games currently used to treat troops with post-traumatic stress disorder are realistic, but not entirely, because extreme realism erases the distance between game and reality that enables therapy to work.[22] Peter Meineck's experiences with using tragedy with contemporary veterans point to a similar conclusion:[23] the veterans see their own experiences reflected in the ancient texts through the vital gap between the contemporary and the ancient that enables them to be close to, but also comfortably apart from, the connection between them.

Distance proved key to the development of tragedy at Athens after the Athenians imposed a huge fine on the early poet Phrynichus for "reminding them of their own troubles" in portraying a recent historical event – the capture of Miletus – that hit too close to home.[24] Thereafter, with the exception of Aeschylus' *Persians*, a story dramatizing the suffering of safely defeated enemies,[25] tragedy dramatizes Greek mythology, avoiding directly contemporary reference but focusing on a distant past in which the contemporary world is evoked by mythological kings praising democracy (E. *Supp.* 429–55), or Iliadic queens exploring the nature of Zeus with the latest intellectual techniques (E. *Tro.* 886). Audiences could empathize with the troubles of those presented to them on stage, but because those troubles were rooted in a long-ago world, they could, if necessary, be safely "left hanging on the mythical, other-worldly pegs provided by the play's structure."[26] The distance offered an essential comfort zone,[27] poised between closeness and distance.[28] If indeterminacy is essential in enabling tragedy to offer its audience a comfort zone, it will inevitably contain the possibility not of challenging, but of reaffirming, spectators' beliefs, especially if those beliefs were as self-evidently attractive as they would seem from Chapter 1's discussion.

Even the indeterminate space between ancient and contemporary that the characters of tragedy inhabit is not fixed: sometimes the tragedy will approach the contemporary and then retreat, in Christiane Sourvinou-Inwood's famous formulation of "distancing" and "zooming" devices, whereby a tragedian sometimes deliberately differentiates the world of his tragedy from that of the audience and sometimes brings the two together,[29] in a continually shifting process. In the same way, each individual spectator brings his own experience and prejudices, and can himself zoom or distance, decide to accept, resist, or experience some intermediate reaction to what he sees. If the sentiments of the tragedy match a spectator's experiences and prejudices, the zooming process may be unproblematic, but more challenging ideas may be rejected.

The highly poetic Greek of tragedy also combines distance and closeness, as did its stylized form whose "familiar patterns and performative routines provide a further dimension to the 'comfort zone.'"[30] The aesthetic stylization of Greek tragedy means that its events are always at least one step removed from lived existence, and any of the audience can look away (literally or mentally) from anything unappealing to contemplate and, if they need to, "escape" through the reassurance that they are merely watching a performance. Such gaps open up options of entirely submitting to belief in what the dramatist presents, entirely resisting it, or partially accepting and resisting.

Christiane Sourvinou-Inwood offers an intriguing example of how tragedy's indeterminacy may tread a path between fear and comfort. In Aeschylus' *Eumenides*, set in Athens, the Erinyes' threat to blight Athens (780–7) "marks a grave danger for Athens in the world of the tragedy." But she argues that the audience is "insulated" from feeling the danger too closely, through the chorus' self-referentiality earlier in the play: these Erinyes are also a "chorus of Athenian men in the here and now", with the result that their threat ultimately "does not affect the world of the audience; it was a danger in the past that has been overcome."[31] Furthermore, one of her main arguments is that tragedy and Athenian religion are indivisible from one another,[32] and if, as she claims, a disconcerting divine unknowability is central to Greek religion, some sort of comfort zone for audiences to experience human insecurity in a world controlled by the alarming gods that tragedy repeatedly presents is desirable and perhaps necessary.

The distanced time of tragedy is often combined with spatial distance. In comedy, contemporary Athens is central, though in a fantasy world where nothing irrevocably painful happens, except to annoying politicians or intellectuals, and usually resolution, abundance and festivity end the performance. Tragedies, however, are frequently set in cities other than Athens – 32 in Thebes alone[33] – maintaining spatial as well as temporal distance from spectators.[34] *Prima facie*, a play set in "Athens", even safely mythological Athens, would seem to deny its audience the spatial distance offered by a play set in "Thebes". If tragedy works between the poles of critique and comfort, a play offered to Athenians which is set outside Athens might offer greater opportunities for questioning and critique of social and other institutions than a play set in their own city. Since Sophocles' *Oedipus Tyrannus* and *Antigone* are set in a city which is not Athens and Athens has no apparent role in it at all, the distance between "ancient" Thebes and contemporary Athens may enable spectators to conduct self-examination and examination of their city through the questions such plays raise about relationships between gods and man, the family versus the city and so on, within a useful emotional and intellectual comfort zone.

But when Athenians view a play about "Athens", the distance necessary for tragedy to work becomes smaller, and it is reasonable to wonder whether there are some unspoken limits on how tragedians are "allowed" to portray their city while keeping the comfort zone intact. Perhaps what is said about Athens itself may tend towards a more idealized image, or at least offer spectators the *chance* to find that image if they needed to. And in fact, every extant tragedy in which the dramatized Athens has an active role does appear to portray the city in a broadly positive manner, or at least – crucially – the city's actions are *capable* of being read as conforming to the images of Athens sketched in Chapter 1. Critique of those images is also available for those who wished to see it: thus Euripides' *Suppliants* contains many topoi familiar from funeral speeches, such as the city's unique devotion to suppliants, its free democracy and its vigorous defence of Greek ideals,[35] but Athens' help to Adrastus does not stop the wars in Thebes and certainly does not save Evadne and her father from abject misery. These failures may colour the play as a whole for some spectators. However, others might argue that when Athens intervened to preserve Greek customs, it was successful on its own terms, even acquiring a useful alliance with Argos, sanctioned by Athena, as its reward: Athens could not save Thebes, but it did not intend to do so, nor could it, given the dominant tradition in which the Epigonoi avenge their fathers. Pelling discusses interpretations of the latter part of the play which downplay Evadne's suffering by attributing her "extreme and non-civic grief which marks the un-Athenian activity" to her Argive origins, considering such interpretations "too facile an approach to analysing the Other" because only a "complacent" audience would feel that an idealized Athens would never have to contend with such extreme grief.[36] In that formulation, such readings do seem highly unsatisfactory. But perhaps by displacing extreme agony onto Argives, Athenian spectators might enter into Evadne's grief and pain more fully *because* of the gap between them, since, as Athenians, they are protected from too problematically close an identification with her.[37] Thus the play creates its own comfort zones for those who preferred affirmation and escape routes from criticism of Athens, even when a more critical view is also possible. Tragedy must allow its spectators, if necessary, not to be "reminded of their own troubles" and retain a more comforting view of what it means to belong to the city which helps the suffering but which always, itself, remains "outside the tragedy" (ἐκτὸς . . . συμφορᾶς, E. *HF* 1249).[38] Tragedy is political, but one strain of the political will include the affirmative image of Athens outlined in Chapter 1. Perhaps we have relied too much on Thucydides' sceptical attitude to all idealized portrayals of his city, and overestimate the Athenians' ability for self-critique.

This is a time of great intellectual sophistication as modern thinkers wrestle with issues such as privilege, the complexities of transgender experience, or even how the discipline of Classics may promote sexism and racism.[39] Such issues are hugely important for many. For many others (mostly, but not entirely, non-academics), not only are they not interesting, but pointless at best and destructive at worst. In 424 BCE, Aristophanes' *Clouds* portrayed Socrates and his philosophy, in which self-criticism and reflection are central, in a similarly contemptuous manner, as either trivial – measuring how far fleas jump (143–53) – or dangerous, teaching young men to use dishonest rhetoric to damage fundamental societal institutions (1399–1444). Evidently, Aristophanes considered that this portrayal of Socrates, the "gadfly" who afflicted the comfortably smug "horse" that he considered the Athenian democracy to have become (Pl. *Apol.* 30e), would make his audiences laugh and judge his comedy to be the best. And if that is so, then it would seem likely that he was appealing to the prejudices of a people who were not unanimously interested in deep self-examination. This is certainly not to defend anti-intellectualism, in either ancient or modern worlds, but merely to offer a minor corrective to views of Athenian tragic spectators as universally willing and able to interrogate themselves. While Socrates, Thucydides and other Athenian intellectuals were disposed to cast a critical eye on their city, and doubtless themselves as well, equally, other Athenians enjoyed watching the merciless portrayal of Cleon in Aristophanes' *Knights* but then duly voted him back in as general, baffling Thucydides and others, just as many in the United Kingdom and the United States have been baffled by popular enthusiasm for Brexit and Donald Trump. Academics are more naturally disposed to a Thucydidean view of the world, but this disposition may lead us to a slightly distorted view of tragedy's broader audience.[40]

Athens or places in Attica feature in five extant plays whose production dates range from 458–401 BCE: Aeschylus' *Eumenides*, Euripides' *Heraclidae*, *Suppliants* and *Heracles*, and Sophocles' *Oedipus at Colonus*. Additionally, Euripides' *Hippolytus*, set in Trozen, concerns Theseus, the king of Athens, and is itself a retelling of a story he treated in another, now fragmentary, play, while Aeschylus' *Persians*, though set in Persia, is an unquestionably Athenian play. There is a remarkable degree of consistency among the portrayals of Athens in almost every extant tragedy. Moreover, these portrayals conform in various ways to the image of the idealized Athens discussed in Chapter 1, which even marks, as best we can tell, certain fragmentary plays with Athenian setting or content, such as Euripides' *Erechtheus* or the *Peirithous* attributed to Critias or Euripides. In particular, the

Theseus of tragedy has many characteristics of the ideal Athens,[41] and Euripides' *Heraclidae* and *Suppliants*, the fragmentary *Erechtheus* and Aeschylus' fragmentary *Eleusinioi* all dramatize the canonical deeds of Athens that almost every *epitaphios* narrates as Athenian "history". In *Heraclidae*, Athens rescues Heracles' children from his enemy Eurystheus,[42] while both *Suppliants* and *Eleusinioi* dramatize Athens' intervention to bury the bodies of the dead Seven against Thebes.[43] For a modern reader, the tales of the funeral orations may seem "trite, chauvinistic, and full of historical distortions"[44] and not worthy of being taken seriously, but they were "*true for the Athenians*, in that [they] conform[ed] to the idea that they wish[ed] to have of themselves."[45] If this is right, then the essential "truth" of such stories for an Athenian audience should not be dismissed: certainly fourth-century orators took them entirely seriously, invoking them as "proofs" to support the cases they were arguing.[46]

The extant Athenian plays portray a city active in helping those around them, especially oppressed suppliants.[47] Athens is good and does good because of a military power that it deploys only where necessary, matching that power with moral knowledge. The city can also transform others for change, if imperfectly or impermanently, but most importantly, it is always rewarded for its actions, often by an alliance committing the descendants of those Athens has helped to unending loyalty to their one-time benefactors. Although many interpreters find complexity and ironies in such portrayals,[48] the indeterminate and multivalent nature of tragedy compels ironic portrayals to coexist with more straightforwardly optimistic readings. And even if the tragic portrayal of Athens is in some respects ambivalent, its enemies receive an unambiguously negative characterization. Different spectators will have brought different needs and interpretations to the plays. Some would have seen cracks in the idealized city: one would love to know what Thucydides thought of *Heraclidae*, for example. But characters like Thucydides might already have been disaffected and brought to such plays what they wanted to see in them.[49] The indeterminate space of tragedy always offers room for a safe space as well, avoiding or refuting criticism of the idealized city for those unwilling to engage with it.

Scholars must interrogate texts more analytically than a non-professional Athenian spectator might do, even one who actively sought education in the theatre. Moreover, only deep readings of ancient texts can even begin to bring us to enter into ancient mentalities. But for that reason, along, perhaps, with our own individual scholarly and psychological temperaments, our reactions to tragedy may potentially distort understanding of the reactions of a significant number of ancient spectators to what they saw, so that it might sometimes be useful to retreat briefly from complexity, paradox and irony.[50] Our tendency to prefer complexity and irony may paradoxically also be a relic from a less critical Hellenophile past, when the Greeks were the pinnacle of civilization and we believed in "golden age" Athens. If we impose upon every Athenian spectator a modern and arguably anachronistic interest in questioning and subversion, we create a remarkably sophisticated audience.[51] There must also have been some, and perhaps many, less exalted viewers for whom tragedy was a source of entertainment, horrified fascination and questions, but also a potential degree of comfort where their own city and its history was involved. As Theseus' descendants, they could view a theatrical representation of how their ancestor's wisdom, virtue and power had generously helped others, preserving and strengthening Athens in the process, and reflect on ways in which they too could promote or were promoting his legacy.

2.2 Aeschylus' *Persians*

Just eight years after the people of Athens evacuated their city, fought a navy many times larger than theirs and then returned to find their homes burned and sacked,[52] some of them sat in the theatre, perhaps on seats made from the timbers of Persian ships,[53] with the ruined temples of the Acropolis in their view, to watch a fictionalized representation of the agony of the enemies who had once destroyed their city, on learning that their once invincible forces had been unexpectedly humbled at Salamis.

Aeschylus' *Persians* is unique among surviving tragedy (and highly unusual among all known tragedies) in dramatizing events that actually happened in the lifetimes of its audience, including that of Aeschylus himself, who fought at Salamis. Aeschylus' earlier contemporary Phrynichus had experimented with tragedies based on contemporary history, notoriously in the *Capture of Miletus*, but also in the *Phoenician Women*,[54] produced just four years after the battle of Salamis, in 476. We know very little about it, but the *Hypothesis* to Aeschylus' play states it was modelled on that of Phrynichus. Aeschylus' opening line appears to echo that of Phrynichus, which the *Hypothesis* quotes, though Phrynichus' prologue was spoken by a eunuch arranging cushions on a seat: soft cushions contrast with the manlier wooden benches on which the Athenian counsellors sat.[55] Since both were dramatizing a contemporary event familiar in certain aspects to their entire audience, the two plays doubtless shared many verbal and thematic elements, especially those of foreignness and feminized lamentation that infuse Aeschylus' portrayal of Athens' enemies,[56] and it is likely that Phrynichus' chorus were wives of men in the Phoenician navy.[57] Although almost nothing of Phrynichus' play survives, so that we have no idea of its general tone, even the tone of Aeschylus' extant play is highly contested.[58] Is *Persians* a story of Persian suffering or a dramatic representation of the triumph of Greek over barbarian?[59] If the former, is Aeschylus making a serious statement about the dangers of overreach and divine punishment – a warning as relevant to Greeks, and especially Athenians, as it is to foreigners?[60] If the latter, is this simply a patriotic, and relieved, celebration or an outburst of *Schadenfreude*, mocking an effeminate, cruel and now humbled enemy? Is the victory celebrated one of a panhellenic, unified force, or is it an Athenian triumph in which Athens is the saviour of Greece, to delight a majority-Athenian audience?[61] Broadly speaking, older scholarship tends to favour a patriotic interpretation of the play which degrades the Persians to a greater or lesser extent,[62] while many more recent writers have detected a surprising humanity and sympathy for Athens' enemy that largely transcends narrow nationalism or promotes a message of a common human vulnerability for fictional Persians and contemporary Athenians alike.[63]

It is not surprising that critics have arrived at such different conclusions about Aeschylus' tone, if indeed tragedy offers multiple opportunities for individual spectators to find whatever they need in it, but the complexity of the play is especially understandable given how notably ambivalent Greek, and especially Athenian, attitudes were towards Persia.[64] The Persians had inflicted horrific harm on Athens and had nearly conquered Greece, and the Athenians naturally claimed that they had won a sensational victory over ferocious opponents.[65] On the other hand, the Greeks' preferred image of themselves as righteous warriors projected an image onto the Persians that was its opposite: if Greeks, and especially Athenians, are manly heroes, Persians must be emotional, feminine,[66] decadent and impious.[67] But however the Persians themselves are viewed, the play unambivalently claims that *hybris* attracts divine punishment, and one emotion that was surely universal among the Athenians ever since the retreat of the Persians and the gradual recovery of their violated city is a sense that justice had been done and that Athens (and Greece) were divinely favoured, presumably for the future as well. But what other feelings might have been possible for the first spectators of *Persians*? Vindictive pleasure, empathetic sorrow, or something in between?[68]

"To write a *kommos* for a defeated enemy (especially a *kommos* for the Persian invaders to be performed in a public Athenian festival) is in itself a remarkable event."[69] This is absolutely true but cannot tell us how the audience *received* such a piece.[70] Could the Athenians have viewed Persian lamentation, however heart-wrenching, and felt unadulterated[71] sympathy, given the horrendous disruption that they had directly inflicted on many spectators just eight years previously?[72] A very imperfect parallel might be a piece of art which portrays the humanity of a vulnerable Hitler:[73] even some 70 years later, it is not easy or uncontroversial to do so.[74] Along with an unquestionable emphasis on portraying the punishment of *hybris* by Zeus, parts of Aeschylus' play, above all 230–45 and 398–407 (cf. 284, 347–8, 473–4), can hardly be viewed as anything other than highly patriotic, and patriotic in a way that aligns with the dominant portrayal of the Persian Wars in Greek literature of various times and places, and especially Athenian literature.[75] The queen's supposed ignorance of Athens (230–45)[76] instantly establishes the Athenians in particular as the plucky underdogs whose virtues will eventually triumph over all the odds. The same sort of questions by foreigners are used for similar effects for the Greeks in Herodotus, to reflect "Greekness" back to the Greeks, affirming their differences from, and usually superiority to, Persian ways.[77]

Any dramatization of the Persian invasion could only be written from the side of the losing Persians, not from that of the Athenians viewing their sacked city, and the genre of tragedy by definition involves a degree of sympathy, pity (considered an especially Athenian quality in the idealized Athens)[78] and an awareness of human vulnerability.[79] Herodotus too sometimes viewed the Persians' doomed expedition empathetically in a grand context of human vulnerability (e.g. 7.46–7). Serious genres like epic and tragedy sometimes condemn excessive pleasure in the downfall of an enemy,[80] and when the prevailing narrative of the Persian Wars focused so consistently on Persian *hybris*, it might be foolish for a tragedian to encourage his audience to feel triumphalistic joy over an enemy's suffering. Perhaps the sight of Persian suffering did stimulate a humane and generous response in many spectators.[81] And yet, an uncomplicated, empathetic response is always easier for those "outside the tragedy", and in this play, Athens cannot retain its usual place "outside the tragedy" because of the historical and geographical closeness of the wound that the Persians had inflicted on this very audience.[82] Of course, some spectators might have pitied the Persians as human beings just like themselves in some regards, but both what spectators saw on stage in the context of their own lived experience, and the construction of the play itself probably made pure empathy, free of any triumphalism, more difficult.

The construction of the *Persians* is notable both for its relative lack of action and its portrayal of events that everyone not only knew about but that most had actually experienced. Irony in which the audience knows more than the characters on stage is fundamental in tragedy, but a play based on contemporary Athenian history takes dramatic irony even further. The phrase "all the strength of Asia has gone" (13; cf. 59–60, 252) has one meaning for the chorus, anticipating the return of their victorious army, and quite another for the audience, who have an unusually clear knowledge that there will be no such glorious return because of what they did to that army in righteous revenge. In such a context, the spectators may focus less on wondering what will happen next in the play because they know it, and more on gazing on, recognizing and enjoying (in the broadest sense) scenes which focus on their enemies' misjudgement, lamentation and suffering, from their position of superiority and surely a considerable degree of identification with those whom the Persians curse as enemies.[83] Looking upon another's sufferings is innate to tragedy, but looking upon the sufferings of those who destroyed your home, confident of victory, but who are now humbled and frightened (64, 115–25) as you are no longer frightened, might cause spectators to experience an overwhelming sense of relief, that their victory was divinely ordained and that the workings of the universe are reassuringly comprehensible through the victory of the righteous underdogs.[84] Aeschylus enables this pleasure with a graphic description of Persians being unheroically clubbed to death like fish, recalling the (deserved) fate of the suitors in the *Odyssey*.[85] The description is so violent that in the mouth of an Athenian it might seem excessive, but in the mouth of a Persian messenger, such danger is avoided even as Athenian triumph is fully celebrated. Again, *Pers.* 532–47 describes the reaction of the newly widowed women, who "tear veils with soft hands (537–8)",[86] lamenting the loss of the sensual joys of youth. The luxuriousness of Persia, now destroyed by blood, thirst and hunger, that runs throughout the play represents the cosmic danger of excess that runs through Greek thought[87] and in particular shapes Herodotus' understanding of the Greeks' victory.[88] This passage also contains distinctly sexual overtones that feminize the Persians and make Greeks and especially Athenians represent the masculine courage and restraint that tends to win divine favour. All the while, the audience watches these scenes from a safe position of superiority and relative security,[89] with physical memorials of what the Persians had done to their city all around them:[90] the Persians' pain is horrific, yet surely not completely undeserved.

Tendencies innate to tragedy shape Aeschylus' portrayal of Xerxes and the Persians so that they can appear potentially sympathetic even in the context of an essentially patriotic play. They cannot be completely without redeeming features, since their fall would not be a tragedy,[91] and yet reasons for their suffering must be clear, and an Athenian audience could hardly want them to succeed or find unadulterated merit in them. The tone of the play might be compared with that of Horace *Odes* 1.37 celebrating the battle of Actium, which mingles denigration of and repulsion towards a foreign queen who nearly destroyed the poet's homeland, with an acknowledgement that she was, after all, an impressive foe. Horace's apparent respect for her is still tempered by dominant tones of relief and pride in her defeat.[92] It is not accidental that the battle of Salamis, celebrated by this play, has subsequently been used by many nations as a charter myth for brave resistance against a seemingly invincible enemy: such nations are always David fighting Goliath because it is so attractive to any victorious power to see their victory both as against all odds and as deserved.[93]

This is a profoundly patriotic play. It is also a profoundly imperial play in being imbued with many of the ideas, if only in embryo, about Athenian power that shape the view of Athens discussed in Chapter 1 and that will run through various texts and artefacts of the fifth century. While the exactitude of Aeschylus' portrayal of Persian languages and culture is in some doubt, he has certainly made some attempt to offer Persian names, certain Persian terms and possibly some Persian customs to his audience.[94] Such attempts at ventriloquizing and imagining Persia have an imperial dimension.[95] By ventriloquizing Persians and presenting them to Athenian spectators, the Athenians take possession of Persia through their imaginations, in a kind of metaphorical colonization, just as they would literally take possession of previously Persian territory to form the Delian League, in an easy and natural assumption of undisputed leadership with the allied Greek army's victory. Every commentator notes Aeschylus' emphasis on the wealth and manpower of Persia (3, 9, 45, 52–3, 73, 83, 159, 250, 533 etc.) and the repetition of certain prefixes or suffixes to emphasize the excessive numbers of Persian soldiers[96] and ships – 1207 against a mere 300 Greeks (337–43) – with an implied connection to the excessive arrogance of the Persians which will bring about correspondingly catastrophic losses.[97] The equation of the vastness of Persia's forces with the vastness of the disaster is replicated in Herodotus, for whom the sheer number of Persians is a similar obsession in his grand account of rivers running dry and millions crossing the Hellespont.[98] While Aeschylus certainly shows some respect for the Persians, they are also explicitly portrayed as mere babblers (406), cruel (371), servile to their leaders, fearful, luxurious and lacking in understanding.[99] Xerxes is also ambivalent, portrayed both in orientalist fashion as cowardly, luxury-loving and cruel, yet also as a kind of everyman, ambitious, rash and now humbled and grieving.[100] The Greeks, by contrast, are consistently well disciplined, courageous and intelligent (374–5, 394–405, 417). Such portrayals will become standard as Athenian imperial ideology develops. Persians combine the two contradictory vices of savagery and refinement, the Greeks avoid both vices, while the Athenians combine every virtue.[101]

Particularly effective in conveying the relentless waves of enemy invaders repelled by the Greeks (and especially by Athens, from an audience perspective) is Aeschylus' use of catalogues. Early catalogues of individuals and types of soldiers (21–60, 302–28) recall the magnificence of Herodotus' later account of Xerxes surveying his army (7.60–97), or the catalogue of ships in the *Iliad*. These contrast with the catalogue of 480–514 which details the Persians' painful retreat through a list of places in hostile country (cf. Hdt. 8.115.2, 117, 129) all the way to Thessaly, where they finally find refuge after a journey very different from their march towards Greece. At 765–87 Darius lists the previous rulers of Asia, a dynasty whose continuing power is now in jeopardy thanks to Xerxes' impulsiveness. Particularly poignant for the Persians but a source of pleasure for Aeschylus' audience is the catalogue of places that Darius once easily conquered (864–902),[102] especially the islands, which by 472 belonged instead to the Delian League.[103] Finally, Xerxes is held to painful account as the chorus question him on the whereabouts of a final catalogue of dead Persians (957–1001). The catalogues with their specific listing of names contrast with the anonymity of the "Greeks" or "Athenians,"[104] conforming to the democratic ideology of the *epitaphioi*.[105]

At 178 the queen refers to the "land of the Ionians," evidently meaning Greece in general rather than Ionia proper, but other references to the superior naval power of the "Ionians" surely recall Athenian naval prowess at Salamis (950–1, 1025; cf. 563), especially for Aeschylus' audience. This ambiguity between Athens and Ionia[106] prefigures the claim made by Athens especially forcefully later in the fifth century to be the mother city of the Ionians, whose position in Xerxes' forces in 480 Aeschylus is careful to obscure or absolve.[107] Thus the *Persians* may precede by some 60 years Euripides' *Ion* as an embryonic charter myth for the Delian League.[108]

Aeschylus' Persian characters frequently invoke Athenian history or truths that Athenians would have considered uncontroversial. That Athens' enemies voluntarily endorse what Athenians know about themselves enhances the power and credibility of Athens' self-image. Atossa herself (474) calls Athens "famous",[109] and when the Persian messenger claims (347) that the gods save the city of the goddess Pallas, here conflating Athens with the entire Greek army, he endorses one of the great truths that would shape the Athenians' relationship with the rest of the Greek world long after the Persian Wars. At 284–5, Salamis is called "hateful", in a convoluted but satisfying allusion to Herodotus' famous story (7.141.3–4) of the alarming oracle that advised the Athenians to trust in the wooden walls, ending with an address to "divine" Salamis, whose meaning is explained by Themistocles' assurance that Salamis would have been called "cruel", rather than divine, had the Athenians been destined to suffer as the Persians actually did suffer (7.143.1). The messenger's use of direct speech to recall the Greeks' exhortation to battle (402–5) stirringly recalls the triumphant resistance of that day, and the story is all the more powerful by coming from the mouth of an enemy of Athens. The chorus will "remember" Athens (285; cf. 824), just as Herodotus

5.105.2, taking the glory of the Greek resistance for Athens, tells the story of Darius asking to be reminded of the Athenians at every mealtime.[110] The play often blurs the Greek resistance with the Athenian resistance,[111] because it has been influenced by the Athenian conception of the Persian Wars. The battle of Marathon is obviously not Aeschylus' main focus, but the way that 490's triumph came to shape so strongly all the claims of the *epitaphioi* in which Athens is the "first" or "only" city in some noble attribute[112] has also shaped Aeschylus' portrayal of 480's allied Greek triumph as essentially the unique triumph of a specifically Athenian democracy, free speech, intelligence and order over their opposites. The only Greek state specifically named is Athens (cf. Hdt. 7.104), and when Atossa seeks information from the chorus about the location and nature of the city (230–44), they explain that Xerxes' purpose in attacking Athens is to subject the whole of Greece to the king: to defeat Athens is to defeat Greece (234), a theme very prominent in later ideologically inspired speeches on Athens.[113] The exchange contains multiple contrasts between Athenians and Persians, all of which would have been unarguable truths to the audience, with an ideological dimension beyond mere facts: Athenians fight with the manly weapons of shields and spears (239–40), Xerxes as king has no one to check his despotic power, but the Athenians are subject to no one (241–2; cf. 213–4).[114] While Persia is wealthy with gold belonging to individuals, Athens has a "stream of silver, a treasure from the earth" (238), which, through agreement among the Athenians to use it for communal purposes, was used to create the navy which defeated Persia and brought Athens preeminence (Hdt. 7.144.1–2).

Edith Hall argues that the conceptual polarization between Greek and barbarian essentially began with the Persian Wars and then shifted into a contrast between Athenian democracy and barbarians' forms of ruling or tyranny, as *Pers*. 230–44 illustrates. Once Persia no longer threatened Greece, Athens' claim to lead the Delian league was based on their belief in Athenian political superiority, which in turn underlay justifications of Athenian imperialism.[115] Herodotus already links Athens' service in the Persian Wars with the justice of its primacy among the Greeks.[116] In the context of growing Athenian power, it is therefore significant that Aeschylus' Persians fear for their own imperial power: at 584–94 they prophesy that free speech[117] is coming to a people no longer yoked under a king's power and that their subjects will soon pay them no more tribute. Such fears indicate that, as early as 472, when they could not yet be sure that Persia had truly learned its lesson,[118] Athenian writers could express confidence in their city's powers as world liberators in a mode, already familiar from their pre-Persian War shaping of the Theseus legend,[119] that becomes central to Athenian self-publicity and public education long after 404 BCE. Darius, a successful conqueror in life and now a supernatural being who has special access to prophetic truth, is made to warn Persia not to engage with Greece again (790–842), because the land itself protects them and will bring only hunger and misery on future invaders (794; cf. Hdt. 7.49). By predicting what will happen at Plataea (816–22) – the future for those portrayed on the stage, the secure past for spectators – framed in terms of *hybris* and impiety (820–22), he projects authority and reassurance to the audience that

Persia will not attack Greece a third time, since his people must "remember" Athens and Greece (824). Just three lines later, he speaks of Zeus "the punisher." Given the notable emphasis in later Athenian discourse on Athens as preserver of Greek law and custom by punishing the wicked and rewarding the good, as though they were agents of Zeus,[120] it is striking that these two sentiments appear so closely together in a document of 472 BCE.

Murray attributes Aeschylus' suppression of individual Greek names to religious scruples: not men but gods created the Greek victory.[121] Certainly the hostility of the gods[122] to an imperfectly comprehending Persia is emphasized throughout the play.[123] Both Aeschylus and Herodotus moralize and mythologize the Persian Wars through narratives of events which illustrate a fundamental Greek law of human existence already expressed by Solon (fr. 6W, 13W) according to which excessive prosperity engenders first a destructive *hybris* and then divine punishment.[124] Atossa is said to sleep with a Persian god[125] and to be the mother of a god (157–8), and although Xerxes is generally called godlike rather than an actual god (80, 150–1, 634), he attempts the "divine" act of linking lands separated by sea with his bridge over the Hellespont, "yoking" a "holy" entity as though it were a "slave" (65–71, 745; cf. Hdt. 7.36.1–5).[126] His transgression of divine-human boundaries, combined with the excessive resources that he briefly controls, makes his punishment entirely predictable, as even his wiser father admits.[127] The active malignity of Aeschylus' gods (909, 920, 942–3) causes them to trick the Persians at Edonia by freezing the river Strymon as they crossed it – Herodotus more prosaically claims that they used a bridge (7.24.1) – until the sun melts the ice and drowns them, in a fitting revenge of water on those who had tried to yoke the sea (495–507).[128] Human ignorance (*Pers.* 454; cf. 361, 372–3) is inextricably bound up with divine malignity, and Aeschylus endorses the conventional Greek belief that the gods sometimes actively encourage humans to make destructive decisions.[129] In a particularly striking use of dramatic irony at 215–25, the queen's advisors completely misinterpret the warnings contained in the dreams and omens sent her by the gods (176–214), and Aeschylus' spectators briefly experience an almost divine clarity and certainty in their interpretation of their meaning.

Since Aeschylus and Herodotus view the Persian Wars through the same theodicy, their narratives of the Persian Wars share many details, though their emphases are different.[130] Aeschylus, our oldest witness to the Persian Wars, is an important source for Herodotus,[131] but given the momentousness of the events and our relatively slender collection of extant sources[132] for an event of such importance in the Greek world, the tradition is unlikely to have been straightforward, as the multiplicity of anecdotes in Herodotus suggests: both probably drew on some common sources,[133] and stories of what happened quickly acquired a significance beyond mere battle narrative. Simonides' recently discovered poem on the battle of Plataea (11W²) shows that the Persian Wars acquired a mythological and even theological overlay almost immediately,[134] and many Trojan War myths are realigned with the Persian Wars, as Trojan (or Amazon) conquests are reworked to bestow the heroic splendour of myth on contemporary history (and vice versa). Polygnotus' mural in the *Stoa Poikile* (Paus. 1.15.2–3) juxtaposes Theseus fighting

Amazons, the Trojan War and the battle of Marathon (with Theseus and Heracles as participants), while the frieze of Athena Nike shows the battle of Plataea,[135] and stories of Greek triumph over non-Greeks adorn countless Athenian public artefacts.

An expanding Athens gradually swallowed up much of the credit for the Greeks' success in the Persian Wars, but immediately after the war many cities and even individuals laid claim to saving Greece.[136] At Athens, says Pindar, he must extol the battle of Salamis, but Spartans prefer to hear songs of Plataea (*Pyth.* 1.72–80.) There were also panhellenic offerings, above all the bronze snake column which named 31 Greek cities as architects of the victory, with Lacedaemonians, Athenians and Corinthians placed first (*ML* 27; cf. Hdt. 8.121, 9.81). Aeschylus straddles both tendencies: he speaks of "Greeks" and emphasizes Greek unity in contrast to Herodotus' narratives of fractured relations between cities and individuals in the Greek resistance, but still privileges Athens and expresses Athenian self-assertion in the face of many other claims of outstanding service in the Persian Wars. Like Herodotus, Aeschylus expresses what the *epitaphioi* also emphasize, and what even Thucydides offers with a rather different emphasis (1.73.4–74.2; cf. Lys. 2.2), that Athens is unique among the Greeks and saved them.[137] By contrast, Theopompus (*FGrHist* 115F153) considered that Athens exaggerated its record in the Persian Wars,[138] Herodotus gives huge credit to Sparta in the mouth of Demaratus (Hdt. 7.102–4), while even Sparta's defeat at Thermopylae could be made into the decisive element that saved Greece.[139] In his Persian War poetry, Simonides shares the credit for the victory among several cities,[140] and in the early years after the war, Syracuse[141] and others[142] also attempted to claim credit for saving Greece. The Athenian tradition eclipsed them all.

2.3 Aeschylus' *Eumenides*

While Aeschylus' *Persians* reflects the mood of the Athenians in the aftermath of the Persian Wars, his *Eumenides* is imbued with the extraordinary self-confidence that propelled them through the glory years of the Pentecontaetia, which cemented Athenian power as a political entity, along with the imperial mentality that would continue not only long after other Greek cities had tired of honouring Athenian efforts on their behalf but even long after the end of the empire. The *Oresteia* was presented only a few weeks after the tumultuous end of the first year of the first Peloponnesian War, at a time when Athenian energy and success seemed unbounded. By 459, Athens was preparing to fight Corinth and perhaps the entire Peloponnesian League under Sparta. While besieging its old enemy Aegina, Athens had also defended Megara successfully, not with regular hoplites but with a force of under- and over-age soldiers (Thuc. 1.105.2–106). Though still at war with Persia, and having sent 200 ships to Cyprus, the Athenians heeded Egypt's appeal for aid against Persia and sent those ships to aid them (Thuc. 1.104.1).[143] IG1² 929 lists 177 of the Erechtheis tribe alone who died in the campaigns of 459. Meanwhile at home, they were no less busy, as Athenian oligarchs were encouraging a Peloponnesian army to invade Attica (Thuc. 1.107.4). In an ensuing battle at Tanagra (1.108.1), Sparta was victorious, but it was a Pyrrhic victory, and after they went home with many casualties, Athens took control of central Greece.[144]

Given this flood of activity and temporarily almost limitless success, it is not surprising that many topoi of Athenian self-assertion discussed in Chapter 1 run through 458's play. Characteristic of empire is the desire both to extend without limits in time or space and to naturalize its claims by asserting that it has always existed in some form. Both these elements shape the story of *Eumenides*, in a relatively early example of the Athenians' increasing tendency to appropriate non-Athenian mythical characters for their own ends to glorify the city. As early as the sixth century, Athens laid claim to a valuable identity as benevolent and civilizing by appropriating Eleusis and its myths.[145] By the late sixth and early fifth centuries, the Athenians promote Theseus as their heroic representative and gradually mould him to match the greatest panhellenic civilizing hero Heracles, so that some of his deeds resemble Heracles' or he is inserted into some of Heracles' exploits, such as combat against the Amazons. Later in the fifth century, Heracles himself and Oedipus, heroes whose connection with Athens is not deeply rooted compared with their connections elsewhere, are coopted by Athenian tragedy as examples of outcasts whom Athens, defender of the oppressed, takes into the city.[146] The story of Orestes' dealings with Athens broadly fits into this mould.

Aeschylus may not have been the first to bring Orestes to Athens to be tried for matricide,[147] but he was probably the first to imagine his jury not as a group of gods[148] but as a group of Athenian citizens.[149] While both versions date to the fifth century, it seems more likely that Aeschylus would have jettisoned a divine jury to give more glory to Athens and create a charter myth for the establishment of the court of the Areopagus as a homicide court,[150] than that he would have changed a story glorifying Athens to glorify the gods instead.[151] Making the jury human glorifies the power and potential of Athens to an exceptional degree: the goddess of wisdom herself states that she alone should not decide on the case and enlists Athenian citizens to carry out an initial (though not final) judgement (*Eum.* 470–82).[152] Orestes' reception in Athens also foreshadows a motif that will become especially popular in representations of Athens in later fifth-century tragedy, in which Athens accepts suppliants whose past history brings with it potential dangers. Heracles' children, advocates for the burial of those who failed to sack Thebes, Heracles and Oedipus are all "clients"[153] of Athenian prowess, both in war and peace, and all either have human enemies who could attack Athens for receiving them, or have themselves committed terrible crimes, so that accepting them could bring divine vengeance on Athens for harbouring someone polluted. In every suppliant play, representatives of Athens must deliberately decide to incur risk by helping them, using their judgement (backed up by military prowess if necessary) to determine the right course of action. Athens does choose to help, every time, and is rewarded for so doing. The *Eumenides* differs structurally from true suppliant plays in some important respects,[154] but similar patterns run through it.[155] Orestes the matricide is pursued by the Erinyes, who consider him irredeemably polluted. It is their word against his as he repeatedly claims that his pollution has worn off and he is no longer dangerous to others (235–9,

280–88, 443–52), but even if he is right, welcoming him is potentially dangerous to the Athenians since the Erinyes threaten dire punishment if he is acquitted (710–1, 719–20, 732–3). The Athenian jury must make the decision, and they do so through the exceptional wisdom that Athena commends: at 1002 the Eumenides state that the Athenians are even "revered" by Zeus.[156] The chorus of jurors is silent except to vote, and the arguments put forth on both sides are notoriously partial, but Athena's speech after the vote has been cast exemplifies the rational wisdom that is attributed to this idealized jury henceforth, and which characterizes Athens and its representatives in panegyrical texts.[157]

The decision to acquit Orestes brings Athens an alliance with Orestes and his city (754–77), the first reward of many promised to the Athenians for their intellectual and moral courage. The alliance with Argos (unilateral, like all Athens' alliances in tragedy),[158] which is enthusiastically emphasized in the text (289–91,[159] 669–73, 762–74) must recall the recent Athenian-Argive alliance of 461, but the play pushes alliance with Argos back to a time when gods like Athena and Apollo were thought to mingle with humans on almost equal terms of respect and awe (470–88, 1002), and emphasizes its comfortingly eternal span from the heroic age through the time of 458 BCE's Dionysia to an unending future.[160] Even posthumously, Orestes will prevent his people or enemies from harming Athens (763, 774), setting the pattern for later heroic protectors of Athens, such as Adrastus and Eurystheus in Euripides and Oedipus in Sophocles. Claims to eternity also shape the references to Athens' possession of Sigeum (401) as well as Athena's court (484; 572; 683; cf. 670–2).[161]

In later tragedies, the alliances with which Athens is rewarded result from war undertaken to help vulnerable suppliants. While Orestes is not at war with the Erinyes in Aeschylus' *Eumenides*, the glorification of (externally directed)[162] Athenian war-making is notable and intimately connected with its peacetime activities of promoting justice and wise counsel. By acquitting Orestes and ending older, rougher forms of justice, Athens gains a useful alliance with a distinguished city, which will help Athenian activity in the world, whether it is conceived of as helping others or the *polypragmosynē* of which its enemies complain (cf. E. *Supp.* 576–7). Ample external war of the kind that brings glory is specifically sanctioned by Athena, patron goddess of Athens, chief "fixer" in the lawcourts and the daughter of Zeus herself.[163]

Right from the start of this play, Aeschylus hints that the city where Orestes will find reconciliation is especially advanced. His Apollo takes control of Delphi not, as in more dominant traditions, by force,[164] but by a peaceful transition which was perhaps Aeschylus' invention.[165] Apollo goes to Delphi from Delos, via the beaches of Attica, while the "road-making (κελευθοποιοὶ) children of Hephaestus" accompany him with honours, "making tame the land previously untamed" (χθόνα / ἀνήμερον τίθεντες ἡμερωμένην, 13–14). Again, an Athenian author pulls the Athenians into the story by taking possession of a myth originally not theirs. The more common tradition has Apollo coming to Delphi via Boeotia,[166] but here he travels the road that Athens used for sending delegations to the Pythian festival at Delphi:[167] these sacred delegations were preceded on the road by men holding axes "to tame the land" (ὡς διημερώσοντες τὴν γῆν).[168] Thus in two lines Aeschylus concisely invokes the religious and cultural order, peace and civilization of the ideal Athens.

Athens courageously receives Orestes, a potentially dangerous suppliant, and creates a new institution through which he will be restored to his rightful position. Even more courageously, Athena will find a place in Athens for terrifying and physically repellent supernatural creatures of the night.[169] This second alliance that Athenian courage gains for the city is far greater than any human alliance in guaranteeing the eternal peace and prosperity of the whole city. Athena can negotiate this alliance partly because, uniquely among the divinities, she mediates between two sets of interests, as a goddess whose preference is for the male in all things, and as the daughter of Zeus who, unlike Apollo (179–97), can recognize and reconcile the conflict between the interests of the older and younger gods.[170] As a mediator, Athena is the middle term, neither too male nor too female, neither too old nor too young, the daughter of the chief Olympian and, like the chorus, a virgin,[171] hitting that "sweet spot" of the middle that is so prized by Athens, Rome and other powerful nations.[172] Unlike Apollo, she is courteous to the Erinyes yet calls them to account when they deny that Apollo and Orestes have any valid claims (428–30). Both the Erinyes and Athena herself actively espouse a "middle way" between tyranny and anarchy (517–30; 696–9) with a place for "what is terrible" as a guarantor of justice and order in the city forever. Such an ideal conforms to older Greek popular morality but is appropriated here by this most Athenian play and turned into an innovation, created in Athens for the benefit of the whole of Greece, just as the *epitaphioi* claim a general, cultural primacy for Athens.

The imperial, acquisitive Athens that works to appropriate Orestes in myth is also evident in Athena's claim (397–401) that she has come from the Scamander, securing land there as a "choice gift" for the sons of Theseus "in perpetuity" (401). The reference to the Scamander is often interpreted as a reference to Sigeum,[173] which strictly speaking was not the Athenians' possession but rather a loyal member of the Delian League at this time, liberated from Persian control. Athena's words imply a rather more imperial relationship, prefiguring the language of some inscriptions that we see around 450/49 of the cities "over which the Athenians have power".[174] Similarly, the earlier reference to Libya (292–3) may recall Athenian activities in Egypt and in other places.[175]

Athena sets up the first homicide court (682),[176] in an early version of the claims of later panegyrics of Athens that Athens brought justice to the world.[177] Similarly, when Athena claims (702–3) that no other nation, whether Scythian or Peloponnesian, has such a protection for its city,[178] she invokes a second topos, featured repeatedly in Athenian rhetoric, of Athens' uniqueness.[179] The dominant aetiology for the name of the Areopagus and its court connects it with Ares' trial by a divine jury for killing Poseidon's son Halirrothius for an assault on Ares' daughter.[180] Aeschylus, however, states that the Amazons camped on the Areopagus when they came in their grudge (φθόνος)[181] against Theseus (686–7) and sacrificed to Ares: hence its name of Areopagus (689–90). Here again, Athenian imperial acquisitiveness has shaped Aeschylus' play, because the invasion of Athens by Amazons was the mythical prefiguration of the invasion by the Persians, whom Athenian tradition partly assimilates to the Amazons in Athenian tradition as fellow easterners who exhibit a problematic mixture of male and female;[182] and like the Amazons, the Persians used the Areopagus as a base to attack the Acropolis (Hdt. 8.52.1). By creating a new, Athenocentric aetiology, Aeschylus makes a subtle but reassuring reference to the eternally victorious image of the city: the Amazons camped in the heart of the city, but neither they, nor the Persians, will ever match Athenian prowess.

That the votes of the jury are apparently so close and Athena's divine vote apparently saves Orestes[183] also aligns with the preference for a middle way that idealizing texts claim for Athens. Similarly, Athena's endless patience with the Erinyes[184] in their desire to avenge Athens' disrespect foreshadows the kind of ideal Athenian position which will be embodied in later tragedy by the quintessential Athenian Theseus, who prefers persuasion to force but can resort to military power if persuasion fails. Here, Athena points out (826–9) that she "alone" of the gods has the key to Zeus' thunderbolt, "but there is no need of it here." Indeed: but the implication that ultimately her sheer power, sanctioned by Zeus, could dominate the Erinyes if they will not come to heel is clear. Still, though, persuasion and the offer of honour, expressed both in the abstract and with concrete gifts of a place at Athens, sacrifices and first fruits, will be a superior incentive for their compliance (854–5).

The final epirrhematic "duet" between Athena and the Eumenides is imbued with themes of Athenian imperial discourse of the fifth century and beyond. Athena looks forward from the heroic age to the present and future of the citizen spectators,[185] promising that they will gain ever greater honour as time rolls on (853),[186] connecting past, present and future in one glorious, undifferentiated Athenian perfection.[187] Her claims also hint at an Athenian exceptionalism in finding an unending prosperity in a new Golden Age (937–47), which, unlike Hesiod's myth of ages (*Op.* 109–20) will never deteriorate (*Eum.* 853–4).[188] Moreover, the Athenians give the Eumenides a unique home: no other mortals could offer anything similar (857), and significantly, when they accept her offer (916–21) they call the city the "altar-defending citadel of the gods, the treasure of Greek gods" ("φρούριον θεῶν ... ῥυσίβωμον Ἑλλάνων ἄγαλμα δαιμόνων"), in effect "the acropolis of Hellas",[189] acknowledging a clear primacy for Athens. The unique honour given them will guarantee an absence of civil war combined with plenteous war abroad for love[190] of glory. This striking description of war indicates supreme Athenian self-confidence at the time of writing, and Athena calls her city "most loved by the gods" (*Eum.* 869). Athena's patient persuasion and warm welcome are especially striking because these beings never stop being terrifying and hideous (990). Athena actively encourages them into the heart of the city where they will retain their terrifying characteristics but will be directed by Athenian human beings and their goddess to use their powers for good. At the end of the play, they are formally welcomed into Athens[191] and don the scarlet robes of metics[192] over their black clothing (1028). They are not suppliants, but their treatment recalls plays in which an alarming suppliant is incorporated into Athens for the city's own benefit, and above all, at the very end of the fifth century, the figure of Oedipus, who is explicitly aligned with the Eumenides in *Oedipus at Colonus*.[193] Along with the blessings of successful warfare will also come blessings from the earth, sea and heavens, of fertility and abundance (904–9, 939–45), with the plenitude, completeness and eternal combination of the war and peace motifs that is central to Athenian panegyrics of Athens. Lines 945–7 even promise mineral resources, which would include the "stream of silver" (*Pers.* 238) on which Athens' contribution at Salamis and the unimaginable benefits arising from it ultimately depended.[194]

2.4 Sophocles' *Oedipus at Colonus*

The half-century during which Athens dominated the eastern Mediterranean, then struggled to dominate it and finally ran out of steam is bracketed on the one hand by the vision of Athens in Aeschylus' *Eumenides* and on the other by the final portrayal of Athens in extant tragedy by Sophocles' *Oedipus at Colonus*. While there are clear differences in the portrayal of Athens in the two plays, notably in the absence of a human ruler in Aeschylus versus the dominance of Theseus as Athens' king in Sophocles, their portrayals of Athenian virtues and the rewards the city gains from them are as consistently unchanging as the view of the idealized Athens presented in panegyrical literature.[195]

At the start of the play, Oedipus and Antigone arrive at the grove of the Eumenides (39–43) in Colonus.[196] It is holy ground (16), beautiful to see and to hear with its laurel, olive, grapes and nightingale song (cf. 668–94).[197] Oedipus has a unique affinity with the Eumenides in his terrifying aspect (286, 577–8), aligned with the power to curse and bless those who treat him badly or well:[198] as with all other tragic suppliants, Athens will be rewarded for courageously receiving him. While the citizens of Colonus feel reverence and fear even at passing the grove, much less entering it (39–40), Oedipus is not bound by such strictures, but due to his hideous appearance and then the revelation of his identity, he becomes an object of such fear that at first his presumptive hosts treat him badly. At 118 the chorus of old men of Colonus arrives to hunt out the ignorant foreigner whose violation of the Eumenides' grove might harm them and the city. When Oedipus reveals himself, they describe him as "terrible"[199] to see and speak to (140). At this point, he has merely violated the grove, but this violation symbolizes more terrible violations by Oedipus that they have yet to discover. Even so, at this point, they do exercise a degree of cautious sympathy for him as long as he is prepared to move from the grove (148–69), which he does once he has extracted a promise that they will not harm him (176–7). In many Athenian suppliant plays, the arrival of suppliants at Athens is in effect their acceptance, because Athens is the eternal refuge for suppliants. In a manner more like Euripides (cf. E. *Supp.* 195–292), however, Sophocles plays with audience expectations at this moment: though the chorus have promised to protect him, immediately after his painfully slow progress out of the grove, they persistently ask him who he is (203–19). Resistance is impossible and once names such as Laius, the Labdacids and Oedipus are mentioned (226), they command him to leave on the grounds that he deceived them into allowing him to stay, so that no shame or danger will result from breaking their promise (229–33). A suppliant like Oedipus, whose mere name is inseparable from the two worst crimes a human being can commit, is the most frightening possible in the inherently disturbing category of suppliant. Their fear of the danger the city may incur by receiving him (234–6) is not unreasonable. But it is also not becoming to Athenians. As will emerge in the next scene (399–419), this is a Theban sort of fear which has no place in the audience's city.

That this fear is un-Athenian is expressed first by Antigone, who pleads for them to pity her and find respect for her father (237–53). As residents of the city where pity is a national characteristic, they do pity her, but their fear of the gods is too strong to allow pity to cause them to act (254–7). Oedipus then appeals directly to considerations that all Athenian spectators would recognize (258–91, esp. 258–62): reputation is mere words if Athens refuses to live up to its reputation as the most god-fearing city which alone (μόνας)[200] can help the oppressed stranger. Here he appeals to conventional characterizations of Athens: its reputation for pity,[201] physical and moral courage, wisdom (differentiating between deserved and undeserved suffering)[202] and its uniqueness. He claims that what happened to him was suffered rather than done, thanks to the workings of the gods, whose will it is that Athens should now save him.[203] Though Athens is the city that uniquely has the resources to make alliances with the weak, since the Greek world only has room for one benefactor who wins friends by giving rather than receiving benefits,[204] in fact the city always does receive rewards for the risks it takes, even as it makes lordly claims to disdain such considerations. Thus while Oedipus refers now to the unique reward that the Athenians will receive for helping him (282–7), the chorus are significantly incurious about that benefit. Athenian spectators may also have enjoyed watching the representatives of their city be open to Oedipus' persuasion, an essential element in Athenian democracy, by agreeing to summon Theseus to make the final decision.[205]

Theseus represents the tragic Athens which is both a moral arbiter and typically stands "outside the tragedy". He instantly knows who Oedipus is (553), asking him no questions to spare him the pain that the chorus have caused him by their inquiries, and expresses pity for him (556) since he, like Oedipus, grew up in a foreign land and knows that all humanity is vulnerable (562–8).[206] Oedipus' hideous outer form does not represent his character (576–8), and Athens' representative sees beyond his appearance and past actions. Several times (576–8, 626–7; cf. 286–7) Oedipus mentions the gift that he brings, but after he has ascertained that the gift is a matter for the future, after Oedipus' death, Theseus does not press him for details (586): in his speech formally accepting him (631–6) Oedipus' gift is only last in his list of reasons (635), after Athens' reputation for offering δορύξενος / κοινὴ . . . ἑστία ("the common hearth for a spearfriend") and its care for suppliants (631–4), secure in Athens' power to provide unconditional aid.[207] Just once, Oedipus rebukes him for judging his actions without knowing the whole truth and Theseus responds (594): "Tell me: I shouldn't criticize without knowing all the facts", a line whose moderate tone resembles Athena's courteous address when she first met the Eumenides.[208] Such moderation is especially appropriate given Theseus' fundamentally limited, human knowledge that contrasts with Oedipus' broader knowledge (cf. 607–24).[209] But when Oedipus expresses fear for the future, Theseus responds with complete confidence in his city's power to protect him from harm (649–67).

To mark the acceptance of this strange being into the city of Athens, the chorus sing an ode of extraordinary beauty (668–719),[210] which starts locally with the physical attributes of Colonus but ends with a grand reassertion of the claims that recur consistently throughout public discourse about Athens. Colonus is shining,[211] and the chorus reprise elements of Antigone's description of the place at the start of the play, the aural beauty of the nightingales' songs and the visual and sensual beauty of the green glens, ivy and coolness, leaves with many fruits and flowers while the eternally abundant waters of the Cephisus bring the kind of fertility that Aeschylus' Eumenides had once promised the city. Colonus is almost paradoxically both cool and windless, melding two slightly contradictory attributes to form the perfect place, because Athens is the place of perfection which can combine elements which elsewhere are opposed to one another.[212] The gods are here in abundance: Dionysus, the Two Goddesses (683–4),[213] the Muses and Aphrodite.[214] But the greatest glory of all is the olive tree, the profoundest emblem of Greek civilization,[215] which Athens appropriated as its own exclusive emblem of Athenian civilization. Hdt. 5.82.2 (cf. E. *Tro*. 801–3) reports the claim that once olives only grew in Attica and here (*OC* 694–706); Sophocles claims that olives do not exist in Asia Minor or in the Peloponnese. The uniqueness of Athens must suppress any horticultural good sense. The olive is described (695–9) as φύτευμ' ἀχείρωτον αὐτόποιον, / ἐγχέων φόβημα δαΐων, ("unconquered, self-renewing,[216] causing terror to destroying enemies"): in all, an indefatigable tree which represents the unconquerable strength of Athens. It is also a nurturer of children, which itself has an imperial dimension because of the importance for the maintenance of empire that sons carry on their fathers' traditions.[217] Zeus and Athena tend the olives, and such divine supervision speaks to the promise of eternity for the city whose access to the olive is unique. In the traditional myth portrayed on the west metopes of the Parthenon, Athena and Poseidon clashed over the possession of Athens, which had to choose between the gifts the two gods offered them.[218] Here Athens is blessed with the gifts of both gods, olives *and* horses – which Athens was the first to tame (715)[219] – *and* sea power, as the imperial reach takes everything into its grasp.[220]

When Creon attempts to abduct Oedipus' daughters, Athens shows that its reputation for effective action, or the combination of words and deeds, is justified.[221] When Oedipus appeals to the chorus for aid, they admit that they are old, but the strength of the land has not grown old (724–7): the eternal strength of Athens transcends mere individuals. Indeed, these old men are stronger and more authoritative than some other elderly choruses, such as those of *Agamemnon* or Euripides' *Heracles*.[222] They manage to delay the seizing of both girls for a relatively long time (824–85) and their stalwart confidence in the Athenian army and subsequent ode in which they vividly invoke the battle (1044–97) assimilates them to the combatants in the actual battle. Creon addresses them courteously at first and attempts to invoke Athenian values by praising Athens' outstanding strength (733–4) and appealing to democracy by stating that all of Thebes wishes to recover Oedipus (737–8; cf. 849–50). He even claims to feel pity for him and Antigone (740–54). But these appeals to Athenian values are proved entirely counterfeit, when his designs to abduct Oedipus' daughters and then Oedipus himself become clear.

The chorus invoke the strength of the whole city for aid (840, 884), and finally Theseus returns (887), even though he had been in the middle of a sacrifice to Poseidon.[223] When a suppliant needs protection, Theseus or Athens have the moral wisdom allied with the military power to weigh up conflicting obligations. Saving a suppliant in a moment of unusual crisis must trump more quotidian religious observance.[224] At once Theseus springs into action, sending troops to save Oedipus' daughters and his own reputation (897–903), and then gives Creon a grand and outraged rebuke, combining effective words and deeds in a typically omni-competent Athenian mode (1143–4; cf. Thuc. 2.40.3).[225] Even here, Theseus' anger is restrained: Creon must suffer only as he has made others suffer, evil returned for evil but no more, and Theseus accuses him of acting unworthily not only of a law-abiding place like Athens (913–4; cf. 929), but even his own city Thebes, which did not teach him such terrible behaviour (919–23; cf. 911–2, 929–30). Thebes is consistently portrayed negatively in Athenian literature: if Creon's behaviour is not even Theban, he is especially contemptible, so these lines are perhaps not the strange compliment to Athens' enemy that has puzzled some commentators,[226] but rather a severe indictment of Creon, combined perhaps with an expression of an Athenian superiority so secure in itself that it can even grant Thebes some credit in this specific context. Theseus claims that he would never enter a strange territory, even with good cause, without the ruler's consent (924–8). Perhaps some visitors to Athens smiled wryly at this, but his moral outrage was doubtless appealing to the Athenians ("sons of Theseus") in the audience.

Creon attempts to justify his actions with another appeal to Athens' excellence and to divine law under which a polluted man like Oedipus should be entirely unwelcome there (939–49): his claims recall the chorus' concerns earlier in the play, proving that these were in fact wrong.[227] Oedipus is entirely sceptical and accuses him of mere flattery of Athens (1003–5), in a long speech denouncing Creon, exculpating himself and praising Athens' outstanding piety (1006–7). In due course, Theseus' men successfully capture the captors of Oedipus' daughters and return them to him as promised. Creon is allowed to leave (1036–7), humbled but punished no more strictly than is fitting, because idealized Athenian moderation never exceeds what is just and can make an exact moral calibration of what that just punishment will be.[228]

By this exploit, Athens wins yet another dependent client on whom to lavish protection, bringing the city (and spectators) clear psychological benefits: the concrete benefits from Oedipus' body are yet to come. Once more, Athens' uniqueness is praised: Antigone gives Theseus unique credit for her recovery and Oedipus entirely concurs (1117, 1123), adding that in the Athenians "alone of all men" (1126) he has found piety, reasoned moderation (τὸ ἐπιεικές, a word important in Athenian self-praise),[229] and honesty. Theseus responds modestly, since this strange day in Athens has brought up a new matter. A stranger with Argive connections has asked to see Oedipus, and much against his will, Oedipus agrees to see him, yielding grudgingly to Antigone's insistence that he reciprocate the generous treatment that he has found as Theseus' suppliant (1202). While Polynices is a more pathetic character than Creon, reconciliation with Oedipus is impossible and Polynices' supplication to the father he treated so badly has little in common with the suppliant relationship between Oedipus and Theseus.

After Polynices' dejected departure to face certain death, Oedipus' business is over, and the thunder which he knows will be a sign of his end begins. For the chorus, this is alarming (1456, 1463–71), and some of their old fears resurface. But Theseus returns as the emblem of Athenian energy and courage (1500) in one final exhibition of strong and generous care for his client. The second part of Oedipus' mission to Athens now comes into play. From the start he had promised a special benefit to Athens at his death, but the Athenians in their usual manner rather brushed it aside, unlike Creon, whose attempt to take the posthumous benefit promised by Oedipus without giving him proper burial inverted Athenian (and Greek) norms, relying on a false and cowardly piety, quite different from Athens' active, courageous piety. Now, however, Oedipus announces that it is time for him to reciprocate the benefits that Athens has given him (1489–90), and he offers the eternal blessing of his body in Athenian soil, posthumously protecting the land from all Theban incursions and dangers (1518–1525). To gain it, Theseus must never reveal the place where Oedipus leaves the earth: all we know is that it is near the place where Theseus' loyalty to Peirithous was commemorated (1593–4). Theseus' special knowledge will be exclusively passed down the royal line from father to sons (1530–32). Oedipus' last direct words on earth are a wish for the eternal prosperity of Theseus and his land (1555). Rejecting forever his own descendants in favour of the Athenians, Oedipus exclusively grants Theseus, and thus Athens (1640–44), the prosperity which his native city might have acquired.[230] Though Theseus is willing to help Antigone and Ismene, acknowledging what he owes them (1776–7), he cannot let them return to Thebes or give them the account of their father's death that they so desperately want: Athens' prosperity depends on his silence (1760–5). For the last time in tragedy, the Athenian imperial reach has shaped mythology to benefit Athens, even as the play emphasizes the benefits given to, rather than received from, its suppliant client, and reflects back to Athens an idealized view of the city which few, if any, could find unappealing.[231]

Notes

1 For a fuller version of the argument made by this introduction, see Mills (2017). Thanks are due to Brill publishers for allowing me to use a version of it here.
2 See already Arrowsmith (1964) 32–3, quoted by Rhodes (2003) 117: "The Athenians regarded the theatre not as entertainment but as the supreme instrument of cultural

instruction, a democratic *paedeia* complete in itself." Croally (1994) discusses the issue at length, claiming explicitly that "tragedy questions ideology" (43); cf. 11–12 and in general 17–69.
3   Goldhill (1987) and (1990).
4   Cartledge (1997) 6; Euben (1986) 27–29; Allan and Kelly (2013) 79 n.7.
5   Pelling (1997b) 235.
6   Goldhill (1990) 114.
7   Heath (1987); Sourvinou-Inwood (2003) especially 153, 293, 331–2, 513–8.
8   Griffin (1998).
9   Goldhill (2000).
10 Cf. Rhodes (2003) 119.
11 Croally (1994) 224; Dover (1975) is cautious, but see Ostwald (1986) and Wallace (1994).
12 Goldhill (2000) 41 appears to suggest that this was indeed a universal response, but the Athenian audience was distinctly diverse and playwrights had to take such diversity into account: Revermann (2006b).
13 Rhodes (2003) 107–15.
14 Cf. Allan and Kelly (2013) 85.
15 Goldhill (1990) 101–2, 106–14.
16 Goldhill (1997) 61.
17 Pl. *Mx.* 234c–235c (cf. *Gorg.* 502b–c5): cf. Carter (2011a) 61–2.
18 Rosenbloom (2014a) 164–5; Christ (2006) 50 estimates, however, that of the 30,000 Athenians eligible to participate in the Assembly probably no more than 6000 attended any particular meeting.
19 Lee (1999) 80–1; Griffin (1998) 54; Allan and Kelly (2013) 87–8.
20 Rosenbloom (1995) 101–2. At *Rep.* 606b Socrates emphasizes that it is *others'* sufferings at which audiences weep, since (605d) one's own sorrow demands equanimity and restraint. See also earlier, p. 20.
21 Steiner (1996) 545 n.3. Ancient writers discuss the intensely emotional responses to tragedy of some ancient audiences, and the importance of avoiding too close an identification with those suffering on stage: Lada (1993), esp. 100–11; Halliwell (2002) 53, 75–8. One of Plato's criticisms of tragedy (*Rep.* 387b–388e, 393c, 395c–396d, 605b, 605d3–4) is that its intense emotional power can be detrimental to the character of its audiences: Johnson and Clapp (2005) 141–54; Rosenbloom (1995) 101–3.
22 McChesney (2007).
23 Meineck (2012).
24 Hdt. 6.21.2; Arist. *Poet.* 1448b10–20. The exact nature of these troubles is disputed. How and Wells (1912) 72 suggest that the play reproached Athens for deserting Miletus, while Rosenbloom (1993) argues that the portrayal of Miletus' sufferings stirred up fear of Persian reprisals on Athens for helping the Ionian revolt. See also Roisman (1988), but his attempt (18) to downdate the play so that the Athenians watching the sack of Miletus were reliving their own experiences in 480 is unconvincing: Rosenbloom (1993) 171–2.
25 And even this play contains distancing strategies: Grethlein (2013) 75–9, 86–8.
26 Lee (1999) 82.
27 Lee (1999) 82–3. For Pelling (1997b) 220, tragedy necessitates some distance between audience and play, but still "challenge[s] and test[s] prejudices . . . [making the audience feel] pleasurably uncomfortable." But what happens when "pleasurably uncomfortable" shades into merely "uncomfortable"?
28 Lada (1993) 123–4.
29 Sourvinou-Inwood (1989); (2003) 16–19.
30 Lee (1999) 83–4.
31 Sourvinou-Inwood (2003) 237–8, 242–6.

32 Sourvinou-Inwood (2003) 153, 293, 331–2.
33 Rosenbloom (2014b) 1391. Bremer (1991) 57–8 estimates that only 10% of the plots of extant tragedies (27/280) concern mythical material set in Athens. It may be significant that fully nine of these represent Athens as a haven for suppliants, undoubtedly an image designed to appeal to Athenian audiences.
34 See especially Zeitlin (1990).
35 E. *Supp*. 87–91, 321–25, 340–1, 378–80, 404–5, 438–55.
36 Pelling (1997b) 231.
37 Pity is a product of thinking that some similar evil might happen to us (Ar. *Rhet*. 1382b13–17), but responding properly to tragedy requires some detachment as well (Ar *Rhet*. 1386a18–19): cf. Lada (1993) 123; Halliwell (2002) 215–7.
38 Recent research into the relationship of fiction and empathy among contemporary audiences (Hoffman (2001); Jarvis (2012)) suggests that observers of suffering spontaneously imitate the victim's facial, vocal or postural expressions: these changes trigger the brain to produce feelings resembling the victim's. People are classically conditioned to experience distress when seeing it in others as a result of their own experiences of suffering, and can also feel distress through direct association where some aspect of the distress reminds them of their experiences of pain. Conversely, in situations in which audiences believe that victims are partly to blame for their suffering, empathic distress tends to be reduced. If such phenomena also functioned among ancient audiences, it would be understandable why spectacles of Theban or Argive suffering might predominate over those of Athenian suffering.
39 Zuckerberg (2019).
40 Cf. Griffin (1998) 42.
41 Mills (1997).
42 Cf. Lys. 2.11–16; Dem. 60.8; cf. Isoc. 4.54–6; 12.194; 10.31.
43 Cf. Lys. 2.7–10; Dem. 60.8; cf. Isoc. 4.58, 10.31, 12.171, 14.53.
44 Steinbock (2013) 57.
45 Loraux (1986) 171; cf. Steinbock (2013) 57.
46 Steinbock (2013) 61–2.
47 *Hippolytus* is a partial exception in its story of the murder of his son by Athens' greatest hero, but even this plot offers significant mitigating factors for Theseus' actions: Mills (1997) 186–221 and later pp. 97–8. A previous version of the story which appears not to have mitigated the guilt of Phaedra and possibly Theseus caused offence among the Athenians, according to the *Hypothesis* to the extant play (cf. Ar. *Thesm*. 497, 547, 550; *Ran*. 849–50): perhaps it reminded its audience of "their own troubles", albeit old ones.
48 For example, the reading by Fitton (1961) 430–48 of Euripides' *Suppliants*, even though ancient sources consider the play an encomium of Athens.
49 "Each member of an audience, consciously or not, modifies the stimulus he perceives according to his own predispositions": Cooper and Dinerman (2003) 30.
50 Cf. also Sourvinou-Inwood (2003) 291.
51 Allan and Kelly (2013) 83–5.
52 For a vivid account of events from the perspective of Athenian civilians, see now Garland (2017); Rosenbloom (2006a) 22–5.
53 Harrison (2000b) 51.
54 See Garvie (2009) x–xi. On Naples 3253 (the Darius vase), inscribed "Persai", Darius appears to be listening to a messenger, perhaps delivering a warning: around him, men in oriental dress, presumably the council, seem surprised or alarmed. At the bottom of the picture, a treasurer counts up money while from each side come Persian satraps in submissive poses, some bearing tribute. But, the gods show that Persia's fate is sealed: Athena leads Hellas up to Zeus while Apate on the right tries to lure Asia away from the altar on which she is seated for protection. Trendall and Webster (1971) III.5.6 suggest that the vase represents a fourth-century revival of Phrynichus

(cf. Anti (1954)), but this is unproven: cf. Hall (2007) 8. Even so, the meaning of the illustration is clear and congruent with Athenian beliefs about the Persians and especially that the gods were directly involved in their miraculous defeat by Greece.
55 *TGrF* 3F8; Hall (1993) 115–6.
56 Podlecki (1970) 10. Aeschylus' *choregos* was Pericles (IG II^2 2325: Snell (1986) 69), one of the architects of the Athenian empire. Plut. *Them.* 5.4 states that Themistocles, whose decisions were also fundamental in creating the conditions for Athens to assume preeminence in Greece, performed this function for Phrynichus, and it is usually assumed that he did so in 476, the year of *Phoenissae*.
57 Georges (1994) 102–3. In *TGrF3* 9–11, the women of Phoenicia sing and dance exotic choruses representing a female Asia in mourning.
58 *Persians* was not a part of a connected trilogy, making attempts to determine its tone perhaps even harder; for some speculations on its thematic connections with other plays presented in 472, see Garvie (2009) xl–xlvi; Sommerstein (2010) 62–5.
59 Craig (1924) 98; Broadhead (1960) xv–xvi; Collard (2008) xxiii. See also Harrison (2000b) 135 n.1, who offers bibliography and a summary of the scholarly arguments that have been offered for both sides.
60 Hall (1989) 71–2; de Romilly (1974) 16. Some suggest that Aeschylus was warning the Athenians about the dangers inherent in Athens' own nascent empire: Melchinger (1979) 35–6; Rosenbloom (1995) and (2006a), esp. 96–7; Sommerstein (2010) 61.
61 Lattimore (1943) 90–3. Even more specifically, was the play designed to glorify Themistocles and Salamis over Marathon and Cimon?: Podlecki (1966) 15–23. See, however, Harrison (2000b) 31–9, 98–100 and especially 98: "If the *Persians* was indeed interpreted as a message of support for Themistocles it was a message that had power only by harnessing the play's patriotism to a partisan end, by disguising that partisan stance behind themes that all could rally to." For Hall (2007) 12–13, Aeschylus leaves room for various interpretations of the Themistocles question, but his unambiguous heroes are the anonymous citizen combatants of Athens.
62 Hall (1989) 71; see, for example, the commentaries of Prickard (1879) xxviii–xxix and Sidgwick (1903) viii–xi.
63 Goldhill (1988); Loraux (2002) 45; Dué (2006) 57–90; Rosenbloom (2006a).
64 Rhodes (2007) 36–7.
65 Georges (1994) 83–4: the Greeks slaughter the *best* of the Persians on Psyttaleia (*Pers.* 448–64).
66 Aeschylus' Persia lacks an authoritative adult male leader and is repeatedly portrayed as empty of or lacking in men. It is prone to wild lamentation, even from its leader Xerxes (*Pers.* 468), and is a continent wide open for male, Greek domination (*Pers.* 279): Hall (1993) 117–26; Georges (1994) 102–3; cf. McClure (2006) 20–1.
67 Loraux (1986) 160. Hall (2007) 5–7 discusses the relationship of the play to historical reality. Aeschylus could obviously not create a fully accurate documentary about the Persian Wars, but it is a "truthful record of the ways in which the Athenians liked to think about their great enemy . . . a document of the Athenian collective *imagination.*"
68 For a recent discussion, see Harrison (2000b) 98–114, with whom I largely concur, especially in his argument (113–5) that modern readings in which Aeschylus' portrayal of the Persians' plight invites and receive sympathy from its audience are somewhat anachronistic products of modern classicists' desire to validate their discipline by imagining a highly sensitive and self-critical audience of the kind of which I too am sceptical: pp. 50–52 earlier.
69 Goldhill (1988) 193.
70 Though this is not true of Goldhill's, some discussions of the play (e.g. Murray (1972) 35) are hampered by the assumption that patriotism and great poetry cannot coexist, in a kind of syllogism: "*Persians* is a great play; overt patriotism does not produce great art; therefore *Persians* cannot be a completely patriotic play."

72 *Tragedy and Athens*

71 Hopman (1993) argues that there is a distinction between the triumphant narratives of the Greek victory in the play's speeches and the lamentations that the chorus express: but whether identification with those lamentations would have been the *dominant* audience response is uncertain. Many, though certainly not all (cf. later, pp. 54–6), elements of Xerxes' portrayal do conform to standard portrayal of the Persians in the *epitaphioi* and other texts, which juxtapose Persian vices with Athenian virtues: e.g. Lys. 2.56–7; Dem. 60.11; Isoc. 4.89, 120; Pl. *Mx*. 240d.

72 Craig (1924). For Aristophanes (*Ran*. 1026–7) *Persians* was all about seeking victory over enemies: Harrison (2000b) 51–2. We know of several cases where Athenians did not treat their enemy with the moderation that was the city's great boast of itself. Pericles' father crucified the Persian governor of Sestus (Hdt. 7.33, 9.120.4), while Plutarch (*Them*. 13.2 and *Arist*. 9.2) claims that the Athenians endorsed live sacrifice of three children of the royal family at the battle of Salamis: Georges (1994) 82–3.

73 Or possibly Peter Sellars' post-Gulf War version of the *Persians*, in which Iraqi suffering was emphasized. It received some hostile reception especially in the US and reviews in which aesthetic criticism shaded into slightly defensive political criticism: Hall (2004) 176–82; Taylor (1993) and especially Drake (1993). The play was performed just two years after the Gulf War, and perhaps that was too soon.

74 Johnston (2015). Rosenfeld (2014) traces an increasing path of "normalization" of Hitler, as actual memories of the horrors of Nazi Germany have diminished over time, with a distancing effect that enables him to be imagined as sympathetic, comic and so forth, but it has taken decades for such portrayals to become possible.

75 Rosenbloom (1995) 98.

76 Even today, audiences in Athens clap at these lines: Harrison (2000b) 56.

77 Hdt. 1.153.1, 5.73.2, 5.105.2, 7.101–5 and 8.26. In general, though, the Persians were less interested in the Greeks than the Greeks thought they were: Harrison (2000b) 58–9.

78 Dem.24.170–1, Paus.1.17.1; cf. Mills (1997) 106, n. 74.

79 Pelling (1997a) 13–17.

80 Hom. *Od*. 22.409–16, S. *Aj*. 121–6.

81 Cf. Grethlein (2013) 86–92.

82 Rosenbloom (2006a) 22.

83 "The play may seem, superficially, to be lacking in action . . . however, that is to ignore another plot that runs in parallel to it: the play's gradual striptease of Athenian virtues and achievements:" Harrison (2000b) 115; cf. Albini (1967) 252–3.

84 Craig (1924) 100. As late as 419–396, the experience of suffering Persians was still an interesting spectacle. Timotheus' poem about Salamis included speeches of drowning Persians speaking bad Greek: Stoneman (2015) 158.

85 *Pers*. 419–426, cf. 441–64: Said (1988) 332.

86 Compare also the image of Atossa, in abject terror abandoning her luxury (603–9): both images hint at the sack of a city, but not the city that the Persians actually sacked.

87 See, for example, Solon fr. 4W esp. ll.7–8; 13W, ll.9–22.

88 Hdt. 1.32.1; 7.8γ1–3; 7.22–4, 33–6; 8.109.3: Asheri (2007) 37–9; Castriota (1992) 19–28.

89 Cf. Grethlein (2007) 376–8.

90 Was the Dionysia already something of a panhellenic festival in 472, as it became in the later fifth century? If there was already a significant non-Athenian presence in the audience, the play would offer a very early demonstration of the imperial-epitaphic ideology of Athens outlined in chapter one: Hall (2007) 11.

91 Ar. *Poet*. 1453a1–10: although Harrison (2000b) 110–11 denies that this play conforms to any Aristotelian model, a suffering character on stage must somehow be sympathetic enough to draw spectators to engage with his plight.

92 For Craig (1924) 100, the play expresses "a deep sense of danger overpast, of the aggressor's fall." National collective feeling can express sentiments less tainted by jingoism than a person speaking individually can easily manage.

93 Hall (2007) 1. Compare already Hdt. 6.112.3; 9.27.5, 46.2 with Thucydides' account of the Syracusan resistance to Athens, 7.21.4 and 66.2.
94 Broadhead (1960) xxx; Garvie (2009) xii–xv. About 75% of the Persian names are recognisably Iranian, while some words designating Persian types of leaders appear to translate Persian nomenclature: Hall (1989) 76–100. Podlecki (1970) sees echoes of the Behistun inscription in *Pers.* 5–6, 24. Kennedy (2013) 69–76 discusses the congruence between historical portrayals of Darius and that of Aeschylus.
95 See earlier, p. 14.
96 Notably the prefixes χιλιό- ("1000") and μυριό- ("10,000") at 302–18.
97 *Pers.* 429–32; cf. 513–4 with Collard (2008) xxiv–xxv. On the role of repeated prefixes such as ἁβρό- ("delicate") and χρυσό- ("golden") to emphasize Persian excess to underline the themes of the play, see Kelley (1979); Said (1988). Harrison (2000b) 66 traces verbal movement in the play from πολύανδρος ("with many men", 73) to κένανδρος ("empty of men", 118) and ἄνανδρος ("with no men", 166, 288, 298) and then back to πολύανδρος (533, 899) as the scale of Persia's losses comes fully into focus. Similarly, the repetition of the verb οἴχομαι (already at line 1) emphasizes the sheer magnitude of the devastation: Avery (1964) 175.
98 Hdt. 7.12, 44, 56, 59.2–60, 184–7. The connection between vast resources and foolish, and ultimately destructive impiety is especially clear in the sequence of events described in Hdt. 7.34–7.
99 Hall (1989) 79–84.
100 Griffith (2007) 101–4. Bridges (2015) esp. 10–43 offers a detailed account of Aeschylus' portrayal of Xerxes.
101 Hall (1989) 126–7; cf. earlier pp. 16–17. Elements of later Athenian imperial attitudes may shape both Aeschylus' and Herodotus' conceptions of the Persian empire. Atossa explains Xerxes' attack on Greece as an attempt to outdo his father (*Pers.* 753–758: cf. Hdt. 7.68α.2); compare Thuc. 2.36.1. The Persians also claim (91–2, 1017) that both gods and fate sanction the invincibility of their army: Sampson (2015) 30–1; Rosenbloom (2006a) 94–103. For analogous claims by Athens and other empires compare pp. 10, 11, 19, 21, 24 earlier. Sampson (2015) 25 also discusses the Persians' understanding of past and present as continuous and history as "consistent, regular, and paradigmatic", so that imperial prosperity originates from and predicts future prosperity: this is very much the world of the *epitaphioi*.
102 Darius had his own troubles at Marathon, so their claims (858–902) that he was undefeated are untrue. Marathon is mentioned earlier in the play, but not here, no doubt to underline the contrast between Darius and his son, whose losses were, in any case, far worse: Sommerstein (2010) 60–1.
103 Broadhead (1960) 213; Meier (1993) 70. Not all were keen to be liberated: Hdt. 8.111.
104 Ebbott (2000) contrasts the broken, bloodied bodies of the Persians with the order and honour offered to the dead on the Athenian casualty lists.
105 Goldhill (1988) 191. This is one of a series of oppositions throughout the play that present the unique glory of Athens to Athenian spectators by contrasting their communally oriented democracy with the tyranny of rule by one man. Atossa cares exclusively for her son's welfare, unlike the mother of a warrior in the polis who would consider the whole community. Persians have great personal wealth but Athenian silver is spent collectively, and – especially remarkable for the Persians – Athenians are not subject to one ruler (211–4, 762–4.) Demaratus makes a similar statement to Xerxes (Hdt. 7.103–4.) In general, see Georges (1994) 83–111.
106 Kowerski (2005) 80–4.
107 Podlecki (1970) 65, 72, 104; Hall (2007) 111, 162, 166.
108 Harrison (2000b) 108–10. Irwin (2012) offers an intriguing reading of Bacchylides 17, roughly contemporary with *Persians*, that points in the same direction. The conclusion to Herodotus' *Histories* suggests that he considers that the Athenians pick up as imperialists exactly where the Persians leave off: Stadter (1992); Moles (1996).

74 *Tragedy and Athens*

109 Compare Pind. fr. 76; S. *Aj.* 961; E. *Hcld.* 38, *Hipp.* 423, 760, 1459, *Tro.* 207, *Ion* 30, 262.
110 The meaning of each remembrance is of course significantly different: Said (2002) 138. Compare also Hdt. 5.105.2; 7.5.2, 8β1–3, 11.2, 138.1, 139.1; 9.3.1, all of which give pride of place to Athens in Persian hostilities: also Thuc. 6.33.6. On the portrayal of Persian memory, see Sampson (2015); Grethlein (2007).
111 In Atossa's dream of the two sisters, the woman representing Greece wears Dorian dress, and Sommerstein (2010) 48–9 uses this, along with the mention of Plataea, to minimize the presence of Athenian chauvinism in the play. But there is simply too much emphasis on Ionian achievement for this to be entirely true (178, 563, 950–1, 1011, 1025), and while Plataea is mentioned, the less significant engagement at Psyttaleia is given remarkable emphasis: Lattimore (1943) 91–2.
112 Notably, the false claim that they were the first to endure the sight of the Mede (Hdt. 6.112.3): Kennedy (2013) 67–8; cf. earlier, pp. 12, 18.
113 Lys. 2.20, 31, 42; Dem. 18.202–3; Isoc. 4.49, 59, 92–9, 157; Lycurg. *Leoc.* 70, 108: Marincola (2007) 112; cf. di Benedetto (1978) 34.
114 Compare E. *Supp.* 230–45 and the characterization of the Spartans at Hdt. 7.103–4. On the implications of *Pers.* 242 in the broader democratic ideology of Athens, see Garvie (2009) 138.
115 Hall (1989) 16.
116 Hdt. 6.109.3; Harrison (2000b) 62.
117 Free speech is Athens' hallmark: its absence in Persia is shown in the way that the chorus' extreme veneration for Darius makes communication with him impossible (694–702). Aeschylus emphasizes the slavishness of Persia, where masters hear only what slaves believe is safe for them to hear (cf. Hdt. 7.101.3), leading to distortions of truth and memory, so that the Persian elders conveniently "forget" Darius' failure at Marathon: Sampson (2015) 24–5. Even the admirable, intelligent Darius cannot understand that Persia's undemocratic regime is inherently problematic: Georges (1994) 95–8, 110–11.
118 Rhodes (2007) 34–6; Georges (1994) 94–5. The Persians continued to maintain a claim to the territories lost after 480, and even in the fourth century there was still a curse on anyone making overtures to the Persians: Ar. *Thesm.* 336–8; Isoc. 4.157; Plut. Arist.10.6.
119 Mills (1997) 6–42.
120 For example, Lys. 2.20, Pl. *Mx.* 239b, Dem. 60.8 and pp. 5, 18–19, 22, 32, n.101. Di Benedetto (1978) 33–4 comments on the way that the adjective στυγνός ("hateful", 286, 472, 990) links Athens and the divinity who has destroyed the Persians. Christ (2012) 100–4 discusses the psychological attractions for Athenian jurors of an assumed "quasi-divine" power to help distressed litigants.
121 Murray (1972) 47. Compare *Pers.* 809–12 with Themistocles' ascription of the Greek victory not to men but the gods and heroes at Hdt. 8.109.3, perhaps his actual words: Podlecki (1966) 23.
122 Including the "gods" of land and sea which conspire against the Persians: 389–91, 707–8, 792–4; cf. Hdt. 7.48–9: Harrison (2000b) 68.
123 They tend to ascribe the disaster rather vaguely to "some god" or *daimon* (345, 354, 514, 573, 725; though 827 does refer to Zeus.) Broadhead (1960) 116; Collard (2008) xxv.
124 Hall (1989) 69–70; cf. Papadimitropoulos (2008).
125 At *Pers.* 856 Darius is "godlike", but 643, 651, 654–55 and 711 call him a god.
126 Persians fear their king as though he were a god but have no compunction about destroying temples and other sacred things, *Pers.* 809–12; Hdt. 8.109.3 with Kantzios (2004) 15–16.
127 *Pers.* 739–52, 821–31; Rosenbloom (2006a) 43–4, 92–3; Georges (1994) 89, 111.
128 Hall (2007) 144.

129 Cf. *Pers.* 725. Judet de La Combe (2011) 89–90 compares the way that Xerxes is lured into battle with the false dream sent by Zeus to Agamemnon at the start of *Iliad* 2 (cf. *Pers.* 93–9).
130 Lazenby (1988) 185. For example, when Atossa asks if the city was unsacked (348), the word ἀπόρθητος may recall Herodotus 7.141's account of the second, more encouraging oracle given to the Athenians by Delphi: Athens was, of course, sacked (Hdt. 8.53–4), though Aeschylus implies otherwise at 349 ("'With men inside there it is a safe enclosure"), which echoes Themistocles' words at Hdt. 8.61.2 (cf. Thuc. 7.77.7). The unnamed "Greek man from the Athenian army" (355) who tricked the Persians into thinking that the Greeks were going to leave is named as Sicinnus from Themistocles' household in Hdt. 8.75.1. Atossa blames evil company (758–9) for Xerxes' errors: compare Hdt. 7.5–6.1, 3.134.1–3. Compare also *Pers.* 792 with Hdt. 7.49.1 and *Pers.* 807–12 with Hdt. 8.109.3: Lattimore (1943) 92–3.
131 Podlecki (1970) 52, 57, 91; Parker (2007); Said (2002) 137–45.
132 Harrison (2000b) 15–16, 44–8; on the relationship between Herodotus and other literary sources, see also Boedeker (2001).
133 Lazenby (1988). Of course we should expect many inconsistencies and different emphases, since fighting is confusing, people forget and many different versions of reality are possible: Pelling (1997a) 1.
134 Marincola (2007) 105; Garvie (2009) xi; Grethlein (2007) 364–5 with earlier bibliography. On Simonides and the Persian Wars, see the papers in Boedeker and Sider (1996) and (2001), esp. 27–9 for a full text and translation of fr.11; also Kowerski (2005).
135 Hall (1989) 68–70.
136 West (1970); Kowerski (2005) 84–6; Marincola (2007) 122–3.
137 Hdt. 7.139; 8.136.2–3. Xerxes will punish the Athenians first because once he has conquered them, no one will stand in his way; 7.8β2–γ1, 53.2. Harrison (2000b) 62 compares British views of World War II, in which they alone (omitting the peoples of the British Empire) stood between freedom and Nazi tyranny.
138 Marincola (2007) 111–2.
139 D.S. 11.11.6: cf. Marincola (2007) 114.
140 Taplin (2006) 4–5. The tradition about the actual subjects of Simonides' Persian War poetry is confused and is not resolved by publication of the new Simonides, but it is clear from fr.11W^2 and other fragments that some of it took a panhellenic line, praising both Sparta and Corinth and perhaps other cities: Harrison (2000b) 61; Boedeker and Sider (2001) 4; Boedeker (2001) 127; Aloni (2001) 98–100; Kowerski (2005) 64–107.
141 Ephorus *FGrHist* 70F186; cf. Kierdorf (1966) 39–43. In Pind. *Pyth.* 1.75, Syracuse's victory over the Carthaginians and Etruscans "delivered Hellas from grievous slavery."
142 Even the prostitutes of Corinth staked their claim: *FGrHist* 115F285.
143 Athens had been active for some time as the policeman/enforcer of the Aegean. Successful intervention breeds successful intervention, in both myth and history, which reinforce one another to form a view of the world in which the intervening state creates and maintains its own self-image and "mythology": successful interventions deserve reward, in a cycle which acquires its own momentum.
144 Sommerstein (1989) 29, 38–9; (2010) 281–4.
145 Shapiro (1989) 76–7.
146 For an overview of these processes, see Mills (1997) and Kowalzig (2006), who broadens the discussion of this phenomenon to include Ajax and Iphigenia as characters from panhellenic myth whom Athens absorbs.
147 Sources from E. *IT* 947–60ff. tell an aetiological story in which Orestes arrives at Athens on the day of the Choes as a polluted figure to whom no one will speak, and thus the king decrees that everyone should drink in silence and from separate cups

to avoid embarassing him: Phanodemus *FGrH* 325F11; Plut. *Mor.* 613b, 643a; ΣAr. *Ach.* 961, *Kn.* 95. In a different tradition, Orestes is already in Athens in *Od.* 3.307, but goes thence to Argos to kill Aegisthus.

148 As at E. *Or.* 1650–2; Dem. 23.66, 74; Aristid. *Panath.* 48.
149 The absence of any king in *Eumenides* is striking: Athena performs the functions of a ruler (cf. 288), but at a human level, the city is politically closer to the democracy experienced by the audience than it will be in later plays, in which Athens has a king while retaining technically illogical claims to democracy: E. *Supp.* 349–51.
150 See Sommerstein (1989) 13–14 for a brief history of the council of the Areopagus.
151 Sommerstein (1989) 4–5.
152 Chiasson (1999) 142–6. Taplin (1977) 129–34 rejects the idea that tragedians sometimes directly addressed audiences, but *Eumenides* may be a special case (Wiles (1977) 211–2), and the suggestion of Sommerstein (1989) 186, that Athena's call to order (566–73) is addressed to the audience themselves, inviting them into the world of the play in a mingling of past and present by which ancient and contemporary Athenians are drawn together, remains attractive. Meineck (2013) imagines the audience's reaction to watching Athena in action on stage in the shadow of the huge statue of Athena Promachos (Paus.1.28.2) on the Acropolis. If some of the audience experience a blend of past and present at some moments in this play, the stakes will be especially high for them after the trial as the chorus threatens Athens (thus the audience) with hideous consequences if Orestes is acquitted.
153 Athens' treatment of its suppliants is a highly idealized analogy for its dealings with its allies, as stronger to weaker: Tzanetou (2011) 306–11; see also Loraux (1986) 80–3. Loraux' characterization of Athens' competitive generosity (cf. 67–8) recalls Athena's commendation of Athens that its rivalry in doing good is victorious forever, *Eum.* 974–5.
154 Mitchell-Boyask (2009) 89.
155 The "supplication to Athens" topos can be traced at least to the Persian Wars and the foundation of the Delian League at the request of the Ionians who had been spurned by the Spartans: Thuc. 1.96–7.1 with Tzanetou (2011) 311–2.
156 Sommerstein (1989) 25; Chiasson (1999) 142.
157 A court of Athenian jurors acting as *dikastai* aligns the city of Athens with Zeus' function as *dikastēs* (*Pers.* 826). Representatives of Athens will reprise similar roles in later tragedy: pp. 67, 86, 89–90.
158 E. *Hcld.* 1030–6; *Supp.* 1187–204; S. *OC* 1524–34. Athenian inscriptions often refer to allies rather than subjects: *ML* 40.20–5, 31; 56.18–20; 73.14, 32; IG1[3] 60.1–4. For the phenomenon in literature, see Ar. *Ach.* 181, 506, *Eq.* 839, *Nub.* 609, *Vesp.* 673, *Pax* 639, 935–6, *Lys.*1175–80, [Xen.] *Ath. Pol.* 1.14–18, 2.1, 3.2, Thuc. 1.96.1, 2.13.3, 3.19.1, 5.111.4, 6.91.7: Rosenbloom (2011) 365 n.44.
159 On the meaning of ἄνευ δορός (289), see Quincey (1964) 191–3.
160 *Eum.* 289–91, 670 and especially 763. By focusing on the alliance as an eternal protection for Athens (something that few in the audience could object to) and retrojecting it to the heroic age, Aeschylus transcends any specific "party political" reference: Macleod (1983f) 22, 25; Revermann (2008) 251–2. For the importance of unchanging eternity to an imperialistic mentality, see earlier, p. 000.
161 Chiasson (1999) 147–8.
162 On the evils of civil war, cf. 858–66, 976–87, 526–7, 696–7, 980–4.
163 *Eum.* 864–55, 914; cf. 776–7 and 913–15, 1009.
164 On these, see Zeitlin (1996) 100–4; Rabinowitz (1981) 78–84.
165 Bowie (1993) 14–16; Revermann (2008) 241, 247 notes that Delphi's treatment at the start as a "prime locus of conflict resolution" (241) will highlight its subsequent failure to resolve Orestes' position. Only Athens will do that. The number of gods in Aeschylus' prologue is notable. A similar plethora of gods haunts Sophocles'

Oedipus at Colonus, some 50 years later, a play with significant echoes of Aeschylus: pp. 64–6.
166 Sommerstein (1989) 81.
167 Ephorus *FGrH* 70 31b, which credits Apollo with civilizing (ἡμεροῦν) the people by introducing cultured fruits and ways of life.
168 Scholia on *Eum.* 13a.
169 *Eum.* 73, 68–70, 349–51, 360–65, 385–8.
170 Conflict between older and younger gods: *Eum.* 162–3, 490–3, 731–3, 778–92, 808–22. Rynearson (2013) traces the language of seduction that the "psychologically astute" (15) Athena offers beings who are traditionally shunned.
171 See Mitchell-Boyask (2009) 32–3.
172 See earlier, pp. 16–17.
173 Kennedy (2006) 41–3 suggests that the reference is intended to evoke the broader territory of the Troad, an area of battles between Athens and Persia from the 470s and onwards. The region also has non-political resonances, since the Scamander recalls the Trojan War and the contrasting tone of Agamemnon's ill-omened return to Greece at the start of the trilogy: Mitchell-Boyask (2009) 61–3.
174 IGI³ 19: Sommerstein (1989) 152.
175 Kennedy (2006) 43–7 against e.g. Dover (1957). She concludes (50) that the geographical references in *Eumenides* "provide the Athenians with an imaginary map . . . that demonstrates the far reach of Athens [which] . . . justifies and reinforces the patriotism an Athenian might experience at hearing the verbal mapping."
176 Aeschylus' references to contemporary politics, above all the relationship between the studied ambiguity of 690–5 and Ephialtes' reforms of 462/1 have occasioned much debate: see, e.g. Dover (1957); Dodds (1973) 45–53; Conacher (1987) 199–205; Macleod (1983f); Bowie (1993) 10–11 offers a brief account of some key articles in the history of the problem. For the purposes of this discussion, one need only note, first, that the innate indeterminacy of tragedy will allow individual interpretations of the lines: Sommerstein (1989) 217–8. Second, the conditional effect of 693 – αὐτῶν πολιτῶν μὴ 'πικαινούντων νόμους – is also important: *if* the citizens do not change the laws, the city will be strong forever. Whatever "changing" the laws might mean, no citizen could dispute the desirability of the eternal strength of Athens.
177 Pl. *Mx.* 237d, Isoc. 14.1: earlier, pp. 12, 18–19. Kennedy (2006) 58–60 connects the trial of Orestes, a non-Athenian ally, at Athens with certain Athenian decrees, starting as early as the Phaselis decree (*ML* 31; IGI³ 10) datable between 469 and 450, which require allies to come to Athens for trials, as the city gradually expanded its sense of justified jurisdiction over its territories.
178 Both were famous for their laws and good order: Sommerstein (1989) 219–20. Athens now surpasses them.
179 Cf. pp. 17–18 earlier.
180 E. *El.* 1258–60, *IT* 945–6, Hellanicus, *FGrH* 323a 1 and 22, Philochorus, *FGrH* 328 F3; Dem. 23.66, Din. 1.87, Aristid. *Panath.* 46, Paus. 1.21.4, Apollod. 3.14.2.
181 In Lys. 2.5, the Amazons had already enslaved many other people and are moved to attack Athens by hearing of its glory. In the late-sixth-century *Theseid*, the Amazon invasion is more justified as a rescue of their sister Antiope from abduction by Theseus: Plut. *Thes.* 28.1.
182 Mills (1997) 58–9.
183 The exact number of the chorus is a problem: if they were ten in number, Athena's vote brings a six-five majority, in which case it may seem odd that she says that an equal vote will bring acquittal (741). If there were 11 jurors, Athena will equalize the vote to six-six, explaining l.741, but then the human jury must have voted to condemn Orestes (who does, indeed, focus all his gratitude on Athena, 754–6): see Gagarin (1975); Mitchell-Boyask (2009) 78–86.

184 Athena already represents restraint in Homeric Hymn 28: Felson (2011) 264–75; Rynearson (2013) 15–17.
185 The frequent use of deictic pronouns referring to "this" city (834, 852, 884, 890, 902, 915) bring stage action and audience closer together: Chiasson (1999) 146–7.
186 Compare Pericles at Thuc. 2.36.2: Sommerstein (1989) 250–1.
187 Loraux (1986) 60–1, 123 and earlier, pp. 9, 12–13, 21. On the eternal quality of the Eumenides' residence in Athens with all the benefits that it will bring, compare also 891, 898, 964–7, 975, 992. The aetiology which is such a feature of Athenian tragedy is one aspect of the imperialistic drive towards eternity and sameness, free from change. Of course it does not represent an *exclusively* imperialistic impulse. Revermann (2008) 255–6 states, "Rooting current social practice in the past and emphasizing its functionality for times to come gives direction, meaning, and an empowering sense of agency in a life environment that is fundamentally shaped by unpredictability and severely limited human control."
188 Chiasson (1999) 148–9.
189 The title was used to honour other cities as well, notably Corinth (*FGE* "Simonides" 14.3–4) and Sparta (*FD* III.1.50.3–5): Rosenbloom (2011) 365–6.
190 The word used is ἔρως, a word used by Thucydides in an imperial Athenian context, by Pericles (2.43.2) and in his account of the passion which fell on Athens for the Sicilian expedition (6.24.3). This is the desire to possess, an acquisitive desire which fuels imperialism.
191 For the relationship of the end of the play to the Panathenaea, see Bowie (1993) 27–30; Weaver (1996) with earlier bibliography. For the importance of their cult (assuming the identification of Erinyes, Semnai Theai and Eumenides) in Athenian life, see Parker (2009) 146–51. Their precinct, like the Theseion (Suda s.v. Θησεῖον) was a place of sanctuary at Athens (Ar. *Eq*.1312, *Thesm.* 224; Thuc. 1.126.11) and thus tied to Athens' self-image in idealizing texts as saviour of the oppressed.
192 Headlam (1906).
193 Mills (1997) 162–3, 167–8.
194 Against this highly positive reading of Aeschylus' portrayal of Athenian imperialism, see the concerns raised by Kennedy (2006) 61–2; Rosenbloom (1995).
195 For a fuller account of this play, see Mills (1997) 160–85; Bernek (2004) 129–219; on its Athenian imperial aspect, see Markantonatos (2007) 157–67. On the multiple connections between Aeschylus' *Eumenides* and this play, see Bernek (2004) 129–46.
196 On this opening and the way that Colonus is viewed by awe-struck foreigners, see Markantonatos (2002) 172–4. Theseus is king of Athens but also sovereign at Colonus, while already at 106–8, the Eumenides and Athens are closely aligned, so I doubt the suggestion of Kirkwood (1986) 104–6 that Sophocles intends a distinction between the corrupt imperial Athens and Colonus as the repository of true virtue: cf. A. Kelly (2009) 98–102. Von Reden (1998) 177–90 argues for a distinction between deme and city, but the portrayal of the relationship of the two could as easily denote the harmonization of potential opposites that is conventional in Athenian imperial ideology; cf. Blundell (1993) 287–90.
197 The bronze threshold is called ἔρεισμ' Ἀθηνῶν, "the support of Athens" (57): von Reden (1998) 180 compares the designation of Athens by Pind. fr. 76 as the Ἑλλάδος ἔρεισμα: "What referred once to Athens as a whole and her role in the defeat of the Persians was now applied to the spot at Colonus which . . . would confirm the Athenian hegemony within Greece" if Oedipus were to be buried there.
198 Edmunds (1981) 225–9; cf. Mills (1997) 162–3, 167–8; A. Kelly (2009) 71–4.
199 δεινός: Sophocles frequently uses the word to describe Oedipus (*OT* 1297–8, cf. 1267, 1310, 1327; *OC* 141, 212, 500, 1651), and this word is used by Aeschylus' chorus of *Eumenides* (517) to signify the element of the terrible that a city must incorporate within itself if it is to flourish. In that play, Athens will find success by incorporating

the terrifying supernatural beings; just as in *Oedipus at Colonus*, Athens will incorporate the unsettling figure of Oedipus. Understanding the paradoxical necessity of bringing such beings right into the city is difficult, and Athens' uniqueness is shown by its ability to do so.
200 As also 261–2: compare also his reproach at 265 that they fear his name alone (μόνον).
201 Pl. *Mx.* 244e, Dem. 24.170–1: Tzanetou (2005) 102.
202 Isoc. 4.47, cf. 41.
203 His claim is not uncontroversial: Linforth (1951) 153; Gould (1965); Rosenmeyer (1952) 96–7; A. Kelly (2009) 52–9.
204 Thuc. 2.40.2; Loraux (1986) 81–2; also earlier, pp. 22–4.
205 Blundell (1993) 296–8.
206 On the importance of these sentiments in the play, see Mills (1997) 172–3.
207 Cf. Bernek (2004) 158.
208 A. *Eum.* 413–4; compare E. *HF* 1416.
209 Mills (1997) 174–6.
210 Its expression of the glories of peacetime Athens will be matched with the stirring ode, 1044–95, on Athens in battle: Burian (1974) 421.
211 Panegyrics of Athens frequently describe it as "shining". Aristophanes mocks the Athenians' pleasure in hearing such epithets (Loraux (1986) 306–7), though the word used by Sophocles (ἀργής) is different from the usual λιπαρός.
212 See earlier, pp. 16–17.
213 On the relationship of these to Athenian claims to civilization via the Eleusinian mysteries, cf. A. Kelly (2009) 94, 81–3; Markantonatos (2002) 186, 197–220.
214 Compare the emphasis on sensuality and divinity in the encomium of Athens in E. *Med.* 824–45. Markantonatos (2002) 187–8 (cf. 177–8) notes the chorus' inclusion here of certain divinities such as Aphrodite who have no traditional place at Colonus, just as the stranger included Prometheus as a hero of Colonus even though his altar was actually in the grove of Academus south of Colonus.
215 Detienne (1970).
216 Hdt. 8.55.1 states that Athena's olive grew again the day after the Persians burned the Acropolis: Markantonatos (2002) 190–2.
217 Thuc. 2.36.1–3; 6.18.2.
218 Hdt. 8.55; Apollod. 3.14.1: Tyrell and Brown (1991) 180–1.
219 Another sign of civilization: McDevitt (1972). On Poseidon in *Oedipus at Colonus*, see A. Kelly (2009) 68–9; Markantonatos (2002) 195.
220 The stanza may also hint at, with a view to blurring, the potential tension between the elite associations of Poseidon Hippios with the knights (Paus. 1.30.4) and of his shrine as the site of the establishment of the oligarchic constitution in 411 (Thuc. 8.67.2), and his association with the rowers of the democratic polis: Blundell (1993) 290.
221 *OC* 720–885; cf. Thuc. 2.41.3.
222 See Dhuga (2005), esp. 338–41.
223 In mythological tradition, Poseidon is his father, but this play distinguishes Theseus' fundamentally human, limited nature from Oedipus' more tragic and more divine vision: Mills (1997) 176–7.
224 Unlike Sparta: Hdt. 6.106.3; Blundell (1993) 292–3.
225 Markantonatos (2002) 111.
226 Blundell (1993) 301 n.58; Zeitlin (1990) 167; Vidal-Naquet (1988) 337–8.
227 Blundell (1993) 291–2.
228 *OC* 904–8: cf. E. *Supp.* 724–5: Blundell (1989) 250.
229 De Romilly (1979) 53–63; Kirkwood (1986) 100–4; cf. Mills (1997) index s.v. *epieikeia*.
230 Similarly, Eurystheus (E. *Hcld.* 1028–38) grants Athens a benefit which could have been Sparta's.

231 Blundell (1993) 300–1 compares Sophocles' Athens with the ideal city of Pericles' funeral speech, though her claim that the play offers "no legendary justification for ... imperialist expansion" and that Theseus' Athens is "immune to ... πολυπραγμοσύνη" separates two elements of Athenian imperial ideology (the unique virtue of Athens and its drive for power, justified by appeals to that unique virtue) that I consider inseparable. Those disposed to see critique of contemporary Athens in a contrast between Theseus' heroic era and the late fifth century could find it, but Sophocles does not point specifically in that direction, *pace* Blundell (1993) 303–5.

3 Euripides, empire and war

3.1 Introduction

Euripides is traditionally associated with the sophists and other progressive thinkers who continually questioned established conventions. But Athens features in Euripides' extant plays far more frequently than in Aeschylus or Sophocles, and in surprisingly conventional and positive ways; or at least they offer spectators the *option* of conventional and positive interpretations.[1] Moreover, *Heraclidae* and *Suppliant Women* actually bring Athenian "history"[2] to life on stage by dramatizing two of the canonical stories from the *epitaphioi*. For a long time, these plays were condemned as propaganda and therefore automatically artistically inferior because of their apparently uncritical endorsement of Athenian military action.[3] More recent reevaluations focus on potential ironies and contradictions underlying the idealization of Athens that appears at first reading (and, not coincidentally, have somewhat rehabilitated their critical reputation).[4] If these plays encompass both glorification of the idealized Athens and elements which undermine that idealization, what spectators will take from them will depend on the relative weights they give to the various elements in the plays' characteristic combination of traditional Athenian narrative and ominous sequels. Euripides can be made to say that Athenian interventionism preserves Greek law by punishing the bad and rewarding the good, but some cities, especially Thebes and to a lesser extent Argos,[5] are irredeemable, so will never receive the divine and human rewards that Athens receives. A different emphasis yields a more Thucydidean Euripides, who questions the self-image of Athens and suggests that it is born of self-love and wishful thinking. It is, however, important to remember that the Athenian audience of such plays were viewing their ancestors' achievements, and any reading that explores potential ironies in them that undermine the simple portrayal of Athenian virtue should be balanced by remembering their potential for reinforcing spectators' potential identities as the proud successors of Theseus and others. Modern scholars can be suspicious of overtly patriotic sentiments, but we are not Athenian citizen-soldiers. As previously argued, distance is essential for tragedy to work properly with its audience, and when Athens is directly involved in a tragedy, that distance is inevitably diminished. Some spectators, at least, might not have acknowledged every possible shade of grey in what they saw, preferring instead a simpler vision conforming to certain preconceptions that they brought to the theatre, primed by the pervasive images of Athens that they consumed in multiple formal and informal communications. Most of Euripides' spectators were Athenian males, who regularly endured danger to protect their city and retain its dominance in Greece. Certain types of intellectual and emotional reactions from them, tending towards a more favourable interpretation of their city, would be understandable, even though the complexities of tragic texts can inspire a range of reactions in any diverse audience.

Tragic texts raise many questions, but those questions typically originate in the fates of cities other than Athens. A spectator can therefore simultaneously enjoy a conventional image of his own city while appreciating other cities' troubles at a different emotional level: indeed, by displacing extreme grief onto others, a spectator might enter into their pain more empathetically.[6] Some spectators probably saw contradictions or criticisms of Athens in certain tragedies, but no one was compelled to do so, because the Athens of Euripidean tragedy is notably distanced from the mistakes from which tragic suffering springs. Equally, consistent real-life war-making, rewarding though it might be, also entails consistent loss and pain. This too needs expression.[7] Thus tragedy helps its spectators project their own pain onto the Trojan War, or onto non-Athenians, rather than making it directly part of Athenian experience, enabling the city's strength and excellence to remain intact for those who needed it to be so. This process was perhaps especially important for Euripides and his audience, once the brilliant successes that underpin the mood of Aeschylus' *Persians* and *Eumenides* were past, and the Athenians were mired in uncertainty and threats to their superiority in Greece in the later fifth century.

Perhaps these needs help to explain the pervasiveness of idealized Athenian values in extant and even some fragmentary Euripidean tragedy. The most obvious examples, already mentioned, are *Heraclidae* (c. 430) and *Suppliants* (later 420s), both of which dramatize two canonical stories of epitaphic narrative. In *Heraclidae*, King Demophon of Athens, Theseus' son, saves Heracles' defenceless children from his enemy Eurystheus.[8] In *Suppliants*, Theseus defends panhellenic burial customs by forcing the Thebans to allow the burial of those who died in Polynices' failed attempt to sack Thebes.[9] In both tragedies, Athens and its representatives uphold Greek morality, using Athenian military power for the good of Greece, though they claim to prefer diplomatic persuasion. Though set in the distant past, they are full of now-familiar contemporary claims that Athens is the only city that joins strength and righteousness to save others. Aligned with these in tone is *Heracles* (420s–416), in which Theseus plays a less central but still crucial role, while the fragmentary *Peirithous* appears to portray a Theseus who represents Athenian loyalty to friends in distress; the very fragmentary *Theseus* offers an apparently similar characterization. *Ion* (420–10) is marked by the topic of Athenian autochthony, a claim to Athenian superiority and therefore to the rightness of Athenian power in Greece. Although *Trojan Women* (415) is set at Troy and Athens is barely mentioned, it is often interpreted as a coded condemnation of Athens' treatment of Melos in 416, but I will argue that it is unlikely that most spectators interpreted it thus. In only two plays is Athens less successful, and even here the failures are partly alleviated. Athens' royal family experiences significant suffering in the fragmentary *Erechtheus* (late 420s?), but their personal loss saves the city. In *Hippolytus* (428), Theseus causes his stepson's death, but significant mitigating factors surround the play's events.

3.2 *Heraclidae*

When the play begins, Iolaus is at Marathon,[10] seeking help from Theseus' sons. His virtues are apparent immediately in one telling sentence (6–10), in which he remembers the glorious days of helping Heracles with his labours (πόνοι) out of honour and respect for their kinship, even though he could have lived quietly (ἡσυχῶς) in Argos. His rejection of the quiet life and embrace of πόνοι align him with the way of life that texts idealizing Athenian power frequently claim as Athenian.[11] Like Iolaus, Athens is loyal to its friends and intervenes untiringly for the common good, and the reference to πόνοι recalls both Heracles' labours for humanity and Athenian labours for Greece,[12] assimilating Athens and Heracles as saviours. Like Iolaus, the idealized Athens rejects quietness (ἡσυχία) as mere cowardice and selfishness: in Euripides' other overtly political play, it is explicitly condemned by Theseus' mother Aethra, who contrasts Athens' life of glorious πόνοι with cautious, ungenerous cities that practise ἡσυχία (*Supp.* 324–5). Aethra names no specific city, but under her words lies the contemporary debate expressed in similar language between Athens and its enemies. The active foreign policy which Athens considers altruistic generosity by which Athenian power is fully deserved is considered meddlesomeness (*polypragmosynē*) by the city's enemies. Conversely, the reticence of Sparta on which it prided itself as self-control and quietness is termed slowness and selfishness by the Athenians.[13] The contrast is pervasive in the plays of Euripides which foreground Athenian military action.

So Iolaus has previously displayed behaviour conforming to epitaphic ideals. His other great appeal is his weakness. He has the right intentions but not the power to act on them. To help the weak whose cause is just requires a combination of intellectual and moral wisdom to know that their claims are just, the physical power to perform πόνοι to help them, and the generosity to avoid any overt request for something in return. Only the ideal Athens combines these virtues.[14] And so, when the Argive Herald advances menacingly on Iolaus, rips Heracles' children from the altar and knocks the old man to the ground, Iolaus cries out to the chorus (69–72).[15] Immediately they hurry on stage and prevent the Herald from further wrongdoing, asserting Athens' power to treat suppliants according to divine law (101–13; cf. 238, 258, 260, 264). They are old men, a type of chorus whose infirmities are usually emphasized in tragedy,[16] but because they are old Marathonians, like the old men of Colonus in Sophocles, they transcend infirmity when helping others is necessary (120–1) and exemplify the speed – crucial for a city that prides itself on consistently helping friends – that is another attribute of the idealized city.[17]

The Herald's treatment of the suppliants[18] is visually powerful and has a potentially imperial dimension. Vulnerable suppliants had a clear appeal as objects of the Athenian gaze and as clients of Athenian beneficence, and Euripidean tragedy abounds in them. The sight of suffering suppliants could evoke a pleasing emotional response in individual spectators[19] and offer the city a vision of its ability to uphold divine and human laws in pitying the oppressed and, where proper, helping them. We pity in others what we fear for ourselves, so that pity enables identification with others' sufferings, but in the one who has the luxury of pitying, it also creates a convenient degree of distance from the one who is pitied.[20] Like tragedy, pity combines nearness and distance: feeling pity or experiencing tragedy properly requires identification with another's pain while remaining a little distanced.[21] Pity also contains an intellectual element, of judgement that the one who is pitied does not deserve suffering, and the one who pities must have a special insight to know this.[22] Athenians famously have a talent for pity:[23] Paus. 1.17.1 even (wrongly) claims that only in Athens is there an Altar of Pity, and Plutarch ascribes the origin of the use of the suppliant olive branch to Athens' reception of Heracles' children.[24] In the context of Athens' relationship to the rest of Greece, as the city which gives help while magnificently needing no return, pity is understandably a crucial characteristic of the ideal city: indeed, Plato (*Mx.*244e) claims that Athens' only fault is excessive compassion. Athens' strength and freedom necessitate the weakness of others, both in tragedy and in real life, but Athenian virtues soften the imbalance of power:[25] preeminence in pity asserts both Athenian superiority and its benign quality.

Once Demophon and his silent brother Acamas arrive (120), they listen to the conflicting claims of the Herald and Iolaus. For the Herald, no sane city would wish to help Heracles' children because it brings no advantage (144–52), whereas supporting Argos will ally Athens with a powerful city (153–7; cf. 57–8). If they heed Iolaus' pitiable lamentations (οἰκτίσματα, 158), they will incur war with Argos and gain only a feeble old man and mere boys for allies (163–73). He advises Demophon not to do what Athens "usually" does by choosing inferior allies when strong ones are available (163–73).[26] But Athenian spectators, familiar with standard idealizing rhetoric, might well disagree. It is a cherished principle that Athens helps the oppressed at the city's own risk with no thought of reward and alone makes friends by doing rather than receiving good,[27] not needing any allies. Helping the needy is a point of pride. If helping suppliants brings war, it is all to the good: the city's power, along with its virtue, will be tested, and every campaign burnishes the city's reputation. Athens' services to Greece in myth, such as the defence of the Heraclidae, align with Athens' historical service to Greece in the Persian Wars, offering one unbroken line of daring and success from the mists of time to the present day.[28]

The Athenian mission to uphold divine law and protect suppliants is often contrasted with the expedient avoidance of war recommended as good sense by Athens' enemies, such as the Herald (57–8; cf. 19–22, 110, 152; cf. 255, 263). In particular, at 162–8, he claims that Argos' conflict with Heracles' children is not Athens' business. Although he does not use the actual term that the Theban herald in the *Suppliants* will use to Theseus (*Supp.* 576), his complaint that the Athenians are interfering in others' affairs recalls the *polypragmosynē* of Athens, the opposite of staying quiet (ἡσυχία), of which the city's enemies frequently complained. Enemies consider Athens' foreign activity aggression and interference. From an Athenian perspective, it is legitimate and all the more legitimized when Athens' enemies trivialize Athens' canonical services to Greece on behalf of human and divine law as mere "interference".[29]

Iolaus' speech to Demophon has many points of contact with other texts which glorify Athens. By stating that Athens is different in freedom and strength from the other cities which have rejected his appeals (191–6), he invokes the uniqueness of Athenian virtue to which the Herald has already briefly alluded (151) and which is central in characterizing the idealized Athens. He also cites additional factors designed to remind Demophon of proper Athenian behaviour. Heracles' children are their kinsmen as well as suppliants, but most importantly, Heracles once helped Theseus against the Amazons and rescued him from Hades (215–9). Friendship in Greece had a strongly competitive element, and the receiver of benefits was felt to be in an inferior position, necessitating swift reciprocation to redress the balance, although the person conferring the benefit, as the dominant party, could magnanimously claim indifference to what he knew he would in fact receive.[30] Athens' relationship with the rest of Greece is strongly influenced by this mentality, as are Theseus' relations with Heracles in tragedy. In *Heraclidae*, *Heracles* and *Peirithous* by Critias or Euripides, Theseus, originally the recipient of Heracles' help and thus his subordinate, is reconceptualized as the saviour of Heracles or his children, to reset the balance of benefactions in Theseus' favour, even though Heracles was a far greater panhellenic hero and benefactor of humanity.[31] The attempted substitution of Theseus for Heracles as Greece's greatest hero, the saviour of Heracles the saviour (Dem. 60.8), reflects through mythology Athens' real-life ambitions, through active intervention around Greece on behalf of friends/allies/clients/subjects, to put others in the city's debt.[32]

Helping the oppressed is quintessentially Athenian business, and Demophon accepts them without hesitation (236–52),[33] in spite of the Herald's warnings that he will incur war if he is not sensible.[34] Though the Herald is provocative to the end, so that Demophon briefly threatens him (270–1), he commits no actual violence against him, in contrast to the Herald's violence against the suppliants,[35] and sends him packing.

Athenian rhetoric portrays Athens' interventions for other cities as selflessly undertaken, but tragic Athens is always rewarded for the risks the city incurs. In *Eumenides*, Orestes pledges his city's alliance; in *Oedipus at Colonus*, Oedipus promises eternal protection from Theban invasion. Here, Iolaus praises Athens' unique (306) kindness and urges Heracles' children to pledge never to attack Athens (306–19). Since the Spartans with whom Athens was fighting the Peloponnesian War when this play was performed were considered the descendants of the Heraclidae, Iolaus' words are not only highly ironic but also foreshadow the complaints of later Athenian rhetoric that other Greeks' ingratitude to Athens instigated the Peloponnesian War.[36]

Some 350 lines into the play, the events most significant to Athenian spectators appear to be effectively over. The chorus sing a triumphant ode exalting Athens' martial and other virtues and its sincere desire for peace. Iolaus then confidently asserts that Zeus will punish Argive arrogance (387–8; cf. 353, 356), with the implication that Athens will be his agent (cf. 766–8).[37] But we expect the unexpected from Euripides, and now it emerges that military success depends on the sacrifice of a maiden to Persephone. Demophon refuses to kill any Athenian, and this new twist undoubtedly complicates the play's enthusiasm for Athens. Has idealizing rhetoric exaggerated Athens' capacity for altruism (as the chorus hint at 461–3), or is Demophon merely setting reasonable limits on his city's interventions? Athenian spectators, primed by epitaphic rhetoric, would bring certain expectations to this story, and in no other version is Athens forced to incur such a burden. A child of Heracles would undoubtedly be a more appropriate victim than an Athenian, because it is they, not the Athenians, who need victory over Eurystheus. For Athens to sacrifice one of its own for the Heraclidae might indeed be excessive interference in others' affairs. Neither Iolaus nor the Maiden who offers herself for sacrifice condemns Demophon (435–6, 503–6). Yet the dilemma is real and the limits of Athenian altruism are clearly tested: as a good Athenian king-democrat (424),[38] Demophon seeks his people's advice, but they themselves are deeply divided.

And so Heracles' daughter conveniently saves Athens' reputation and her brothers' lives by offering her own.[39] We may well consider this an ironic solution, and elsewhere, Euripides vehemently condemns the practice of treating the young like sacrificial animals.[40] However, this is not the focus of *Heraclidae*. Instead, the Maiden thanks the Athenians for all their help and states that Heracles' children must now offer reciprocation for the labours (πόνοι, 505) they have imposed on Athens:[41] only by this can they match their father's nobility (503–10). Although the losses of the Maiden and her family are acknowledged,[42] emphasis on the grimmer aspects of her fate are largely absent, and her speech recalls epitaphic topoi which extol individual sacrifice on behalf of the city's collective.[43] In particular, if the text is complete,[44] in contrast to E. *Hec.* 518–82 and *IA* 1146–1208, Euripides omits any description of the young woman's death, and she calmly performs the role she has accepted. One might well think that Demophon was preternaturally lucky to have this outcome to his impasse, and the play does undermine the usual idealizing narrative that innate Athenian virtue brings Athenian success, by imagining this success as a result of sheer luck rather than anything more substantial. But one might recall the sentiments expressed by Aristophanes and others:[45] Athens makes bad decisions, but the gods always turn its mistakes to the good. Some spectators could view what happens here with similar self-confidence: a uniquely lucky outcome befits a uniquely virtuous city. From this perspective, Athens is doubly blessed for its services: not only has the city secured Iolaus' pledge of loyalty, but its courage in initially accepting the suppliants inspires them to action that saves it from embarrassment. This interpretation does not preclude enjoying the suppliants' plight and pitying and admiring the Maiden's sacrifice. But in this play, and almost all Euripides' Athenian plays, Athens is essentially a spectator, welcoming and pitying suppliants. It is never itself a suppliant or pitiable.

The end of the play also contains multiple interpretative possibilities. Eurystheus' cruelty and arrogance are duly punished by defeat (825–42; cf. 924–5), but he is not killed on the battle-field because Iolaus wants Alcmena to have her chance at avenging his crimes against her family (879–84). Eurystheus is at her mercy and her rage is too strong for her to care that killing a prisoner of war in cold blood is immoral,[46] even though the chorus explicitly deem it unacceptable to Athens' rulers (964). When Eurystheus finally speaks, he is surprisingly sympathetic, explaining his treatment of Heracles' children and acknowledging Heracles' excellences (998–9) and Athens' mercy in sparing his life (1012). Like Iolaus earlier, he appeals to Greek law: though he would have been willing to die in battle, the law requires mercy to those who surrender, or his murderers will incur pollution. In the transmitted text, the following then happens: the chorus advise Alcmena to obey the city and release Eurystheus. She offers instead to kill him but then surrender his body to his friends (1022–5). This offer plainly does not conform to Greek law, but the chorus leader accedes to it. After Eurystheus' next speech, Alcmena orders her servants to throw him to the dogs (1050–2). Again the Marathonians apparently assent (1053–5): "For our deeds will be clean in the sight of our rulers."[47] Many commentators assume a lacuna between 1052 and 1053 and often fill it with material absolving the chorus from a stunning cynicism which contradicts every Athenian ideal expounded earlier in the play. The ending as transmitted is undoubtedly incoherent, and some lines may certainly be missing.[48] But is it possible to make any sense of the transmitted text?

How important are the handful of lines given to the chorus? Should they have as much weight as Alcmena's revenge, which is given far more space,[49] or is their ultimate failure to support Greek law the focus of the end of the play, so that Athenian ideals are ultimately mere talk?[50] This is certainly possible, but Euripides' last remarkable twist does allow a less damning interpretation for some spectators. Though Iolaus' earlier promise that Heracles' descendants will never attack Athens is known by Euripides' spectators to be false, Eurystheus promises to reward Athens with posthumous protection by residing in Attic soil, following an oracle of Apollo (1015, 1032–3), while being implacably hostile to those (Alcmena, thus her Spartan descendants) who killed him (1034–6, 1044). Even when the future descendants of Heracles' children attack the city – Eurystheus himself condemns their ingratitude (1036)! – Athens itself will be safe. Since the Athenians *can* only get this oracle-sanctioned blessing through Eurystheus' death now, as Eurystheus himself understands (1026–9),[51] they can hand his death over to Alcmena and reap the benefits he offers, knowing that Alcmena's descendants will suffer for it. Some spectators at least might have found Eurystheus' promise of protection more important than the chorus' apparent rejection of Greek laws, since this ending also reflects Athens' increasing interest in cult places of Attica during the Peloponnesian War, partly for strategic reasons and partly to gain supernatural protection from enemies.[52] Christiane Sourvinou-Inwood[53] argues that ancient spectators would have viewed the end of the play through the religious schema of "appropriation of the enemy hero", of which there are many examples in Athenian history and tragedy, and might have focused on the reassuring elements of an ending in which Eurystheus assures their eternal protection. The play ends on a jarring note, but mostly because of the opposition of Eurystheus and Alcmena.[54] This is where the conflict began, and reconciliation is impossible. Meanwhile, Athens has done what it could do, and there is little doubt over whose good fortune is greatest, where Eurystheus is dead, Alcmena cursed, and the descendants of the Heraclidae accused of outrageous ingratitude.[55]

3.3 Suppliants

The slightly later *Suppliants* also mingles pro-Athenian rhetoric with pessimism,[56] but again, Euripides detaches Athenian action from any inextricable link to tragic suffering. In this play, the mothers of the Seven against Thebes, led by Adrastus, come to Eleusis[57] to supplicate Theseus to help them retrieve the bodies of their dead sons from the Theban victors, who are dishonouring divine law by keeping them unburied, laying this charge on Theseus "alone" (27). Only he is capable, just as only Athens is capable in the world of the *epitaphioi*. The audience might reasonably have expected him to follow Demophon and accept their supplication immediately, since burying the Seven was one of Athens' most famous actions in patriotic mythology. Instead, Euripides surprises us with a lengthy dialogue (110–61) between the increasingly cowed supplicant Adrastus[58] and Theseus, in which Theseus emphasizes his foolishness in aligning with Tydeus and Polynices against divine will and in being too influenced by bellicose young men (161).[59]

Adrastus responds with familiar appeals to Athens' unique reputation, in contrast to Sparta's "rough and shifty" nature.[60] Athens "alone" can undertake this deed (πόνος) because the city is famous for pitying the wretched (188–90). Theseus, still unmoved, responds with a speech about the essential beneficence of the gods (experienced by Theseus alone in this play) and human foolishness, of which he accuses Adrastus in his desire to marry his daughter to Polynices. This self-righteous Theseus rejects any alliance with a person he considers impious and incompetent, fearing that Adrastus' misfortune will taint his own city. This is not the expected Athenian response, and Adrastus reproaches him (253–5): he did not come to find a judge (δικαστής) or punisher (κολαστής),[61] but help and healing.

Theseus' old mother Aethra pities the old mothers of the chorus and persuades her son to change his mind, though even already he feels some pity for the lamenting women (288).[62] In a stirring speech, she reminds Theseus of what it means to be an Athenian. She would have stayed quiet (ἡσυχῶς, 305), as a good woman should, if the Thebans were not violating Greek law (311)[63] by refusing burial to the dead, and as an Athenian, Theseus is bound to help the unjustly treated (304–5). She reminds him that πόνοι[64] benefit Athens (323), in contrast to those excessively cautious, quiet cities which "look darkly."[65] The instability of human life makes pity essential and the triumphant Thebans (and, briefly, Theseus) have forgotten a cardinal tenet of Greek popular philosophy which is central to tragedy, that human good fortune is always fleeting.[66] Old Aethra remembers (329–31), and she will make Theseus remember as well.

Theseus' first, "un-Athenian" response, which is later echoed by the Theban herald,[67] helps to throw into stronger focus the rightness of his change of mind and openness to persuasion and helping the vulnerable as a good Athenian should. Once he is convinced, he becomes the voice of moral authority in the play, notably in his endorsement of Aethra's expression of the instability of human fortune (549–63), asserting rhetorical and military superiority over clients and enemies alike. He does, however, remain distant from Adrastus: he helps him according to Athenian principles, but Adrastus does not share his campaign, and Theseus refuses to let him speak until it is over (513; 590–3). The Athenian imperial ideal has a two-fold influence here. The idealized Athens does everything easily, unlike Sparta (Thuc. 2.39.1, 4), but what it does must *look* difficult. The choice to help suppliants must be a sufficiently difficult πόνος for its successful completion to glorify Athens and show off its unique excellence. And so, the potential danger to Athens that may result from helping someone like Adrastus, whether by the potential taint of his misfortune, which could incur divine sanctions, or from reprisals against Athens by human enemies, is always in the background.[68] Theseus cannot ignore Adrastus' dubious past, but acknowledges the higher priority, that it is innate to him to act nobly, punishing the bad, never shirking πόνοι (339–42). And so he finally acts like an Athenian and agrees to help Adrastus, whether by persuading[69] the Thebans to return the bodies or by compelling them (346–8).[70] Like Demophon, he is king and democrat, seeking the people's sanction yet confident that he will receive it (349–51). Thanks to Theseus, Adrastus finds redemption through Athens on a human level. The pattern is similar in *Eumenides*, *Heracles* and *Oedipus at Colonus*, where again, Athens offers aid to those who have suffered divinely imposed traumas.

A choral ode of gratitude to Athens is followed by a debate between Theseus and a Theban herald, which, like the equivalent scene in *Heraclidae*, addresses contemporary Athenian democracy and imperialism. Both use standard commonplaces: for the herald, democracy is rule by the unskilled mob, swayed by unscrupulous demagogues, while Theseus responds with an equally stereotyped condemnation of tyranny, given 29 lines to the Herald's 18. Theseus does not directly address the herald's criticisms, and this omission is sometimes interpreted[71] as indicating Euripides' own scepticism about Athenian democracy. But even if some spectators drew such conclusions, others might not have needed an explicit refutation of "obvious" lies – they could do that for themselves – and instead would have enjoyed listening to a righteous Athenian representative and ancestor attack tyranny.[72] Some also interpret the herald's claim (479–93) that foolish hope promotes the wars that are destroying Greece as a comment on the Peloponnesian War and perhaps Athens' role in it.[73] *Suppliants* undoubtedly shows the horrors caused by endless war-making, but there are good and bad wars, and Theseus is simply fighting to uphold panhellenic law (538; cf. Thuc. 2.37.3). Athenian activism is strongly endorsed in Theseus' heated exchange with the herald in which he boasts of previous πόνοι of punishing the violent and proud (ὑβρισταί; cf. *Hcld.* 18, 457), while sparing the good (*Supp.* 575). The herald responds, "You and your city are always interfering."[74] The term he uses clearly alludes to the charges of *polypragmosynē* laid against Athens by enemies. In the mouth of an unambiguously repellent character, such *polypragmosynē* is plainly vindicated to the ears of Athenian spectators, and Theseus asserts that all the labours (πόνοι) that such a policy creates brings his city much (πολλά) happiness.

Theseus' subsequent victory will prove militarily and morally complete. Since he fails to persuade Creon to obey panhellenic law (670–2), the battle begins. Theseus is a powerful combatant who could have stormed and taken Thebes. However, his mission was merely to reclaim the dead and, unlike the Thebans, he chooses simple justice over excessive revenge (720–5).[75] The image of the just conqueror who chooses to exercise less power than he has at his disposal, through moderation even to enemies, represents the idealized imperial combination of power, mercy and wisdom.[76] This narrative aligns effectively with the expectations of those spectators who were well disposed towards idealizing portrayals of Athenian power. Military success, no less than moral success, demands intelligence, foresight and an awareness that human prosperity is precarious. Many non-Athenian generals of Euripidean tragedy rely on temporary fortune and oppress those who are temporarily less lucky,[77] but Theseus is different. Moreover, his firm yet merciful treatment of Thebes even causes Adrastus to reflect on his own mistakes, in rejecting Eteocles' moderate terms (μέτρια, 740),[78] with disastrous results.

Through enlightened *polypragmosynē* and self-control, Theseus demonstrates complete superiority. Not only does he help the suppliant mothers by returning their dead, but he rehabilitates Argos after its impious mission, apportioning punishment and reward to clients in an almost divine role. Theseus crowns his self-controlled prowess in war with a deed of outstanding compassion, as a model of Athens' idealized omni-competence, by gathering the decomposing bodies with his own hands and preparing them for cremation (762–8). His efforts enable Adrastus at last to be sufficiently rehabilitated to be allowed to pronounce a funeral oration over the dead (857–917).[79] Once more, however, Theseus takes over (925), in praising Polynices, arranging a separate burial for Capaneus (935) and then rebuking Adrastus for inviting the mothers to view the traumatic sight of their dead sons before they are cremated (942–7). Adrastus succumbs again with a final lament at human bellicosity and a wish to live peacefully with the peaceful (ἥσυχοι μεθ' ἡσύχων) with no πόνοι (952–4): if the phrase invokes contemporary politics and favours conduct closer to that of Sparta than Athens, it is in the mouth of a consistently discredited character. Theseus never expresses such sentiments: for him and his city alone, warfare has been beneficial.

Argos is on its own wretched track that even Athens cannot change, and Theseus and Athens fade out of focus as Capaneus' grieving widow commits suicide in a tragic self-sacrifice that causes yet more suffering. Misery is added to misery as the stage fills with the sons of the dead, carrying their ashes in urns and threatening revenge (1144). The conflict is over for Athens but not for Argos. Though Theseus in altruistic Athenian mode offers further help to Adrastus (1180), asking nothing

Euripides, empire and war 91

in return except remembrance of Athens' services and a rather vague "honouring" (1172), Athena intervenes to ensure that her city's πόνοι are properly rewarded with the accustomed military deterrent. She makes Theseus impose much stricter terms, extracting an oath from Adrastus not to attack Athens (1191–5, 1208–13), and sealing it with a dedication at Delphi, solemnized by a sacrifice. The knife used for the sacrifice is buried under the pyres of the Seven and will rise up if the Argives dare any future invasion. In 421/20 BCE, Athens and Argos signed a treaty, but Euripides' fictional treaty is entirely one-sided: Argos makes pledges to Athens but Athens promises nothing in return. By prophesying to the Epigoni that they will one day sack Thebes, Athena sanctions continued misery for Argos and Thebes, but not for Athens. This play contains multiple strands: spectators can feel the pain that war imposes on others, by empathizing with them through their own experiences, but they can also maintain a reassuring sense of their own city's impregnable success. As in *Heraclidae*, Athens' imperial mission cannot help everyone, especially those on their own historic-mythologically sanctioned course, but it does help Athens, both now (the mythological past) and for the future (the audience's own present and futures.)

3.4 *Heracles*

Though it is less exclusively focused on Athenian action, Euripides' *Heracles* resembles *Heraclidae* and *Suppliants* in its portrayal of Theseus. Like Oedipus in *Oedipus at Colonus*, Eurystheus in *Heraclidae*, and even the Eumenides in Aeschylus, Heracles, another non-Athenian hero, finds a new home in Athens which benefits both newcomer and recipient city.[80] When the play begins, Heracles is in Hades on his final labour to capture Cerberus (23–5), and a tyrant controls Thebes, rendering his family completely helpless.[81] The first third of the play repeatedly complains that in spite of this greatest panhellenic hero's services to humanity and the gods, no human or god will help them, whether through apathy or inability (339–47; cf. 53–6, 84–5, 217–30, 312–15, 430, 498–502, 551, 558–61, 568–70). Sorrow turns to joy as Heracles returns from the dead, explaining that he had been initiated into the Eleusinian mysteries (613),[82] which helped him with the task of capturing Cerberus; while in the underworld he also helped Theseus (619–21). Soon, however, Hera, angry that Heracles has successfully accomplished his labours, sends Lyssa (815–73) to send him mad and kill all his family except his aged father Amphitryon.

When he regains his sanity and learns what he has done, Heracles can only think of suicide (1146–52), and at Theseus' arrival (1154, foreshadowed in retrospect by 619–21) he veils his head, fearing that his presence will bring religious pollution on him. Theseus has recently learned that Thebes is under tyrannical rule and, because of Heracles' previous kindness to him, has come to help with proper Athenian speed:[83] even the greatest panhellenic hero sometimes needs Athenian assistance. Theseus repays Heracles' services to him to redress the balance between them as soon as possible (unlike what Heracles' earlier false or feeble friends did), by offering him immediate assistance, and will reset the balance decisively in favour of Athens when he eventually offers Heracles a home at Athens (1336–7).

Once Theseus has understood from Amphitryon what has happened, he instantly attributes the disaster to Hera's machinations (1191) and bids Heracles uncover his head. His judgement is speedy and correct, as befits the representative of an intelligent, compassionate and active city famous for helping the unjustly treated (Thuc. 2.37.3) and for its ability to distinguish between deserved and undeserved sufferings (Isoc. 4.47). For Theseus, Heracles' help to him in Hades trumps everything now, just as his friendship with Heracles trumps any fear of pollution (1219–21, 1236).[84] Theseus tries to absolve Heracles of blood guilt, by focusing on human solutions to his woes, largely ignoring divinity as at best indifferent and at worst actively hostile to humans, and a useless model for human moral struggle (1314–21). This is a very imperfect solution, since it completely bypasses the play's central question of theodicy, but Theseus, as an exemplary human being, avoids engagement with that theodicy because such unsatisfactory divinities make human acceptance at Athens Heracles' only real hope. Panegyrics of Athens emphasize that the city worships the gods and is beloved by them in turn, but another strain of thought ascribes to Athens an almost divine status in wisdom and agency,[85] and the ability partially to mitigate divinely created suffering, as is seen in Theseus' treatment of Heracles here.

Once more, Athens is the pitying helper, a role only possible for a city fundamentally detached from the tragedy, as Heracles himself notes. When Theseus urges him to be strong (1242–8) he complains that Theseus cannot understand his experience because he is "outside the disaster" (ἐκτὸς . . . συμφορᾶς, 1249; cf. 1410–17). The very excellence of Athens limits the city's ability to offer anything other than incomplete human solutions in a world controlled by obscure and hostile divinities. Heracles considers such solutions insufficient, finding Theseus' explanations simplistic and superficial (1255–321; 1340–51) – as he must, if he is to seem sympathetic to his audience.

Yet, ultimately, the great saviour of humanity does consent to be saved by becoming Athens' newest mythological recruit. Theseus has already repaid Heracles for his service in the underworld by coming to his aid, but Heracles now asks him (1387) to help him bring Cerberus to Argos. Cerberus' capture is Heracles' greatest feat, a symbolic conquest of death, but here it is partly transferred to Theseus (though left carefully in the future).[86] The symbolism of this transfer for Athenian claims to preeminence in the Greek world is clear. Euripides' *Heracles* lays much stronger emphasis on Athens' help to Heracles than on any benefits that he will offer to Athens,[87] effecting further minimization of Heracles' services to Theseus and glorification of Athenian generosity.

3.5 *Peirithous* and *Theseus*

Theseus' visit to the underworld was dramatized in the now-fragmentary, late fifth-century *Peirithous*, ascribed to Critias or Euripides.[88] In early myth, Theseus and his friend Peirithous visit Hades to abduct its queen and are punished by sitting on thrones which cling to their flesh, leaving them eternally in the underworld,[89] but from the early sixth century a version is known in which Heracles rescues both men.[90] A further popular development in Athenian narrative is a version in which Peirithous is blamed for the impious adventure and forced to stay in Hades forever, while Heracles rescues Theseus alone, as a reward for loyally accompanying his friend.[91] The *Hypothesis* to *Peirithous* distinguishes Peirithous' fate (bound to a rocky seat and guarded by serpents) from Theseus' but states that Theseus remained in the underworld out of loyalty to his friend (cf. fr.6), considering it shameful to abandon him, and both were eventually rescued by Heracles on his quest for Cerberus.[92] The most extensive fragment of the play (fr.7) indicates that Theseus once more represented the idealized Athens which is ever-loyal to its friends. He refuses to betray an unlucky friend (7.5–7), and Heracles commends his words as worthy of him and Athens: "For you are always an ally of the unfortunate." The crime of early myth is here softened into misfortunes of the kind which the ideal Athens always alleviates, as Theseus chooses a life in Hades alongside his friend, recalling both his earliest incarnation as the saviour of the children of Athens in the labyrinth, and the self-sacrifice of the mythical heroes and heroines who die for their cities, or the anonymous soldiers in real life whose sacrifices for Athens the *epitaphioi* commemorate. It appears that Theseus also offered to help Heracles with Cerberus (fr.7.10–14; cf. *HF* 1386–8), an offer which he declines, fearing that Eurystheus will consider a shared labour invalid. The *Hypothesis* seems to say that Theseus' loyalty to Peirithous so impressed the gods of Hades that they allowed both men to go. Like *Peirithous*, Euripides' very fragmentary *Theseus* may also have replicated conventional images of the idealized Athens and its representatives. A badly preserved hypothesis[93] mentions Theseus' righteous conduct in assisting those in the labyrinth,[94] his success there, and Ariadne's desire. It also seems to say either that Theseus did not marry her or that Dionysus married her,[95] and possibly that Theseus was ordered to marry her younger sister (presumably Phaedra).[96] If so, the play did not follow the usual story in which Theseus abandons Ariadne[97] but the version preserved in Pherecydes (*FGrH* 3F148) and illustrated by some vases[98] on which Athena or another god compels Theseus to leave her. This version appears to have originated in Athens, once Theseus became Athens' ideal representative. Since loyalty to friends is a cardinal trait of the ideal city, Theseus must not betray Ariadne, and Athenian stories which absolve him from the charge are necessary.[99]

3.6 *Ion*

Euripides' *Ion* reflects different claims of the idealized Athens, and scholarly tradition remains divided on the degree to which Euripides endorses or critiques them. Central to the Athenians' self-perception were two myths of origin which served different functions in asserting Athenian identity. First, the unique autochthony of the Athenians is frequently moralized in idealizing speeches which claim that the Athenians came from the soil of Attica, and no other people inhabited their land before they did, making Athenian civilization the oldest in Greece, with purer ancestry. Autochthony also makes them more just than others (especially the Spartans) by never having ejected others from their land to inhabit it.[100] But the Athenians also consider themselves Ionian, and their claim to be the Ionians' mother city legitimizes their control over the Ionians of the Athenian empire.[101]

When Apollo raped Creusa, the daughter of the Athenian king Erechtheus,[102] she gave birth to a son, who was spirited away to Delphi and grows up as the servant of Apollo's temple, ignorant of his parents' identity. Creusa subsequently married Xuthus, an Achaean ally of Athens, but they are childless and are now visiting the oracle to seek its advice. In the play's prologue, Hermes reveals that through Apollo's agency, Xuthus will accept the temple attendant as his son so that he can return to Athens with an heir. The boy will be named Ion and become the founder of the Ionic settlements in Asia (69–75).

Autochthony is central to much of the play, starting at its prologue in which Hermes emphasizes Ion's Erechtheid ancestry and Erechtheid lore.[103] Later (585–647), when Xuthus has accepted Ion as his son and wants to bring him to Athens in celebration, Ion hesitates, imagining that a people with such pure blood will despise a foreign-born son of an unknown mother (589–90).[104] His concerns are well founded, since Creusa's allies, the chorus (703–4, 719–24; cf. 1058–60, 1069–73) and her old servant (808–11, 819, 837), are very hostile to incorporating an apparent foreigner into the royal line and Creusa plans to kill the interloper with one deadly drop of the Erechtheids' ancestral gift of the Gorgon's blood (845–6, 976–8, 999–1019). Euripides raises real questions about Athens' treatment of non-citizens and about the claims of idealizing texts (e.g. Thuc. 2.39.1) that the city is truly open to foreigners.[105] But once the tokens from his babyhood presented by Apollo's priestess prove his identity (1427–36), Ion, Athenian royalty through his mother and of divine origin through his real father, will represent the ideal Athens excellently in his unique combination of contradictory statuses. Ion's right to rule Athens, which conveniently removes the foreigner Xuthus' descendants from the succession, is affirmed by Athena as *dea ex machina* (1571–5), who prophesies that Ion's sons, eponyms of the four Ionian tribes, will settle the Cyclades, colonize Europe and Asia and lend strength to Athens, divinely sanctioning Athens' power over the Ionians (1575–93). Moreover, Creusa and Xuthus are destined to have two more children, Dorus and Achaeus, the eponyms of the Dorians and Achaeans. Hesiod (fr.9) makes Dorus Xuthus' brother, but Euripides demotes him so that the Ionians will be the senior race in Greece with a uniquely divine ancestry.[106] This arrangement aligns Athens' antiquity and distinction with the autochthony topos in which Athenian civilization is older than that of other cities, and also makes Athens a kind of mother city of the whole of Greece, in a move analogous to Athens' mythological grab for Heracles, Oedipus and others. Still, the complexities of this play are undeniable. Athena credits Apollo for a "happy" ending (1595–1600), but many commentators struggle to believe that the claim can be taken at face value[107] since Euripides emphasizes the pain and estrangement he causes to Ion and Creusa, above all in the graphic description of her rape (859–922). Moreover, Athena prevents Ion from confronting Apollo directly (1546–52, 1601–2) while Xuthus never knows who his new son's father really is. Equally, however, Athena eclipses Apollo at the end of the play, and Ion and Creusa ultimately express satisfaction with what has transpired (1606–12), so that a reassuring ending can be found by those spectators who seek it. Like Hera in *Heracles*, Apollo acts disappointingly by human standards (1557–8; cf. 436–51): but whether he *should* be judged by those standards is left unclear, because the emphasis of the play shifts so decisively at its end to the glorious future awaiting Ion and his descendants. Euripides' Athenian plays frequently oppose a human and humane Athens which offers some resolution and positive comfort to broken human beings, with violent and enigmatic gods. Although Euripides is not entirely innovative in portraying such gods – Homer's gods can be ruthless[108] – perhaps one reason for the anti-religious impression he left on his contemporaries and many moderns is the tendency of his Athenian characters to epitomize the highest human virtues as they rescue the victims of divine anger or simple indifference.

3.7 *Erechtheus*

In *Erechtheus* (c. 422–11),[109] of which only fragments, albeit substantial ones, remain,[110] the Delphic oracle requires king Erechtheus of Athens to sacrifice one of his daughters to save his city from Eumolpus of Thrace,[111] who is trying to annex Athens for his father Poseidon. This is another story from Athens' glorious history,[112] which reminds its audience of past triumphs over invaders and that Athens was once the source of strife between two of the greatest Olympian gods (fr. 360.43–9). In fragments 352–6 a speaker, possibly Erechtheus, may confront a representative of Eumolpus and affirm just war-making[113] over its opposite, resembling Theseus or Demophon in the extant plays.[114] The chorus appear to be elderly Athenians (369): it is unfortunate that we lack a context for their ostensibly un-Athenian praise of ἡσυχία (369.2). In fr.360, quoted by the orator Lycurgus, Erechtheus' wife Praxithea affirms the claims of the city over the individual. She ascribes Athens' excellence to its people's unique autochthony (5–13; cf. *Ion* 589–90), and states that if the preservation of the whole city depends on sacrificing one life – a daughter, since she has no son, but would have sent him out (22–7) – that is the higher good (14–21, 38–42).[115] These democratic sentiments mingle with a more aristocratic sensibility as she contrasts the common glory of ordinary soldiers with the individual glory that her daughter will gain (32–5; cf. *Hcld.* 534). Fr.364, decrying a pleasant life or κακὴ ἀτολμία, claims that "Good things increase for men from labours (πόνοι)": unfortunately, it is just one line, but it echoes the idealization of Athenian *polypragmosynē* discussed earlier.[116] Whether Praxithea's daughter was equally enthusiastic about dying for Athens is unknown,[117] but Praxithea's pious belief (35–7) that she will still retain her other two daughters is proved wrong. At some point they commit suicide in a pact with their sister (370.69–70) by throwing themselves off the Acropolis,[118] while Erechtheus himself is killed by Poseidon (370.59–60), presumably in revenge for killing Eumolpus. Almost like Creon in *Antigone*, she loses all her beloved family in a very short compass, and at the start of fr.370, she laments her losses (23–44). Then, however, Poseidon sends an earthquake (45–54) before Athena as *dea ex machina* takes control and rebukes him for excessive violence (55–7). She then instructs Praxithea, the city's "saviour" (χθονὸς [σώτειρα Κηφισοῦ] κόρη, 63: cf. 360.51–2)[119] to bury her children in recognition of their nobility (γενναιότης, l.69) in fulfilling their oath (63–70), promising that as the Hyacinthidae,[120] they will be worshipped by, offer protection to and receive sacrifice from every Athenian expeditionary force henceforth (73–89).[121] Extant tragedy typically acquires foreign protectors for Athens: here, unusually, the heroes are homegrown. Erechtheus will receive a precinct on Athena's own acropolis (90–4) and be known as Poseidon Erechtheus, offering an aetiology for the Erechtheum which was built in the last quarter of the fifth century. Praxithea will become the first priestess of Athena Polias (95–7).[122] These transformations effect a reconciliation between Poseidon and Athena (cf. S. *OC* 695–719) which will bring significant future benefits to Athens. At 99–100, Athena refers to future orders of Zeus, and though the text now becomes very fragmentary, 100–116 apparently link this Eumolpus with the more familiar Eumolpus of Eleusis, perhaps offering an aetiology for the Eleusinian mysteries, since Demeter is mentioned (103, 109) as are "secrets" (ἄρρητα, 110) and the Kerukes (115), who shared priestly duties at Eleusis with the Eumolpidae.[123]

Erechtheus is highly unusual in its portrayal of significant Athenian pain, as Praxithea incurs far more suffering than she imagined when she first offered her daughter for her city. It is intriguing that no extant fragments of the play contain any report of the actual sacrifice, just as Euripides' presentation of the Maiden's sacrifice in *Heraclidae* somewhat diminishes emphasis on its horror,[124] and the play also aligns with other Athenian myths of individual self-sacrifice for Athens.[125] Unfortunately, of course, Euripides' dominant tone cannot be securely determined from fragments, however relatively extensive: did he glorify the Athenian royal family's sacrifice or did he treat it ironically, or ambivalently? Many have been hesitant to imagine an ironic treatment,[126] given the centrality in Athenian life of the cults and temples whose aetiology Euripides establishes at the end of the play. This ending would have especial resonance if the play was indeed performed as the Erechtheum was being constructed on the Acropolis, and Lycurgus, who quotes fr.360, interprets it as a straightforward expression of patriotic duty.[127] That the play appears to endorse πόνος for the good of the city recalls the familiar and necessary glorification of individual sacrifice for the collective that the *epitaphioi* promote.[128] Whether or not it *unequivocally* endorsed such uplifting sentiments, if *Erechtheus* followed the pattern of every other play discussed so far, spectators would have had the *option* to foreground them, whatever other reactions were possible, and in fact, quite unlike the losses incurred by Thebans or Argives in other plays, Praxithea's individual loss brings unalloyed religious and military benefits to the collective body of Athens. Above all, the sacrifices of Athenian expeditionary forces at the sanctuary of the Hyacinthidae will guarantee future success for Athens, offering as potent a reassurance as anything granted by the foreigners incorporated into Athens.[129]

3.8 *Hippolytus*

It is clear by now that tragedies featuring Athenian characters are typically marked by the language of Athenian imperialism.[130] Euripides' *Hippolytus* is an exception. This Athenian king saves no suppliants and even answers his stepson's appeals for mercy with a deadly and irrevocable curse. This play is anomalous for multiple reasons, not least because Euripides dramatized the *Hippolytus* story twice and the two plays are plainly in dialogue with one another. The extant *Hippolytus* is set, not at Athens, but at Trozen,[131] the scene of Theseus' childhood, where he has now returned for a year in exile for killing his cousins, the Pallantidae (34–5). It is usually assumed that the Athenians were scandalized by the sexually provocative Phaedra of the lost play, a claim that can be supported by extant fragments, though they are scanty,[132] and the new *Hypothesis* does not exclude this, though it solves few other questions and raises many others. By contrast, the extant Phaedra is the complete opposite of a sexual predator. She risks her own physical and mental well-being to resist feelings she considers immoral, but she is ultimately betrayed by her well-meaning Nurse. Euripides' prologue explicitly absolves Phaedra: Aphrodite states that she intends to destroy Hippolytus for his disrespect to her and has deliberately made Phaedra, virtuous though she has been until now, fall in love with him to ruin him (47–50). Phaedra is purely collateral damage in the humbling of Hippolytus and since she is doomed from the start, her plight automatically invites the audience's pity.

Changes to the Phaedra-Hippolytus relationship affect the characterization of Theseus and his relationship with his stepson. In all known versions of the story except that of the extant *Hippolytus*, Phaedra falls in love when Theseus is absent in the underworld, presumably attempting to capture its queen with Peirithous.[133] Although this myth may be told to minimize Theseus' guilt, it is not one of the deeds for which Theseus and Athens are commended in speeches glorifying Athens. In the extant play, however, he is absent on a vaguely described expedition (792–3; cf. 280–1) which may both remove him from any impropriety and also help Phaedra's reputation – only a reckless woman would deliberately fall in love with her stepson when her husband was only temporarily away.[134] Though the structure of the myth means that Theseus must kill a Hippolytus who by definition is a victim of injustice, this Hippolytus is arrogant, foolish to believe that humans and gods are equals (94–107), and strange in denying normal sexuality. His pride in his own supposed self-control (σωφροσύνη) and rejection of political life (986–1020) might well sit unfavourably with an Athenian audience.[135] Theseus causes his son's death, but he is different from the cold-blooded and wrath-prone kings of plays such as *Antigone* because of his trust in his wife (817–50). When he reads Phaedra's letter accusing Hippolytus of rape but cannot question her because she has already killed herself in a misguided attempt to protect her honour,[136] his reaction, though disastrous, is understandable. In the light of the letter from the woman he loved, Theseus considers Hippolytus' complete rejection of sexuality to be a sham and uses the first of the three curses that his divine father has given him against his stepson.[137] As soon as he has uttered it, however, he adds a sentence of exile, as though he is unsure of the curse's efficacy (895), and thereafter all emphasis is on the exile (973, 1048, 1094–7) until the messenger arrives with the news of Hippolytus' accident while driving his chariot into exile. Theseus' reaction is telling: "Oh gods and Poseidon, so you really were my father!"[138] Although he had previously refused to pity Hippolytus (1089), he does not gloat over his sufferings now (1257–60).

Theseus curses his son and causes his death, but he too is a victim of the gods' designs and horrified when Artemis rebukes him for his gullibility in believing Phaedra, and vindicates Hippolytus' virtue and even Phaedra's attempts at behaving nobly (1283–325). But immediately afterwards, she acknowledges that even Theseus can be forgiven because (as the audience knows) this was Aphrodite's desire, and divine law forbids gods from frustrating other gods' purposes (1325–37). Theseus has made a mistake but he can find pardon, as even Hippolytus acknowledges on his deathbed.

This play is the closest extant tragedy gets to bringing an Athenian hero squarely "inside disaster". It does not get as close as it might have. Though Euripides' chosen plot necessitates that Theseus must kill his son, his filicide is given notable mitigation, and *Hippolytus* is also highly unusual in detaching Theseus from the usual rhetoric glorifying Athens. Its Trozenian setting and the reference to the killing of the Pallantidae are features of Theseus' heroic youth, and he describes himself not as having saved the Heraclidae or the bodies of the Seven against Thebes, but as the hero who slew Sinis and Skiron (976–80), deeds connected with his youthful journey from Trozen to his father in Athens, rather than the mature Theseus who represents the idealized Athens. Nor does Hippolytus appeal to Athenian ideals of mercy in his confrontation with his father. Instead, Euripides has systematically detached Theseus from his usual connection with the ideal Athens and aligned him with more traditional parts of the Theseus myth.

3.9 Trojan Women

Euripides' *Trojan Women*, produced in 415 BCE, has often been read as Euripides' response to the previous year's siege and massacre at Melos, considered by Thucydides and others as the supreme example of Athens' abuse of power.[139] In more recent years it has become the paradigm anti-war play in which the traumatized Trojan women represent all victims of war. Perhaps some Athenian spectators at the play's premiere did interpret Euripides' words as a condemnation of Athenian action, but significant caveats complicate any idea that Euripides deliberately equated the Greeks at Troy with the Athenians at Melos, not least simple chronology, since he is unlikely to have been able to conceive his play, submit his proposal to the archon to get a chorus and then write and rehearse it between the sack of Melos in late 416 BCE and the Dionysia of 415.[140]

The *Trojan Women* certainly condemns war-making (95–7, 400), but in a non-specific way which need not target contemporary Athens specifically.[141] In fact, like Hermione in *Andromache*, the hated figure of Helen is frequently dubbed "Spartan,"[142] and the chorus' speculations about where they will be sent as prizes for the Greek contingents are revealing. Their first choice is "Theseus' land", with Thessaly second and Sicily or southern Italy as third (214–29). There is no compelling dramatic or mythological reason why they should name these specific places,[143] but all are of clear contemporary relevance to Athenian spectators,[144] and are characterized by beauty and a prosperity that may even hint at a kind of moral superiority as well.[145] By contrast, the place they most dread is Sparta (210–13), and the second is Corinth, another enemy of Athens: since Helen is Spartan, such fears are mythologically appropriate, but since Athens notoriously had little part in the Trojan War,[146] contemporary conditions seem more immediate than the mythological background. Moreover, Athens is a city to which foreigners would naturally wish to come (cf. E. *Med.* 824–45), and Sparta is the opposite.

The choral ode of 799–859 describes Salamis, later called "holy" (1096), as close to the holy hills where Athena first made olives appear (801–3), reprising the familiar claim in Herodotus and later *epitaphioi* that olive trees originated in Attica and were Athens' marvellous gift to the rest of the world.[147] Athens is also given its traditional, even clichéd, epithet of "shining" (803).[148] There is no reason to assume any ironic intent in Euripides' invocation of these topoi of the idealized Athens, and in any case, the rest of the ode has a different focus, replaying once more the Greeks' assault on Troy.

In her confrontation with Helen (895–1059), Hecuba, who believes the gods to be better than we know them to be, condemns her for lust and greed for Paris' eastern gold in her longing to escape Spartan poverty (991–96).[149] Hecuba even accuses her of wanting to have people prostrate themselves in front of her. While her charges make sense in a purely mythological context, the figure of the deprived Spartan seduced by wealth may have some presence in the Athenian imperial imagination: perhaps some spectators remembered the Spartan general Pausanias who went eastwards and adopted Persian ways.[150] Whereas Athens offers every attraction but not to excess, as the city which is by definition in the middle and naturally attracts foreigners, Sparta is a city of extremes and therefore lacking in certain respects, causing its inhabitants to look elsewhere for what it cannot provide.

Perhaps some spectators did connect what they themselves did at Melos with Euripides' portrayal of the sack of Troy. No author controls what his audience takes from his work. It would take impressively honest and self-critical spectators to do this. But I am not sure that we can assume that most were like this,[151] if just because Euripides has made it sure that the condemnatory reading is not the only one possible. The play's potential references to contemporary politics are at least as favourable to Athens and hostile to Sparta as the reverse, and many are explicable in a purely mythological framework. This is what might be expected in the context of the conditions in which Euripides was writing. If Herodotus is to be believed, any playwright who wrote too specifically about Athenian pain or failure might experience what Phrynichus suffered for violating the unspoken convention that Athens should be "outside the disaster" (E. *HF* 1249). Tragic playwrights competed for a much-desired first prize. If Euripides did want to prick Athenian consciences over Melos, he would have to tread a very fine line and allow "escape routes" for those who did not want to view this tragedy as an indictment of their own actions. In any case, although Thucydides portrays the treatment of Melos with utmost moral seriousness, Aristophanes found "Melian hunger" material for a one-liner in the roughly contemporary *Birds* (186), and it may be that only after the Peloponnesian War did Melos come to represent the worst excesses of Athenian power. Modern audiences are also essentially "outside the disaster," if in a slightly different sense. We are so far distant in time (and, typically, scholars, not soldier-spectators) that the sack of Troy and the Melian massacre seem easily comparable. For Euripides' contemporaries, "within the tragedy", or their polis' ideology, parallels between the two may seem less compelling, if only through the marvellous human capacity for not seeing what we do not want to see.[152]

Notes

1. Cf. pp. 45–52 earlier.
2. Thomas (1989) 206–13; Loraux (1986) 3.
3. Zuntz (1955/1963) offered the first major modern rehabilitation of their reputation.
4. Vellacott (1975) esp. 178–92; Burian (1977); Walker (1995); Allan (2001); Mendelsohn (2002); Tzanetou (2012). On tragedy's inherent ambivalence and multivocality, see also earlier, pp. 47–50.
5. Zeitlin (1990), esp. 145–7.
6. Cf. pp. 49–50 earlier.
7. Meier (1993) 2–4, 47–8; Pelling (1997b) 228–9.
8. Cf. Hdt. 9.73.2; Lys. 2.11–16; Xen. *Mem*. 3.3.10; Pl. *Mx*. 239b; Isoc. 4.54–60, 5.33–4, 10.31, 12.194; Dem. 18.186, 60.8–9; Ar. *Rhet*. 1396a13–14. Loraux 1986 42–78.
9. Hdt. 9.73.3; Lys. 2.7–10; Isoc. 4.54–9; 12.168–74; Dem. 60.8; Xen. *Hell*. 6.5.46–7; Plut. *Thes*. 29 (on Aeschylus' fragmentary *Eleusinioi*).
10. A potent setting, although it is largely conflated with Athens in the play: Allan (2001) 46–9; Mendelsohn (2002) 63–5.
11. The early part of the play is especially full of conventional expressions, both in words and actions, of the idealized Athens of encomiastic texts: 38, 101–8, 113, 129, 191–8, 206, 286–7, 309–25, 329–32, 362–70.
12. Cf. earlier, pp. 21–2 and for Heracles, see *Hcld*. 331 πόνους . . . μυρίους; *HF* 1275, cf. S. *Trach*.1101: Wilkins (1993) 93. Of Athens, E. *Supp*. 189, 314–23, 573, 576–7; Thuc. 2.36.2, 62.3, 63.1, 64.3; Lys. 2.55; Isoc. 12.128: Boegehold (1982); Carter (1986): 10–13; Raaflaub (1994) 109–10; Mills (1997) 64–5. Aristocratically biased texts such as Hom *Il*. 9.323–7, Pind. *Pyth*. 12.28 and *Ol*. 5.15 connect struggle and the common good. The Athenian democracy, as it aspired to a common aristocracy, viewed its relationship to the Greek world through images like these: Wilkins (1993) 131–2.
13. Thuc. 1.70, esp. 70.8, sets the "typical" Athens against the "typical" Sparta. On the fifth-century debate and the vocabulary in which it is expressed, see Ehrenberg (1947); Kleve (1964); Adkins (1976); Allison (1979); Mills (1997) 67–9; Carter (1986) 42–7, 57–8 traces connections between Sparta, ἡσυχία, σωφροσύνη, εὐνομία and moderation.
14. See pp. 18–19 earlier.
15. He calls them "those who dwell in Athens from of old", 69, referring to the longevity of Athenian civilization, another element in Athenian self-glorification. Similarly, Athens is called "famous" (κλεινῶν) at *Hcld*. 38: cf. Pind. fr. 76; S. *Aj*. 961; E. *Tro*. 207, *Hipp*. 423, 760, 1459, *Ion* 30, 262.
16. A. *Ag*. 72–82; E. *HF* 107–14, 435–41. Their choral songs (esp. 748–83 and 892–927) express remarkable confidence throughout the play: Allan (2001) 203.

17 Compare S. *OC* 884–903; Thuc. 1.70.4, 2.39.4; cf. Lys. 2.23, 26; Isoc. 4.87, 12.170; Hyperid. 6.24. Athens' speed and daring, contrasted with Spartan slowness and caution in the Persian Wars, could be used to justify Athens' possession of the empire: Lys. 2.23: Loraux (1986) 158–9; Thomas (1989) 222.
18 On their role as suppliants, see Allan (2001) 39–43.
19 On the relationship between pity and pleasure, see Heath (1987) 8–10; Falkner (2005) 166–7.
20 Ar. *Rhet.* 1368a17–29: Rosenbloom (1993) 164–8.
21 Ar. *Rhet.*1385b33–5, 1386b17–24: earlier, pp. 49–50.
22 Ar. *Rhet.*1385b14–16, 26–7, 1386b1–3; cf. Isoc. 4.47; Sternberg (2005a) 2; Konstan (2005) 55.
23 Thuc. 3.39.2; Dem. 24.171; Plut. Mor. 790c; Plin. *NH* 35.69: Stevens (1944); Macleod (1983d) 74–5; Pelling (1997) 17 n.75; Mills (1997) 76–8, 105–6. On pity more generally, see Rosenbloom (1993) 165–7; Konstan (2001) 50–1, 60–6, 77–82, 88–90, 128–3; Tzanetou (2005).
24 Plut. *Thes.* 22, where they meet Theseus, not his sons.
25 Tzanetou (2012) 75–80.
26 Cf. Isoc. 4.53; E. *Supp.* 321; Thuc. 6.13.2.
27 Thuc. 2.40.4; Mills (1997) 63–9; Loraux (1986) 67.
28 Hdt. 9.27.2–5; Pl. *Mx.*240a6–7: cf. earlier, pp. 12–14, 21.
29 Compare *HF* 266–7 discussed later.
30 See earlier, pp. 22–5; cf. Mills (1997) 63–6.
31 *HF* 222–3, 1169–428; S. *Trach.* 1010–14. The process begins as early as the later sixth century: Allan (2001) 25 n.19.
32 Kowalzig (2006) 97–8.
33 On Athenian speed, cf. n.17 earlier.
34 The word used (σωφρονῆς, 263) is one of the "Spartan" terms that can be opposed to Athenian *polypragmosynē:* Finley (1938) 45.
35 The Herald is a one-dimensional anti-Athenian villain, and Athenian spectators need not be concerned at Demophon's brief and unfulfilled threat: in fact, the chorus mockingly imagine that when he returns to Argos, he will vastly exaggerate his ill-treatment (292–6). In Philostr. *VS* 550 the Athenians actually kill the Herald.
36 Isoc. 4.54–63, esp. 62; Pl. *Mx.* 244b–c; Aristid. *Panath.* 228: Allan (2001) 218. Imperial nations often complain of ingratitude: earlier, p. 24; cf. p. 9.
37 Compare E. *Supp.* 341; Lys. 2.7–11, 16; Dem. 60.11; Pl. *Mx.* 240d; Isoc.12.170, 174; Hyperid. 6.5. For Zeus the punisher, cf. A. *Pers.* 827.
38 Cf. 826–7 with Allan (2001) 198.
39 Erechtheus' daughters offer a similar service for Athens: later, pp. 95–6. On the ritual significance of human sacrifice see Burkert (1983) 58–72, Wilkins (1993) xxiii–v, Larson (1995) 101–30.
40 E. *Hec.* 518–82, *IA* 1146–208. Allan (2001) 162 and 170 against Wilkins (1993) 189.
41 Tzanetou (2012) 84–91 reads this scene in the context of Athens' relations with its allies: Athens offers its protection, but the allies owe something in return.
42 *Hcld.* 541–2, 579–80, 591, 602–7.
43 Mendelsohn (2002) 87–94; Roselli (2007) 132–5; Tzanetou (2011) 323.
44 See Wilkins (1993) xxvii–xxx; Allan (2001) 35–6.
45 *Nu.* 584–9; and earlier, pp. 23–4.
46 In the early years of the Peloponnesian war, Athenians, Plataeans and Spartans were all guilty of killing prisoners without trial: Thuc. 2.5.7, 67.4; 3.68.1.
47 τὰ γὰρ ἐξ ἡμῶν / καθαρῶς ἔσται βασιλεῦσιν.
48 Zuntz (1963) 41–2; Burian (1977) 19–20; Wilkins (1993) xxx–xxxi, 193; Allan (2001) 223–4.
49 Alcmena is the grandmother of the suppliants who are the Spartans' ancestors. Did some spectators see her as a typical Spartan?

50 Allan (2001) 207; Burian (1977) 15–19.
51 Burnett (1976) 10–14. For Pelling (1997) 227, the strange realignment of sympathies at the end of the play "is not Athens' fault"; "the ideal remains . . . an ideal: it is usually, if not quite always, real life which is at fault" (234).
52 Krummen (1993) 215–17. DS 12.45 reports that the Spartans spared Marathon because it was the scene of the defeat of Eurystheus. Perhaps they were not entirely ungrateful after all.
53 Sourvinou-Inwood (2003) 324–5.
54 Wilkins (1993) xxv.
55 Sourvinou-Inwood (2003) 325.
56 Gamble (1970) and Fitton 1961) emphasize its pessimistic elements.
57 Mendelsohn (2002) 135–46 discusses Eleusis' literary and religious significance here; cf. Krummen (1993) 203–8. Imperial politics may also underlie the setting, since Aethra appears to refer to the festival of the Proerosia (28–9) and an inscription (*ML* 73) records Athens' requirement that its allies offer first fruits to the Eleusinian goddesses at this festival, in an apparent attempt to promote Eleusis as a panhellenic sanctuary: Storey (2008) 19. According to Lycurgus fr.86 and the Suda (εἰρεσιώνη) the Athenians saved the world from famine, and this was the *aition* for sending first fruits to the Proerosia: as Goff (1995) 73 states, this "represents a redemptive Athens with the Greek world in its debt."
58 Mendelsohn (2002) 150–1 comments on his submissive and womanish position.
59 The mothers themselves admit that they are at Demeter's temple "not according to ritual" (63; cf. 93). Generally, however, the tragic Theseus takes a broader view of piety (E. *HF* 1399–400, S. *OC* 886–90).
60 *Supp*.187: Σπάρτη μὲν ὠμὴ καὶ πεποίκιλται τρόπους. Explicit, rather than the more frequent implicit, condemnation of Sparta is also expressed in *Andromache* (esp. 445–52, 471–5, 486–93, 595–601), performed c. 425, and an ancient commentator on l.445 specifically connects this hostility with the Peloponnesian War. In general, except in *Helen*, Euripides' Menelaus is "arrogant, brutal, unscrupulous, deceitful, treacherous, cowardly, weak" and a Spartan: Poole (1994) 3–25.
61 Cf. earlier, n.101, p. 32, n.37, p. 101; cf. pp. 18–19, 22–23.
62 On Aethra's political role in the play, see especially Goff (1995) 70–4. Like Athena, in *Eumenides*, she combines female (motherhood) and male (knowledge of ideal Athenian belief and action.) Mendelsohn (2002) 164 n.29, cf. 166–7, argues that she uses "masculine" speech and logic, even as she acts out of female solidarity. Admittedly, Aethra is Trozenian but perhaps she too has some Athenian power to combine opposite virtues. Equally, Theseus has a feminine role in burying the dead: Mendelsohn (2002) 185–7.
63 Burying the dead is already important in the *Iliad*, and failure to do so was strictly punished: Vaughn (1991) 41–4.
64 Connecting this word with Heracles' labours, Storey (2008) 42–3 traces a Heraclean connection throughout the play: at 113, Adrastus addresses Theseus as καλλίνικος, a typically Heraclean epithet, while at 714–17, Theseus wields a Heraclean-style club.
65 *Supp*. 324–5: αἵ δ'ἥσυχοι σκοτεινὰ πράσσουσαι πόλεις / σκοτεινὰ καὶ βλέπουσιν εὐλαβούμεναι.
66 Memorably expressed by Solon to Croesus, Hdt.1.32: Mills (1997) 107–10. The relative immunity of tragic Athens to human vulnerability is another aspect of the city's uniqueness.
67 At 472, the herald claims that Theseus has no business with Argos, as Theseus told Aethra (291), and at 496–7, he claims that their impiety makes them ineligible for Theseus' help.
68 Compare the structure of Oedipus' reception at Athens in *Oedipus at Colonus*, earlier, pp. 64–5. The topos of helping dangerous suppliants works differently in *Medea*. The chorus characterizes Athens in familiar idealizing language (835–55): the Athenians

are Erechtheids, blessed children of gods, their land is unsacked, they have wisdom, culture and virtue, even moderate (μετρίους, 839) breezes: how can such a city receive an infanticidal mother (846–65)? But Athens will remain unharmed because it will have the wisdom and strength to remove Medea once she proves dangerous: Plut. *Thes*.12.2–3; Paus. 2.3.8; Diod. Sic. 4.55.4–6: Mills (1997) 228–9, 239–45.
69 As in Aeschylus' *Eleusinioi*: Plut. *Thes*. 29.4–5; Isoc. 12.168–71; Paus. 1.39.2.
70 The more common version, doubtless due to its prevalence in the funeral orations which honoured the deaths of Athenians in military service: Mills (1997) 90–1.
71 For example, Fitton (1961) 433; Grube (1941) 234.
72 For an earlier incarnation of Theseus as speaker of truth to tyrannical power, compare Bacchyl. 17.20–46.
73 Fitton (1961) 435–6.
74 πράσσειν σὺ πόλλ' εἴωθας ἥ τε σὴ πόλις (*Supp*. 576).
75 Some see an allusion to 424's battle of Delium here, in spite of significant differences between history and tragedy. Both situations concern Theban violation of panhellenic burial customs, but even if Euripides comes uncomfortably close to presenting spectators with "their own troubles" (Bowie (1997) 52–3), he provides ample escape routes for those who reject any troubling interpretations, since this Athens is a detached "policeman", arbitrating between two other Greek cities: Mills (1997) 93–5.
76 Cf. p. 23.
77 Inconstancy of fortune: *Hcld*. 22, 746–7, 895–900, 928–35; *Supp*. 608–9, 739–44; *HF* 103; *Tro*. 1203–6; *Hec*. 283–5; oppression: *Supp*. 124, 176–82; *Tro*. 69–86.
78 On the ideological implications of this word, see earlier, p. 17.
79 Its tone has occasioned considerable debate, since Adrastus transforms the originally monstrous and impious Seven against Thebes into civic paragons: scholars who believe that Euripides is satirizing or criticizing the funeral oration in some way include Fitton (1961) 438–40; Smith (1967) 161–4; Burian (1985) 148–9; Mendelsohn (2002) 188–96; see also Bernek (2004) 293–9 esp. 297 n.95. For the textual difficulties here see also Collard (1972); Grube (1941) 237–8; Mastronarde (1979) 116–17. For a less ironic reading, see Zuntz (1963) 13–16; Collard (1972); Mills (1997) 124–5. Theseus himself commends the Seven (925–8), and Adrastus' speech may simply be part of the humanizing rehabilitation of the dead: they have suffered for their actions, but their punishment is limited by their deaths (cf. Thuc. 2.42.3). Historical *epitaphioi* also ascribe virtue to the dead, while offering little explanation for so doing. They are praised *because* they are dead: Yoshitake (2010).
80 For Euripides' innovations in Heracles' myth, especially his migration to Athens, which is incompatible with the usual versions of his death on Mount Oeta or apotheosis, see Bond (1981) xxvi–xxx.
81 The tyrant, a character invented by Euripides, uses notably "un-Athenian" language, such as εὐλαβεία (165–6; cf. *Supp*. 325), and Amphitryon condemns his ἀμαθία (172), another term sometimes opposed to Athenian virtues (Thuc. 1.68.1, 2.40.3, 3.37.2): Mills (1997) 131–2.
82 One of the benefits shared by Athens with humanity: Isoc. 4.28–9.
83 At 266–7, the chorus connect *polypragmosynē* with the virtue of helping friends, but because they are old and feeble, their good intentions cannot be translated into the effective intervention that Theseus instantly offers.
84 At 1400, he goes even further, inviting him to wipe his slaughtered family's blood on him.
85 Isoc. 4.28–9, 33, 39–40; Pl. *Mx*. 237d–238b; compare the topos of Athens the punisher.
86 Compare also *Peirithous* fr.7.8–14: Collard and Cropp (2008a) 655.
87 Contrast *Hcld*. 1026–36; *Supp*. 1191–5.
88 See Collard and Cropp (2008a) 636–57; Mills (1997) 257–62.
89 Paus. 10.29.9; cf. 9.31.5, 10.28.2; 1.17.4.

90 The scene is on an inscribed shield band from Olympia of c. 580: Kunze (1950) 132–5.
91 Distinction between Theseus and Peirithous: Apollod. 2.5.12, *Ep*.1.23–4; Diod. Sic. 4.63.4; Plut. *Thes*. 35. Loyalty of Theseus: Isoc. 10.20; Ael. *VH* 4.5.
92 Collard and Cropp (2008a) 640–1.
93 *P. Oxy* 4640 col. i 1–18: van Rossum-Steenbeek (2003) 7–17; Collard and Cropp (2008) 418–19.
94 Frr. 385 and 386 appear to come from a lamentation by the Athenian children, presumably hoping to be rescued by our hero.
95 *P. Oxy* 4640 col. 1 l. 16–17 refers to someone κελεύσασα – Athena?
96 Collard and Cropp (2008) 416–17, 427, who suggest that fr.388 which refers to "another kind of love" belonging to a "soul that is just and temperate and good" comes from a speech of Athena, decreeing that Theseus and Ariadne must part. Ariadne's desire is mentioned in the *Hypothesis*: did Athena condemn it to distance Theseus from any possible reproaches of disloyalty?
97 Hes. fr.147, 298 MW; cf. Plut. *Thes*. 20.1–2; Athenaeus 557b.
98 E.g. Trendall-Webster III.3.50; *LIMC* III *Addenda* "Ariadne" 93–8.
99 Mills (1997) 14–18.
100 See p. 17. On the theme in *Ion,* cf. Zacharia (2003) 44–76.
101 Solon fr.4aW; Hdt. 5.66.2; 7.94.1; 8.22.1, 44.2; Thuc. 1.95.1, 6.82.3–4; Paus. 7.1.2–5: Meiggs (1972) 293–8; Zacharia (2003) 50–5. From the 440s, the allies were required to send a cow and panoply to the greater Panathenaea "like colonists": ML 46:41–2, 69:56–8, 49:11–13; cf. ML 40:3–5. Those who refused were punished: ML 46, ll.40–3. By the 420s, they were also required to send first fruits of wheat and barley to Eleusis (*ML* 73) to acknowledge Athens' gift of wheat to the world. Such requirements blurred distinctions between allies, subjects and colonists to the Athenians' advantage: Dillon (1997) 143–5; Barron (1964) 45–8. *Ion* was probably performed between 420 and 410: some connection between the play and the revolt of Athens' Ionian allies in 412/11 is often conjectured.
102 Whose ancestor, Erichthonius, was literally autochthonous through being born from the earth. Erechtheid identity runs through the play: 10, 20–6, 265–82, 999–1003, 1060; cf. 1163–5. Athens itself is also praised: 30, 184–7, 262–3, 590, 1038. Through the Erechtheus myth the Athenians can claim to be born from the earth as possessors of unique racial purity and also "children of blessed gods" (E. *Med*. 825) as descendants of Erichthonius' father Hephaestus: Zacharia (2003) 63.
103 *Ion* 8–26; cf. 283, 1030. The recognition tokens that reconcile mother and son are an olive wreath and a gold serpent necklace (1429), recalling Erichthonius' origins.
104 Ion's own concern for purity is notable, proving his innate, if as yet unknown, nobility: 94–106, 150, 154–75, 643–5. He commends the noble births of Creusa and her ancestors, 237–40, 262–3, 267–82, 619–20, but calls her a "foreign woman" (1221) when he accuses her of murder, and fears discovering that his true parents are low-born: 1382–4; 1473–6.
105 Wolff (1965) 175; Loraux (1993) 205–7. Rabinowitz (1993) 207–8 discusses the darker side of autochthony, while Hoffer (1996) considers violence central to this play, reflecting the inherent violence of the Athenian empire. But such violence remains at its edges and even Apollo will be largely forgiven by his victims: Wolff (1965) 177. Walsh (1978) 305–10 argues that the play consistently undermines the characters' obsession with rigid purity, racial and otherwise, as good comes out of bad and relationships shift from friendly to hostile and back again in an unstable world.
106 Cole (1997) 88; Bremmer (1997) 12. The claim will have especial appeal to any Ionian spectators: Swift (2008) 28.
107 Loraux (1993) 209–10; Rabinowitz (1993) 219–22. Wassermann (1940) exonerates Apollo from all criticism. Conacher (1959) usefully summarizes previous judgements: for more recent bibliography, see also Swift (2008) 106 n.1.

108 Lefkowitz (1989).
109 For a full discussion see Sonnino (2010) 27–34, who prefers an early date.
110 Collard and Cropp (2008) 362–401; O'Connor-Visser (1987) 148–76; Cropp (1995) 148–94; Sonnino (2010) 133–8 offers a speculative reconstruction of the plot.
111 The play emphasizes that he is Thracian and thus barbarian: Gotteland (2001) 161–5. His nationality reflects the history of the Persian Wars, but older stories make Eumolpus an Eleusinian: Calame (2011) 12–13; Parker (1987) 200–4. On the popular tragic theme of child, and especially girl, sacrifice to preserve the city, see Burkert (1983) 64–6; Allan (2001) 164–6; Larson (1995) 101–10.
112 Dem. 60.8, 27; Lycurg. *Leocr.* 98–104; Pl. *Mx.* 239a–b; Isoc. 4.68, 12.193. The word πόλις is uttered repeatedly and the play is set in the heart of the city: Sonnino (2010) 131–3.
113 Fr.356 also affirms a preference for a small army rather than many bad men (πολλοὺς κακούς), perhaps with a nod at the plucky little Athens of the Persian Wars.
114 Collard and Cropp (2008) 364–30; Sonnino (2010) 224–7.
115 Cf. Thuc. 2.44.3; Ar. *Lys.* 589–90 takes a less sanguine view. For self-sacrifice for the city as patriotic behavior suitable for both men and women cf. p. 86 and Wilkins (1990) 179–82.
116 Above all, E. *Supp.* 575–6; Loraux (1986) 148–9, 277; Cropp (1995) 180.
117 Sonnino (2010) 119–24 (cf. 289–93) argues that fr.350, in which someone asks in ignorance about a ritual involving (apparently) sacrificial cakes, are the words of Praxithea's daughter, whom her parents deceive into being sacrificed, working from Aristides' story (*Panath.* 87) that Erechtheus' wife dressed up her daughter as for a religious festival and brought her to her father to be sacrificed. This would be a radical portrayal of the Athenian royal family in tragedy, but it must remain unproven at this time.
118 The motif derives from the story of the Cecropids: Sonnino (2010) 124, 354–6.
119 For the supplement, see Sonnino (2010) 377.
120 Technically daughters of a Spartan immigrant rather than Erechtheids, but they too sacrificed themselves for Athens (Apollod. 3.15.8): Sonnino (2010) 90–100.
121 For the aetiologies contained in this prophecy, see Collard and Cropp (2008) 396–7; Wilkins (1993) xxiv. Raaflaub (2007) 16–17 and (2001) 326.
122 Collard and Cropp (2008) 398–9; Calame (2011) 3; Sonnino (2010) 395–7.
123 Sonnino (2010) 402–6.
124 O'Connor-Visser (1987) 177–80.
125 As well as the Hyacinthidae with whom Erechtheus' daughters are identified here, King Codrus (Lycurg. *Leocr.* 84–7)) and the daughters of Leos (Paus.1.5.2, D.S. 17.15.2) are other Athenians who gave up their lives for Athens.
126 E.g. Wilkins (1990) 189; Collard and Cropp (2008) 367: *contra* Sonnino (2010) 110–19, 342–3, 351–2.
127 Gotteland (2001) 165; Calame (2011) 4.
128 Calame (2011) 6–8, who notes the importance of the deictics, 5–6, 35, 52, which blur mythical and contemporary Athens: compare A. *Eum.* 834, 852, 884, 890, 902, 915. On tragedy's emphasis on the nobility of military self-sacrifice for the common good and its relationship to contemporary Athens, see also Christ (2006) 65–87.
129 Cf. Phanodemos FGrH 325 F4 and Philochorus FGrH 328 F12 with Burkert (1983) 65–6.
130 For a fuller discussion of the two Hippolytus plays, see Mills (1997) 186–221, partly superseded by the publication of a fragmentary *Hypothesis* of the lost *Hippolytus* (P. Mich, inv. 6222A): Luppe (1994) and (2003); Hutchinson (2004); Kannicht (2004) 459–75; van Rossum-Steenbeek (2003); Magnani (2004).
131 As is also suggested for the lost play: P. Mich. Inv. 6222A fr.C, l. 4 mentions Trozen. I continue to believe, against Gibert (1997) and some others (cf. Kannicht (2004) 460), that the lost play is the earlier of the two: cf. van Rossum-Steenbeek (2003) 17.

132 The *Hypothesis* of Aristophanes of Byzantium claims that the extant play "put right" what was "unseemly and blameworthy"; in the other play. Collard and Cropp (2008) 467–8; Barrett (1964) 11, 30–1 with fr.428, 430, 421, 433, 435; Ar. *Ran.* 1043, 1052–4, *Thesm.* 491–8.
133 P. Mich. Inv. 6222A fr.A 7 appears to mention Thessaly, Peirithous' home: cf. *TGrF* V, 465.
134 Mills (1997) 203–4. Plut. *Mor.* 27f–28a states that the Phaedra of the fragmentary play tried to justify her love with an appeal to Theseus' own sexual transgressions.
135 Gregory (1991) 62–3; Carter (1986) 52–6. He is an ἀπράγμων, detached from the vigour and enthusiasm for πόνοι that are praised as Athenian in other tragedies discussed here, though he is not merely an anti-Athenian type: Barrett (1964) 173.
136 In the other play, she kills herself only after the truth is revealed, making her considerably more culpable: Apollod. *Epit.* 1.19; cf. Asclepiades (*FGrH* 12F28) with Collard and Cropp (2008) 467–8.
137 It is not certain but possible that in the other *Hippolytus*, he used the third curse (Σ Hipp. 46; Sen *Ph.* 944: Mills (1997) 213–14. Collard and Cropp (2008) 470, 486–9 ascribe fr.953f also to the lost Hippolytus play and if so, Hippolytus' exile featured in this one as well.
138 ὦ θεοί, Πόσειδον, ὡς ἄρ' ἦσθ' ἐμὸς πατὴρ ὀρθῶς.
139 Raaflaub (2001) 334–9; Croally (1994) 12, cf. 253.
140 Van Erp Taalman Kip (1987).
141 Sparta is as likely a target for those who wished to see it as such: Roisman (1987) 46–7.
142 *Tro.* 34, 250, 869; cf. 133, 1110–13; compare E. *Andr.* 29, 128, 209, 486. On the way that the play "blocks" identification between Athens and Helen, see Rosenbloom (2006b) 248–9.
143 Roisman (1987) 43–7, who suggests that Euripides shared his contemporaries' excitement about Athenian designs on the western Mediterranean.
144 Roisman (1987) 42–3; cf. Westlake (1953) 190.
145 Visvardi (2011) 275–6.
146 Thuc. 2.41.4; Plut. *Per.* 28.7.
147 Cf. earlier, p. 19.
148 P. *Isthm.* 2.20; Ar. *Ach.* 640; cf. later, p. 111.
149 Sparta can be both unattractively poor as here, and luxuriously rich, as at *Andromache* 147–54.
150 Hdt. 5.32.1; Thuc. 1.95.3, 128.3, 130.1–2, 132.1; Roisman (1987) 44–7. For the corruptible Spartan in Euripides, see also Poole (1994) 19–21.
151 Green (1999). But for Cartledge (1997) 32, Euripides invites spectators to a "remarkable depth of self-scrutiny" to which he compares a radical British playwright equating the bombing of Baghdad in 1991 with Nazi bombing of London in World War II.
152 Green (1999) 101–3.

4 Aristophanic *Archē*

4.1 Comedy, truth and Athens

Comic writers want to make spectators laugh. A comic world will therefore recognizably reflect that of the audience[1] but generate humour by introducing distortions – absurdity, subversion of norms, or violation of taboos that control behaviour in normal society.[2] Aristophanic comedy is characterized by the democratic attempt to appeal to all comic preferences, from the bottom of the toilet to the peak of intellectual wit, along with a fantastic, sometimes surreal inventiveness, as men ride dung-beetles to the heavens, or dogs are tried for larcenous behaviour with cheese. Old Comedy at Athens is also marked by religious origins which encompass obscenity and invective against individuals.[3] Ridicule with phallic aggression is a venerable tradition of many religious festivals, especially those honouring Demeter and Dionysus,[4] and has important social functions. The hostility[5] that underlies such ridicule is often considered to be broadly beneficial, by enabling complaint about some aspect of life that is annoying but unpunishable, or giving voice to those whose voices are somehow marginalized.[6] For Aristotle (*Poet.* 1449a32–3) comedy represents "inferior people" and necessitates a certain "ugliness".[7] But another characteristic of Aristophanic comedy is its combination of violent ridicule, intended to raise laughter, with the offer of apparently serious advice to its audience.[8] At some moment in every play, Aristophanes claims that he teaches his spectators. In particular, his *parabases* frequently claim that following his advice will actively help them (e.g. *Ach.* 655–8), or that he has previously offered them excellent advice so deserves first prize now. These claims are partly comic,[9] but they must also have some serious point.[10] Aristophanes himself draws attention to a deliberate connection of humour and seriousness at *Ran.* 391: its author's aim is to say many funny and many serious things, and to win the prize by playfulness and mockery ("πολλὰ μὲν γέλοιά ... εἰ/πεῖν, πολλὰ δὲ σπουδαῖα / ... παίσαντα καὶ σκώψαντα νικήσαντα / ταινιοῦσθαι").

Comedy's self-aware combination of humour and sporadic earnestness makes Aristophanes' own political position almost impossible to establish,[11] and in turn offers significant challenges for any assessment of how comedy portrays Athens' power and possible Athenian reactions to that portrayal. In typical tragic structure, the hero somehow perverts the proper cosmic order and must be removed, causing suffering for those around him or her. In Aristophanic comedy, by contrast, others have violated that order, and his hero, often portrayed as uniquely sane in a mad world, must solve the problems they have caused: once he does, the play ends in rejoicing, feasting, drinking and so on. Often the deed that restores order is fantastic, but the circumstances around it – above all, a grinding war – are extremely real.[12] This combination of dramatic fantasy and political reality greatly complicates any understanding of audience reaction to Athens' portrayal on the comic stage.[13] Notoriously, Aristophanes won first prize for excoriating Cleon in the *Knights*, yet a few weeks later, Cleon was duly elected as general by largely the same body of citizens who had enjoyed Aristophanes' vicious theatrical attack on him.[14] Equally, though, the advice given to Athens at the end of the *Frogs* was apparently taken seriously, winning Aristophanes the unusual honour of a second performance.[15]

Such apparent contradictions in comedy's effects beyond the theatre may reflect the conditions in which it was performed, separate from "real life" in a theatre within a specifically festival context,[16] where invective and ridicule were traditional, and thus to an extent conventional.[17] Spectators of Old Comedy might come to expect violent abuse of those of higher social status, knowing that they could enjoy participating as spectators in the kind of speech that might bring them shame or legal trouble in a non-festival context. But once such abuse becomes conventional in comic theatre, it may lose some of the power to regulate social action in this specific context that it continues to have in the world outside the festival.[18] Thus the portrayal of Cleon in *Knights* ultimately caused him no political harm because spectators visited the theatre already primed for laughter at the abuse of their leaders. This consideration is especially important in considering Aristophanes' treatment of Athenian democracy and the empire. In tragedy, Athens is typically idealized: in Aristophanes, it is a prime target of mockery. If Cleon ultimately did not suffer from the tirades levelled against Paphlagon in the *Knights*, would Aristophanes' unflattering portrayals of Athens have engendered serious soul-searching among many Athenian spectators? Even biting satire does not necessarily represent social reality,[19] and established comic convention may take the sting even out of Aristophanes' sharpest criticisms.

Sometimes the confident, idealized Athens of the texts lurks unexpectedly underneath ostensible criticism. In *Clouds* (presented at the Dionysia in 423), the cloud chorus say that they created major celestial events to warn the Athenians not to reelect "the Paphlagonian tanner, hateful to the gods", but they took no notice. "For they say that bad judgement is in this city; but the gods turn all your mistakes to a prosperous outcome."[20] What starts as criticism turns into a stealth boast, recalling images of the idealized Athens as the city most dear to the gods, while its context in the genre of comedy, marked by conventions of abusive language on the one hand and comic fantasy on the other, deflects any serious challenge to Athens' positive self-image.[21] The prevailing belief, promoted so often in word and image, in an idealized and unassailable Athens, which *Clouds* 581–9 reflects, may mitigate any concern that there is anything seriously rotten in the state, enabling spectators to laugh at Aristophanes' criticisms without damaging their belief in the essential excellence of Athens and of themselves that they bring to the theatre:[22] thus, for example, a potentially alarming failure of democracy at the start of *Acharnians* is portrayed for laughs.[23]

An apparent counter to the argument that comic criticism and abuse had few serious effects, either for playwrights or audience, is offered by Σ Ar. *Ach.* 378, which states that in *Babylonians*,[24] performed at the Dionysia in 426 BCE, Aristophanes ridiculed the allotted and elected offices and Cleon: Cleon then indicted him or his producer for insulting the people.[25] In *Acharnians*, performed at 425's Lenaea, Aristophanes claims that Cleon dragged him into the council chamber and shouted at him, accusing him of mocking and abusing the city in front of foreigners.[26] Fragments of *Babylonians* are scanty: Dionysus was arrested in it (fr.75) and approached by Athenian demagogues hoping to be bribed (75; 68): fr.84 also connects demagogues and bribery. This is unflattering to the demagogues but in the context of other Aristophanic plays, does not seem outrageously offensive.[27] The Babylonians of the title are probably the chorus, whether or not they were eastern followers of Dionysus.[28] Most commentators state that they were enslaved and thrown into a mill, while fr.71 compares "those from the mill" with the "many-lettered Samians". Later writers offer various interpretations of the term "many-lettered":[29] the most striking is that it refers to the branding of rebel Samians by the Athenians after they had crushed Samos' revolt in 440–39.[30] Joking about an act of physical violence on rebellious subjects is certainly unpleasant but arguably no more so than joking about starving Melians (*Av.* 186). Some commentators therefore go further, arguing that the branded slave chorus was somehow identified with Athens' oppressed allies and that Cleon's anger was aroused by Aristophanes' exposure of Athenian abuses of power:[31] unfortunately, the fragments as we have them cannot offer unequivocal proof of this claim. Still, the connection of the Athenians as office-holders and politicians, a political embarrassment in front of strangers and the Dionysia, remains intriguing. Perhaps some kinds of comic comment on Athens did have a dimension of seriousness: [Xen.] *Ath. Pol.* 2.18 says that the people forbade criticism of ordinary people, only allowing the rich to be pilloried,[32] and if the ancient commentator who mentions Cleon's lawsuit had read the play and is right that it targeted all sorts of office-holders, even minor ones, attacks on such people, as well as Cleon, might have aroused the ire of the so-called people's watchdog (*Eq.* 1017–9, 1023–4). It remains odd, though, that the thinly disguised character of Paphlagon and the unflatteringly portrayed Demos in *Knights* were less offensive than what *Babylonians* supposedly claimed about Athenian politics. Perhaps what was said was less important than where it was said, and different conventions applied to comedy presented at the Dionysia from those at the Lenaea,[33] at which comedy was performed from the late 440s on. At the Dionysia, Athens was on display to non-Athenian visitors,[34] but the Lenaea took place before the main sailing season and its audience contained fewer non-citizens (Ar. *Ach.* 502–3). The political tone of the Lenaea plays, *Acharnians*, *Knights*, and to a lesser extent *Wasps*, is somewhat different from that of Dionysia plays such as *Peace* and *Birds*. Their humour relies on more specific knowledge of Athens than does that of the more broadly based comic ideas of

Birds and others, and they are arguably more directly critical of Athens than are the Dionysia plays.[35] Among "family", the tone of comic discourse was perhaps different from the show put on at the Dionysia, although the demands of the genre mean that Athens could never entirely avoid comic ridicule. Since contemporary Athens is central to comedy, Athens' idealized image, so important in motivating Athenian attitudes and actions, can itself be an object of comedy, and even in the grimy comic Athens, the ideal city will intermittently be visible, even amid all the distortions that the genre of comedy performs on it.

4.2 Remnants of the ideal

Though they shared a largely common audience,[36] Aristophanes presents a very different world from that of tragedy or funeral speeches. The texts and art which portrayed an idealized Athenian power justified by innate Athenian virtues were highly appealing to the Athenians: they were created by, and in turn shaped, the Athenians' self-image in the broader Greek world. Comedy subverts that self-image and mocks Athenian pride in it.[37] Athens is no longer the "education of Greece", or the generous benefactor of the world through the Eleusinian mysteries, no longer the eternally just city of law which even gave laws to the rest of Greece. In comedy's mirror image, it is the city of corrupt litigiousness,[38] foolish, bellicose, materialistic and greedier for eels, pretty girls and wine than for the nectar of philosophy or saving suppliants.

The idealized Athens influences comic Athens, but it is warped in various ways through comedy's distorting mirror. First, Aristophanes frequently relies for comic effect on nostalgia for the "good old days" when Athens was supposedly better,[39] and references to those days are frequently expressed in ways that recall the *epitaphioi* and other idealizing texts. Second, a consistent theme of such texts is that Athens' excellences justify Athenian power and their premises actually underlie Old Comedy in multiple and somewhat surprising ways, above all in Aristophanes' consistent assumption that the Athenian people deserve benefits from the city's power, even if the reality is marred by the predations of Cleon and others. The idealized Athens is a city burdened by principled military action for others. Comedy, with its preference for the shameful and the distorted to elicit laughs from the audience, turns the contemporary Athens of the Peloponnesian War into quite the opposite, but the comic Athens retains a relationship with the ideal Athens.[40] Either contemporary Athens has deviated from an ideal which still remains possible if they could just eject useless politicians and return to the fantasy of pre-War perfection, or belief in the ideal Athens explains uncritical assertions that the people deserve the political and economic power arising from the empire.

Aristophanes' Athens partly recalls that of Thucydides, who rejects its claims to moral superiority and portrays idealized descriptions as ultimately deluded. Both present a consistently unflattering portrayal of Cleon,[41] but Aristophanes' claims, unlike Thucydides', are framed by the conventions of comedy in which abuse, fantasy and the festival setting mark off what is said in the theatre from life outside it. A framework in which ridicule and condemnation are expected may, as argued above, temper criticism of Athens or of its people, especially if they brought to the theatre a deeply held sense of their city's basic excellence. The privilege of the fool is to make statements that can always be qualified as "just comic" in a way that similar statements in the assembly, the court or the history book cannot be.[42]

As I will discuss in Chapter 6, Thucydides strips away the justifications of Athenian power contained in idealizing material to reach what he sees as the truths that underlie them. In comic mode, Aristophanes mocks the Athenians for a susceptibility to flattery that is closely connected with images of the idealized Athens. In particular, parts of the parabasis of the *Acharnians* (628–64, esp. 628–45) recall the image of Athens that emerges from idealizing sources, even as Aristophanes distorts them. Here, the Athenians are described as ταχυβούλους and μεταβούλους (630–2), "swiftly thinking" and "changing their minds": speed and intellectual versatility are typical of the ideal Athens,[43] but such traits are characterized less favourably here, as indicating an inability to fix on good decisions, which is connected with excessive enjoyment of flattery from foreigners[44] (as χαυνοπολῖται, 635),[45] who can easily get whatever they want out of Athens by calling it "violet-crowned" (ἰοστέφανοι) and "shining" (λιπαραί). The first of these terms is an honorific dating back to a poem by Pindar which praised the Athenians for their service in the Persian Wars,[46] a time when the foundations of the idealized Athenian self-image that underpinned the drive to Athenian imperial power were being laid. Aristophanes ridicules the Athenians' allegedly ecstatic responses to these epithets, claiming that they made them "sit on the tips of their little buttocks" (638), and that "shining", another quintessential Athenian epithet, with both a literal and a metaphorical dimension, is an epithet fit merely for sardines (640).[47] Both Thucydides and Aristophanes question the overidealized image of Athens, but for Thucydides, Athens appears irredeemable. In Aristophanes, the ideal still seems possible, and he frequently invokes an older generation, especially those who fought at Marathon, as ideal Athenians to whom contemporary Athens could still aspire,[48] if only different people were in charge. Marathon is perfect for nostalgically imagining an idealized past because it is the world of Aristophanes' grandfather, distant, but not completely out of reach.[49] The clearest example of such nostalgic fantasies comes at the end of *Knights* where Demos is cleaned up so that he lives in – and, now that he understands the toxic effects of demagoguery on him/the city, lives up to – the traditional description of "noble, shining violet-crowned Athens" (1330), precisely those adjectives which Aristophanes mocks in *Acharnians*. The humorous framework makes the ideal distant, but it still exists.

4.3 *Wasps*

All of Aristophanes' plays commend peace,[50] with its benefits of abundance and leisure, but he never recommends relinquishing the empire, the primary cause of the war.[51] The tough old soldier chorus of the *Wasps* mentions the capture of Naxos

(355) without any apparent regret, even though Thucydides 1.98.4 considers it the first sign of Athenian overreach. Philocleon and his fellow jurors actively enjoy their city's power, both in the courts, which bring them status, material rewards and even pleasure in watching defendants squirm in court,[52] and over Greece itself (518, 576). Philocleon makes no claims to the justice of the idealized Athens[53] but rather considers his happy status as that of a king (549), and even Zeus (620; cf. 639–41). Any criticism he and the Athenians might face for exploiting their subjects is filtered through Cleon, the "voracious whale" (34–6; cf. 1031–5) who is accused of exploiting the people of Athens as much as the allies, and spectators are shown an Athenian people who are victims (595–6) deceived by one politician as repellent as he is powerful.[54] Bdelycleon himself inveighs against Cleon's greed, not the empire itself, by adding up all the income the city receives from the various contributions of the allies (655–62; cf. 518–20). What did the audience think when they heard his (wildly exaggerated) financial and territorial claims of nearly 2000 talents in tribute and 1000 tributary cities from the Black Sea to Sardis (700–7)?[55] From the agonistic perspective of the ancient world, such dominance might have seemed impressive and admirable, but Bdelycleon's further calculation, that of the nearly 2000 talents Athens receives, just 150 come to the jurors (663–4), and worse, even the allies scorn the people for their gullibility and instead lavish a delicious list of imperial delights on the city's leaders (676–7),[56] is designed to stimulate hostility to Cleon and others for tossing them mere scraps (672) of the vast rewards that should be entirely theirs. The fruits of empire are not immoral, but the greed of Athens' leaders is: if the allies are their victims, so are ordinary Athenians. Moreover, some of the language of these accusations against Cleon and the rest echoes that of the *epitaphioi*. Bdelycleon states that those who have laboured by land and sea receive nothing for their pains: the phrases "by land and sea" (πολλὰ μὲν ἐν γῇ πολλὰ δ' ἐφ' ὑγρᾷ, 678) and "πολλὰ πονήσας" (685) recall texts recounting Athens' efforts on behalf of the rest of Greece.[57] The topos of reward for virtue is central to Athenian imperial mentality: the empire is deserved because of Athens' efforts on behalf of Greece, and here, Bdelycleon argues that imperial plenty should enable those who fought at Marathon to receive what they deserve in the form of the comforts that Cleon and his ilk are in fact wresting from them (707–11).[58] Similar claims are made by the chorus, whose old age links them with the idealized Athens: at 1075–1121 they reminisce about the prowess and hard work by which they defeated barbarians (1078–90), and ascribe the consequent power and excellence of Athens to their Attic autochthony (1078, 1090).[59] Their past achievements in crushing the Persians and being "most responsible" for acquiring the tribute mean that they deserve, but are not receiving, significant benefits from that tribute.[60] They express great displeasure at being at the mercy of greedy young men who take benefits they do not deserve (1114–21; cf. 1139, 1187–9.)[61] The complaints of Aristophanes' characters are comic fantasy but reflect some social reality as well: most people tend to believe that they deserve more for their efforts than they are given. Here, comic resolution is found at the end of the play, where the reformed Philocleon will finally renounce Cleon and the rest (1224ff.).

4.4 *Acharnians*

Of all of Aristophanes' plays, *Acharnians* has one of the closest relationships with contemporary life and at first glance seems to express strong anti-war sentiment. What might a man from Acharnae, who had borne the brunt of Spartan attacks for several years (Thuc. 2.19–21.3), think of a play in which a farmer much like himself makes his own private peace with Sparta and regains all the pleasures of pre-War life while refusing them to others for not having supported peace? Did it cause him to wonder whether this draining war was worth the lives and resources it had already squandered?[62] Or did he enjoy Aristophanes' humour, acknowledge that times were hard now but expect a time when he too would enjoy peace again, because surely Athens' loss was unthinkable, in spite of the war's already alarming length, an unimagined six years?[63] After all, Aristophanes' dramatic solution to the real crisis is funny and so preposterous that it is hard to see how it could have any actual bearing on the life of a spectator.[64] Although the chorus are at first outraged at Dikaiopolis' treachery (280–365), the context and some of the content of their outrage is clearly comic or comically exaggerated (284–5, 299–302, 320, 331–41, 351). Dikaiopolis' account of the beginning of the Peloponnesian War is also exuberantly exaggerated (515–43), and since he immediately wins over the support of one of the semi-choruses, serious political content in the dispute seems hard to find. To praise peace is not necessarily to condemn fighting a particular war,[65] and Dikaipolis' solution for himself is pure comic escapism, whose relationship to any votes on actual policy that spectators would subsequently have taken is not easy to determine. Lamachus as an authority figure can easily and enjoyably be mocked for his obsession with war,[66] but such mockery is not synonymous with wishing to end the war as such,[67] and it is the injustice of the privileges granted Lamachus and his fellows that is the play's real complaint (596–619). Moreover, blame for the war is carefully ascribed not to the Athenian people, or even corrupt politicians, but to unspecified ἀνδράρια μοχθηρά, παρακεκομμένα ("nasty little counterfeit[68] men"), who began the denunciation of Megarian goods from which the war blew up (*Ach.* 524–5). Much of the comic invention in this play – the peace treaties that taste like wines, the use of Euripides' *Telephus* – distances us from the sadder reality of the war,[69] though there is also a bellicose relish to 544–54, as Dikaiopolis imagines Athens mobilizing for a naval campaign with an "extraordinarily evocative"[70] enthusiasm that recalls images of the vigour and speed of the idealized Athens.

Points in *Acharnians* resemble certain elements in *Wasps* in allowing aspects of the idealized Athens to shine through as something desirable and even possible again. The contemporary city is far from ideal, due to such plagues as greedy politicians (65–90), but a core of virtue remains, exemplified by the Acharnian chorus who are veterans of Marathon (181). Marathon symbolizes Athens' unchanging excellence and its archetypal benefaction to the Greek world that entitles the city to power and the benefits that should flow from it.[71] But something has gone wrong with the system of reward that should obtain for those who have served the city well, and the chorus speaks on behalf of the old men who are not being properly rewarded for having made the city great (676–718; cf. 595–617).[72] Instead, they are at the mercy of clever young orators with scanty records of services to the city, who humiliate them in trials, in spite of their having toiled (συμπονήσαντα, 694) for the city at Marathon. Neither they nor the city are flourishing at present, but the ideal remains, and with new leadership, Athens might be able to regain unquestioned primacy in the Greek world owed for services previously rendered, and those who rendered those services might gain their fair share of the rewards. While Dikaiopolis' solution to Athenian political woes has no application to real life, an Athenian audience does see him finally surmount all obstacles to enjoy the abundant food, drink, leisure and sex associated with high political and social status.

The past is idealized in many forms of human communication. In the *epitaphioi*, an idealized past is used to inspire audiences to emulate the deeds of old. In comedy, the past can be used to remind audiences of better days, but the idea that things were better in the old days is also a rich source for humour. Aristophanes' half-humorous, half-admiring characterization of older men is difficult for moderns fully to grasp. Though the choruses of *Wasps* and *Acharnians* represent an ideal, their cranky old ways of these tough old gentlemen rather past their prime (e.g. *Ach*. 219–22) can also provide laughs: the audience can laugh at them while also finding them sympathetic and admirable because they represent a noble ideal.[73] By contrast, Lamachus represents the unjustly privileged of the city against whom the underdog hero (whose general appeal is evident) stands firm (595–619). One can imagine the audience's vindictive pleasure[74] both at the discomfiture of a representative of the political and military elite being denied delicious thrushes and eels (966–70) by Dikaiopolis, and at the contrasts between Dikaiopolis' "expedition" to the priest of Dionysus' house with all its peacetime pleasures of food and sex (1089–93) and Lamachus' miserable provisions for war – ostrich plumes in a helmet versus delicious pigeon meat, locusts instead of thrushes (1105–17) – as well as his eventual fate keeping watch for Boeotian plunderers in the cold with a broken ankle while Dikaiopolis lives it up indoors (1071–227).

Abundance of resources from multiple places is a boast of the Athenian empire[75] and Dikaiopolis represents the drive to acquire them. When the play begins, he laments the deprivation that war has imposed on him by forcing him out of his deme. When he takes the solution to his problem into his own hands, he represents what might be called the natural Athenian order of things, and the chorus comment (978) "all good things come to him of their own accord" as they see everything (cf. 874–5, 878–80) that his individual treaty brings him.[76] Dikaiopolis displays an impressive greed and longing for good things for himself,[77] and this confident greed reflects something of the spirit of Athens' relationship with the allies, as it lays claim to their resources for its own benefit.[78] Aristophanes does not appear to condemn him for such instincts, and we are clearly meant to cheer him on (as the chorus does, 836–41) when he refuses to share his pleasures with Lamachus. Abundance of food, especially in lists of food, is both comic[79] and imperial:[80] Eupolis fr.330 connects Athens' abundance with its reverence for the gods, and the economic privileges of the ideal Athens both result from Athenian power and act as its justification. The emphasis on feasting at the end of plays like *Acharnians*, *Knights* and even *Lysistrata* symbolizes a reversion to proper order in many different ways, including the "natural" order where Athens can offer its citizens abundance through living up to its idealized reputation once more.

4.5 *Knights*

While Aristophanes does not seek to condemn Dikaiopolis, the "little man" for seeking every material pleasure, the demagogues – no friends of the people, whatever they claim – are the target of his most violent abuse.[81] In Aristophanes' *Knights* (Lenaea, 425), the Athenians are characterized as Demos, an old, bad-tempered gentleman languishing in the clutches of the disgusting flatterer slave Paphlagon, a thinly veiled portrait of Cleon (42–57), who will be ousted by the Sausage-Seller, who outdoes him in excessive pandering to Demos. Paphlagon, the loud-voiced,[82] corrupting influence on the people, is relentlessly abused for devouring public funds,[83] harassing magistrates and the rich and timid with lawsuits to line his pockets, while grovelling to the people/Demos.[84] He is condemned for his predatory approach to the tribute, but again the tribute *per se* is not the problem, but rather his relentless exploitation of citizens and allies alike for his own profit. Rapacity towards the allies is condemned, but in the context of the greed of the leaders (797–804): the benefits of empire and Athenian dominance as such are not considered wrong.[85] But in spite of the imperfections of the individual Demos, the play also expresses pride in the bigger picture of Athenian power. At *Eq.* 163–76 Demosthenes shows the Sausage-Seller its manifestations: the market, the harbours and the Pnyx, the ports, islands and merchant ships, claiming that an oracle states that all these πέρναται ("will be administered/sold") one day by the Sausage-Seller. He even points even as far as Caria and Carthage, on which Hyperbolus apparently had designs: later in the play, at 1300–15, an old trireme is imagined rejecting outright his plans to sail there with 100 of her sisters. Plans to control the Western Mediterranean and beyond were expressed in public discourse at Athens at various times,[86] but here, it is expansionism promoted by a detestable demagogue that seems to be condemned:[87] elsewhere, the play seems more favourable to Athenian expansion. The chorus (838–40) prophesies with apparent approval that the Sausage-Seller will become the greatest in the land, controlling the city and ruling the allies, and while the Sausage-Seller condemns Paphlagon's prophecy that Demos is to rule all of Greece, giving verdicts in Arcadia itself for the princely sum of five obols a day (797–809), his condemnation rests on Paphlagon's despicable character rather than on a general condemnation of Athenian domination.

The chorus of knights embodies an alternative vision of Athens. Although they are rich young aristocrats, not the old, non-elite men of *Wasps* or *Acharnians*, they resemble them in their special association with the older Athens. Their identity derives from being sons of fathers who served Athens well,[88] and they invoke their fathers' excellence and willingness to fight on land and sea,[89] successfully and altruistically,[90] unlike the self-interested contemporary youths (575–6). Like some other broadly admirable Aristophanic characters, they are comic too, pleading to retain their long hair and tiaras if ever peace comes and the πόνοι stop (578–80), but they promise to defend the land and the gods selflessly and there is no moral equivalency between them and Paphlagon as they invoke Athena, goddess of the ideal Athens, as τῆς ἱερωτάτης ἁπασῶν / πολέμῳ τε καὶ ποιηταῖς / δυνάμει θ' ὑπερφερούσης / μεδέουσα χώρας ("ruling over the most sacred of all lands, outstanding in war, poetry and power", 582–5). They also represent an idealized alliance of all social classes against Cleon, with no division between sailors and hoplites, hinting at the idealized, unified city of the *epitaphioi*.[91] Poseidon is god of horses, and the knights' patron, but he also loves triremes (550–5), while at 595–610, which recalls an engagement fought at Corinth (Thuc. 4.42–5), Aristophanes assimilates the knights' horses to sailors. This marvellous image blends comic surrealism with an underlying seriousness in encapsulating a socially united and successful past that Athens can still regain if the awful Paphlagon and his like are renounced.[92]

Aristophanes portrays the undignified relationship between Demos and the politicians unsparingly. Paphlagon and the Sausage-Seller both woo Demos with extravagant claims of eternal devotion and concern which depend on extortion from the public accounts (e.g. 763–72, 1030–4). From 1163 to 1223, each makes grander and grander promises to the "tyrant" (1114) Demos,[93] until at the climax of the competition, the Sausage-Seller reveals that his basket is empty because he has given Demos everything, while Paphlagon's is revealed to contain a splendid cake for himself with just a tiny slice reserved for Demos (1209–25). What did the Athenian audience – the *demos* – think of this sordid *erastes-eromenos* relationship? Aristophanes' wild exaggeration is obviously intended to make them laugh, but his portrayal of the *demos* as Demos is also quite insulting. The charge (715–8) that Paphlagon chews Demos' food before he gives it to him, so that he gets three times as much as Demos, recalls Aristophanes' frequently stated claim that the people are exploited by their leaders, but Aristophanes also seems to blame those same people for political naïveté (752–5) and willingness to accept cheap scraps and wild promises (642–63; cf. 682). Throughout much of the play, the Sausage-Seller plays along with Paphlagon (773–85, 871–911, 1163–215), while attempting to expose his dysfunctional relationship with Demos. Demos is too easily seduced (788–9; cf. 751–5) while Paphlagon is corrupt and exploitative and does not "love" Demos at all (732, 792–7; 823–35; cf. 1340–1). At 1111–50 Demos claims, not entirely convincingly, that in fact he controls the demagogues, rather than being their victim, by letting them "feed" him and then fattening them up to destroy them. Neither side comes out with any glory, and this squalid relationship takes us very far from the *epitaphioi*.

And yet, Demos is a veteran of Marathon and Salamis (781–5), in spite of his current plight. Though Aristophanes dismisses the battle of Marathon as merely something about which Athens talks loudly (and by implication incessantly,

782),[94] the last part of the play traces a gradual return to the Athens of the *epitaphioi*, partly through a series of oracles (1000–1100). It is not a linear process because oracles are inherently ambiguous both in their language and interpretations, and here, Aristophanes' oracles refer through a comic filter both to Paphlagon's misdeeds and to the idealized Athens. At 1011–13, Demos wishes to hear his favourite, the one "about me becoming an eagle among the clouds."[95] This oracle, which refers to an apparently genuine proclamation from Delphi,[96] is eventually capped by the grander, invented prophecy by the Sausage-Seller that Demos will rule over the earth, over the Red Sea and in Ecbatana, licking cakes dotted with pickle (1088–9). Though such oracles in their grandeur and number are plainly ridiculous (cf. 801–4, 961–5), their connection with the attested oracle glorifying Athens and their commendation of Athenian expansionism is significant, suggesting that such promises of expansion were part of public discourse on Athenian power. In the context of this comedy, they are also significant because the Sausage-Seller not only uses Paphlagon's oracular tricks against him to win the contest for Demos' favour, but his prophecies of Athenian glory are in a sense fulfilled as Athens is finally cleansed of corruption and at least partly restored to the excellence of the idealized Athens. At 1316, Demos appears, rejuvenated and handsome, dressed in traditional clothes (1331),[97] and is said to dwell in the ancient, violet-crowned Athens (1323, 1327–9)[98] of Aristides and Miltiades. The description of "shining, violet-crowned" Athens that was mocked in the *Acharnians* for seducing the Athenians is now fully endorsed (1329–30). Though Demos smells of peace libations (1331), such a peace will not require the price of compromise with Sparta, since Demos is to be monarch of Athens and even of Greece (1330), keeping intact a purified Athenian empire, worthy of its deeds at Marathon (1333–4).[99] Demos, now ashamed of his former gullibility, is absolved for having been deceived by Paphlagon (1355–7), whose only punishment is to be required to become a sausage-seller (1395–401), as befits Athens' image as the city of moderation.

4.6 *Peace*

Peace, performed at 421's Dionysia, promotes generally panhellenic and actively anti-war sentiments, which are natural in the play's chronological context, just before the Peace of Nicias was ratified.[100] Athens and Sparta are blamed equally for the war, but particular blame is placed on the two conveniently dead "pestles", Cleon and Brasidas, rather than ordinary Athenians,[101] while the War god threatens to pulverize all the cities of Greece without distinguishing one side or another (242–52, 266). Even here, however, we find no real repudiation of Athenian imperialism, and some strikingly unsympathetic jokes about their enemies. When the statue of Peace is being pulled up, the Boeotians (464–6) and Argives (475–7) are rebuked for doing nothing to help, matching their contemporary political stances,[102] but more shocking to a modern ear is the dismissive portrayal of the Megarians, who are "doing nothing" because they are starving (483).[103] The references to Megarian hunger will be echoed in *Av.* 186 (414 BCE), which jokes about Melian hunger caused by Athens' siege of the island: here, even Thucydides' outrage at Athenian violence, let alone glorifications of Athens as the city of eternal mercy to the oppressed, seems very distant.[104] Hermes' crack at Athens (503–7) for doing nothing to help but spending all the time in litigation, and his advice to "withdraw a little towards the sea", that is, abandon ambitions for power on land, seems mild in comparison. Aristophanes keeps the people of Athens largely free from blame for the original disappearance of peace. Hermes' account of the origin of the Peloponnesian War first blames prominent men such as Pheidias and Pericles (605–6), but then the allies or "cities which you rule" (619) are blamed for trying to bribe Sparta to help them because they feared the tribute.[105] Those Spartans, being greedy and treacherous to outsiders (623), standard Spartan characterizations,[106] then threw out Peace and embraced war. Of course, if the allies fear the tribute, then Athenian imperialism *is* an important cause of war, but the emphasis on Spartan failings helps to obscure Athens' responsibility for Greek turmoil, especially since any blame that could clearly be attached to Athens is placed upon the demagogues, notably the dead Cleon, who enriched themselves at the expense of the poor (635–6) and the allies. Once more, even if the allies are oppressed, so are all the poor who sit in the audience.[107] Peace, interpreted by Hermes, directly condemns the Athenians for refusing Spartan overtures after Pylos (665–7), and Trygaeus acknowledges that Athens was wrong, but, as he says, "our brains were in our shoe-leather", referring to Cleon's frequently reviled trade as a tanner:[108] once again, a man dead for three years is blamed for Athens' misfortunes and misdeeds. Once Peace has returned, Trygaeus longingly imagines an agora filled with all the good things, especially from Megara and Boeotia, that war has taken from Athens and that will now return (999–1005), but even in this moment of reconciliation, hints of its potential fragility remain through the figure of Hierocles, who recites humorous oracular warnings of Spartan deviousness (1064–5, 1067–8) and questions the advisability of peace (1075–6, 1077–9). Trygaeus rejects him, affirming the foolishness of continuing the war and regretting what might have been in terms of shared imperial rule of Greece, had Athens behaved differently after Pylos and Sphacteria (1080–2). But even in this pacifistic ending to a pacifistic play, there is no hint that the subject cities themselves could shake off all Athenian interference: rather, Athenian pleasures can be, or might have been, retained by being willing to share power with Sparta. The mixture of joyful celebration of a coming peace, continued suspicion between Athens and Sparta and the comic fantasy of reconciliation dependent on dividing Greece up between the two cities recurs at the end of *Lysistrata* (1112–77.)[109]

4.7 *Birds*

No consensus exists on whether Aristophanes wrote *Birds* as a cautionary tale about Athenian imperialism, or whether it is essentially a comic fantasy.[110] The play recounts the adventures of two Athenians, Peisetairos and Euelpides, who abandon Athens to start afresh in the kingdom of the birds. Ultimately, however, they can only recreate a kind of Athens: the new city is given Athens' familiar epithet of "shining" (λιπαρόν, 826),[111] and at first Euelpides suggests Athena Polias as its patron goddess (826–8). *Prima facie*, this plot could be as much a comic amplification of the old adage, "wherever you go, there you are" as any critique of Athenian imperialism.[112] Its structure is typical of Aristophanic comedies in portraying the frustrations of the little man and his eventual triumph, but with a significant difference. At first, the pair simply want to leave Athens for a place not greater but more pleasant (124), free of the stereotypical litigiousness and busyness of their home town (40–4, 109–10)[113] – and a place where they do not owe money (115–6). But almost at once, far from remaining one of the "little people", Peisetairos sees opportunities in the new city and shares them with the peaceable birds:[114] already at 181–97, he suggests a plan for the birds to force the gods to pay tribute to them, a scheme that will come to fruition later in the play. They acknowledge him as a talented rhetorician (317), and as befits his name, he is brilliantly persuasive, by stirring up keen longing among the birds for the time when supposedly they, rather than the gods, ruled the earth (465–539).[115] Like Aristophanes himself in *Knights* or *Wasps*, Peisetairos recalls an idealized Golden Age, to which the present compares unfavourably (523–39).[116] It proves a seductive vision for the birds, whose chorus immediately lament their forefathers' inability to transmit their honours to them (540–3),[117] and they accept Peisetairos as their saviour (547). He promises (586–626) that men who acknowledge the power of the birds will acquire all sorts of blessings from them, some realistic but others absurdly extravagant, such as the promise that birds can add 300 years to human lives (606–8): his wilder promises resemble those of the demagogues of whom Aristophanes complained in earlier plays.[118] Like the Athenians after the Persian Wars,[119] the birds strive for as much power as they can get when Peisetairos offers such exciting opportunities. They are instantly persuaded to see the gods as rivals (630–8) and at 637–8 offer their ῥώμη in exchange for the γνώμη of Peisetairos.[120] The play consistently claims that the birds bring many blessings and deserve worship (e.g. 708–36, 1058–70). At 1102–18, in the context of the usual appeal to the judges for the first prize, they promise multiple avian benefits if the prize is theirs, but copious bird-droppings for the opposite: like Athens, they will favour the "deserving" and punish the "wicked". Once encouraged by Peisetairos (550–69), the nascent avian empire builds walls with vigour and efficiency. *Av*. 1133–5 emphasizes that they need no help from anyone:[121] "The birds, no one else, no Egyptian brickmaker or stonemason or carpenter was there, but just the birds with their own hands built it." The portrayal of the unified joint effort of tens of thousands of birds (1136–41), their ingenuity (1144–6, 1155), the sound of preparation like a dockyard (1157), and its extraordinary speed (1164–5) is reminiscent of the characterization of post-Persian War Athens, especially the building of the Themistoclean wall. With the wall comes a powerful and well-organized military force (1179–81) with which they can blockade the gods and maximize their own power and plenitude (555–69, 1060–71). A once quiet community takes, like ducks to water, to *polypragmosyne*, assuring their own prosperity by externally directed belligerence and imperial longing,[122] based on reclaiming what was once (supposedly) theirs and what they (supposedly) deserve. There are certainly some apparent parallels here with some ideological currents in Athens that this book has discussed, especially the ancestral, "right" and "natural" sovereignty of the birds which recalls Athenian claims based on autochthony and the attraction to a Golden Age.

Though Nephelokokkygia was intended as a utopian city, a non-litigious Athens, neither the city itself nor those who visit it can be other than what they have tried to leave behind. An indigent poet appears the moment that the city is dedicated (905–54), followed by an oracle-monger (959–91) who even describes the new city as an Athenian-style "eagle in the clouds" (977–8; cf. *Eq.* 1011–13). He is followed by Meton (992–1020) the town-planner, while at 1035, a decree-seller brings new laws on weights and measures (1040). There is no peace here, nor is it even possible to avoid Athenian power. At *Av.* 145, Tereus had suggested founding the new city by the Red Sea, but Peisetairos demurred, in case Athenian law might actually extend there one day. Now his fears prove justified as a sleek Athenian visiting commissioner (1021) comes to Nephelokokkygia to investigate and report.[123] When Peisetairos offers him his pay, he is happy to accept it without working for it (1027) but runs away when Peisetairos tries to "pay" him with blows (1034), returning at 1046 to indict Peisetairos for outrage against him.

The play offers a comic exploration of imperial expansion, but whereas Aristophanes uses comedy to condemn unequivocally the demagogues of Athens in plays like *Knights* and *Wasps*, condemnation of Athenian *polypragmosynē* is not so clear here. The new city greets the goddess Iris aggressively, accusing her of illegal immigration (1199–223). When she asserts the gods' traditional power and warns of their anger, Peisetairos threatens preposterous violence against them via his winged comrades and even threatens to rape her. In the *Clouds*, Socrates was burned to death for milder impiety (1503) than this. But Nephelokokkygia remarkably suffers no ill-effects at all.[124] Instead, the new city is highly successful, attracting many would-be citizens. After a comically fulsome address to Peisetairos, 1271–3, a herald reports that this most famous city (1277) has many suitors (*erastai*, 1279)[125] wanting to live there bird-style: no wonder, since it contains some stereotypically ideal Athenian qualities of wisdom, desire, the Graces and peace.[126] Earlier in the play, Peisetairos had sent unwanted visitors packing, and now he successfully repels a parricide, the dithyrambic poet Cinesias, and an informer (1410–69) who wants wings to carry out his despicable trade: he does not welcome them but keeps his city clean of them. Even more success comes with the news that the birds' blockade on the gods has worked (1515–24): they are starving and send a deputation to treat with their new masters. To these divine ambassadors, Peisetairos continues to use his persuasive power, claiming that the gods will benefit from restoring the power currently held by Zeus to the birds (1606–26), since they will improve terrestrial morality by punishing humans for transgressions which now the gods cannot see or remedy. He also asks for Basileia (1634–5), the ultimate prize, following advice given to him earlier by Prometheus, the gods' eternal opponent (1534–5, 1543, 1547).[127] Eventually every divine ambassador, even Poseidon, is talked into accepting his terms (1683–4) and the play ends, in standard comic fashion, with a celebration. Here, Peisetairos will marry Basileia with Zeus' approval, and he has won supreme power (1753). The gods have lost their dominion, and all the emphasis is on the success of the birds and of Peisetairos, without any overt condemnation from Aristophanes.

I suggest that this play is shaped by a world-view in which imperial expansionism is just how the world works. Perhaps it is even how the world should work,[128] since it can be argued that *Birds* is a kind of defence of *polypragmosynē*.[129] According to Peisetairos, the birds originally lost their kingdom to the Olympians by being *apragmones*, and no Athenian (or even Athenian ally) could seriously imagine that it is better to be dominated than dominant where possible. As the play proceeds, Peisetairos' and Euelpides' initial desire for a quiet life proves impossible, given human or avian nature, since empire appears to be the natural order. If it is the natural order, it cannot really be condemned,[130] even if it is not so clear whether Aristophanes explicitly justifies imperialism and its methods.

Birds was performed at the Dionysia, to an audience of Athenian citizens and representatives of the subject cities. Having seen the power of the city of Athens paraded in glory before the play, these subjects then saw comic representatives of a city with imperial pretensions. The Athenian commissioner clearly represents Athenian *polypragmosynē*, as the non-Athenian spectators doubtless recognized, but whether they read him as an example of the Athenian jackboot or of the pettifogging official that nobody in any society has ever loved must remain open.[131] Nor is it certain that Athenian spectators would have felt embarrassment at this portrayal of Athenian officialdom: like the oracle-monger and others, the Athenian official may read as a stereotypical bureaucrat or irritation of contemporary life, like the others that plague the new city, and his role in the entire play is just 100 lines among nearly 1800 which tend in a very different direction. The praise of the charms of the new city and its popularity among prospective immigrants, combined with its relentless aggression and drive to acquire world domination, do seem to offer a clear and not completely flattering parallel with imperial Athens.[132] Moreover, certain lines point towards actively disturbing elements in the new city. At 1583–5, we learn that Peisetairos is barbecuing the birds who have rebelled against the friends of the people, evoking images of a tyrannical city. And yet, the joke is allotted just two lines, and given the Athenian passion for birds' meat of every kind, it is a very obvious quick-fire joke: Aristophanes could have emphasized Nephelokokkygia's dark side more explicitly than he does.[133] Similarly at 1225–8 Peisetairos claims, "It will be terrible if we rule others but you gods disobey and don't yet understand that you must obey the stronger in your turn."[134] A modern audience is likely to read these lines through the filter of the Melian dialogues, or to align Peisetairos the tyrannos here with Athens the tyrant city of Thuc. 2.63.2,[135] but the context is a comic conflict with Iris, and in spite of language which elsewhere would deserve punishment for its impiety, nothing bad happens to Peisetairos, who, even more than Aristophanes' other "little" men, gains everything he desires at the end of the play with no dire consequences. The *Birds* was performed just after the start of the Sicilian expedition, 415–4 BCE, in a mood of extraordinary confidence at Athens, and its plot and tone may reflect that confidence.[136]

The laugh-driven focus of comedy means that attempting to uncover Aristophanes' attitude to the Athenian empire is a challenge. Even greater is the challenge of imagining what truths his audience would have taken from his plays. That said, several clear imperially related themes do recur in Aristophanes, and these have a relationship to the Athenian mentality that I have attempted to outline in previous chapters. Ideals are not funny in themselves but can be made fun of. Aristophanes, for all his exuberant comic genius, handles the idealized Athens quite gently. While he mocks the Athenians for their pleasure in enjoying descriptions of their city which seem radically different from the grubby reality of the late fifth century, it is specifically Cleon and other prominent politicians who are the architects of that reality. On the whole, the ideal Athens, though perhaps gently mocked in the persons of the Marathonomachoi or the Knights, is still a possibility, and certainly, the city's right to power in Greece is never seriously challenged.

Notes

1 In some contrast with tragedy, which maintains distance between its world and that of its audience: Taplin (1996) 11.
2 McLeish (1980) 93; Bowie (1993a) 10–11.
3 Aristotle *Poetics* 1449 ascribes its origins to the prelude to "phallic songs". See also Handley (1985) 362–7; Reckford (1987) 444–91; Csapo (2012), esp. 26–30.
4 Burkert (1985) 104–5, 238, 244, 282. On the relationship between obscenity, ritual strife in cult and Old Comedy, see also Rosen (1988) 3–7; Henderson (1991) 1–19; Halliwell (2008) 158–206. There are limits. Athenian comedy ridicules other gods but never Athens' patron goddess: Revermann (2006a) 30.
5 Spectators derive pleasure from Old Comedy through the exposure of someone else, pleasurably gratifying their own hostile impulses, especially if that exposure is witty: Henderson (1991) 9–11; Zimmermann (2006) 13–16. The physical aggression of Aristophanic comedy is also notable: *Eq*. 247–95, *Lys*. 266–386, *Av*. 343 etc.
6 Reckford (1987) 41–2. Comic heroes are typically people of humble social status, like the majority of the spectators, who prevail over their social or political superiors in comedy's imaginary world. Comic poets never ascribe Athens' problems to ordinary, "decent" people but to elite wastrels, greedy politicians, irresponsible intellectuals and so on: Henderson (1998) 269–71.
7 Shame and laughter are linked within a privileged setting in both ritual and theatre. The deliberate obscenity of some ritual speech is a paradoxical transgression of normal religious *euphemia*, framed and protected by its religious setting and converted into worship. Old Comedy offers a parallel process, as speech which would normally be shameful is aired in a special context: Halliwell (2008) 215–16; (1991) 69–70.
8 Whitman (1964) 2–9; Henderson (1996) 85–8; Revermann (2006a) 145–59. Apte (1985) 151–76 discusses humour in the drama of preliterate societies as a source of both entertainment and education.
9 Heath (1987a) 10–12.
10 The *Life of Aristophanes* T1 ll.42–3K-A claims that when Dionysius of Syracuse wanted to study Athenian politics, Plato sent him Aristophanes. For Aristophanes' importance as evidence for Athenian popular attitudes, see Pritchard (2012).
11 Rosen (2010) 230–40. Thus for Gomme (1996), we can say nothing about Aristophanes' politics (cf. Chapman (1978)), but for De Ste Croix (1996) 44–5, he is a clear

conservative, hostile to radical democracy and the Peloponnesian War, and relatively pro-Spartan. Given the difficulties of understanding even the extant plays of Aristophanes, I will not discuss the comic fragments.
12 McLeish (1980) 60–6.
13 De Ste Croix (1996) 44 compares Aristophanes to a political cartoonist who uses humour to make a serious message more palatable, but one specific image is different from a dramatic story of 1200 lines or more. For a subtle and helpful account of how reality and unreality coexist in Aristophanes, see Ruffell (2011).
14 Heath (1987a) 5–6; Olson (2010) 42–4. Debunking authority is central to comedy, but authority is not necessarily weakened thereby, and Aristophanes' mockery of Cleon and Lamachus even after they are dead (e.g. *Pax* 47–8, 269–72) suggests that the political satire in comedy had a humorous function beyond an active attempt at influencing contemporary politics: McLeish (1980) 58; Halliwell (1993) 335–9.
15 Allan (2012) argues that the play even influenced Theramenes' failed *dokimasia*.
16 Reckford (1987) 21; Revermann (2006a) 29.
17 The legal status of free speech in Athenian comedy is murky: sources claiming that it was restricted are very late and often rely on demonstrably false assumptions (Halliwell (1991) esp. 54–7). One of the two most plausible sources, Σ *Av.* 1297 claims that the decree of Syrakosios (415/4) banned ridicule of individuals in comedy, but *Birds* itself makes this claim questionable (Sommerstein (1986) 101–4). Sommerstein (1986) and others argue that this decree was intended to ban mentioning the names of those accused in the scandal of the Mysteries, but Halliwell (1991) 59–63 discusses real difficulties both in interpreting this *scholion* and in imagining how it could have worked effectively. The only likely curb on comic free speech is the briefly valid decree of Morychides preventing public comic ridicule, c. 440, but repealed in 437 (Σ Ar. *Ach.* 67). This decree, if historical, may have been connected with the conditions of the Samian War and, like Cleon's attack on Aristophanes for embarrassing the city in *Babylonians* (see later) may have originated from Athenian concerns over relations with the allies: Halliwell (1991) 57–8, 64–5. However, the evidence for the decree is thin and late, and even if it was made law, it was valid for just four years. Given the highly combative tone of Old Comedy, if there had been serious constraints on what comedians could say about the prominent, one would have expected more accounts of complaints brought by their victims, so I agree with those who argue for a culturally sanctioned freedom of speech at comic festivals. Halliwell (2008) 243–4 even argues for a legal status for such speech through the ritual connections of comedy with αἰσχρολογία (shameful speech): cf. Halliwell (1991) 51–4; Heath (1987a) 15–18; *contra* Henderson (1998) 265–7.
18 Halliwell (2008) 246–8.
19 Olson (2002) 201.
20 *Nub.* 581–9; cf. *Lys.* 56–7 and Eupolis *Poleis* 219, which complains about Athens' choice of inferior generals, but Athens' bad choices are not ruinous, since the city is "more lucky than smart."
21 Just as tragedy may have "escape routes", so may comedy, though of a different kind. Loraux (1986) 305 contrasts the invitation of Pericles' funeral oration to Athenians to fall in love with their city, with Aristophanes' attempt to deter them from using such passionate vocabulary. Citizens in love with the city may then fall in love with themselves and be prey to destructive demagoguery. On the image of the lover of the city, compare Thuc. 2.43.1 with Ar. *Ach.* 143; *Eq.* 732–4, 1340–4; Gomme (1956) 136–7; Wohl (2002), esp. 73–113 on Aristophanes' Cleon.
22 Cf. Pritchard (2012) 42–3. Compare also the claim of [Xen.] *Ath. Pol.* 2.17 that in real life too, the people tended to reject responsibility for decisions that turned out badly; cf. Ar. *Eccl.* 193–6, 823–9.
23 Olson (2002) xlviii; cf. Heath (1987a) 12–14, esp. 13: "Aristophanes again and again devised plots which assume that Athens is in the most desperate of straits. . . . If Aristophanes really felt so desperate throughout his career, it is astonishing that he could

write such funny plays. But of course he did not; he chose to portray Athens in this unflattering light because his audience, *knowing it to be untrue* [Heath's emphasis] (for they certainly were not in the throes of despair throughout his career), laughed when he did so."

24 On *Babylonians*, see Norwood (1930); Welsh (1983); MacDowell (1995) 30–4, 43–5; Olson (2002) xxvii–xxix.
25 He might not have been formally tried. Some details in the comment suggest that the scholiast's knowledge of what happened was limited and derived from Aristophanes himself: MacDowell (1995) 43–4; for scepticism as to the historicity of the event, see Rosen (1988) 59–82 and (2010) 232–5; cf. Pelling (1999) 148–50.
26 Ar. *Ach.* 377–82, 502–6, 633–42.
27 Storey (2003) 221–2.
28 As Norwood (1930) 5; see, however, Welsh (1983) 137, 140–1.
29 Hesychius σ 150; Suda σ 77.
30 Frr.90 and 99 also refer to branded slaves. Plut. *Per.* 26.3–4 claims that both Samians and Athenians branded their enemies, partly exonerating the Athenians and entirely denying Duris of Samos' lurid accounts of Athenian abuses against the Samians (28.1–3). He also states (28.3) that on his return from Samos, Pericles gave the funeral oration, for which he won "the greatest admiration." One would love to have heard his account of the idealized Athens in that speech, especially since Ion reports that he expressed pride in taking just nine months to crush the most powerful Ionians.
31 Murray (1933) 25; Norwood (1930) argues persuasively against the claim. Welsh (1983) 143 suggests that Aristophanes compared the chorus of Babylonians, Persia's "slaves", with the allies' relationship to Athens, thereby arousing Cleon's anger. Aristophanes' claim (*Ach.* 642) that he helped Athens by showing "how the peoples in the cities are democratically ruled" (τοὺς δήμους ἐν ταῖς πόλεσιν δείξας ὡς δημοκρατοῦνται) is sometimes interpreted as evidence that *Babylonians* condemned Athens' rule over the allies, but the line has no innately sinister meaning: Norwood (1930) 2–5; cf. n.47 later.
32 Cf. Ar. *Pax* 751: Olson (2002) xxx.
33 Russo (1994) 1–4; MacDowell (1995) 16, 30–1; Revermann (2006a) 165–6; see, however, Pelling (1999) 149–50.
34 Goldhill (1997) 61; earlier, pp. 46–7.
35 McLeish (1980) 27–8; Goldhill (1987) 61.
36 Loraux (1986) 310; on the difficulties of determining the exact composition of the audience at the Dionysia, see, e.g. Ruffell (2011) 261–3. But there was a general overlap between those in the theatre and those who would attend other official functions in Athens.
37 Loraux (1986) 304; Bowie (1993a) 10–11.
38 Especially in the figure of Philocleon in *Wasps*, but also *Av.* 40–1; *Pax* 503. While the *epitaphioi* concentrate on Athens' pity and mercy, *Peace* claims that the Athenian national character was harsh: 349–50, 607, 934–6.
39 Whatever his actual political beliefs, Aristophanes' conservative stance is at least partly for humorous effect: Whitman (1964) 13; Rosen (2010) 242–3. Comic longing for a better world need not always look backwards: Crates' *Theria* imagines a future of automated tools, in which no slaves will be needed.
40 Loraux (1986) 304–5.
41 Perhaps because of shared political and social background: De Ste Croix (1954) 31–7; Rhodes (2006).
42 Henderson (1996) 68.
43 Cf. S. *OC* 886–90; Lys. 2.23, 26; Isoc. 4.87, 12.170; Hyperid. 6.24: Mills (1997) 67, 142–3, 179. For other, unflattering versions of the topos, see Thuc. 2.65.3–4, 3.38.5; Isoc. 15.19.
44 Their own orators also encouraged their pleasure in self-praise: Ober (1989) 314–24.

45 Compare Dikaiopolis' cynical response to the Thracian Sitalces' extravagant claims to love Athens, *Ach.* 141–52, even to be its ἐραστής . . . ἀληθής (143): cf. *Ach.* 370–4. MacDowell (1995) 31–3 tentatively attributes the references to Athenian flattery by foreign envoys to a scene in the *Babylonians*, but the past general conditional clauses, "κἀπειδή τις εἴποι . . . ἐκάθησθε" (637–8) and "εἰ δέ τις . . . καλέσειεν . . . ηὕρετο" (639–40) should surely refer to repeated instances of flattery, rather than a specific scene.

46 Pind. fr.76. The term could be applied to other places but became standard for Athens: Ar. *Nu.* 300, fr.112.2; Hdt. 8.77.1; E *Alc.* 452, *Tro.* 803, *IT* 1130–1: Olson (2002) 238. Pindar knew the susceptibilities of an Athenian audience even then: his poem netted him 10,000 drachmas and Athenian proxeny (Isoc. 15.166).

47 The meaning of *Ach.* 642, "showing the peoples in the city how they are democratically governed", must remain ambiguous. Sinister meaning has been imputed to the line (*contra* Norwood (1930) 5), but the causal connection between exposure of Athenian oppression of the allies (one of whose grievances was the tribute) and the lines immediately following (643–4), "That is why they will come from the cities bringing tribute to you", is unclear.

48 Loraux (1986) 304–5. *Eq.* 565–70 commends the city's forefathers for their victories on land and sea and care for the city, while Athens' triumph at Marathon is invoked (*Eq.* 781) in the context of a currently degraded people. At *Eq.* 581, Athena is invoked as ruler over "the holiest land, outstanding in war, poets and power" and she is allied with Victory; note also the lyrical description of Athens at *Nu.* 299–313. In Eupolis *Demes*, Solon, Miltiades, Aristides and Pericles all come back to help Athens, the "famous" city: on Eupolis, see especially Storey (2003).

49 Handley (1993) 418–20; cf. Loraux (1986) 307–8.

50 Comedy's exaltation of peace, and especially the importance of saving one's own skin that Dikaiopolis expresses, are connected with the comic imperative of subversion, particularly the subversion of the epitaphic ideal of dying bravely for the state: Loraux (1986) 304–6. *Acharnians* is in effect the obverse of *Heraclidae*: Goossens (1962) 219–22.

51 Olson (2010) 63–4.

52 *Vesp.* 383, 390, 548–602, 606–30, 942; cf. 322, 340.

53 Pericles' claims about Athens can be directly contradicted: compare *Vesp.* 495 with Thuc. 2.37.2: MacDowell (1988) 200.

54 For Olson (2002) li–lii, it is quite "brilliant" that an audience of democrats who collectively had all the power could be persuaded that they are all victims of powerful adversaries. The appeal of such an argument is obvious.

55 Cf. *Eq.* 173–4; the actual total was 300 cities, and the tribute was much less than 150 talents: MacDowell (1988) 228–9.

56 On lists in imperial discourse, see earlier, p. 11.

57 On the connotations of πόνος, see earlier, pp. 21–2.

58 Forrest (1963) 1 n.3; De Ste Croix (1996) 61; Meiggs (1972) 391–6.

59 Despite his criticisms of Athens' susceptibility to flattery, Aristophanes, no less than the demagogues, sometimes panders to his audience.

60 *Vesp.* 1098–1101: πολλὰς / πόλεις Μήδων ἑλόντες / αἰτιώτατοι φέρεσθαι / τὸν φόρον δεῦρ᾽ ἐσμέν, ὃν κλέπτουσιν / οἱ νεώτεροι.

61 At *Ach.* 66, 90, Dikaiopolis complains of an embassy which received extremely generous pay of two drachmas a day; cf. *Ach.* 137, 610–17.

62 Olson (2002) xxxviii–xxxix.

63 Cf. Forrest (1963) 2–3; Newiger (1980) 236–8.

64 As is true for all the comedies which "solve" a contemporary problem: Olson (2010) 62–3.

65 From a Greek perspective, war is the natural state of things (Plato *Laws* 626a), but this does not preclude complaint: Dover (1972) 84–5; Forrest (1963) 2–3.

66 *Ach.* 575, 581–9, 964–7, 1080, 1179–85, and especially the obscenity of 591–2.
67 Forrest (1963) 4–6.
68 The term παρακεκομμένα implies that they were not legal citizens.
69 For which Olson (2002) xxxii–xxxvi; Edmunds (1980) 10.
70 Olson (2002) 215.
71 Cf. Ar. *Eq.* 781–5, 1334; *Vesp.* 711; *Nu.* 986, fr.429; Eupolis fr.233; Hdt. 9.27.5; Pl. *Leg.* 707c: Olson (2002) 128. Theopompus dissents: *FGrH* 115F153.
72 Aristophanes' *Holkades* fr.429, produced perhaps between 424 and 422, appears to offer a reward of "a loaf for the oldsters on account of their trophy at Marathon" (trans. Henderson (2007) 319).
73 Handley (1993) 422; Pelling (1999) 138–9.
74 Though the idealized Athens is the city of supreme compassion (Thuc. 3.39.2, Dem. 24.171, Plut. *Mor.* 790c etc.), comedy leaves little room for pity.
75 See earlier, pp. 11–12.
76 Olson (2002) xliv–xlv; Edmunds (1980) 16.
77 Whitman (1964) 61–3. Compare the desire (ἔρως) that drives Peisetairos (also emblematic of Athens) in *Birds*: Arrowsmith (1973) 129–35.
78 Note also his deal with the Boeotian in which he gets much the better bargain – Copaic eels for a sycophant (900–58): Edmunds (1980) 19.
79 With Ar. *Ach.* 1098–1112, compare Ar. *Horae* fr.581 and Hermippos *Porters* fr.63. Cratinus' *Ploutoi* frr.172, 175–6 imagines an age of abundance in Cronos' age; cf. Telecleides *Amphictyones* fr.1; Pherecrates' *Metalles* imagines a miraculous and abundant underground world, frr.113, 137.
80 Thuc. 2.38; [Xen.] *Ath. Pol.* 2.7–8; Xen. *Vect.* 1.2–8 puts an anti-imperialistic slant on the topos of imperial abundance. Aristophanes' *Holkades* contains a chorus of merchant ships that brought goods to Athens from all over the world. Wilkins (1997) 253–5 discusses the imperial significance of different types of bread in Athenian comedy: Athens' imperial possessions provided access to different types of wheat and thus to a unique Athenian abundance of bread. That Athens is also concerned to portray itself as a place of modest appetites, as well as the city of abundance (Wilkins (1997) 262–6), is yet another way in which the perfect imperial city seeks to transcend contradiction.
81 *Eq.* 92–4, 326, 355–62, 375–80, 392.
82 *Eq.* 137, 274–6, 304–11, 487, 863; cf. *Vesp.* 596; Ar. *Ath. Pol.* 28.3.
83 Images related to food dominate the play, especially those of harvesting (326, 392) and devouring (355–62; cf. 375–80, 824–7, 1035).
84 *Eq.* 201–3, 258–263, 267–8.
85 Cf. 839, 1035. Compare *Nu.* 203, which refers to measuring land for cleruchies as "democratic" and useful.
86 Thuc. 4.65.3–4; 6.15.2, 34.2.
87 Anderson (2003) 2, n.5.
88 *Eq.* 565–90, 595–610; cf. Thuc. 2.36.1–4: Sommerstein (1981) 3–4.
89 *Eq.* 567–70; cf. Thuc. 2.40.3, 5.
90 The topos is quintessentially epitaphic: Harriott (1986) 65–6.
91 Loraux (1986) 141, 275–8, 293, 331.
92 Edmunds (1987) 253–6.
93 With a different context, compare Thuc. 2.63.2.
94 Cf. Hermippus fr.75; Thuc. 5.89.1, 6.83.2; Loraux (1986) 305.
95 It is reprised at 1086–7, where Demos will be an eagle and rule the whole world.
96 The oracle is quoted at Σ *Eq.* 1013a: "Having seen much and suffered much and toiled much, you will become an eagle amid the clouds forever:" cf. *Av.* 978. The eagle may represent Athenian hegemony or its effortless evasion of capture. Parke-Wormell ii.53–4 date it after the battle of Oenophyta in 457 when Athens' ally Phocis controlled Delphi: Dunbar (1995) 548.

97 Although the Marathonian generation were famously tough, they had a softer side, just like imperial Athens, in contrast with Sparta's obsession with war: Thuc. 2.38.1, 39.1, 40.1, 41.1 and p. 18 earlier. In his hair, the reborn Demos wears a golden cricket, an item worn by older Ionian men celebrating their kinship with the Athenians (Thuc. 1.6.3). Thus Edmunds (1987) 257–60 interprets Demos' transformation in the light of Athens' treatment of their Ionian allies. "Old Demos has, then, become an Ionian. Or rather he has become an Athenian of the period in which – so Aristophanes pretends – Athenian and Ionian were still the same thing." By assimilating Ionia into Athens, Aristophanes reflects the reality of Athenian policy: "The soft-but-tough Ionian Athens is the imperial city in its pristine form" (260).
98 *Eq.* 1329: λιπαραὶ καὶ ἰοστέφανοι καὶ ἀριζήλωτοι Ἀθῆναι.
99 Edmunds (1987) 259–60.
100 Newiger (1980) 227–8.
101 *Pax* 211–19, 269–84.
102 The Boeotians disdained the Peace of Nicias for requiring them to return the border fort of Panactum to Athens: cf. Thuc. 5.17.2, 26.3, 32.4. Argos was neutral in real life (Thuc. 5.28.3), although its peace with Sparta was about to expire.
103 They also rejected the Peace because it did not require Athens to give up Nisaea, captured in 424: Thuc. 5.17.2.
104 On Megarian hunger, compare *Ach.* 733–5, 751 and in general 750–835, while for cruel humour mocking other cities' suffering at Athenian hands, compare the earlier discussion, of *Babylonians* 71b on the "lettered" Samians. Equally harsh are frr.245–7 of Eupolis' *Poleis* which characterize three cities, Tenos, Chios and Cyzicus. The feminine gender of the word "city" in Greek sets up an easy set of associations for a Greek audience. Cities are like women, portrayed as exploitable, sexually (cf. 247.2–4, 244, 223) and otherwise, and requiring domination, as slaves by masters or as animals to be tamed. Their masters are the Athenians, whose self-presentation as masculine, dominant and capable was an essential part of the larger ideology of the Athenian empire. Thus fr.246 commends Chios as a readily obedient horse, while Cyzicus is claimed to offer abundant money and easy sex. Just as Greeks considered female subjection to men natural, so Athens' rule over the non-Athenian city states could be considered natural and even beneficial for them: Thuc. 5.91.2.1, 105.2, Xen. *Oec.* 7.18, 28 with Rosen (1997) 154–8, 161–3. Nothing compels us to assume that Eupolis was condemning such sentiments: modern critics may have more tender sensibilities than did ancient Athenian audiences, or may want more self-critical, more sensitive, even more ideal Athenians than this book suspects that they were.
105 They were afraid that demagogues might win over the people by promising new projects at public expense which would be financed by an increased tribute: Sommerstein (1985) 160.
106 Cf. *Pax* 1064–8, *Ach.* 308, *Lys.* 628–9; E. *Andr.* 445–53, *Supp.* 187; Hdt. 9.54.1; Thuc. 1.77.6, 95; 5.105.4.
107 Compare *Eq.* 66–8, 326, 775, 802, 1408; *Vesp.* 281–9, 644–6, 669, 971.
108 ὁ νοῦς γὰρ ἡμῶν ἦν τότ' ἐν τοῖς σκύτεσιν: Sommerstein (1985) 164.
109 On whose comic and fantastic aspects, see Heath (1987a) 6–8.
110 A direct connection with Athenian imperialism, specifically viewing it as an attempt to dissuade Athens from the Sicilian expedition, was suggested already by Süvern (1827), but for Koechly (1857) only some 30 years later, the city of the birds was no warning but an ideal for Athens to aspire to, and the debate continues. For bibliography, see Hubbard (1991) nn.3–4 and (1997) 27 nn.20–1; Konstan (1995) 31–2. Though Arrowsmith (1973); Hubbard (1991) 158–92 and (1997); Katz (1976) and others read the play politically in various ways, others doubt that it is making any serious political comment: Murray (1933) 135–63; Sommerstein (1987) 1–6; Dunbar (1995) 1–6; see also Henderson (1997) 142–5. The play certainly refers approvingly to some elements of contemporary Athenian imperial policy: l.186 jokes about

Melian hunger, and Nicias is praised for successes at Syracuse (362–3) and chided for slowness (639, 1360–71): Henderson (1997) 143. At 879, the Chians are tacked onto the prayer for the Nephelokokkygians: Thrasymachus (85F3 DK) states that Athens included Chios in all prayers for its own well-being because of the island's loyalty.

111 Cf. *Ach.* 639, *Eq.* 1330.
112 Arrowsmith (1973) 126–9; Konstan (1995) 30; MacDowell (1995) 222–3, 228.
113 Their longing for a better place is "a kind of primitivist nostalgia, a desire for civilization without its discontents, that is conveniently projected by a colonizing population onto what they perceive as simpler beings, whether beasts or native peoples": Konstan (1997) 11.
114 Like the typical Aristophanic hero, he is disenchanted with Athens as it is, yet his rhetorical skills and appeal to the (winged) masses and his ambition are typical of the Athenian elite: Henderson (1997) 137–8. A combination of opposites is typical of the ideal imperial Athens, and Peisetairos exemplifies an analogous combination of opposites. Henderson explicitly compares him with Alcibiades (140), though perhaps it is more that Alcibiades, like Peisetairos, is himself an Athenian imperial "type".
115 Henderson (1997) 136–40.
116 Hubbard (1997) 25 considers return to the Golden Age an "obsession" of Old Comedy; cf. Storey (2010) 211–3.
117 A kind of anti-epitaphic moment (contrast Thuc. 2.36.1–2, 62.3.)
118 Henderson (1997) 139 notes the resonances of the name Euelpides with Thuc. 6.23.2, 24.3.
119 Arrowsmith (1973) 143 compares the birds' acceptance of Peisetairos with the way in which the allies entrusted themselves to Athens to form the Delian League.
120 Compare Gorgias 76 F6 15, "δισσὰ ἀσκήσαντες μάλιστα ὧν δεῖ, γνώμην <καὶ ῥώμην>"; and in general, the imperial combination of the two in Athenian rhetoric about the idealized Athens.
121 Compare the uniqueness of the lone state Athens, earlier, pp. 17–18.
122 Konstan (1995) 30: "These paradoxical intersections are a reflex of tensions in Athenian ideology at the time of the Peloponnesian War," while 40–1 notes the reciprocal relationship between the birds' plenitude and their ever-increasing need for domination. On desire (ἔρως) in this play and as the driver of the Athenian empire, see Arrowsmith (1973) 129–35; Konstan (1995) 30.
123 Such inspections were law for all allied states: *ML* 40.13–15 (c. 453/2) and *ML* 46.5–11 (c. 447/6) with Dunbar (1995) 562–5 on this scene. On the roles and numbers of Athenian imperial magistrates abroad, see Balcer (1977).
124 Dunbar (1995) 12–13.
125 For "famous" as Athens' epithet, see earlier, pp. 56, 100, n.15, and for a city's *erastai*, cf. Thuc. 2.43.1.
126 Compare 1320–2 with E. *Med.* 824–45, S. *OC* 668–94; Dunbar (1995) 4–5.
127 A popular figure in Athens, representing the ingenuity which Athenians considered innate to their own character: Dunbar (1995) 12–15.
128 Cf. Henderson (1997) 136–40, who sees the play's ambiguities as reflecting the "fantasy world of the Athenian corporate imagination: fantasies of national solidarity and imperial conquest" (136).
129 Bowie (1993a) 175–7.
130 Similarly, at *Pax* 410–13, it is considered "natural" that the Moon and Sun are scheming to take over the cults of the gods for themselves.
131 Dunbar (1995) 562–3; cf. 567–8.
132 "As a world of natural bounty, free of contention, it stands for the sufficiency of the golden age. But this plenitude at the same time inspires an ambition for universal conquest of domination and is thus a figure for Athenian expansionism": Konstan (1997) 15.

133 For Bowie (1993a) 167–71, this is a very troubling moment, aligning Peisetairos with tyrants, but Aristophanes tends not to be subtle in drawing morals of good and bad, and against any scattered hints of tyranny may be set Peisetairos' great success. The claim of Hubbard (1997) that Nephelokokkygia is "a dystopian nightmare of grandiose proportions" (25) seems exaggerated.

134 δεινότατα γάρ τοι πεισόμεσθ', ἐμοὶ δοκεῖ,
εἰ τῶν μὲν ἄλλων ἄρχομεν, ὑμεῖς δ' οἱ θεοὶ
ἀκολαστανεῖτε, κοὐδέπω γνώσεσθ' ὅτι
ἀκροατέον ὑμῖν ἐν μέρει τῶν κρειττόνων.

135 Konstan (1997) 15–16; Henderson (1997) 145 cautions against automatically bringing Thucydides to bear on this passage.

136 Sommerstein (1987) 4–5: cf. Thuc. 6.24.3, 31.6. See also Henderson (1997) 142–5 and esp. Major (2013) 129–32, who states (132): "It is an unpalatable idea to say that Aristophanes, at least as far as what he projects in *Birds*, belonged to the uncritical supporters and was thus on the wrong side of history. But that it is unpalatable does not make it less true."

5 Thucydides
What was really said?

5.1 Introduction

A large body of evidence has now been amassed, and all of it tends broadly in the same direction. Tragedy and oratory, especially the *epitaphioi*, along with post-fifth-century material and some comparative material from imperial nations geographically and temporally distant from Athens have been used to sketch a portrait of a people confident in their position in Greece, who appealed to a glorious past through which they understood their present and which promised a continuously glorious future, as proof that their exalted position was just. But the portrayal of Athenian power that emerges from the only contemporary source that focuses consistently on it is startlingly different. Altruism, courage and civilization are crowded out by fear, self-interest and tyranny. Thucydides was much closer to contemporary Athens than any subsequent source,[1] and he was a remarkably brilliant and perceptive historian whose claim that he had made every effort to establish the truth about the Peloponnesian War should be respected, both because of the clear results of his exceptionally painstaking and often accurate research[2] and thought, visible on every page of his writing, and because this is what he claims. He was not writing in bad faith or deliberately foisting a defective "possession forever" on unsuspecting posterity.

But all historiography is in some sense subjective, since it must rely on an individual's attempt to arrange and streamline events – often apparently random and contingent to those actually living through them – so that they make narrative sense to readers. A historian must inevitably select some events as significant and worth emphasizing while ignoring or minimizing others. Within the events chosen for emphasis, there will be elements that are themselves given extra prominence or analysis, and others that are not, and so on. It is also difficult to imagine how any choice could be made on purely objective grounds. Thucydides' history must have been subject to all these factors because it is impossible to write history otherwise. Indeed, there are instances even in his narrative which seem at first glance to be unimpeachably factual, authoritative and comprehensive, due to his deliberately dry narrative tone, where a degree of subjectivity may have influenced his content. For example, in her discussion of some oddities in Thucydides' portrayal of the Epidamnus affair, Mabel Lang concludes (176)[3] that

Thucydides viewed the facts in the light of his own very acute historical understanding and so presented them not in their raw and unrelated state but *as they should have been* [my emphasis] in order to produce both the observable results and rather less obvious states of mind and opinion. In this case Thucydides, *keeping as close as possible to what was actually done* [my emphasis] by both Corcyreans and Corinthians, has made clear the innocence of the Corcyreans and the rightness of Athenian interference on their side, as it seemed to the Athenians who made the decision.

Lang's findings are but one small example of areas in which Thucydides seems to have deliberately shaped his narrative to convey his own understanding of what certain events of the war meant, as well as how they happened.[4]

5.2 Thucydides' methods

Historians inevitably place their own stamp on their work, but in his statement of his methodology of writing history (1.22.2–3), Thucydides seems to minimize the likelihood that his account is at all subjective, implying a closer and less complex connection between actual events and his narration than seems straightforwardly true:

τὰ δ' ἔργα τῶν πραχθέντων ἐν τῷ πολέμῳ οὐκ ἐκ τοῦ παρατυχόντος πυνθανόμενος ἠξίωσα γράφειν, οὐδ' ὡς ἐμοὶ ἐδόκει, ἀλλ' οἷς τε αὐτὸς παρῆν καὶ παρὰ τῶν ἄλλων ὅσον δυνατὸν ἀκριβείᾳ περὶ ἑκάστου ἐπεξελθών. ἐπιπόνως δὲ ηὑρίσκετο, διότι οἱ παρόντες τοῖς ἔργοις ἑκάστοις οὐ ταὐτὰ περὶ τῶν αὐτῶν ἔλεγον, ἀλλ' ὡς ἑκατέρων τις εὐνοίας ἢ μνήμης ἔχοι.

And as for what actually happened in what was done in the war, I did not think it right to use any random person who turned up as a source, nor to rely on my own ideas, but I went through the events at which I was present and got information from others with as much accuracy as I could. And my investigations were hard work, because the eye-witnesses at each event were not unanimous about what happened, but either could not remember properly or were biased (my translation).

If Lang and others are right that Thucydides sometimes deliberately shapes his narrative, whether by omission, specific emphases or juxtapositions to convey his own view of events, but we also trust his good faith as an accurate reporter, then we must acknowledge the existence of a truth that underlies and sometimes is not identical to specific events. In a sense, Thucydides is the victim of his own scrupulousness. Precisely because this "self-conscious professional"[5] assures us that he has made every effort to find the truth,[6] expectations automatically become much higher for him than for other historians, and disappointment and unease at "catching him out" correspondingly greater.[7]

If even the narrative of apparently objective facts itself has sometimes been moulded by Thucydides,[8] the problems will be significantly magnified in the speeches,[9] where he understandably admits to some degree of invention. It is in the speeches that most of the material relating to Athenian attitudes to the Athenian empire can be found, so they are vital in corroborating or emending the picture of Athenian discourse about Athens laid out so far. Again, Thucydides is a victim of his own scrupulousness because, unusually among ancient historians, he does offer some statement of his methodology in recording his speeches, though not in choosing or placing them, and he has clearly been highly selective in his choices of speeches and their position in his narrative. Had he said nothing, or rendered every speech in indirect discourse, we would have happily assumed that the speeches were largely invented and have considered them of less historical importance than is currently the case. As it is, Thucydides admits the obvious point that not every speech represents exactly what was said at the time:[10] he could not have been present at all of them (although one might make some educated guesses at those he might have heard),[11] and in any case, verbatim recall of a speech is impossible. However, he also explicitly states that the speeches do have a clear connection with what was actually said.[12] At 1.22.1, he says:

καὶ ὅσα μὲν λόγῳ εἶπον ἕκαστοι ἢ μέλλοντες πολεμήσειν ἢ ἐν αὐτῷ ἤδη ὄντες, χαλεπὸν τὴν ἀκρίβειαν αὐτὴν τῶν λεχθέντων διαμνημονεῦσαι ἦν ἐμοί τε ὧν αὐτὸς ἤκουσα καὶ τοῖς ἄλλοθέν ποθεν ἐμοὶ ἀπαγγέλλουσιν· ὡς δ᾽ ἂν ἐδόκουν ἐμοὶ ἕκαστοι περὶ τῶν αἰεὶ παρόντων τὰ δέοντα μάλιστ᾽ εἰπεῖν, ἐχομένῳ ὅτι ἐγγύτατα τῆς ξυμπάσης γνώμης τῶν ἀληθῶς λεχθέντων, οὕτως εἴρηται.

And as for what each side said, either when preparing to go to war or already in the midst of it, it was difficult to remember properly, both for me in those I heard and for other sources from various places who reported to me: but what I thought each should say in the various circumstances, sticking as closely as possible to the general line of thought in what was really said, this I have written down.[13]

This sentence is a notorious quagmire in Thucydidean studies,[14] but it is important to not to read it in isolation from 1.22.2–3, since there, Thucydides regards even his own experiences and ideas of the war as potentially misleading or incomplete, and states that he has tested them rigorously with evidence gathered from other witnesses. But in his account of the speeches, the phrase ὡς δ᾽ ἂν ἐδόκουν ἐμοί is placed prominently in the sentence, signalling that these contain more of his own creation than the tried and tested factual account of events does. Because it is Thucydides' only statement on how he composed his speeches, it elides into one uniform principle many different possible relationships between his second-hand accounts of the speeches and the irrecoverable words of specific individuals' speeches at a particular event. Of course, some speeches must have a higher degree of Thucydidean invention than others do, but there is no clear means of establishing which is which.[15] The sentence also appears to say two different things.[16] First, he has used his own judgement in the rendition of the speeches because of ignorance or other difficulty, and so he has created the words that he thinks his speakers should say in the context (ὡς δ' ἂν ἐδόκουν ἐμοὶ ἕκαστοι περὶ τῶν αἰεὶ παρόντων **τὰ δέοντα** μάλιστ' εἰπεῖν). However, the second half of the sentence claims that the speeches reflect what individuals said at specific moments, so do represent historical accuracy to some degree:[17] (ἐχομένῳ ὅτι **ἐγγύτατα** τῆς ξυμπάσης γνώμης **τῶν ἀληθῶς λεχθέντων**.) Within the sentence are two further phrases, whose meanings are uncertain: τὰ δέοντα and τῆς ξυμπάσης γνώμης:[18] τὰ δέοντα, translated above as "what [I thought] each should say", could also be translated "what was necessary" or "what was appropriate," and, while a basic translation is clear,[19] its meaning is still on any reading an ambiguous phrase.[20] The phrase "τῆς ξυμπάσης γνώμης" has often been emphasized as especially important in determining Thucydides' understanding of the relationship between literal truth and invention in his speeches,[21] but with somewhat limited usefulness. It is typically translated as "the general sense" or "purport" (*LSJ*), but while the adverbial phrase "τὸ σύμπαν" certainly does mean "on the whole" or "in general" (e.g. Thuc. 4.63.2), no unambiguous use of the adjective "ξυμπάς" clearly means this,[22] as opposed to "entire". Moreover, γνώμη has a range of different meanings in Thucydides,[23] comprising judgement or opinion (1.70.3, 75.1, 95.2, 113.2, 140.1; 2.55.2; 3.37.4, 38.1; 4.19.4, 40.1; 7.15.1), especially opinions delivered publicly and sometimes as formal propositions (1.90.3, 93.5; 3.36.6; 4.56.2; 8.68.1); will, disposition or inclination (4.68.3, 5.44.1, 6.45.1); and lastly, in a rather smaller category, intention, purpose (3.92.1, 1.128.7, 8.90.3) or resolve; and *LSJ* translates it at 1.22.1 as "purport". It is not clear that any possibility from these translations helps to elucidate Thucydides' practice in recounting speeches, though given his well-known tendency to stretch language in unconventional ways, translating the phrase as "the general sense" (which certainly offers a plausible means of interpreting the speeches) cannot definitively be rejected. But a translation that claims that Thucydides' speeches offer "the *whole* opinion" (or "will" or "intention") of every speaker[24] seems hard to credit when one looks at individual speeches: there is a world of difference in style and content between what Thucydides' speakers say and the persuasive speeches known to have been delivered by speakers in court or other arenas. Wilson[25] makes the attractive suggestion that Thucydides means that he took a speaker's complete γνώμη into account (though this cannot be true in some cases, such as the speeches at Melos) and based what he made the speakers say on that, using an analogy from writing a history of the Second World War requiring a speech of Churchill for which the historian does not have a verbatim transcript but a list of the points the speech made. The historian can include every point, or make a sort of summary, the "general drift", or offer some of the points made as representative of the speech as a whole. To render everything from an hour-long speech would clearly make a written version too lengthy, while summarizing one main thesis seems inadequate to render a significant speech. Thus it remains to imagine a speech composed of a representative (determined by the historian) selection from the speech. Churchill's "representative" arguments in this context might include the judgement that the English Channel would protect Britain from invasion, while omissions or minimizations would be more emotional elements such as a "long tirade about Hitler and Mussolini . . . and a spirited appeal to the British people." While a historian would naturally prioritize political, factually based elements of a speech over emotional appeals, their omission may distort understanding of the content and function of the original speech.

Thucydides clearly states that he does not reproduce exactly what was said – in any case, an impossibility – and is using his understanding to flesh out speeches into a whole, while simultaneously laying claim to truth. But there is more than one kind of truth, and the apparently clear end of the sentence, τῶν ἀληθῶς λεχθέντων, may be more complex than it first seems, especially in conjunction with the emphatic start of the sentence, ὡς δ' ἂν ἐδόκουν ἐμοὶ, picked up by οὕτως εἴρηται at the end. The truth of "what was *really* said" according to Thucydides' opinion could mean something rather different from particular words said on a particular day by a particular speaker.[26] In the light of the rest of his historiographical "manifesto", I suggest that it is possible that Thucydides' versions of speeches could have differed, in content, inclusions and omissions, from what their original speakers actually said, without making him guilty of dishonesty or contradicting what he claims at 1.22.1.[27] The phrases italicized in the earlier quotation from Mabel Lang's account of Thucydides' method in shaping his account of events at Epidamnus resemble Thucydides' own account of his methodology in the speeches, in that he was working to reveal a truth, rendered both in his narrative and the speeches, that sometimes differs from specific events and may not literally reflect every word spoken at a particular time. Nonetheless, it is a truth.

In several speeches, above all at 5.89.1, the Athenians acknowledge, and almost seem to embrace, the gap between the idealized city of public discourse and the behaviour they are contemplating. It seems at the very least surprising that the original version of such speeches[28] would not merely have omitted any attempts to justify Athenian action persuasively – Athens' "official" history consistently justifies Athenian power through multiple appeals to the excellence of the city – but actively rejected those justifications. Such belligerent speeches hardly seem designed to have any effective persuasive function for their audiences and call into question the belief that Thucydides was reproducing anything close to everything that was said on every occasion. But if these sentiments are Thucydides' idea of what the Athenians *really* meant, or even a carefully selective account of what they said,[29] their tone and content are more understandable: this is τὰ δέοντα of what was really said according to Thucydides, stripped of what he considered all irrelevant niceties.[30]

Chapter 22 of book one is closely connected with 1.21.1, in which Thucydides condemns both the poets' exaggerated claims and his less careful historian predecessors, before staking his claim to a vastly more accurate historiography. But even worse are the general public whom he condemns in chapter 20.1–3 for willingness to believe whatever is appealing, or unthinking reliance on common knowledge, rather than putting strenuous effort into finding the real truth, as he proposes to do. The polemical and rhetorical dimension of Thucydides' claims in these chapters have important implications for the work as a whole. Thucydides states that his methods will bring a higher standard of truth to writing history than anyone has yet offered. He does not claim that everything he writes is the literal truth, and on any reading, admits that the speeches have a greater proportion of his own material than the narrative does,[31] but he does claim that his methods are superior. From that intellectual standpoint, the claim that his versions of the speeches contain τὰ δέοντα, however this is translated, offers the distinct possibility that material that he considered not τὰ δέοντα – and a writer as brilliantly intense as Thucydides might have a very specific understanding of "what was necessary" – was simply omitted. His claim is also a claim to superior judgement (ὡς δ' ἂν ἐδόκουν ἐμοὶ) about what matters and what does not.[32] Nearly all the speeches that Thucydides recounts would have been significantly longer in their original form, and a principle of selection that focuses on τὰ δέοντα suggests a predetermined sense of what is important and what is less so. This principle would theoretically lead to the composition of speeches that focus on certain topics and ignore others. This is in fact what we find:[33] speeches all written in Thucydides' very distinctive, difficult, and highly wrought style,[34] speeches with significant cross-references with one another, even in speeches temporally and geographically distant from each other,[35] or with other parts of Thucydides' history, as opinions in one speech are confirmed by actions in another part of the narrative.[36] Thucydides' speeches also focus on generalities to a remarkable extent. In the light of this, Thucydides' treatment of Athenian attitudes to the *archē*, which only sparingly mentions the laudatory elements of drama and the *epitaphioi*, is striking.[37]

Thucydides was highly aware of the innovatory quality of his history.[38] At 1.23.5, he claims that his account of the Peloponnesian War will be so authoritative that no one in the future will ever need to discuss its causes.[39] Aligned with this confidence in his authority as a historian is his well-documented preference for presenting only the finished picture to the public, in effect forcing his audience into accepting the truth of his interpretations.[40] Authority and a supposedly plain summary of fact have a strongly rhetorical, not to say subjective dimension: as Hornblower himself, generally a believer in Thucydides' essential accuracy, notes: "Thucydides makes us believe that his actually subjective reports are objectively accurate."[41] Acknowledging these tendencies need not impugn Thucydides,[42] but it is important to be aware of the kind of intellect, shaped by several interrelated tendencies, that he brings to his task, as indicated in the "manifesto" of 1.20.1–1.22.

To recap: at 1.20.1, Thucydides claims that most men receive tradition, especially that of their own country, uncritically, citing Athenian misunderstanding of the true story of Harmodius and Aristogeiton (1.20.2–3), a cherished foundation myth of the democracy, to which he will return at 6.54–59,[43] and then non-Athenian issues, reiterating that the masses (οἱ πολλοί) take no pains to investigate the truth. At 1.21.1, he contrasts his own efforts with such lazy thinking, stating that "someone" using the proofs that he has offered would not go astray, and contrasts his work with the poets' exaggerations or logographers'[44] compositions which favour appealing stories, even though their antiquity and encrustation by legend (τὸ μυθῶδες) makes them unfit as proper history. At 1.21.2, he moves on to the Peloponnesian War itself, claiming that although those involved in a struggle tend to overrate its importance, this war really was greater than those preceding it. Chapters 1.22.1–3 discuss his historical methods in both speeches and narrative, emphasizing his own efforts to establish the truth: he did not believe the first source that he found (unlike the majority he condemns in 1.20.1) or even his own impressions, but uses both personal observation and what others saw, subjecting all information to (unspecified) tests of accuracy, which was difficult, given his sources' partiality or inability to remember what really happened. At 1.22.4, he distances himself from those who want mere enjoyment (cf. 1.21.1), preferring to appeal to those who desire accurate knowledge of the past to help interpretation of the future, since "what is human" tends to recur in human life. Temporary gratification is rejected in favour of creating a "possession forever." Chapter 23.1–5 explains why the Peloponnesian War was exceptionally worth his efforts, in particular because it eclipsed the Persian Wars in importance,[45] and he ends with another claim which has generated an equal amount of discussion with 1.22, that the "truest cause" of the war was the one "least clear in words" – Spartan fear of Athens' power.

These short paragraphs reveal a focus which permeates Thucydides' work.[46] He distrusts majority opinion, considering it uninformed,[47] and believes that the masses prefer pleasant stories to the truth. His condemnation of pleasure in storytelling is associated with broader condemnation of an addiction to rhetorical pleasure that, in his opinion, caused Athenians to become easy prey for demagogues and prone to irrational thinking, above all in the Sicilian expedition.[48] By contrast with this intellectually flabby audience, the readership he envisages for his history must be "intolerant of cliché and of all that is maudlin or old-fashioned", "tough-minded", able "to contemplate a radical reinterpretation of the past", and "rethink old certainties."[49] Just as the stern historian condemns Athens' preference for what is easy and pleasing, so in comic mode, Aristophanes mocks the city's delight in hearing flattering clichés about themselves (*Ach.* 635–45).[50] In the funeral orations, the people were bathed in such flattery: the universal greatness of Athens (whose greatness justified the Athenian empire) was fundamental to the "official" history of Athens recounted there, and most Athenians believed in it "passionately."[51] Moreover, much of Athens' idealized history was based on precisely those old stories that Thucydides condemns as historically worthless (1.21.1): myths both in the traditional sense and in their definition by Stewart Flory as "patriotic stories in particular and sentimental chauvinism in general." Reliance on such stories is a serious problem because their exaggerated claims can have such a strong effect on reality.[52] Unlike the writers of tragedy or speakers of the *epitaphioi*, Thucydides' history is not publicly sponsored and can freely criticize dominant traditions.[53]

If Thucydides considers such material as appealing merely to uninformed opinion,[54] it is understandable that the tightly woven, economical history that he creates would not have included such topics as τὰ δέοντα, so that they become significantly under-represented. A second reason for such potential under-representation is foreshadowed in Thucydides' words at 1.21.4, in which he regards human nature as essentially unchanging (cf. 3.82.2), so that what happens now is useful for understanding what may occur in the future.[55] This viewpoint leads him often to use one event as paradigmatic of a whole series of similar events,[56] using individuals and incidents as archetypes to which readers must repeatedly return as reference points.[57] Similarly, the speeches promote what Thucydides regards as τὰ δέοντα, in order to reveal the real, underlying motives and assumptions of his speakers, which provide the paradigms that Thucydides uses to convey his truth to readers. Furthermore, appeals to "human behaviour" remove what Thucydides says from the partisan and particular and bring it into the realm of apparently objective, unassailable truth.[58] This tendency has often been noted in Thucydides' work,[59] along with a rather pessimistic view of human nature,[60] in which expediency will generally best altruism or morality.[61] Thucydides is typical of the philosophers of his time[62] in privileging knowledge of the permanent over particular events, whose importance lies in exemplifying certain permanent laws or tendencies.[63] Ironically, the funeral speeches and other expressions of the ideal Athens posit an equally constant, though qualitatively different, characterization of the Athenians through time.[64]

Thucydides' tendency to write paradigmatic history and his belief in a particular form of human nature must affect his portrayal of Athens. After Pericles' funeral speech, he sees no need to recount anything similar,[65] although in lived reality Athenians would have continually heard, seen and participated in praise of their city. And since he believes that human nature seeks what is expedient, it cannot, by definition, fully embrace altruism or justice or any of the virtues which the idealized Athens claims in what the Athenians heard so regularly. Having offered his one example of the idealizing rhetoric in Pericles' funeral speech, he will go on, both in his narrative and in other speeches, to undermine it consistently. Thus, when Athenian speakers at Melos refuse to justify Athenian power by appealing to Athens' record in the Persian Wars, they

> are in reality not very likely to have said precisely that. But Thucydides, having no way of knowing what was really said at Melos, availed himself of the occasion to cut through propaganda and ideology and impart to posterity the essence of empire and Realpolitik.[66]

This *is* "the truth of what was really said", especially if history depends on effort, scepticism, and not recording the first thing that was literally said,[67] but it may create significant distortion at another level.

These suggestions may shed some light on Thucydides' claim that the cause of the war was the element most formally kept out of sight – Sparta's fear of the growth of Athens' power (1.23.6): τὴν μὲν γὰρ ἀληθεστάτην πρόφασιν, ἀφανεστάτην δὲ λόγῳ, τοὺς Ἀθηναίους ἡγοῦμαι μεγάλους γιγνομένους καὶ φόβον παρέχοντας τοῖς Λακεδαιμονίοις ἀναγκάσαι ἐς τὸ πολεμεῖν. This claim is unlikely to be a literal truth – at 1.33.3, the Corcyraeans mention Athens' power, and it is central to the Corinthians' speech (1.68–71)[68] – but Hornblower suggests that in this context, Thucydides' superlatives should be interpreted more as comparatives: various competing issues (including Athenian justifications of their expansionism) featured in discourse around the Peloponnesian War, but Athens' power was mentioned rather less often in the run-up to the war than those reasons for the war that were commonly discussed.[69] Athens' enemies doubtless conceptualized Athens' power differently from the way that the Athenians did, and if talk of the growth of Athens' power tended, in Athenian mouths, to be sweetened or weakened by public appeals to idealized Athenian virtue to justify Athenian power, then there is a sense in which the harder truths about that power are indeed less visible in public discourse. For Thucydides, the important concepts are not "helping friends" or "upholding justice" but terms like expediency and safety, both of which simultaneously depend on Athenian power and compromise it, according to those speakers, both Athenians and enemies (e.g. 2.63.1–2, 3.11.3), who claim that Athens is so hated that giving up the empire is impossibly dangerous. One might well see how sentiments like these are what was "really" meant, even if more pleasant sentiments were often expressed.[70]

Thucydides' account of the Pentecontaetia alludes to many Athenian triumphs and also some disasters, but, as the Corinthians claim (1.70.3), even in danger they are always hopeful, and even at Athens' most vulnerable moments, its citizens' *modus operandi* involves resisting with renewed vigour, never surrendering. Thucydides recounts no speeches related to such moments of crisis, but many of the topoi of Athens' glorious mythological and historical deeds would be highly appropriate in such situations to reassure the Athenians that they, or their ancestors, had been in dire straits in the past but had eventually triumphed. A speaker could invoke the dark days of their ancestors before Salamis and the native Athenian character that always wins through in the end: there are faint hints of this kind of material in Nicias' reported speech at 7.69.2 and what Pericles says at 1.144.3. It is easy to imagine how appeals to the past could be made at such difficult times, using the "ready-made" examples of Athenian virtues that permeate so many public art forms of the fifth century and beyond. Thucydides, sceptical of such appealing stories, the ὀνόματα καλά (5.89.1), minimizes their presence in his work and problematizes them, but as the next chapter will show, they remain paradoxically important for him, because they represent an image of Athens that was so familiar and broadly acceptable among all Athenians.

5.3 Thucydides and mythology

Thucydides' techniques of reworking some stories of Greek and Athenian mythology is especially revealing. Since such stories are unverifiable by his criteria of contemporary observation, but he does not dismiss tradition wholesale, he rationalizes them and aligns them with his historical paradigms of how human history "really" works, creating an ἔργον underneath the λόγος.[71] Thus his account of Agamemnon (1.9.3–4) focuses on the importance of money and power in explaining how he became commander-in-chief at Troy.[72] Even more telling is his treatment of Theseus, the hero of democratic Athens, whose traditionally heroic monster-killing exploits[73] were easily expanded and reframed in the early sixth century[74] and especially after the Persian Wars as examples of the energetic altruism which was central to the ideal Athens as a model for real-life Athenian interventions in the Greek world.[75] From the ancient myth of Theseus in Crete, Thucydides mentions both Minos (1.8.2–3) and Theseus (2.15–16.1) but keeps them separate.[76] Theseus is exclusively active in domestic policy and closely tied to Athens and its public festivals and buildings. Though credited with the synoikism of Athens and for a mixture of intelligence and power such as Thucydides affords only a handful of others (2.15.2; cf. 8.68.4), this Theseus is neither the brave, volunteer Minotauromachist of early myth nor the glamorous king-democrat of tragedy. By comparison, Minos is an international figure. While Herodotus doubts the historicity of the Minoan thalassocracy (3.122.2), Thucydides' Minos is a historical king, head of a colonizing sea-power which expelled evil-doers, in particular the pirates. Thucydides' readers are evidently intended to draw a parallel between Minos' thalassocracy and that of Athens,[77] but it is striking that in the later narrative of the Pentecontaetia Thucydides makes no explicit parallel between Minos' anti-piratical activity and that of Athens, since ridding the seas of pirates appears to have been another early justification for Athenian sea power.[78] Thus Plutarch (*Cim.* 8.3–5) describes Cimon's successful campaign against Dolopian pirates on Skyros from whom he eventually "liberated" the Aegean before triumphally repatriating Theseus' bones to Athens from Skyros.

However, Thucydides' omission of any direct parallel between the activities of Minos and Cimon is less surprising if he was trying to distance his narrative from Athenian justification of their city's ever-expanding power. Emphasis on the increasing irrelevance of what was done in the Persian Wars is notable in Thucydides' accounts both of the Spartans' treatment of the Plataeans (3.53–9) and of the Athenians' of the Melians (5.85–116).[79] The Plataeans appeal to Spartan mercy by reminding them of their service at Plataea some 50 years previously (2.71.2–4; 3.54.3, 55.5–6, 57.1–4, 58.1, 4–5, 59.2–4), but in vain.[80] Similarly, the Athenians reject all justifications of their power based on their self-sacrifice for Greece in 480 (5.89.1). From the Persian Wars came the Delian League, which became the Athenian *archē* with its power and psychological self-confidence, as Athenian "myths" of exceptionalism in virtue, courage and fortune are solidified. Frequently in Thucydides, by contrast, the world-view defined by the momentous events of 490–479 seems gradually to be growing obsolete.[81]

The portrayal of Minos' thalassocracy as a forerunner of the Athenian empire[82] is also striking in the context of the Athenian rhetoric which characterizes Athenians both as early colonizers (e.g. Isoc. 12.43–4) and as fighters against evil-doers (E. *Supp.* 341; Dem. 60.11; Pl. *Mx.* 240d). Thucydides' Minos is even more remarkable in the context of contemporary Athenian theatrical tradition: whereas Homer characterizes Minos as powerful and mysterious (*Il.* 13.450–4; *Od.* 19.179), Plutarch (*Thes.* 16.3) states that Minos was always reviled in the Athenian theatre, and in the dialogue ascribed to Plato called *Minos* (318d–321a), Socrates claims that the tragic Minos is "vicious, cruel, unjust and uneducated." He further claims that tragedy is a medium particularly pleasing to the people, in which Minos is placed on the "rack of tragedy", as the people take revenge for the tribute he imposed on them (321a). So the portrayal of Minos, stripped of his Minotaur and his sinister power and given certain attributes on which the Athenians prided themselves, is an interesting divergence from popular portrayals of Minos as an enemy of Athens and Athens as liberator of the Aegean.[83]

Thucydides offers an equally singular account of the myth of autochthony that from earliest times guaranteed the unique justice of Athens and brought a stream of suppliants to the city. While he endorses the broad outlines of the popular view, noting (1.2.5–6) that in early times, Attica was free from faction and uniquely did not change its inhabitants (cf. 2.36.1), he argues that Athens' early stability had nothing to do with autochthony, purity or morality, but resulted from Attica's poor soil that was unattractive to invaders. In its turn, this poor soil led to a stability at Athens that did indeed prove inviting to victims of war from other parts of Greece, but he names none of these famous exiles, apart from a very brief reference to the story of the children of Heracles at 1.9.2, several chapters after his account of Athens' acceptance of victims of war in its early history. So in 1.2, Thucydides tells essentially the same story that Athenians heard each year at the funeral speeches or in some tragedies, but without the strong moral and panegyric overlay contained in those versions.[84]

5.4 Believing Thucydides

In spite of the questions that this chapter has raised about Thucydides' reliability, one should not minimize his extraordinary achievement or distrust much of his narrative. It would indeed be "perilously arrogant"[85] to claim a greater knowledge of what really happened than Thucydides had. But the opinion of an extraordinary intellectual like Thucydides by its nature might not align with those of ordinary Athenians.[86] Contemporary evidence for an entirely different attitude towards Athens' power exists, and not all of it comes from sources other than Thucydides. As the next chapter will show, vestiges of mainstream Athenian imperial discourse occur in Thucydides' own writing, even though it will often be undermined in some way. Hornblower himself has shown that Thucydides' relative neglect of religion is unlikely to reflect typical Athenian opinions.[87] Religion is an area of human existence which tends towards conservativism and conformity, and, to judge from the body of evidence amassed in previous chapters, conservativism and conformity also may shape Athenian attitudes to Athens' power and its rightness. It may therefore be legitimate to wonder whether Thucydides' opinion, authoritatively though it is expressed, misrepresents typical sentiments in areas of Athenian life beyond religion.

Many modern critics have made partial steps along this path,[88] but respect for Thucydides' extraordinary achievement and all the ways in which it is trustworthy, and the implications of a less reliable Thucydides, have made it troublesome to follow.[89] But, in the light of the evidence amassed in previous chapters, I believe that Thucydides' portrayal of Athens' power may not reflect general Athenian opinion, and that few Athenians would have allowed, publicly or privately, that their power was unjust.[90] Rather, the disconnect between, as it were, Pericles' funeral speech and the Melian dialogues is entirely typical of the imperialistic (or perhaps just human)[91] mentality explored in Chapter 1. When Thucydides says that he has composed the speeches ὡς δ' ἂν ἐδόκουν ἐμοὶ ἕκαστοι περὶ τῶν αἰεὶ παρόντων τὰ δέοντα μάλιστ' εἰπεῖν, ἐχομένῳ ὅτι ἐγγύτατα τῆς ξυμπάσης γνώμης τῶν ἀληθῶς λεχθέντων, we can take him at his word, while remembering the intellectual framework which he brought to those speeches.

Notes

1 In spite of the abundance of sources contemporary with the fifth-century *archē*, none specifically focuses on Athenian power in the way that Thucydides does, while inscriptions are a product of the empire but are tricky to date and interpret: Low (2008) 6–7; Strasburger (2009) 193. Herodotus and Xenophon offer details of earlier and later stages of the empire, but without any specific focus. Later sources such as Diodorus, who draws largely from Ephorus, and Plutarch and Aristotle often preserve older traditions. Hose (2006) offers a useful checklist and concludes (690) that with the exception of Old Comedy, whose claims find their way into later historical accounts of fifth-century Athens, Thucydides' account remained authoritative and was never seriously challenged historiographically except in his account of the coup of 411. On comedy as an occasional contemporary supplement or corrective to Thucydides, see Forrest (1975); Rusten (2006).
2 See, e.g., Hornblower (2008) 109–12.
3 Lang (1968).
4 The juxtapositions of Pericles' funeral speech and the account of the plague (cf. 2.37.3 with 53.1 and 2.36.3 with 51.3, 53.4), and of Melos and Sicily, are two obvious cases where Thucydides has shaped his narrative to conform to an *a priori* theory of what specific historical events meant in a larger human context. Even when his narrative appears rationalized, certain "tragic" ways of thinking seem to have shaped its arrangement: Rood (1998) 80–2; cf. Gomme (1954) 144; Rhodes (1994) 161–6; Hornblower (2008) 217–25. Rubincam (1991) shows that even Thucydides' report of casualty numbers, factual though they look compared with Herodotus', depends on certain subjective factors. In the narrative portions of the history, he attributes to his characters motives which are generally agreed to be his own invention: Hornblower (1987) 78–81; Hunter (1973) 12–21, 33–4, 92–9. Commonly acknowledged omissions or inaccuracies in Thucydides include his underestimation of the Megarian decrees (Hornblower (1991) 110–12) and the omission of 425's increase of tribute. Rood (1998) 150–1 explains this omission in the context of Thucydides' notable preference for explaining events through appeal to a generalized human nature – here, the human tendency to be seduced by wishful thinking (a common Thucydidean theme) – rather than through a specific, individual event such as a tribute increase. Persia's role in the war is also underrepresented: Andrewes (1961).
5 Hornblower (2011) 13.
6 But Plant (1999) compares Thucydides' claims to truth with those of his sophistically trained contemporaries in court whose pretensions to the truth were less noble.
7 Rhodes (1994) 161–4. The claim of Kagan (1975) 77 that "we cannot allow the possibility that a speech is invented in any important way without destroying the credibility of Thucydides" (cf. Cogan (1981) xi) is ultimately unhelpful. In fact, on p. 89, Kagan undermines this earlier assertion by admitting that Thucydides' speeches are highly compressed: the context is Diodotus' impersonal speech on the topic of human nature, claimed to be unrealistic by Wassermann (1956) 34, 39, but if the compression applied by Thucydides included removing the commonplaces of appeals to pity,

then we are left with quite a misleading account of what was really said by on this occasion.
8 See also Woodman (1988) 16–23, who cites modern examples of the difficulty of using eye-witness testimony in determining war history.
9 For example, see Hornblower (1996) 81–93 on the speeches of 4–5.25. Other useful accounts of the speeches include the essays in Stadter (1973); Hedrick (1993); Debnar (2001); Pelling (2009); Strasburger (2009).
10 Indeed, if Hansen (1993) esp. 172–3 is right, the battle exhortation speeches in Thucydides are largely fiction: it seems unlikely that a general about to go to battle would have produced a long, formal speech and utterly unlikely that the second commander, an enemy whose speech Thucydides by definition could not have heard, would respond in detail to specific points made by the first one.
11 Gomme (1937) 171–7.
12 Andrewes (1962) 65–6.
13 For a useful sketch of how assessments of Thucydides' reliability have changed over the years, see Rusten (2009a) esp. 4–8; Connor (2009); also Badian (1993) 125–9. For a defence of the view that the speeches are essentially what their original speakers said, see Gomme (1937) and (1959) 143–8; Kagan (1975). For greater scepticism, see Wallace (1964); Hunter (1973); Woodman (1988); Low (2008) 5–6.
14 The bibliography is immense: see, e.g. Luschnat (1970) 1162–83 and (1974) 766–8; West (1973) 147–8; Garrity (1998) 362, n.2. Scardino (2007) 399–415 offers a full and useful discussion of these paragraphs.
15 Andrewes (1962) 68; Hornblower (1996) 276–84 analyzes Brasidas' speech, teasing out which parts are probably Brasidas and which Thucydides.
16 Hornblower (1987) 45–6 with references to earlier discussions.
17 Hornblower (1991) 59–60; cf. Laird (1999) 144–6.
18 For a useful discussion, see Wilson (1982).
19 Thucydides uses the phrase quite consistently: 1.70.8, 138.3; 2.43.1, 60.5; cf. 4.17.2, 5.66.3.
20 Wilson (1982) 97 settles for "in the way it seemed to me likely that each of them would speak." This is a reasonable translation but it does not solve the fundamental problem of how far Thucydides' speeches reflect or do not reflect the historical truth of what was said on an occasion. Hammond (1973) 49–50 interprets the phrase as close to "the universals", principles which derive from particulars: again, this allows for a degree of subjectivity from Thucydides in determining what these essentials are. Similarly Orwin (1994) 209–12 suggests that it means what anyone would say to be persuasive in the circumstances, again allowing Thucydides considerable leeway for invention.
21 Badian (1992) 187–9; Wilson (1982) 96–9 cite a representative range of earlier opinions.
22 Along with Thuc. 1.22.1 for this meaning, *LSJ* cites Xen. *Anab.* 7.8.26. Pl. *Leg.* 630b, *Gorg.* 477c and *Rep.* 525a, but only in the last of these does "general" seem preferable to "entire".
23 Orwin (1994) 208–10; Huart (1968) 304–10, who translates 1.22.1's phrase as "l'idée générale."
24 Definitely not, as some have argued, "opinion as a whole" or "the consensus opinion" since such a thing surely did not exist: Badian (1992) 189. De Ste Croix (1972) 9–16 interprets Thucydides' statement as "the main thesis", which gives Thucydides considerable latitude in creating the speeches, but many speeches do not lend themselves to such a simple summary as "main thesis" would imply, and this interpretation significantly denies Thucydides' own claims to accuracy: Wilson (1982) 98–9.
25 Wilson (1982) 99–100.
26 Raubitschek (1973) 39–40.
27 Bradeen (1960) 260–2 invokes Thucydides' statement of "adhering as closely as possible to the general sense of what was really said" to argue that the "exceptionally

truthful" Thucydides of De Ste Croix (1954) cannot be seriously misrepresenting what was actually said; but, quite apart from the questions of selection raised by Wilson, an "exceptionally truthful" historian might well scrutinize publicly expressed sentiments designed to persuade their audiences in order to find what he considers to be the stratum of truth underlying public discourse and potentially contradicting it in some way. Compare Greenwood (2005) 64–5 (cf. 82): "There are numerous instances in the *History* where Thucydides portrays speech culture (particularly in Athens) in a way that suggests the use of speech to cover up what was really going on and to mislead audiences. Even if it had been possible to record the speakers' words with precision, one gets the sense that Thucydides would still have been more concerned with the interpretation of the ideas behind the words."

28 This speech in particular is unlikely to have been one that Thucydides heard himself, so that a potential gap immediately opens up between what was actually said and his account.
29 Cf. Pelling (1999) 117–22. Rokeah (1982) 391–2 considers the use of δέον and δέοντα, concluding that this phrase indicates that Thucydides only reported material which he considered relevant to his account of the war, in effect "censoring" what he considered unnecessary. This is especially plausible given typical lengths of Greek speeches. Pericles' funeral speech is the longest in Thucydides but takes less than 20 minutes to deliver. Extant Attic orations are much longer: Finley (1967) 53.
30 Thus I broadly agree with the formulation of De Ste Croix (1954) 2 (cf. Badian (1993) 146), who argues that some speeches represent what the speakers would have said if they had spoken entirely honestly. Similarly Jones (1957) 66–72 states (66) that if Thucydides accurately reports the content and tone of some Athenian speakers, then they would be "very remarkable, if not unique" in openly avowing that they were guided by self-interest with no concern for morality, and that they must have undergone a complete transformation in the fourth century from which actual speeches with a very different tone are preserved. Thus "Thucydides, in order to point his moral, put into the mouths of Athenian spokesmen what he considered to be their real sentiments, stripped of rhetorical claptrap" (67). For criticism of the claim of Grant (1965) that Greek diplomacy was not very diplomatic, and that even Thucydides' less conciliatory speeches must represent what was actually said, see earlier, p. 25.
31 Rood (1999) 46–8.
32 Compare the theoretical speech of Churchill discussed by Wilson earlier in which historically relevant material is selected from a longer speech, even though the act of selection entails the potential for historical distortion.
33 De Ste Croix (1972) 11; Pelling (2009) 183–4.
34 Even allowing for the relatively subtle stylistic differences between the speeches of Nicias and Alcibiades discussed by Tompkins (1972); see also Scardino (2007) 698–700.
35 Hence studies such as Immerwahr (1973), who argues that the speeches serve to illustrate what he calls "the pathology of power" in Thucydides. Of course, speech and action ought to align with one another at some level, and similar problems, discussions and solutions were arising in different parts of the Greek world roughly contemporaneously: Andrewes (1962) 68; Immerwahr (1973) 23.
36 Hornblower (1996) 395; Rood (1999) 44–5.
37 Andrewes (1962) 68–9; Heath (1990) and especially Strasburger (2009).
38 Hornblower (1991) 4, 147–8 and (1996) 90, 115–6, 122, 358–60, 492; Thomas (2006) 102–4.
39 See Ober (1998) 62; Badian (1993) 127.
40 Gomme (1954) 119–20; Connor (1987) 6.
41 Hornblower (2011b) 68, 81–3; cf. Goldhill (2002) 43; Badian (1993) 161–2.
42 "The partiality of Thucydides could scarcely have been exposed but for the honesty of Thucydides": de Ste Croix (1954) 16; cf. 3; Hornblower (2011a) 25–7.

43 On this and its significance for Thucydides' methods and beliefs, see Stahl (2003) 1–8.
44 This term is usually taken to mean "prose author", but Grethlein (2013) 208–9 argues that it means "orator": such a translation would support my contention that Thucydides is deliberately writing against the pro-Athenian views that are so prevalent in Athenian public oratory as well as poetry, which, as Grethlein notes (209) are the most important "media of memory" in Athens.
45 Connor (1987) 156.
46 For useful general accounts of this focus, see Crane (1998) 36–61; Scardino (2007) 416–41.
47 And he will supply "the facts not known" to banish such ignorance: Stahl (1973) 70.
48 Ober (1989) 58; Edmunds (2009) 106–9; cf. Rogkotis (2006) 65–75.
49 Connor (1987) 13; cf. Rood (1998) 292.
50 Cf. p. 111.
51 Thomas (1989) 196–200 (206); Ober (1998) 80–1; cf. (1989) 314–24.
52 Flory (1990) 194; Parry (1981) 55–6.
53 Boedeker (1998) 198. His claim at 1.23.1–4 that the Peloponnesian War surpassed the Persian War is significant, because images of the idealized Athens and its justified power are connected with Athens' portrayal of its achievements against Persia on behalf of Greece.
54 Cf. Thuc. 2.65.4, 8.1.1; cf. 8.97.2. At 1.20.2, Thucydides attributes the ignorant belief that Hipparchus was the tyrant when Harmodius and Aristogeiton made their attack to the *plēthos*, the Athenian mass as opposed to the elite. Thucydides considers that his tried and tested facts are clearly more reliable than the incomplete and inaccurate "democratic knowledge" that most people have: Ober (1998) 54–8.
55 Hunter (1973) esp. 176–84; De Ste Croix (1972) 29–33; Crane (1998) 295–303; Greenwood (2005) 44–5.
56 Connor (1987) 144; Collingwood (1946) 28–31; cf. 42–5; Macleod (1983) 88–102; Crane (1998) 56–61. A striking example of this tendency is found at 3.87.2, where he states that the second outbreak of the plague was more severe than the first, but offers no further details, leaving us to imagine them from what he has already told us.
57 Pouncey (1980) 16–20.
58 Wallace (1964) 253–8.
59 Edmunds (1975) 158–63; Pouncey (1980) xi–xii, 20–2; Orwin (1994) 5; Rood (1999) 74–5, 80–2, 97–8, 129–30. But as always with Thucydides, there are contradictions. Hornblower (1987) 34–44 discusses the tension in Thucydides between extreme selectivity and the tendency to include what seem to a modern reader to be a mass of inconsequential details.
60 On this concept and its relationship to "national character", see Luginbill (1999), esp. 21–35.
61 Thuc. 2.67.4, 3.81.3–5; 6.85.1; Ober (1998) 67–8; Andrewes (1960) 6; Cogan (1981) 185–8.
62 Especially the sophists: Reinhold (1985) 22–3; cf. Finley (1967) 55–117, 34–5 discuss the common ground between Thucydides and Euripides. See also Pelling (1999) 82–9.
63 Collingwood (1946) 28–31; Wallace (1964) 260; Hammond (1973) 50; Rood (1999) 287; Rood (2006) 237–8 argues that Thucydides wanted the same control over his narrative in terms of consistency and valuing truth over pleasure that an ideal statesman like Pericles had in political life (1.140.1, 2.61.1).
64 See pp. 9, 12–14 earlier.
65 Hanson (2005) xv.
66 Bakker (2006) 119–20; cf. Raaflaub (2002) 152.
67 Compare, too, 1.10.1–2, which claims that sight alone is not a reliable guide for making inferences about a city's power. Most people, after all, can use their eyes, but from Thucydides' viewpoint, partly shaped by the perspectives of the sophists whose interest

in the relationship between appearance and reality is well known, sight cannot necessarily be trusted: Kallet (2001) 54–7.
68 Rhodes (1987) 154–7; Richardson (1990) 156.
69 Hornblower (1991) 66. The phrase occurs here and at Thuc. 6.6.1 in the context of Athens' drive for expansion, where the contrast is between the Athenian desire to rule Sicily (the ἀληθεστάτη πρόφασις) and the (specious, according to Thucydides) reason that they claimed, that they wished to help their kinsmen and allies (a classic example of idealized Athenian "altruism"): Rawlings (1981) 68. Some important treatments of the complex word "πρόφασις" include Rawlings (1975), who argues that it essentially means "cause", and Heubeck (1980); Pearson (1952) who argue for something more like "explanation"; see also De Ste Croix (1972) 51–63; Dover (1981) 415–23; Richardson (1990). Rhodes (1987) 160 plausibly argues that, as at 1.20.3, Thucydides is contrasting his real knowledge with superficial popular accounts.
70 Swain (1993) discusses this tendency in the context of Thucydides' famous account of the breakdown of society (and language as one manifestation of this) in Corcyra, 3.82.4, noting (36) Thucydides' fondness for the word εὐπρέπεια and its cognates as meaning "what seems good but is not": 1.37.4, 39.2; 3.11.2, 38.2, 44.4, 82.4, 8; 4.60.1, 61.8, 86.6; 6.6.1; 7.57.7; 8.66.1, 76.3, 109.1.
71 In his interest in this distinction, he is typical not only of his age, but also of a long Greek tradition: Parry (1981) 15–57; Swain (1993) 35–6.
72 Compare 2.29.3, 102.5–6; 4.24.5; 6.2.1–3: Hornblower (1991) 9–10.
73 For literary and iconographical evidence for the story of Theseus and the Minotaur in Crete, dating as early as the eighth century BCE, see Mills (1997) 1–42, esp. 13–18.
74 Illustrations of these expanded stories can be found perhaps as early as 520 BCE and especially after 510 and are generally believed to reflect the existence of an Athenian epic poem about Theseus: Mills (1997) 19–25.
75 Such exploits are sometimes attributed to the Athenians (Lys. 2.7–10; Isoc. 4.55–6; Dem. 60.8), sometimes to the Athenians and Theseus (Isoc. 12.168–72; cf. 10.25), sometimes to Theseus (Euripides' *Suppliants*; Plut. Thes. 29.4–5) or his son (Demophon in Euripides' *Heraclidae*), but they all exemplify the same Athenian essence arising out of, and necessary for, the continuation of the Athenian imperial psychology outlined earlier, pp. 21–2.
76 As does Herodotus, whose Theseus (9.73) is also not the idealized representative that Athenian tradition promoted: Munson (2012) 202–3.
77 Cf. Irwin (2007) 198–200.
78 Hornblower (1991) 18–23.
79 Connor (1987) 156.
80 Hornblower (1991) 445–6, who compares their appeals with Nicias' "archaic" speech at 7.69.2. Thucydides' speakers often show little patience with these appeals but they may have been more frequent than he tells us: cf., for example, 1.26.3.
81 Cf. Rood (1998) 246.
82 The position of Starr (1955) 289–91 that the Minoan thalassocracy is a fiction may be extreme (Buck 1962), but Athenian imperial myth-making around Theseus may have expanded images of a Minoan thalassocracy controlled by a tyrannical Minos whom Theseus was imagined to have vanquished, just as Athens would vanquish the Persians in more recent history.
83 Cf. Irwin (2007) 199–204, who argues that Thucydides portrays Minos' thalassocracy as an ambiguous version of the Athenian thalassocracy whose power may be either condemned or seen simply as "natural" law.
84 Thucydides does, however, affirm Athens' claim to being the first "real" Greeks, by associating barbarism not with race but with violence and insecurity, and claiming that the Athenians were the first to lay down arms and live a softer life: Georges (1994) 136–7.

85 Hornblower (2011a) 26.
86 De Ste Croix (1972) 11–12; Ober (1994) discusses Thucydides' active resistance to democratic hegemonic discourse. I agree with De Ste Croix (1954) 31–7; and Rhodes (2006) (cf. (1987) 161) that Thucydides was basically sympathetic towards aristocracy and oligarchy, as befitted his background, and this, combined perhaps with his own "passionate and troubled spirit" (Lesky cited by Connor (2009) 30), made him question the self-glorifications he heard. It is tempting to wonder what effect his failure at Amphipolis which he describes with such detachment (4.105–106.2; 5.26.5) had on him: Tritle (2006) 487 attributes Thucydides' cynical Realpolitik to his own disappointments as soldier and politician; cf. Westlake (1969); Pouncey (1980) 3–8.
87 Hornblower (2011a); cf. Furley (2006) 421.
88 Compare the work cited in n.4 earlier. Additionally, Low (2007) 228 points out that non-Thucydidean sources, especially Athenian inscriptions, are so different in tone from Thucydidean speeches that, in spite of Thuc. 1.22.1 (an "elusive, internally inconsistent and argumentative assertion"), such speeches cannot reliably be used as authentic records of the tone of interstate diplomacy in fifth-century Greece. Connor (1987) 39 n.41 suggests that Thucydides attempts to correct what he considered the simplistic view of his contemporaries that the Megarian decrees caused the war by deliberately de-emphasizing them: see also Hornblower (2011a), while (2011c) suggests that bias against the Argives may shape Thucydides' history. Thucydides characterizes the Peloponnesian War as "like no other" (1.23.1) in its magnitude and suffering. At various points, he inserts editorial judgement about the superlative qualities of certain events (1.50.2; 3.113.6; 5.60.3, 74.1; 6.13.1, 31.2), and superlative claims cluster particularly strongly around the Sicilian expedition (7.29.5; 56.4; 71.7; 75.7; 87.5; 8.1.2; 96.1: note also his claim, "an embarrassment" for champions of Thucydides the objective scientist (Hornblower (1991) 63), that disastrous natural phenomena were more common in the Peloponnesian War.
89 Cf. Kagan (1975) 77 quoted earlier; Hornblower (1996) 17.
90 As Brunt (1978) 162.
91 See, for example, Festinger (1957).

6 Thucydides' Athens
Λόγῳ μέν ... Ἔργῳι δέ

This final chapter will explore Thucydides' portrayal of Athenian power in selected speeches in the histories,[1] with particular emphasis on tracing points of connection, whether through endorsement, modification or outright disagreement, with images of the ideal Athens that have been sketched in previous chapters.

6.1 Book one

The importance of the council at Sparta in book one (1.68–88) is shown by Thucydides' decision to grant it four speeches, rather than the usual one or two. Consistent verbal and conceptual parallels run through these, and in particular, the speeches of the Corinthians and Athenians establish a framework through which the Peloponnesian War can be interpreted by exploring the national characteristics of its two main antagonists.[2] It is conceivable that Thucydides himself heard these speeches,[3] but what we read in book one is clearly the result of significant selection and shaping. The first speech considers Athens from an outsider's position, although much of what the Corinthians say about Athens corresponds to portrayal of the "typical" Athens in other parts of Thucydides and other sources: that Athens' enemies endorse such claims gives Thucydides' own portrayal of Athens objectivity and authority. The second speech considers Athens from an Athenian point of view. In neither case is the standard portrayal of the idealized Athens simply replicated, but it lies behind both speeches, and there is a truth to both which is not necessarily the complete or *literal* truth of what was said by specific men (not "the Corinthians" or "the Athenians")[4] on a specific day.[5]

The Corinthians begin by sketching some typical attributes of Sparta, which serve as a foil for their memorable portrayal of the Athenians in 70.2–9. Many terms with a Spartan ideological resonance are used:[6] the Corinthians state that Sparta's stability and good sense (σωφροσύνη), considered a product of Sparta's admirable constitution (cf. 1.81.1), and which Archidamus will endorse again at 1.84.2–3,[7] have caused ignorance (ἀμαθία) in Sparta's understanding of events abroad (68.1–2), since they completely misunderstand Athens' predatory intentions. Corinth also emphasizes that the Spartans are not living up to their reputation or aspirations to be liberators of Greece (69.1): Sparta could have prevented Greece's "enslavement" to Athens, but by their slackness, Sparta is in effect responsible for that enslavement. Although the Corinthians focus on Sparta, some themes of their speech already align with certain concepts in the discourse of the idealized imperial Athens, as Sparta's qualities, portrayed negatively by the Corinthians here, are the mirror image of typical qualities of the idealized Athens. From Athens' claim to have liberated Greece from Persia arose justifications of Athenian power in Greece, and also the list of Athenian national virtues – notably speed and tireless altruism – which themselves saved Greece and justified Athens' power, in an echo chamber of self-affirmation, of which Thucydides is highly sceptical. Sparta, on the other hand, according to the Corinthians here, could themselves act as liberators of Greece from Athenian enslavement, but its national virtues of slowness, good sense and stability hopelessly hamper successful liberation. At 1.69.4 the Corinthians accuse Sparta of a unique unwillingness to action – ἡσυχάζετε[8] . . . μόνοι Ἑλλήνων: whereas the Athenians aggressively use their power, Spartans are essentially defensive and delay, never making their move, so that they alone (μόνοι) let an enemy become twice its size before crushing it. Sparta, then, is a powerful city which does not use its power to its full extent. In flattering mode, Athens frequently characterizes itself as just such a city, a city that could exert its power more than it does but chooses not to out of self-restraint,[9] but the Corinthians consider the Spartans merely ineffectual in the face of Athenian aggression. Their characterization of Sparta as unique[10] also mirrors the claim to uniqueness that permeates Athenian imperial rhetoric.[11]

Although it is unadorned by the usual flattering glosses, Corinth's description of the Athenian "national character"[12] aligns both with the idealized image of Athens and the factual narrative that Thucydides offers throughout the histories.[13] The Corinthians describe Athens as "completely different [from Sparta],[14] lovers of innovation and swift both to imagine and to accomplish . . . adventurous beyond their power, risk-takers beyond their judgement and always hopeful in danger (70.3)[15] . . . quick and always abroad."[16] For the Athenians, nothing is impossible. The moment they conceive of something, they feel it is rightfully theirs[17] and nothing is ever enough, for "they alone are able to call what they hope for something achieved because of their speed in execution."[18] They spend their whole lives in labours (πόνοι), considering leisure with nothing to do (ἡσυχίαν ἀπράγμονα) much worse than unrelenting hard work (ἀσχολίαν ἐπίπονον).[19] Several words here are familiar from earlier discussions of the idealized imperial Athens, such as the πόνοι supposedly undertaken for others' benefit[20] or terms like ἡσυχία and ἀπραγμοσύνη, commended by Spartans or by more conservative Athenians hostile to the πολυπραγμοσύνη full of πόνοι that is a hallmark of Athens' power, whether idealized or in actuality. The Corinthians end with the memorable claim that the Athenians are born to take no rest themselves and give none to others (70.9): this is the mirror image of Theseus' boast in Euripides' *Supplants* (577) to the Argive Herald's accusation of πολυπραγμοσύνη: "τοιγὰρ πονοῦσα πολλὰ πόλλ᾽ εὐδαιμονεῖ."

The subsequent narrative of the Pentecontaetia bears out Corinth's claims, as does much of Thucydides' narrative.[21] Sparta is slow and passive while Athens is active, innovative and self-confident. Thucydides' account of Athenian activity from the battle of Eurymedon to 446's revolt of Euboea (1.110–13)[22] shows a whirlwind of Athenian activity, where any failure is indeed just temporary, even the calamity in Egypt,[23] and Athens seems invincible (notably at 1.105.1–6). Thucydides' account moves swiftly, text emulating Athens' own speed, and his account is comparatively impressionistic.[24] The stream of constant activity lacks dates and contains few individual names,[25] so that one action blurs into another, creating and naturalizing an unstoppable, unalterable force. In effect, although it is very different from the traditional list of familiar Athenian achievements in the *epitaphioi*,[26] Thucydides' Pentecontaetia functions like the epitaphic catalogues to create a unified essence of Athenian action, if with different moral emphases. Both Athenses are swift, but the ideal Athens is swift to defend the needy and Greek law, while Thucydides' Athens is swift to seize advantages, predatory and sometimes violent.[27] Already at 1.96.1, Thucydides appears to de-emphasize the liberating mission of the early Delian League implied by later sources, who report that the Athenians and the Ionians swore to have the same enemies and friends, symbolizing the eternal nature of their pact by sinking iron lumps into the sea. The solemnity of this gesture suggests something deeper and more idealistic than simple revenge on Persia.[28] By contrast, Thucydides claims that revenge on Persia was just the pretext (πρόσχημα) for the League, and Herodotus using similar language (πρόφασιν τὴν Παυσανίεω ὕβριν προϊσχόμενοι, 8.3.2) claims that Pausanias' *hybris* was a convenient pretext for Athens to seize control of the League. Right from the League's inception, it would seem that idealizing rhetoric from Athens could be countered by less-flattering claims.[29]

The Corinthians' portrayal of Athens finds frequent confirmation in Thucydides' subsequent narrative and contains many claims that the Athenians themselves would probably have endorsed, but neither the Corinthians' sour tone nor the generally neutral, factual tone of Thucydides' narrative[30] reflects the tone of Athenian commentary on Athenian achievements,[31] at least to judge from the Athenians' reply to the Corinthians. Some have thought it too provocative to be a historical record of Athens' response,[32] but, at its outset, the Athenians express sentiments which would not be out of place in traditional rhetoric of justification of Athens' power, the kind of claims that we frequently find in other contexts. Their first assertion is that they have won their possessions "not improperly" (οὔτε ἀπεικότως) and that the city itself is noteworthy (1.73.1; cf. 75.1). Similar claims are made by Euphemus at Camarina (6.82.1, 83.1), and these align with the portrayal of the idealized Athens whose virtues justify its position.[33] But both in Euphemus' speech and in the Athenians' speech here, Thucydides also includes elements which undermine these justifications.[34] By book six, Euphemus denies that Athens deserves its power because of the city's actions in the Persian Wars: these are merely "nice phrases" (6.83.2; cf. 5.89.1). In book one, however, the Athenians still look to the past to justify the present: at 1.73.4, they state that Athens alone[35] at Marathon ran risks against the barbarian, part of the narrative already in Herodotus (6.109.6) that most Athenians would certainly have endorsed, and that their lone stand saved Greece (1.73.4–74.3).[36] At 1.74.1, they claim that they provided almost 400 ships, a little less than two-thirds of the whole.

If this claim is not just a mistake in the manuscript, it may be an exaggeration of the kind frequently found in idealizing Athenian narratives, like the false claim to being alone at Marathon.[37] Had they followed others in yielding,[38] Greece would have been captured (1.74.4): the claim is already found at Hdt. 7.139.1, where he says that "most" (presumably non-Athenian) Greeks will find it displeasing (ἐπίφθονον), a word not only used in a negative form by Euphemus (ἀνεπίφθονον, 6.83.2), but also in adverbial form (ἐπιφθόνως) at 1.75.1, where they complain of Athens' unpopularity in Greece. The Athenians also state that they provided the three things that most helped to win Salamis – the greatest number of ships, the best admiral (cf. Hdt. 8.124) and the greatest enthusiasm that motivated them to abandon their very city, a city that did not even exist anymore,[39] uncomplainingly doing what was right for the other Greeks who had abandoned them. Herodotean echoes are strong in this passage, though whether because these were authentic to the speech or because Thucydides was deliberately invoking his predecessor is uncertain.[40]

The connection between the Athenians' speech in book one and that of Euphemus in book six is clear, and many commentators have seen a downward moral progression in Thucydides' account of the empire, from a privileged position that is at least partly based on merit, to one in which mere power and a desperate need to retain it are central.[41] But the seeds that blossom horribly in book five's Melian dialogues are already sown in book one, due to the nature of imperial power which must be wrapped up in justificatory language, language which, even in book one, is considered by Thucydides to be misleading and obsolescent.[42]

In fact, much like Euphemus in book six, though more subtly, the Athenian speakers of book one invoke and simultaneously undermine the standard claims of idealized Athenian history. Later *epitaphioi* typically place the Persian Wars after the standard list of mythological Athenian deeds, so that Athens' service to Greece is incorporated into a timeless Athenian virtue where every deed forms an unbroken line between the past, present and potentially future virtues and power of Athens. This rhetoric colonizes time and makes the imperial goal of "empire without end" extend temporally and spatially: Athens has always been this way, through nature, training and experience, so its power should never end. But the Athenians of book one minimize the idea that their power is justified by what they were supposed to have done in remote antiquity (1.73.2).[43] Such a rejection deviates from the norms surrounding the justification of Athenian power and foreshadows a similar omission by Pericles in his funeral speech. The Athenians also emphasize the excessive familiarity even of the events of 480, suggesting that by 432 their narrative is traditional to the point of tedium, giving Athens' universally known services to Greece (Hdt. 7.139.1) a surprisingly unenthusiastic cast: "Though we are rather tired of continually bringing it forward – we ran risks to get advantages which you shared" (73.2).[44] The tired repetition of "getting into the ships" (ἐσβάντες ἐς τὰς ναῦς, 73.4, 74.2; cf. 72.4)[45] has often been noted.[46] Even the claim that Athens conferred on Greece as much as it received (1.74.3) acknowledges that Athens did do well out of the Persian Wars in a somewhat different tone from that of idealized portrayals of Athens, which typically minimize the benefits of empire for Athens, emphasizing instead Athenian contributions to the welfare of Greece. So, even in a speech referencing many elements of Athenian popular history, Thucydides' presentation undercuts traditional popular justifications of Athens' power.

Such justifications also depended on the claim that the Athenians present here, that the allies requested their leadership (1.75.2; cf. 1.96.1),[47] but this familiar assertion is suddenly strikingly undercut by their statement at 75.3–4 that Athens' motivations for acquiring and keeping the empire were fear,[48] honour and self-interest, because they are almost universally hated. Would Athenians have admitted this even privately, much less among a hostile audience?[49] Thucydides makes this claim more than once (1.75.1, 4; 2.8.5, 11.2), but the evidence is ambiguous.[50] The charter of the second confederacy[51] does repudiate elements of the fifth-century empire such as cleruchies, tribute and garrisons, all of which would be potentially objectionable as signs to the allies of their subject status, but Thucydides' own narrative is selective. At 3.82.1 (cf. 3.47.1), Thucydides explains that democracies tend to support the Athenians, and oligarchies the Spartans, but, because of his tendency to offer one explicit paradigm intended to serve multiple contexts, he does not consistently emphasize these significant social divisions when discussing individual rebellions, and sometimes one must read his narrative very carefully to see that some rebels are actually oligarchs hostile to the democracies that Athens tended to support.[52] Thucydides' narrative portrays Athens as a city driven by the desire to dominate. Early in Thucydides' account of the Pentecontaetia, Naxos attempts to leave the alliance (c. 470, Thuc. 1.98.4), and he ominously describes Athens' retaliation the first time a member of the Delian League was subdued (by Athens and other allies) as "enslavement": but Naxos was a very important island which needed to be in the right hands,[53] so perhaps its subjection seemed more legitimate to others, including the allies, at the time than it seemed to Thucydides in retrospect. When the Athenians made their move against Samos, they were aided by the semi-independent Chians and Lesbians (1.116.1).[54] Even the apparent test case of Melos is suspicious:[55] the Melian dialogues were conducted by the leaders away from the people, suggesting that the interests of each group were not the same; allies were the majority in the army sent to subdue Melos,[56] which eventually fell to treachery from within (5.112). At 7.82 Gylippos offers terms to islanders and "some few" accept, but Thucydides is no more specific than that, and while at 8.1–2, Thucydides states that the Athenians are scared of being attacked by angry allies, and some of its most important allies, such as Chios, Lesbos, Euboea and others, do revolt,[57] no attack on Athens actually materializes, and Athens fights on for another eight years.[58] While it is naïve to believe that the allies were actively enthusiastic about Athenian power, since Athens did dominate and exploit them,[59] not to mention committing atrocities in the Peloponnesian War,[60] multiple cases do suggest that claims that by 431, all of Greece, especially Athens' allies, hated the city are exaggerated.[61] All in all, then, although Thucydides' Athenians claim that they cling to their empire (whose possession now seems unjust, in contrast to the language of worthiness with which the speech began)[62] from less honourable motives, these claims may not necessarily represent completely accurately what was literally said on this occasion.

The Athenians go on to claim (1.75.5–1.76.1) that pursuit of self-interest in dangerous affairs is not blameworthy (ἀνεπίφθονον) – again, a contrast to the epitaphic or tragic Athens which does right without fear of danger or thought of advantage – and that if the Spartans had had the opportunity, they would have done what Athens did. Athens is briefly no longer the unique city of idealized portrayals, but just one powerful, amoral city among others,[63] since it is human nature (1.76.2) once power is offered to accept it and then refuse to relinquish it, because the stronger will always rule the weaker, an idea that Thucydides has already laid down (1.8.3) and will cite throughout the history as an established fact of human nature.

After this, however, the Athenians return to their "script" with another appeal to their merits and the further claim that those who, acquiescing to the imperatives of human nature, accept power when it is offered them, yet then refuse to exercise that power as much as they could, are uniquely praiseworthy for behaving more moderately than others would have done in the same circumstances (1.76.3–77.6). Here, Thucydides' Athenians return to the territory of the ideal Athens, even as the surrounding material undermines such idealism.[64] The ideal Athens is preeminently the place of mercy, moderation and pity,[65] and once more (cf. 1.69.4) the imperial image of the merciful master who stays his hand and does not exercise the full power he has at his command is ironically invoked.[66] So too is that other imperial complaint of ingratitude: the Athenians' moderation and preference for law over force (1.77.2–5), uniquely transcending human nature, even as they simultaneously appeal to human nature to justify their power, are not sufficiently appreciated by the allies (77.3). These Athenians portray their power in a very Thucydidean way which diverges from the sentiments expressed in other Athenian-centred literature, even as one can see the traditional sentiments underlying certain points in their speech. This first Athenian speech shifts back and forth between appeals to traditional ideas that Athens deserves its power, and undermining those appeals by the invocation of the sheer force and violence that underlie the empire and that will lurk in all the speeches that claim to justify what Thucydides considers essentially unjustifiable.

6.2 Book two

Although Thucydides sets his own stamp on Pericles' version of the funeral oration, nothing in it is entirely at odds with later *epitaphioi*,[67] and many of his claims are paralleled either in those *epitaphioi* or in idealizing rhetoric of later empires.[68] Pericles begins his account (2.36.1) by invoking the continuous excellence of Athenian power from past to present:[69] he omits specific reference to the autochthony which is normally included in the topos (e.g. Dem. 60.4), though it may be implied, and commends his audience's fathers for having augmented what they received from their ancestors to build the empire as it now stands, not without labour (οὐκ ἀπόνως).[70] At 2.36.3 he notes that his audience have themselves increased Athens' possessions to make it "the most self-sufficient, whether in war or peace" (καὶ ἐς πόλεμον καὶ ἐς εἰρήνην αὐταρκεστάτην). All other cities, other claims, are crowded out in this simple phrase: Athens needs nothing else, no one else,[71] and is supreme in the two fundamental areas of Greek existence. By implication, this process of growth must similarly progress from this generation to subsequent generations. Whereas the Athenians at 1.73.2 rejected claims to worthiness based on the standard mythological deeds of the *epitaphioi*, starting instead with their service in the Persian Wars, Pericles rejects even mentioning the Persian Wars as "talking to those who already know" (2.36.4),[72] substituting instead an account of Athenian national character,[73] containing multiple areas both of agreement and disagreement with the outsiders' account of Athens which the Corinthians offer in book one.

The uniqueness of Athens, often with an implied comparison to Sparta (2.39.1, 39.3, 40.3, 41.3), is one of Pericles' most insistent boasts throughout the funeral speech (37.1, 38, four times in 2.40.2–5, 42.2). The claim to Athenian exceptionalism has many analogies in the rhetoric of later nations and features in the praise of Athens in many other fifth- and fourth-century texts of various kinds.[74] At 37.1, Pericles claims that Athens is an inspiration to all, whose constitution is copied by others rather than copying them,[75] and his rosy picture of the ideal equality in the democracy resembles the Euripidean Theseus' stirring paean to democracy (E. *Supp.* 434–43). Such claims are used to vindicate the rightness of Athens' dominance in Greece: exemplary virtue justifies supreme power, which itself proves its own virtue and rightness.[76] They also exemplify the imperial claim to possession of every virtue, even those which apparently contradict one another,[77] another major theme which recurs throughout the speech. Athens is a democracy but also ruled by an elite, in that the best people, however poor, have the opportunity to offer their talents to the city.[78] A similar claim to complete imperial virtue is also made in Pericles' statement (37.2–3) that while Athens offers its citizens personal and political freedom, that freedom is never abused, but through fear[79] they obey the laws, whether they are actual laws or "unwritten", especially those relating to the unjustly treated (οἱ ἀδικούμενοι). Anyone who had seen the actions of Athens in tragedy could imagine some specific examples of what Pericles means here.

While the Corinthians had expressed grudgingly admiring bafflement at Athenian hyperactivity, regarding it as inevitably excluding other important parts of human life, in chapter 38 Pericles claims the "middle" position. The Athenians have ample leisure and ample resources because of the city's greatness[80] and can enjoy others' products as much as their own.[81] Athenian national character[82] is at the heart of Athens' difference from other cities (39.1, 4), and thus at the heart of its worthiness to rule through an irresistible superiority, as it allows openness and generosity even to enemies and even at the risk that they might take advantage of the city's openness:[83] the emphasis on openness to foreigners which Athenians saw on the tragic stage, including the reception even of potential dangers to the city like Medea and Oedipus, links what Thucydides' Pericles says with other fifth-century representations of endless Athenian generosity to prove the impregnable power of the unique city that surmounts dangers that every other city fears. Sparta works for success, through endless effort from cradle to grave:[84] Athenians are effortlessly superior through their nature, not training.[85]

Though it is exceptional in its epigrammatic form, Pericles' famous claim at 2.40.1[86] is a familiar claim to unique Athenian perfection, combining some traditionally opposed elements in a telling τε . . . καί construction, rather than the μέν . . . δέ dualities that are so fundamental to Greek thought and speech, claiming a unique (μόνοι, 40.2) fusion of word and deed in multiple dimensions, public and private, deliberation and action (40.2–3).[87] The man who does not participate in vigorous political activity is uniquely deemed ἀχρεῖος ("useless"), rather than ἀπράγμων ("minding his own business"), a complimentary term at Sparta and among conservative Athenians, with an implied commendation of the πολυπραγμοσύνη of Athenian imperialism as innate to the national character of the state, whose power proves its virtue. In others, daring is a product of mere ignorance (ἀμαθία) like that commended by Archidamus in book one, but not at Athens (40.3). Athenian activity enables Athens, unlike others (40.4), to acquire friends by doing rather than receiving favours,[88] one of the claims of the speech whose connection with the idealized portrait of Athens in fifth- and fourth-century literature and subsequent imperial claims from Rome to Britain to the United States is clearest. As earlier chapters have shown, it is central to the image of Athens, especially in tragedy,[89] that the city is the one who gives, without thought of the return or expediency through its confidence and freedom (cf. Thuc. 2.40.5). This ideal contrasts with the Athenians' emphasis on self-interest and fear elsewhere in Thucydides, especially in Euphemus' speech in book six which offers distorted echoes of Pericles' funeral speech.[90] Each Athenian is uniquely versatile[91] and self-sufficient, making the collective city unassailably superior:[92] and that superiority is proven by the state's power (41.2), a power promoted by the institution of the funeral oration itself among others. Athens alone (41.3) proves even greater when tested than it is reputed to be, and alone makes assailants not ashamed when conquered, or makes subjects unquestioningly accept the city's worthiness to rule. The proof of power is the proof of virtue and vice versa, in an unbreakable circle, so that Athens has forced every land and sea[93] to be traversed by Athenian daring[94] and has left imperishable monuments "whether for evil or good."[95]

This is the least ambivalent of all Thucydides' explorations of Athenian power in the speeches, but he brilliantly conveys the fragility of the supposedly impregnable Athenian national character almost immediately as plague visits the city (2.51–2), and acts in an all too democratic and versatile manner, sparing no one and being subject to no universal remedy. Supposedly innate Athenian respect for laws will easily evaporate.[96] Other claims of Pericles prove illusory as well: deliberation will prove no match for ἔρως and ἐπιθυμία in book six.[97] It is intriguing briefly to wonder about the content of funeral speeches delivered in plague years. Could the speaker have invoked the usual topoi of Athenian virtues, conforming to the conventions of the *epitaphioi* that we know from elsewhere, in spite of the context of the horrors that Thucydides describes?[98]

At 2.60–64, Pericles gives his last speech[99] to an assembly of Athenians frustrated with his leadership and the progress of the war. Belief in an effortless Athenian superiority has been badly shaken, and while Pericles assures them that their city and people are still great, and πόνος is still essential, the claim that it is supreme over land and sea (2.41.3) has been modified to focus on the sea alone (62.2), and, rather than merely expounding on a timeless Athenian national character, Pericles must instead urge his countrymen to be active in maintaining that greatness and the vigour with which they were brought up as Athenian citizens (61.4).[100] Thucydides offers different filters through which to observe his city's power. This is the final speech of the Athenian leader whom Thucydides respects most,[101] and its finality gives his unattractive portrayal of the empire considerable authority. The πόνος (62.1, 63.1) brought by the war is no longer directed to save others, but something less voluntary, more ominous, that the Athenians have no choice but to continue. Empire necessitates a πόνος of continuous expansion, because of the shame involved in losing (or even not adding to) the gains made to it by ancestors (62.3) and because static power becomes vulnerable: Pericles' earlier fantasy of effortless Athenian superiority (2.39.1–3) is far away. While the idealized Athens assumes the life of πολυπραγμοσύνη voluntarily with apparently limitless competitive generosity in helping others,[102] Pericles denies here that it can be voluntary (or, by implication, limitless) because it is no longer possible to *choose* to reject such a life. Athens cannot enjoy the virtue of the ἀπράγμων (63.2; cf. 3.40.4) because what they have is like a tyranny: by the time of Cleon's speech (3.37.2) it is one.[103] Once empire is acquired and solidified it cannot be relinquished: if it was wrong to take it,[104] it is dangerous to abandon it. Empire, like tyranny, is attractive for the agency it offers (cf. 5.69),[105] but brings with it dangers, as both Pericles (2.63.1) and the Athenians in book one acknowledge (1.75.3–4). Such dangers are not only external but also internal, in that empire can cause catastrophic self-deception if its possessors come to believe that their position is simply what they deserve because they believe so completely in their own idealized self-image. Pericles ends this speech with a final, slightly wistful reminder of the glory of Athens' unique power, that they have ruled the most Greeks, fought the greatest wars and had the greatest and best-provisioned city (cf. 2.38.2): even now, he scorns the ἀπράγμων as inferior figure to the δρᾶν . . . βουλόμενος, and regards present hatred as a worthy sacrifice for future fame (2.64.4–5). This is a particularly brilliant example of Thucydides' understanding of the deeply seductive quality of imperial power over others, alongside the deleterious effects on the Athenians that this "Athenian dream" has had.[106]

6.3 Book three

An unambiguously unflattering view of Athens' power is offered by the speeches of the Mytilenean debate, above all by Cleon.[107] Though Pericles claimed that the democracy generates virtuous citizens who were free in their private lives and allowed freedom to others (2.37.2), Cleon claims that this very feature of democracy makes empire impossible because empire depends on harsh power relations, not virtue and freedom (37.1–2). The ideal Athens is known for its compassion to deserving suppliants and a unique ability to feel pity,[108] along with an ability to punish the wicked and the wisdom to know the difference. But for Cleon, pity (οἶκτος) weakens the city by making it vulnerable to disaffected subjects, and both he and his rival Diodotus appeal strictly to Athens' self-interest, excluding all appeals to pity.[109] It seems most unlikely that there were no appeals to pity in the Mytilenean debate. If these speeches, like others in Thucydides, were highly condensed[110] and if Thucydides considered talk of pity expendable and omitted it in the interests of condensing the Mytilenean debate to more general, and for him, more interesting ideas explored there, what was actually said at the debate might be decidedly different from the narrative Thucydides offers. Thucydides himself notes that others beside Cleon and Diodotus spoke (36.6), and though Cleon urges the assembly to reject pity, that he mentions it at all suggests that others did raise the issue (cf. 3.40.1). Moreover, the Athenians do repent after the first assembly (49.1) and the ship they send to countermand the original order quickly overtakes the first, whose slow pace was due to misgivings about its cruel task (49.4).[111] Thucydides' evident selectivity here may again function to undermine a central attribute of the idealized Athens. Through Cleon, Thucydides claims that stories which portray Athens as the city of pity are merely a dangerous illusion in the light of its sheer power, because the empire is a tyranny (37.2),[112] and power is the only criterion for a successful empire. Through Cleon, Thucydides also deconstructs the difference drawn between Athens and Sparta that underlies many claims in Pericles' funeral speech. Cleon echoes Archidamus in preferring unchanged bad laws to good ones without authority (3.37.3, 4; 1.86; cf. 6.18.7); σωφροσύνη and ἀμαθία (both "Spartan" words) to clever insubordination; and non-intellectuals to intellectuals. Pericles considered debate and deliberation quintessentially Athenian: some later idealizing portrayals claim that language is most developed at Athens, and since language distinguishes humans from beasts, the implication is that Athenians are more evolved human beings than others.[113] Cleon dismisses such things as mere rhetoric,[114] dangerous if Athens is to retain its power (3.38.2–7).

Cleon offers an even more striking rejection of the idealized Athens at 3.40.2, where he claims that three quintessentially Athenian attributes – pleasure in words (ἡδονὴ λογῶν), οἶκτος (pity) and ἐπείκεια (moderation)[115] – are most dangerous to empire. This city of pity and moderation[116] portrayed to Athenians must by definition be an unsuccessful imperialist, even though the ideal Athens not only combines pity and power, but they must actually work together, as the pity Athens feels for suppliants is translated into effective action against their enemies, leading to reward for the good and punishment for the bad, and the restoration of moral order. The idealized Athens balances sentiment and reason: the city's representatives feel pity but also evaluate suppliants' speeches to determine whether it is right to help them,[117] through their superior sense of justice. Cleon rejects the entire process, and his justice is the sham justice of a tyrant. His further claim (40.3) that compassion (ἔλεος, with ἐπιείκεια later in the paragraph) is only for those who can reciprocate it also undermines images of the ideal self-sufficient

Athens which treats others generously without hope of or need for recompense.[118] Instead, Cleon claims that only by punishing Mytilene severely now can Athens retain its power (3.39.6, 40.5, 7). "Parcere subiectis et debellare superbos": imperial rulers can choose who is humble and who is proud, and the *epitaphioi* and tragedy contain many examples of Athenian success in making such choices, often using the principle stated by Cleon himself (3.40.1) that mercy is due to humans who go wrong (ξυγγνώμην ἁμαρτεῖν ἀνθρωπίνως), but Cleon rejects this principle as damaging to Athens' power.

Cleon's message is clearly unattractive, but he cannot merely be disregarded as a "bad Athenian". His arguments have clear and disturbing links of content and language with the those of other, less bad Athenians,[119] and some of his statements about the debasement of Athenian politics resemble Thucydides' own judgement.[120] The verbal echoes between Pericles' and Cleon's speeches are clear,[121] while his claim that if the Mytileneans were right to rebel, Athens is wrong to rule and must relinquish empire and cultivate virtue without danger if this fact is unpalatable,[122] is essentially Pericles' argument at 2.63.1–2 (cf. 1.140.5; 2.60.2). His assertion (3.39.5) that Athens was foolish in having been too lenient with the Mytileneans[123] also recalls the Athenians' claim (1.76.3–4) that they rule more moderately than they could do, given their power. Thucydides' hostility to Cleon is clear, but his speech explores a vision of Athenian rule which is not completely absent from more favourable visions.

Cleon's opponent Diodotus[124] is less harsh as Cleon and reaffirms the value of good counsel and λόγος for anyone not ill-educated or stupid (3.42.1–2),[125] complaining at length of the deleterious effect on the city of arguments such as Cleon's. Even so, his position is not fundamentally different. He too privileges expediency (44.1–2) over συγγνώμη (44.2) or justice (44.4),[126] and no less than Cleon rejects the virtues of οἶκτος and ἐπιείκεια (3.48.1) that are so dear to the ideal Athens.[127] Like Cleon, he acknowledges the importance of hope and, significantly, ἔρως[128] in leading people to strive for their freedom: in fact, he is almost sympathetic to them for so doing (46.5; cf. 39.2), but revenue is important for Athens (46.2–4) and must take precedence over other considerations.[129] Diodotus' recommendation (3.46.6) that prevention is better than cure, demanding intense vigilance to stop rebellions before they happen, exemplifies what it means to be a tyrant city, whose power is simultaneously vast and fragile, never the easy, freely possessed and used dominance of the ideal city.

6.4 Book five

Even though the Athenians punish Scione severely for its rebellion (5.32.1), Thucydides showcases Melos,[130] portraying its fate as the logical outcome of the vast imbalance of power between Athens and the allies that ran even through the early books of the history. Though he claims that Melos was neutral, and deliberately removes any hint of provocation on their part, his own narrative and inscriptional evidence (*ML* 67, Side ll.1–7, 13–17; cf. 69, col. i., l.65)[131] make Melian neutrality questionable.[132] We learn also that the Melian leaders do not speak with

Athens before the people (84.3). Thucydides does not explain why: perhaps the people might have yielded to Athens if they had had the choice.[133] Of course this does not mitigate the Athenians' actions but it does give them a slightly different context, as does Thucydides' report that a large allied force (5.84.1) was apparently willing to help Athens bring Melos to heel.[134]

The episode recalls the earlier treatment of Plataea (3.52–68) in the emphasis laid by the victims on the past and their oppressors' dismissal of the relevance of their claims, but the rhetorical format is strikingly different. The dialogue form,[135] with its short point and counterpoint, is especially effective in illustrating one of Thucydides' anti-idealizing arguments, that although Pericles' Athenians claim to place great value on language and deliberation, ultimately, these have far less importance than Athenian force,[136] as the Melians note from the start. Thucydides was probably not present at the dialogue (Dion. Hal. *Thuc.* 37–41), making these speeches a creation based on his own idea of "what was fitting" in the circumstances.[137] While 1.73.2 and 2.36.1–4 rejected the old myths but acknowledged recent history and Athens' part in the Persian Wars, the Athenians at Melos both reject the traditional claim that their services in the Persian War justify their position in Greece,[138] stating that it is pointless to make "a long speech that no one would believe",[139] and deny that they are retaliating for wrongdoing by Melos (even though Melian hostility could surely have been characterized, however flimsily, as some kind of transgression if they had wanted to do so).[140] In this world, appeals to traditional ideas of justice or to past services are all subordinated to expediency. Only sheer power matters.[141]

The Melians, who speak in more traditional terms than the Athenians do,[142] attempt to use speech (λόγος) to counteract the actuality (ἔργον) of Athenian power, but that power prevails every time.[143] Moreover, they know that this outcome is likely from the very start of the dialogue (86.1), where the supposed Athenian reasonableness (ἐπιείκεια)[144] of conducting a dialogue is shown to be a sham, given the military forces arrayed against them.[145] After the Athenians have defined their motivation for threatening Melos as based on pure expediency, the Melians attempt to save themselves by trying to outdo the Athenians in appeals to expediency, claiming, for example, that a common ability to invoke what is reasonable and just (τὰ εἰκότα καὶ δίκαια, 90.1) is expedient for all.[146] The Athenians prove indifferent: they simply wish to rule without πόνος so that Melos may be preserved (91.2), a policy supposedly advantageous to both sides (93.1). Continued Melian neutrality makes Athens look weak (95.1, 97.1): again, the tyrant city's power is oddly fragile.[147] At 98.1, the Melians try again to link expediency and justice:[148] by attacking them, Athens will make many more enemies in the future – an argument that resembles Diodotus' (3.45–47) – and at 100.1, they argue that if Athens is willing to risk so much to preserve its power, then surely they would be cowardly not to try to resist it, an argument that ironically recalls Athenian resistance to Persia at Hdt. 8.143.[149] But every argument they make is countered with the Athenians' simple appeal to the immense imbalance of power between Athens and Melos: good sense (ἤν γε σωφρόνως βουλεύησθε) demands that the Melians simply submit (101.1, 103).[150] When the Melians express trust both in the gods, who will support just men fighting against the unjust, and men, in the form of the Spartans who will save them out of kinship and a sense of shame, the Athenians consider them woefully naïve. The gods, made in Athens' image, rule by a supposedly eternal law of nature, which existed before them and will exist after them:[151] they are only doing what anyone would do if they had the opportunity,[152] while the Spartans – and the Athenians are right – will rescue Melos only if it is to their advantage to do so (105.3–4).[153] Sparta does indeed yoke expediency and justice (105.4), but in a very different sense to what the Melians suggest Athens should do at 98.1. The Athenians who help their friends, expecting nothing in return, are far away,[154] but the funeral speech itself is invoked with chilling effect at 111.4 when these Athenians claim there is no dishonour in submitting to submit to what Pericles also called the greatest city in Hellas (2.41.3)[155] when it offers moderate terms (μέτρια).[156] This is not quite the moderation praised as typical of the ideal Athens. For Thucydides, the sheer power of Athens makes such idealizing claims a fraud.[157]

6.5 Book six

For Thucydides, the events at Melos represent the ultimate manifestation of Athenian power devoid of all the pretty words (ὀνόματα καλά) of the *epitaphioi* and tragedy. But he well understood their seductive quality,[158] and returns to them in the account of the Sicilian expedition that immediately follows the Melian massacre. At 3.86.3–4, the Athenians had responded to the people of Leontini, who appealed to them as fellow Ionians and allies for help against Syracuse – just the kind of appeal to which the ideal Athens would be susceptible. Athens does indeed send assistance, on the pretext (πρόφασις) of the common ground between them, but really to explore the possibility of controlling Sicily and to stop Peloponnesian imports of wheat. Book six begins with an account of Sicilian history and geography of which Thucydides claims most Athenians, unlike himself,[159] were ignorant: since Athens had been interested in Sicily for almost 20 years,[160] the literal truth of his claim seems questionable,[161] though it illustrates Thucydides' belief that most people are ignorant of their own history and believe whatever sounds most attractive.[162] Thucydides states that Athens' truest reason (ἀληθεστάτη πρόφασις: 6.6.1; cf. 1.23.6) for intervention was conquering Sicily,[163] but the idea of again helping kinsmen and allies εὐπρεπῶς was also attractive: the adverb here does not quite mean "speciously", since such considerations did matter, but it has something of the quality of the ὀνόματα καλά of idealized Athenian action which, as Thucydides consistently shows, are flimsy in the context of a relentless Athenian drive to power.[164]

The Egestaean envoys seeking help from Athens against their neighbour Selinus cite the alliance made by Athens during the time of the Leontine War, appealing both to more idealistic claims and to Athenian self-interest, via the attractions of nipping Syracusan aggression in the bud: they also promise that they can pay for the expenses of the war (6.6.2). The following spring, Athenian envoys return from Egesta with 60 talents of silver (6.8.1) and an encouraging, if false, account of Egesta's general financial position (6.8.2), whereupon the assembly votes to dispatch 60 ships to Egesta. At a second meeting[165] to discuss the logistics of the expedition, Nicias, chosen against his will as general and sceptical of what he considered a flimsy pretext for making a play for all of Sicily,[166] tries to dissuade the Athenians from the action. He outright rejects the traditional Athens that helps friends (6.9.1, 13.2), calling the Egestaeans foreigners (9.1) and even barbarians (11.7), and urges extreme caution given Athens' potential vulnerability (10.1–4): when the Thracian Chalcidians are still rebellious, the Athenians should not be rushing off to help supposedly wronged (ὡς ἀδικουμένοις) Egestaeans. He advises his audience to ignore the dishonest talk of the Egestaeans, who will not thank Athens if they succeed[167] and who will drag their friends down with them if they fail (12.1). Nicias concludes by decrying Athens' policy of making alliances with those who can offer them little in return (13.2): the identical claim is made by the repellent herald in Euripides' *Heraclidae* 176–8, where it is rejected by Demophon.[168] So much for the self-sufficient Athens that makes friends by doing, rather than receiving, good from them (2.40.4–5).

Athens was greatly damaged by its disastrous foray into Sicily, whose attempted conquest was a purely imperialistic reach but could be represented at various points (1.44.3; 3.86–8; 3.103–115; 6.6.1) as aid freely offered to friends and allies, by a city living up to its idealized reputation. But already at 4.58–64, Thucydides uses Hermocrates, a Syracusan who understands the gap between the ideal Athens and the reality very well (cf. 6.76–7),[169] as a mouthpiece for questioning Athens' supposed commitment to its idealized values.[170] For him, Athens' supposed interest in helping the Chalcidians, who have never given them anything (recalling the claims of Pericles, 2.40.4–5, and others) is really motivated by desire for the good things in Sicily (4.61.3),[171] and in a highly Thucydidean explanation, Hermocrates ascribes Athens' actions to the fundamental desire to rule, for which he feels even sympathy (πολλὴ ξυγγνώμη), because it is so human. Because this drive is so fundamental for Thucydides and influences some of his view of the repeatable nature of human history, the altruism that supposedly motivates the idealized Athens cannot be credible to him. Hermocrates' assessment of Athens' true intentions proves correct. When the Sicilians ally with one another and Athens' services to allies prove unwanted, the generals go home and are banished or fined for failing to take Sicily, because the Athenians had become so carried away by prosperity that they had confused hope with reality (4.65.3–4). This is a revealing case of the Athenians believing their own "publicity": if many members of the assembly believed in the eternally vigorous and successful "can-do" spirit that the Corinthians (1.70.7) and Pericles ascribe to Athens, because this kind of characterization, based on a selective version of past history, was offered to them through multiple verbal and visual media, it is easy to see how they might have felt that the generals in Sicily had deprived them of what was rightfully theirs by a lack of daring, Athenian spirit and the concern to surpass their fathers' achievements.

Such a spirit pervades the response to Nicias' speech by Alcibiades, many of whose predictions will prove false.[172] Alcibiades is driven by personal ambition and greed (6.15.2–3), but the arguments he uses to encourage the invasion of

Sicily are embedded in the idealized portrayal of Athens as unique among Greek cities, and he closely identifies himself with the fortunes of Athens (6.16.2).[173] He claims that the Sicilian cities will be easy to subdue because they are different from Athens, unsettled in their institutions and full of mingled peoples (17.2–3). While some of what he says turns out to be correct,[174] his argument is notably shaped by the ideologies of Athenian autochthony and idealized democracy that underpinned Athens' sense of its superiority and fitness to rule.[175] He alludes to the achievements of fathers who expanded Athenian power, thanks to their naval superiority (17.7), while at 6.18.1 he claims that Athens is bound by oath to help allies, whether or not they have offered reciprocal services, because (18.2) the principle of helping (supposed) friends indiscriminately is how both they *and others*, strengthening his argument by presenting his policy as a universal imperative, have always won power.[176] This sentence unites the image of the idealized Athens with what Thucydides sees as its power-hungry reality. Thucydides is probably reporting a very abbreviated speech, sticking to what he considered τὰ δέοντα, and it is tempting to imagine that the brevity of 18.2 might conceal an original speech offering more specific examples of help given by Athens to deserving suppliants in the past, based on the familiar stories of idealized Athenian action.[177] This must remain speculative, but Thucydides' version of this speech does clearly combine elements of Pericles' two last speeches in book two, one describing the idealized Athenian empire, the other, its extreme vulnerability,[178] as Alcibiades moves from the confidence of 18.2 to an argument from fear at 18.3. Alcibiades asserts that it is impossible to put limits on empire: once the Athenians do so, they will face the danger of being ruled and the whole empire is likely to collapse, so that the ἀπραγμοσύνη commended by Nicias is damaging and even un-Athenian (18.7). This ambivalence between absolute power and absolute vulnerability is not only typical of the tyrant in Greek thought (cf. 2.65, 3.38 and 6.87.2), but also endemic to imperialism as a whole. *Imperium sine fine* must always aspire (and likely fail) to stretch over time and space,[179] but the impossibility of the task makes every empire vulnerable.[180]

With Alcibiades' speech and the urging of the Egestaeans and Leontine exiles combined – did they also appeal to Athenian tradition, like Oedipus at S. *OC* 258–62? – the Athenians fall in love with the expedition (6.24.3)[181] and commit 200 triremes, 5000 hoplites and other armaments to it.[182] Hope and greed (24.3) crowd out any concerns about the feasibility of the venture.[183] The city that withstood Persian oppressors is now the oppressor, and its fate in the harbour at Syracuse resembles in some significant ways the Persians' experience in 480 BCE.[184] The Athenians become to the Syracusans what the Persians once were to the Athenians (6.33.5–6),[185] with a similar moral,[186] confirming Thucydides' claim (1.22.4) that through τὸ ἀνθρώπινον, the past can be replayed in future events. Syracuse itself has embryonic stirrings towards imperialism,[187] and the cycle moves on. Athenians become Persians,[188] while Syracusans start to become Athenians,[189] whose experience, innovation and courage grow throughout book seven (e.g. 7.36.2–6, 59.2, 66.3–67.4) as those of the Athenians correspondingly diminish.[190] In particular, Hermocrates, who has a fine understanding of

Athenian psychology, confirming Thucydides' claims that the Syracusans most resembled the Athenians in institutions and character,[191] becomes a sort of Dorian Themistocles, intelligent, energetic and practical (6.34).[192] He states plainly that the Athenians' pretext (πρόφασις) is alliance with Egesta but their real target is Sicily (6.33.2; cf. 76.2, 77.1), specifically Syracuse, because the rest of Sicily will easily fall once Syracuse is taken.[193] He reassures the Syracusans that they can withstand the invaders since few armies have ever prospered in distant campaigns: indeed, Athens' own power arose from Persia's failure in such a campaign, and Syracuse may similarly benefit (33.6). At 6.34.4, he urges them not to follow their accustomed "love of quiet" (ἡσυχία)[194] but confront the Athenians directly to show that they mean business: the unexpected sight of Syracusan daring (τόλμα) will alarm them.

The last of the speeches which interrogate Athenian imperial values is that of Euphemus at Camarina (6.82–87), who both answers Hermocrates and replicates the structure of Alcibiades' speech in what he says about the empire. He begins with the claim that Athens has, and rules, its empire reasonably (εἰκότως, 6.82.1; cf. οὐκ ἀπεικότως, 1.73.1),[195] arguing also that as Ionians, they must act always in self-defence against hostile and numerous Dorians (82.2).[196] He then refers to the Persian Wars (82.3), claiming that Athens acquired ships and rid itself of the ἀρχή and ἡγεμονία of the Spartans, as though Athens had liberated Greece from Sparta rather than Persia.[197] "Being appointed" Greek leaders of the king's former subjects through their strength, they must continue to lead to avoid falling under Peloponnesian domination. Moreover, it was not unjust to subject the Ionians and islanders because (82.4) the Ionians opposed their own mother city, not daring to sacrifice their own property as the Athenians did, but desiring slavery and wanting Athens' enslavement as well.[198] After this simultaneously aggressive and self-defensive narrative, whose emphasis is utterly different from all other accounts of the Persian Wars and the origin of the Delian league,[199] Euphemus returns to the Athenian "script" at 83.1 by stating that Athens deserves to rule Greece because it provided the greatest fleet and greatest enthusiasm for the fight.[200] But the last words of this paragraph ("desiring strength against the Peloponnesians")[201] prepare for a dramatic shift. Euphemus suddenly discards any traditional justification of Athenian rule. We will not "use nice words" (καλλιεπούμεθα, 83.2; cf. 5.98.1) that we rule reasonably (εἰκότως; cf. 82.1, 1.73.1) because we overthrew the barbarian single-handedly (μόνοι) or because we risked all for others' freedom. In fact, in 480 Athens acted entirely in its own interests. He states that it is ἀνεπίφθονον ("not to be complained about") that everyone should provide for their own safety: the term links us with the very first time that a crack was placed in the idealized Athens, in the Athenians' first speech, 1.75.1 (cf. Hdt. 7.139.1).[202] Now all claims to altruism or fighting for justice without fear of the consequences are gone, and safety is after all what matters (83.2–4). Athens retains the empire through fear, self-interest and self-preservation: even the element of honour, cited at 1.75.3, is now gone (85.3). At 85.1, Euphemus equates a tyrant with an empire,[203] arguing that nothing is unreasonable if it is expedient, and no one a kinsman unless he is trustworthy, but that such categories are not fixed: friends and enemies are determined according to the occasion (καιρός), a radical departure from the claims to constancy and stability that the *epitaphioi* promote. Euphemus lays out the imperial dilemma explicitly in 87.2: we rule in Greece so as not to be subject and are compelled to continuously interfere (πολλὰ πράσσειν) because there is so much to guard against (πολλὰ φυλασσόμεθα). The πολυπραγμοσύνη claimed as innate to the Athenian character and vindicated by tragedy for its advantages for oppressed suppliants and even Athens' happiness itself (E. *Supp.* 577) turns out to be imposed upon them and is certainly no source of happiness.[204] The Athenians' energetic activity created the empire, but it can only be retained by ever-increasing and ultimately unsustainable activity, and so, uniquely among Thucydides' speakers, Euphemus must invite his listeners (87.3) to find what is advantageous for themselves in Athens' power, rather than judging (since justice is now evidently irrelevant) or attempting to change Athenian policy or character. At 87.4, he develops the claim: "all men in every place, even where we are not, who either apprehend or meditate aggression, from the near prospect before them, in the one case, of obtaining our intervention in their favour, in the other, of our arrival making the venture dangerous, find themselves constrained, respectively, to be moderate against their will, and to be preserved without trouble of their own."[205] Here, the claims to universal power, to Athens as a force for moderation, salvation and work on behalf of others, the trope of Athens as policeman of the Aegean, could almost come straight out of the portrayals of Athens in the *epitaphioi*, but they are entirely undermined by their context, and the contrasts within Euphemus' speech expose the contradictions within statements of traditional Athenian imperial virtues like little else in Thucydides.

6.6 Book seven

By the end of book seven, the extraordinary reversal in Athens' fortunes is clear, both from Nicias' speeches (generally agreed to contain significant Thucydidean invention)[206] and from Thucydides' narrative itself, which recalls and contrasts happier Athenian campaigns.[207] As Athenian power increasingly declines, Nicias rallies his troops before the final conflict in the harbour, by appeals to considerations that many of Thucydides' earlier speakers have scorned in weaker adversaries. In particular, his desperate appeals recall the Athenians' contemptuous dismissal of similar appeals by the Melians.[208] At 7.61.3 (cf. 7.77.3–4), he lays emphasis on fortune and hope for the future; at 63.3, he implores the sailors not to be perplexed by misfortunes, while at 63.3–4, he appeals to the allies to remember all the benefits Athens has given them, even the pleasure they received from being considered Athenian through their language and imitating their ways. Since they freely share their empire with the allies alone,[209] those allies must not betray[210] them now (63.4). His pleas recall Pericles' claims at 2.36.3, 37.2 and 40.4, although the Athens whose strength, benevolence and self-sufficiency enable them to act for others uniquely without seeking reciprocation[211] is long gone. Even in Nicias' attempts to encourage his troops by recounting the practical measures they have taken against the Syracusans, they have clearly lost their edge and are reacting to others' innovations (67.2) rather than bending others to their will with their own innovative spirit, and the Syracusans take easy countermeasures against them (65.2). The exhortation to fight for salvation and fatherland (7.61.1) is revealing: this would normally be a topos for those defending their land, as Nicias himself warns the Athenians at an earlier stage of the expedition (6.68.3).

By contrast with Nicias, Gylippos is confident and excited that his army will be remembered as the first to resist the Athenians' unprecedented power (7.66.2; cf. 2.64.3).[212] At 66.3 (cf. 67.4), he comes close to the kind of psychological "colonization" discussed in Chapter 1, by entering into the Athenians' minds, explaining that when men are crushed in what they thought they excelled in, they typically crumble more easily than their actual strength would warrant, and that this is "probably" (εἰκός) what the Athenians are experiencing. By contrast, his army, daring but originally unskilled (67.1),[213] now match innate daring with learned skill.[214] Many in the Athenian army are more used to land than sea, which will create confusion (63.2),[215] and in a narrow harbour, Athens' larger navy will not help them (67.3).

Thucydides does not even trouble to record directly Nicias' next speech, born of acute alarm at the forthcoming battle (7.69.2),[216] calling it ἀρχαιολογεῖν.[217] Evidently, he considers his readers capable of imagining Nicias' words through the appeals that they themselves might have heard in similar contexts.[218] Nicias talks "as men are apt to do", which partly entails reverting to the vision of Athens that most of Thucydides' other speeches have made so hard to endorse. Thus he exhorts them to be true to their fathers, their own fame or the hereditary virtues by which their ancestors became glorious, echoing Pericles even as the circumstances of the two speeches are utterly different,[219] by reminding them that their country is the most free and everyone is allowed to live however they wish, and using "other arguments that men tend to use in such crises, which can be made to serve on all occasions alike." This is Nicias' own brief funeral speech[220] for a fantasy combination of power and virtue that Thucydides perhaps thought was near death, but, τὰ ἀνθρώπινα being what they are, has proven remarkably resilient.

Notes

1. For a full list of speeches in Thucydides, see West (1973). I will focus on 1.68–71, 73–78, 2.35–46, 60–64, 3.37–40, 42–48, 5.85–113, 6.9–14, 16–18, 33–34, 76–80, 82–87, 7.61–64, 66–68, 69.2, and 7.77. They are not discussed in their entirety, but only insofar as they illuminate the relationship between Thucydides and idealized images of Athenian power.
2. Hornblower (1991) 107–8.
3. Stroud (1994) 276.
4. The ascription of speeches to "the Corinthians/Athenians" rather than individuals makes them especially significant as the "*logos* of the city": de Romilly (1963) 242 (cf. 274).
5. For example, it is often thought that the relegation of the Megarians' complaints to one brief paragraph (1.67.4) before the Corinthians' great programmatic speech, 68–71, may not reflect the emphasis laid on them at the council.

6 Debnar (2001) 227–9; Georges (1994) 146. For a collection of words typical of Sparta and Athens, used by Thucydides to denote their respective national characters, see Luginbill (1999) 87–94. Cf. also earlier, pp. 13–14, 16–20.
7 Archidamus reaffirms the value of being slow (the opposite of the speedy Athenians) as a reason for Sparta's freedom and glory, considering it the basis of their thoughtful good sense (σωφροσύνη ἔμφρων) and their courage and good counsel, and ἀμαθία as beneficial in inculcating due obedience to law. At 3.37.3, Cleon, portrayed in certain respects as an "anti-Athenian", commends ἀμαθία μετὰ σωφροσύνης ("ignorance with good sense").
8 On this term in Thucydides and its association with the ἀπραγμοσύνη uniquely rejected by imperially minded Athenians, cf. Huart (1968) 367–73.
9 Thuc. 1.76.3–4; E. *Supp.* 723–5; Pl. *Mx.* 242c–d. For the connection with this image and imperialistic psychology, see p. 23 earlier.
10 Compare Archidamus' claim for Sparta at 1.84.2.
11 See pp. 17–18; cf. Thuc. 1.70.7, 73.4, 102.3; 2.39.1, 40.3–4, 44.5. Similarly, Thucydides' Plataeans use phrases such as μόνοι Βοιωτῶν (3.54.3), παρὰ δύναμιν (3.54.4, 57.4), and so on, recalling Athens' own narrative of their exceptional stand against Persia. The Plataeans also warn that enslaving the land where Greek freedom was won would violate Greek common law, the same law which is frequently invoked in tragedies glorifying Athens' services to the Greeks and the gods (cf. E. *Supp.* 526–7), and claim that glory comes from compassion and reason, another lesson offered by Athenian tragedy. But for Thebes and Sparta the past proves irrelevant: Macleod (1983c), esp. 106–7.
12 On national character, see Luginbill (1999), esp. 82–104. Daring and its concomitant elements of optimism but also acquisitiveness are central to Athens, as opposed to Spartan σωφροσύνη and its tendencies towards self-control and stability but also inaction: Luginbill (1999) 89–93; Forde (1989) 17–20. Success in the Persian Wars contributed to Athens' hope and daring and brought a psychological confidence that in its turn spurred further hope and daring. Forde (1986) 436–7 (cf. (1989) 22–5) rightly emphasizes that Athens behaved extraordinarily in briefly vacating their city in 480 BCE, abandoning their religious roots and placing human concerns temporarily above divine concerns. However, he is not necessarily right to conclude that justice was therefore unimportant to them, or that the absence of the gods from Pericles' funeral speech is a significant indication of Athenian attitudes towards the divine. On the contrary, their motivations in 480 may perhaps recall the way that Theseus in *Oedipus at Colonus* abandons a sacrifice to Poseidon to help a needy suppliant. In both cases, at least in idealizing mode, they are motivated by confidence in knowing the proper course of action, which the gods will reward with continuing success.
13 Cf. 8.96.4–5 and 4.55.2: Hornblower (1991) 114; Connor (1987) 44–5; Luginbill (1999) 134–72.
14 At 2.39.1, the verb διαφέρω is again used to mark Athens as unique: cf. n.11 earlier.
15 But in Thucydides, hope is typically founded on wishful thinking or even when given a more concrete grounding, not realized: Huart (1968) 141–8. Hope is a dangerous incentive to rashness because it is one of the appetitive emotions, like ἔρως, which both enabled Athens' victories in the Persian Wars and disasters like the Sicilian expedition. Thucydides traces a clear path from Salamis to Syracuse through Athens' relentless dynamism and resilience: Rood (1999) 247. Words with the ἐλπις root appear three times in chapter 70 alone (70.3, 70.7 (twice)). Even when the word itself is not used, the concept was central in Athenian conceptions of their own character and actions, and combined with Athens' innate speed, made the city truly formidable: Gervasi (1981); Luginbill (1999) 26–8, 65–81.
16 Thuc. 1.70.1–4: πᾶν διαφέροντας . . . νεωτεροποιοὶ καὶ ἐπινοῆσαι ὀξεῖς καὶ ἐπιτελέσαι ἔργῳ ἃ ἂν γνῶσιν . . . παρὰ δύναμιν τολμηταὶ καὶ παρὰ γνώμην κινδυνευταὶ καὶ ἐν τοῖς δεινοῖς εὐέλπιδες . . . ἄοκνοι . . . καὶ ἀποδημηταί.

17 Parry (1981) 131 (cf. 162) describes this as the "dynamic harmony of λόγος and ἔργον which is characteristic of the Athenians and responsible for their successes."
18 Thuc. 1.70.7: μόνοι γὰρ ἔχουσί τε ὁμοίως καὶ ἐλπίζουσιν ἃ ἂν ἐπινοήσωσι διὰ τὸ ταχεῖαν τὴν ἐπιχείρησιν ποιεῖσθαι ὧν ἂν γνῶσιν.
19 Thuc. 1.70.8: καὶ ταῦτα μετὰ πόνων πάντα καὶ κινδύνων δι' ὅλου τοῦ αἰῶνος μοχθοῦσι, καὶ ἀπολαύουσιν ἐλάχιστα τῶν ὑπαρχόντων διὰ τὸ αἰεὶ κτᾶσθαι καὶ μήτε ἑορτὴν ἄλλο τι ἡγεῖσθαι ἢ τὸ τὰ δέοντα πρᾶξαι ξυμφοράν τε οὐχ ἧσσον ἡσυχίαν ἀπράγμονα ἢ ἀσχολίαν ἐπίπονον.
20 Earlier, pp. 21–2; cf. 83, 84–5, 89–90; in Thucydides, 2.36.2, 38.1 and in general 2.60–64; Boegehold (1982); Raaflaub (1994), esp. 103–11. Wade-Gery (1958) 265–6 equates ἡσυχία with ἀπραγμοσύνη, the political opposite of Athenian πολυπραγμοσύνη. While Hornblower (2004) 60–3 rightly warns that these concepts transcend narrow reference to Athenian imperialism, and that the actual term πολυπραγμοσύνη is rarely found, so that words like these must be given a nuanced interpretation, the contrast between Athens' and Sparta's "national characters" is so fundamental to Thucydides that it seems appropriate to read these terms here and elsewhere in a political sense.
21 Luginbill (1999) 134–72.
22 Thucydides gives no reason for the revolt, but Athenian land-grabbing is a likely cause: Hornblower (1991) 184–5.
23 Had it been part of his purpose, Thucydides could have portrayed it as a disaster as great as the Sicilian expedition: Hornblower (1991) 173; cf. 176–7.
24 McNeal (1970); Forde (1989) 26. Inscriptions can sometimes supplement Thucydides' silences: Meiggs (1943).
25 Rood (1998) 235–6; de Romilly (1963) 59–65.
26 The orators diverge wildly from Thucydides' version of Athenian history: Thomas (1989) 227–8 compares the very different effects that Thuc. 1.105 and Lys. 2.48–53, telling the same story, produce in the reader; cf. Rood (1998) 246–7. Strasburger (2009) 200 uses these discrepancies to argue that the versions of Athenian history which we see in the later *epitaphioi* must actually have had earlier origins: "I cannot imagine that this official version of the history of the age of Pericles could have been built anew once more after Thucydides, that is in defiance of his authority if it had not already been firmly established before him." See also Loraux (1986) 289–95.
27 The Pentecontaetia sketches a portrait of Athens that will be consistent throughout Thucydides' narrative. Athens is eternally active, even when retreat might have seemed more reasonable than renewing aggressive efforts. For example, when there is plague in Athens and the Spartans are coming to ravage Attica, Pericles sends 100 ships out against the Peloponnese (2.56.1; cf. 7.42.1–6; 8.10.2–4, 95.2). Sparta is slow and slack: 1.86.3, 3.2.1, 15, 25–9; 4.55. At 6.103.3, Spartan inaction nearly causes Syracuse's surrender to the Athenians (cf. Plut. *Nic.* 18.4, 21.3), amply confirming Thucydides' judgement (8.96.5) that Athens was lucky that such a slow enemy faced its dash and vigour: Luginbill (1999) 92.
28 Rhodes (1993) 296 citing Plut. *Arist.* 25; [Ar.] *Ath. Pol.* 23.5.
29 Rawlings (1977) 8, agreeing with Hermocrates at 6.76.3: "To a Greek . . . hegemony was not normally a selfless concept"; Tzanetou (2011) 311–12; Fornara and Samons (1991) 76–104. For the view that imperialism started only after the peace of Callias, see Meiggs (1972) 152–74.
30 Thuc. 2.65.12 and 7.28.3 are exceptions, where, almost in spite of himself, he seems to display admiration for his city's remarkable resilience: Hanson (2005) 280–1; Rood (1999) 24; Andrewes (1960) 6 and (1970) 182–7; Strasburger (2009) 214–5. The drive and vigour of Athens effectively illustrate Thucydides' theory that greed (πλεονεξία) and ambition (φιλοτιμία) motivate human behaviour.
31 De Romilly (1963) 246–7.
32 Gomme (1959) 253–4; De Ste Croix (1972) 12–13, who is surely right that its original form would not have appealed to the Spartans and was different from what we have

here. For de Romilly (1963) 261–72, the speech is more directed to Thucydides' readers than the original audience; for Raubitschek (1973); Pohlenz (1919); Kagan (1969) 293–300, the speech broadly reflects historical reality.
33 On the connection of the two speeches, see de Romilly (1963) 242–8. Raubitschek (1973) 36–8 distinguishes between them: the Athenians appeal to honour, Euphemus, to sheer power.
34 "It is as if Thucydides deliberately let stand some strange remnants of the layer of propaganda that he has destroyed, but to prevent a credulous reader from being deceived, has crushed them under the weight of opposing points of view": Strasburger (2009) 206; cf. Loraux (1986) 289–95.
35 The lone stand at Marathon mingles with a generalized, idealized Athenian uniqueness: cf. pp. 17–18. In Thucydides, 1.73.4 is picked up at 102.3–4, as the Athenians are angry at being sent away *alone* of the allies because of their lone services at Marathon: Rood (1999) 245. Athens did not actually face the barbarians alone, as Herodotus knew well (6.111.2–3, 108) and any Athenian could see on the Stoa Poikile (Paus. 1.15.3: Dem. 59.94–106), and Walters (1981) notes the remarkable power of such stories to survive even when a contradictory story is plainly known, commenting (211), "If myth did have such an influence here on history, we see all the more clearly how unusual and how uncharacteristic of his time Thoukydides' demand for *to akribes* in history was." One might add how pervasive the need for self-deception regarding Athens' power was – surely part of the reason why this demonstrably false claim survived – and how unusual was Thucydides' active rejection of such comforting stories.
36 Again, rejected by Euphemus: Raubitschek (1973) 37.
37 Herodotus claims 180, while A. *Pers.* 338–9 suggests 310: Walters (1981a) 201–3.
38 As Pericles and others tell us, Athens is the unique model, not the one who copies.
39 Thuc. 1.74.3; Hdt. 8.61.1.
40 Hornblower (1996) 128.
41 Raubitschek (1973) 38–9; Rawlings (1981) 120–2.
42 Cf. Flashar (1969), esp. 44–6. The two strains in Athenian action and character are already demonstrated in Herodotus' account of the Persian Wars: daring and brave, self-sacrificing on behalf of Greece, but also self-serving (Hdt. 8.62.2, 9.11.2), violently punishing those whom they consider to have done wrong at Sestos (9.114–21): Flower and Marincola (2002) 14–15; cf. 309–11.
43 καὶ τὰ μὲν πάνυ παλαιὰ τί δεῖ λέγειν, ὧν ἀκοαὶ μᾶλλον λόγων μάρτυρες ἢ ὄψις τῶν ἀκουσομένων;
44 τὰ δὲ Μηδικὰ καὶ ὅσα αὐτοὶ ξύνιστε, εἰ καὶ δι᾽ ὄχλου μᾶλλον ἔσται αἰεὶ προβαλλομένοις, ἀνάγκη λέγειν· καὶ γὰρ ὅτε ἐδρῶμεν ἐπ᾽ ὠφελίᾳ ἐκινδυνεύετο, ἧς τοῦ μὲν ἔργου μέρος μετέσχετε.
45 A similar phrase is found in the Themistocles decree, *ML* 23.13–14: Raubitschek (1973) 38.
46 Gomme (1959) 235; Canfora (1992) 48–9.
47 Cf. Lys. 2.47, 54–7; Pl. *Mx.* 241d; Isoc. 4.100; Aristid. *Panath.* 23–5: Strasburger (2009) 199. Thucydides follows the official line (1.75.2, 95.1, 130.2; 3.10.2), but Herodotus 8.3.2 preserves an alternative tradition: Baragwanath (2008) 200–1.
48 Originally, the Athenians fear the Persians, but now they fear their allies' hatred instead: Stahl (2003) 47.
49 "Although even Athenian politicians occasionally adopted [the claim that Athens was a tyranny] to shake up their audience, and the *demos* basked in the glory of its 'magnificent rule', to be branded a tyrant was still insulting and incompatible with Athens's self-image as benefactor and savior of the Greeks": Raaflaub (2004) 177.
50 Rhodes (1985) 46–8; De Ste Croix (1954) considers Thucydides' claims exaggerated and misleading; see, however, Bradeen (1960); Raaflaub (2004) 160–5.
51 See Tod (1948) no. 123, ll.25–46.

52 At 3.27.3, the Mytilenean *demos* forces terms with Athens. At 3.92.1, Sparta and Athens are weighed equally by the Trachians needing help, while at 4.66 the leaders of the Megarian *demos* betray the city to Athens, rather than accepting rule by the banished party; cf. 4.102–8, with De Ste Croix (1954) 4–5. Thuc. 7.48.2 mentions Syracusans who wanted to betray the city to Athens: see Hornblower (2008) 634–5. Some cities even apparently paid tribute voluntarily: Samons (2000) 195–6. Equally, though, evidence from the Athenian Tribute Lists suggests that the late 450s saw considerable allied disaffection, perhaps after Athens' failure in Egypt, though literary sources give little hint of it: Osborne (2000) 94–7. Morris (2005) 41–2 argues that since that the tribute was basically paid by the elites in the allied cities, their hostility to Athens would be understandable; cf. Forrest (1975).
53 Meiggs (1943) 21.
54 At Thuc. 3.10.5–11.3, the Mytileneans explain their actions by appealing to the difficulty of resisting in the majority votes made at the Delian League, but it is not certain that the action was completely coerced: Gomme (1956) 264. Self-interest rather than ideology probably guided the policies of these islanders: Quinn (1981) 24–5, 40, 55–6; Raaflaub (2004) 162.
55 De Ste Croix (1954) 12–16.
56 On the implications of this detail and the argument that Athens had reason to attempt to subdue Melos, see Andrewes (1970) 156–8. Macleod (1983a) 66–7 argues that the allies participated either because Athens seemed irresistible or out of self-interest, but even this claim weakens any idea that Athens was hated *per se*: moreover, allied participation could be "spun" by Athens as further justification for the campaign.
57 Thuc. 8.5.1–2, 4–5, 8.7, 9–10.1, 14–15.1, 22, 24.2–5, 44.1–2, 95.5–7. Both at Chios (8.9.3, 14.1–2) and at Samos (8.21.1; IG^3 96), internal politics between the people and oligarchs influence policy to Athens, making general sentiment difficult to determine.
58 Meiggs (1972) 351. When the Syracusans offer Athens' allies freedom before the final battle, they refuse; the Samians also stay loyal as well (Thuc. 8.21.1; cf. IG^3 96): De Ste Croix (1954) 10–11.
59 Raaflaub (2004) 128–41 offers a concise summary of Athenian infractions on allied autonomy.
60 Sparta, too, had its share: De Ste Croix (1954) 14–15.
61 Lewis (1992) 383–4, with some reservations. Thuc. 8.64.5 states that once the cities acquired a moderate government and freedom they were unwilling even to be ruled well by Athens, but again, this is not quite the same as hating Athens. Only in a few cases is generalized hostility to Athens really clear: de Ste Croix (1954) 3–11, 37–40; cf. Gillis (1971) 41. Bradeen (1960) and Macleod (1983) 100–1 are less sanguine.
62 This is not the only Athenian speech that begins in idealized mode but pivots away from idealism: compare the speeches of Alcibiades and Euphemus in book six, pp. 160–63 later.
63 Cf. Debnar (2001) 51–6.
64 Raubitschek (1973) 43–8.
65 Cf. Debnar (2001) 160, 184; de Romilly (1979) 53–63; cf. Mills (1997) 77, 173–82.
66 Compare earlier, p. 23.
67 But the omissions (Pericles'? Thucydides'?) of material relating to Athens' "ancient history" and to the gods' care for Athens and vice versa are intriguing: Orwin (1994) 19–20.
68 How far it is Periclean and how far Thucydidean is unclear: for bibliography on the question, see Orwin (1994) 15, n.1. Dion. Hal. *Thuc.* 18 criticizes the positioning of the speech at this point in the book to honour relatively undistinguished combatants and doubts that it represents Pericles' own words. Since there is significant overlap between its general portrayal of Athens and other versions of the ideal Athens, and Thucydides is using this speech paradigmatically to present just once a picture of the idealized Athens, specific questions of authenticity are not crucial for this discussion.

Hornblower (1991) 294–6 considers it Periclean, while Stadter (1973) 118–9 considers it largely Thucydides' own composition; cf. Kakridis (1961) 109–14; Flashar (1969).
69 See pp. 9–14, 19, 21 earlier for the importance of temporal continuity and stability in maintaining and justifying empire.
70 For the implications of πόνος, see earlier, pp. 21–2.
71 Compare pp. 11–12, 17–18. Of course, this claim contradicts what Pericles says at 2.38.2, while Hdt. 1.32.8–9 claims that no individual or city can be self-sufficient (1.32.8–9): Scanlon (1994), esp. 145–9, who notes (146) that human limitation is traditionally contrasted with divine self-sufficiency; cf. Flashar (1969) 31. Self-sufficiency is also associated with the tyrants whose power is quasi-divine, so supposedly have no need for others: Wohl (2002) 53. The plague seriously undermines Pericles' claims: 2.51.3 with Foster (2010) 204–6.
72 "Talking to those who already know" is precisely what the speakers of the later *epitaphioi* do: it is typical of Thucydides to omit such material (Connor (1987) 66 n.37), but it is not certain that this omission represents Pericles' own choice, since this and other places where Thucydides' speakers reject beautiful words or familiar topoi suggest that they were a normal part of Athenian discourse: Strasburger (2009) 208; cf. Loraux (1986) 290.
73 Later *epitaphioi* focus on Athens' services to the Greek world, while Pericles' funeral speech is more inwardly focused on the nature of Athens itself: Strasburger (2009) 210. The ἴδιος/κοινός contrast which is so common in later *epitaphioi* in characterizing the labours borne by Athens for others' benefit is given a very different, internal use at Thuc. 2.43.2; cf. 61.4: "Giving their bodies in common, individually they received ageless praise" (κοινῇ γὰρ τὰ σώματα διδόντες ἰδίᾳ τὸν ἀγήρων ἔπαινον ἐλάμβανον).
74 See earlier, pp. 17–19; S. *O.C.* 258–62 is a particularly clear example.
75 Not always voluntarily, of course: *ML* 40 (c. 450) shows the Athenians setting up a democratic constitution at Erythrae after its attempted revolt from the Delian League.
76 Orwin (1994) 18. They are essential claims for the imperialist: see Chapter 1, esp. pp. 21–4 earlier.
77 See earlier, pp. 13–14, 16–17.
78 In tragedy, Athens also manages to be both a democracy and ruled by a king, for reasons that are slightly different, but with a similar result of the union of opposites to form the best (if factually impossible) city. In fact, most appointments aside from those which were military were made by lot, and Athenian politics were dominated by men from rich families, so Pericles' claim (37.1) that only merit matters at Athens is untrue: Rhodes (1988) 220.
79 Cf. A. *Eum.* 690–2, 517–25. Pericles' empire is freely chosen and retained, owing nothing to necessity, considerations of advantage (rejected by Pericles at 40.5) or any other of the factors the Athenians cite in their speech in book one: Orwin (1994) 27.
80 Μέγεθος is a pleasingly abstract term, far from the vulgar details of economic compulsion.
81 A quintessentially imperial claim: pp. 11–12 earlier. The contradiction with Athens' claims to self-sufficiency at 36.3 is clear, and the fragility of this apparent strength is clearly shown at 7.28.1, as Decelea is fortified and imports become a difficult necessity rather than a source of imperial pride: Taylor (2010) 163–4.
82 For the importance of this conveniently unscientific term in imperial justification, see pp. 5–7, 13–14, 15–17, although Thucydides clearly does consider the conflict between two very different types of national character a genuine reason for, and influence on, the course of the Peloponnesian War: in general, see Luginbill (1999).
83 τήν τε γὰρ πόλιν κοινὴν παρέχομεν, καὶ οὐκ ἔστιν ὅτε ξενηλασίαις ἀπείργομέν τινα ἢ μαθήματος ἢ θεάματος, ὃ μὴ κρυφθὲν ἄν τις τῶν πολεμίων ἰδὼν ὠφεληθείη: 2.39.1.
84 οἱ μὲν ἐπιπόνῳ ἀσκήσει εὐθὺς νέοι ὄντες τὸ ἀνδρεῖον μετέρχονται, ἡμεῖς δὲ ἀνειμένως διαιτώμενοι οὐδὲν ἧσσον ἐπὶ τοὺς ἰσοπαλεῖς κινδύνους χωροῦμεν.

85 Cf. Wohl (2002) 49–52. Hornblower (1991) 303 finds this chapter "puzzling" because it wrongly implies that Athens lacks military professionalism. But it is an expression both of a general imperial self-confidence in amateurism (pp. 23–4 earlier) and of the unique Athenian ability to combine traditional opposites of military prowess and relaxation without having to work too hard for superiority. Here, in fact, πόνοι are minimized in favour of an Athenian lightheartedness that even so makes them no less daring than their rivals. For Vidal-Naquet (1986) 89–90, "nowhere else is the ideology of non-professionalism pushed so far," even being dubbed "supreme insolence". The comparison with Sparta means that Athens must not be focused on military activity to the exclusion of all else. Parry (1981) 165 rightly calls this "a truly aristocratic ideal for the parent of democracies."

86 φιλοκαλοῦμέν τε γὰρ μετ᾽ εὐτελείας καὶ φιλοσοφοῦμεν ἄνευ μαλακίας. His further claim, that Athens uses wealth more for action than for show, is turned on its head in the Sicilian expedition, so that power is but the illusion of power (just as the claims of the *epitaphioi* are themselves beautiful but illusory): Kallet (2001) 18–84.

87 Parry (1981) 159–75; Kakridis (1961) 50–1: compare the qualities ascribed to Themistocles (1.138) and Theseus (2.15).

88 οὐ γὰρ πάσχοντες εὖ, ἀλλὰ δρῶντες κτώμεθα τοὺς φίλους. Athens is, of course, not unique in Greece for this characteristic, but Low (2007) 242–8 discusses a striking contrast between the mutual exchange of honorific decrees between Athens and other cities in the fourth century, and their unidirectional flow, from Athens to other cities but not vice versa, in the fifth century. The allied cities, of course, give tribute, while Athens generously hands out honours, hiding their very real gains under a veneer of benevolence while closing off to their allies a method well established in Greece of acquiring and showing status.

89 De Romilly (1963) 136 notes how closely Pericles' words parallel E. *Hcld*. 198, 245, 305–6, 329–32.

90 Connor (1987) 184 n.65.

91 On this quality (εὐτραπελία) see Scanlon (1994) 152, who notes Aristotle's definition of it as "schooled insolence" (*Rhet*. 1389b10–12). Such "ready and affable dexterity" is part of the imperial culture of the amateur who does not need to try too hard: cf. pp. 23–4.

92 Since the superiority resides in the characters of every single Athenian, it is natural and potentially limitless in time or space, in another example of the common ground between the ideology of the Athenian *archē* and that of later empires. Though these men are dead, the "whole earth" is their tomb even in lands "not their own" (2.43.3): see also Taylor (2010) 117.

93 Certainly from Hellenistic times, but arguably earlier, the formulation "land and sea" is used to claim universal empire. It is a standard formulation for Roman power (e.g. Cic. *Balb*. 6.16), while for the Augustan regime it has a peaceful dimension (Appian *B.C*. 5.542) as well as a more aggressive one, and the monument for the victory at Actium (*pace parta terra marique*) combines both: Hardie (1986) 308–9.

94 πᾶσαν μὲν θάλασσαν καὶ γῆν ἐσβατὸν τῇ ἡμετέρᾳ τόλμῃ καταναγκάσαντες γενέσθαι: Thuc. 2.41.4. On Athenians as road-builders and civilizers compare A. *Eum*. 13–14 and also the story, current in Athens from the late sixth century, of Theseus' journey from Trozen around the Saronic Gulf to Athens, making the route safe for travellers.

95 Pericles uses the language of ruling the sea "to create an imaginary empire that extended far beyond the physical reality of Athenian rule": Foster (2010) 188–9.

96 Compare 2.37.3, 40.3, 41.1, 43.4 (cf. 35.3) with 2.51.3 and 53.1: Flashar (1969) 34–6; Macleod (1983b) 151–2.

97 Connor (1987) 100–5; Raaflaub (2006) 197.

98 Or perhaps something like the rallying cry of 1.144.4: "Did not our fathers resist the Persians, starting out with less than what we have now, and even abandoning what they had, and with greater wisdom than fortune, and greater daring than power, did

not they drive the barbarian back and advance our affairs to their present height? We must not prove inferior, but resist our enemies in every way, and try to hand down our power to our successors undiminished."

99 For a general discussion, see Andrewes (1960).
100 Thuc. 2.61.4 offers another use of the familiar κοινός/ἴδιος contrast in connection with Athens' internal affairs, rather than with the city's benefactions to Greece as is typical of later *epitaphioi*: "Stopping grieving for your personal troubles, hold onto the safety of the commonwealth" (ἀπαλγήσαντας δὲ τὰ ἴδια τοῦ κοινοῦ τῆς σωτηρίας ἀντιλαμβάνεσθαι).
101 The portrayal of Pericles, like those of Cleon, Nicias and Brasidas, is one of the areas where Thucydides' veracity is most questionable: he never has to debate anyone and seems invincible, a portrait that does not represent historical reality: Rawlings (1981) 139.
102 At 2.62.4 Pericles faintly echoes the contrast that he made at 2.40.3, between Athens' fully conscious daring and Spartan courage born of ignorance.
103 Compare the Corinthians, 1.122.3, 124.3 and Euphemus, 6.85.1; also Ar. *Eq*. 1111: Hornblower (1991) 337–8; Scanlon (1987) 286–90; de Romilly (1963) 124–8.
104 Contrast 1.76.2 and 95.1–2, 96.1, where leadership is offered to Athens by grateful allies.
105 Connor (1977) 98–104.
106 Cf. Immerwahr (1973) 27–8.
107 It is commonly agreed that Thucydides' portrayal of Cleon, like Aristophanes', shows a degree of hostility that is arguably unfair, as is his equally partial, but positive, view of Nicias: Hornblower (1987) 166–7 and (1996) 170; Rood (1999) 183–201; Woodhead (1960) tries to redress the balance. On the speeches of Cleon and Diodotus see Andrewes (1962); de Romilly (1963) 156–71; Kagan (1975); Cogan (1981a); Connor (1987) 82–91; Macleod (1983) 92–102.
108 Note his ironic use of "ξυγγνώμην ἔχω" at 3.39.2; cf. 40.1. The word "ξυγγνώμη" is one linked with Athenian ideals of moderation and sympathy, and he denies any such allowance to the Mytileneans.
109 Orwin (1994) 147–54. On pity in Thucydides, see also Lateiner (2005) 80–8.
110 Kagan (1975) 89.
111 Andrewes (1962) 72; Hornblower (1991) 419; Pelling (1999) 122; cf. de Ste Croix (1954) 15–16.
112 No longer "like". The admission that Athens is an actual tyrant also problematizes the repeated appeals to justice in Cleon's speech, e.g. at 3.40.1.
113 Isoc. 4.27–8, 48–9. The tendencies in the Athenian assembly which Cleon criticizes are a debased variation on Corinth's claims (1.70.2) about Athens' love of speed and change: Macleod (1983) 94.
114 As a good Athenian he employs rhetoric to persuade his speakers that that they love intellectual display and rhetoric too much: Wassermann (1956) 32–3; Winnington Ingram (1965) 71, who also notes (74) that Cleon argues from the structure of tragedy (39.4) that good fortune leads to *hybris*, and *hybris* can be punished "with a good conscience – one might almost say it is a Zeus-like function."
115 This "trinity" recalls the more realistic and unlovely set of fear, honour and interest that the Athenians invoke at 1.75.3.
116 This word is used in Athenian panegyric as a quintessential Athenian characteristic: Kirkwood (1986) 101; Mills (1997) esp. 55, 77, 105–6, 173–83.
117 See earlier, Chapters 2 and 3.
118 Macleod (1983) 96.
119 Rengakos (1984) 60–5.
120 Hornblower (1987) 166–7 n.51; Woodhead (1960) 299; Andrewes (1962) 75.
121 Compare 3.38.1 and 1.140.1, 2.61.2; 3.37.2, and 2.63.2; 3.40.4 and 2.63.2.
122 Thuc. 3.40.4: παύεσθαι τῆς ἀρχῆς καὶ ἐκ τοῦ ἀκινδύνου ἀνδραγαθίζεσθαι.

123 In treating them "differently" from others: compare Pericles' use of the adverb διαφερόντως, 2.40.3.
124 On his speech, see Bodin (1940); Wassermann (1956) 34–9; Orwin (1994) 146–54.
125 On λόγος in the war, see Connor (1987) 81–91.
126 At 47.3 and 47.5, he argues that it is more expedient for Athens deliberately to be wronged than to kill those who do in fact deserve the death penalty, in a perversion of the generous altruism of the ideal Athens.
127 Since Diodotus' speech is conditioned by Cleon's, he cannot appeal to pity if he is to beat him at his own game: Winnington Ingram (1965) 77–8; Andrewes (1962) 72.
128 Thuc. 3.45.1, 5. Hope and desire lead the Athenians themselves to the disastrous attempt to increase their own freedom to rule by conquering Sicily, even after condemning the Melians for their excessive reliance on hope (5.103; cf. 6.24.3).
129 For Connor (1987) 88–90, Diodotus is part of a progressive dissociation of advantage and justice in the histories. His view of human nature that law cannot restrain its drive to advantage means that there is no place for right; thus the idealized Athens must be pure fiction at best and a dangerous illusion at worst.
130 Scione was also a blot on Athens' post-imperial reputation: Xen. *Hell.* 2.2.3; Isoc. 4.100, 12.63; D.S. 13.30.6; Arr. *Anab.* 1.9.5. Discussions of the Melian dialogues include Andrewes (1960); de Romilly (1963) 273–310; Bosworth (1993); Morrison (2006) 81–99; Macleod (1983a); Scardino (2007) 467–83; Hornblower (2008) 216–25.
131 Unfortunately, the inscriptions are complicated as evidence, and it has been argued that *ML* 67 may not be securely datable to the Archidamian War, as is often argued (e.g. Loomis (1992) 56–76; Smarczyk (1999)), but actually sometime after the fall of Melos, even to the 390s: Hornblower (1991) 499 and (2008) 232 with bibliography. But Athens had apparently set its sights on Melos as early as 426 (Thuc. 3.91.1–2) and doubtless saw its claims as in some sense justified, assessing it at 15 talents in the tribute reassessment of 425–4 (*ML* 69).
132 Hornblower (2008) 232; on the long-standing connections between Sparta and Melos, see Malkin (1994) 74–8.
133 Canfora (1992) xi; Dewald (2005) 141–2.
134 Hornblower (2008) 226–7: see, however, Macleod (1983a) 66–7.
135 On which, see Canfora (1992) 13–18; Hornblower (2008) 219–25.
136 Cf. Kallet-Marx (1993) 89.
137 Cf. de Romilly (1963) 273–4.
138 Cf. 1.73.2–5: Rengakos (1984) 95, 101–2.
139 Thuc. 5.89.1; cf. 6.83.3, 1.73.2 with Andrewes (1960); Tzifopoulos (1995).
140 Canfora (1992) 50.
141 Heath (1990) 385–91; Grethlein (2013) 237.
142 Connor (1987) 153; Hornblower (2008) 242.
143 De Romilly (1963) 293–4; Connor (1987) 157.
144 A startlingly ironic use of this "Athenian" word (cf. 1.76.4. 3.40.2 and n.116 earlier).
145 ἡ μὲν ἐπιείκεια τοῦ διδάσκειν καθ' ἡσυχίαν ἀλλήλους οὐ ψέγεται, τὰ δὲ τοῦ πολέμου παρόντα ἤδη καὶ οὐ μέλλοντα διαφέροντα αὐτοῦ φαίνεται: Macleod (1983a) 56–7. The Melians also appeal to ξυγγνώμη (another characteristic of the idealized Athens) at 88.1.
146 Cf. Macleod (1983a) 58; Crane (1998) 239–41. We have moved far from the Theseus of S. *OC* 568–9: ἔξοιδ' ἀνὴρ ὢν χὤτι τῆς εἰς αὔριον οὐδὲν πλέον μοι σοῦ μέτεστιν ἡμέρας.
147 Cogan (1981) 163–4; Macleod (1983a) 59 and (1983d) 82.
148 A common practice in rhetoric (Macleod (1983a) 55). As so often in Thucydides, this combination – unlike the combination of opposites in the idealized Athens – proves impossible: Morrison (2006) 87–91.
149 Crane (1998) 241–57; Connor (1987) 155–7.

150 At 7.77.3–4 Nicias will appeal to hope and divine justice with as little success as the Melians do at 5.103: Connor (1987) 201–2.
151 Compare pp. 4, 6–7, 9–11, 12–16, 20–1, 23 earlier on justifications of empire as both natural and eternal.
152 Athens is, after all, not unique. Compare 1.76.2 and Xerxes' words at Hdt. 7.8a1: Connor (1987) 156.
153 The vocabulary of 5.105 recalls that of 1.76.1: Connor (1987) 151 n.32.
154 Contrast again Theseus in S. *OC* 568–9 (cf. n.146 earlier).
155 Andrewes (1960) 7 n.1. Compare 2.64.3–5, whose Pericles is not so distant from the later "Athenian apologists whose claims shock ordinary decency": Orwin (1994) 22; cf. Immerwahr (1973) 28–30.
156 On the resonances of this word with the idealized Athens, see p. 16.
157 Athens' real power is fatally limited: though they have military power on their side at this time, they do not see the implications of what they argue. After being seduced by inherently human hope and desire (3.45.5 with 6.24.3) into reaching for Sicily, Athens comes to resemble Melos, "forced to rely on hope, chance, and speculations about the gods (esp.7.77.4)": Connor (1987) 155; 167–8, n.22. Stahl (1973) 72 compares Nicias' words of warning to the Athenians with the Athenians' to the Melians, and Alcibiades' speech to their irrational hopes: cf. Taylor (2010) 138–9.
158 Rallying cries of justice and fighting for the freedom of a 700-year-old city (5.112.2) also seduced the Melians: Bosworth (1993).
159 Greenwood (2005) 52–3; for Thucydides' sources of knowledge about Sicily, see Dover (1970) 198–210.
160 Thuc. 1.36.2, 44.3; Hdt. 7.161.3; Hornblower (2008) 5–6. On the campaign of 426, see Kagan (1974) 181–93; Westlake (1960).
161 Kagan (1981) 165. It is more reasonable if he means that most Athenians lacked *personal* experience of Sicily: Hornblower (2008) 260; cf. Rood (1998) 163.
162 Smith (2004).
163 Hornblower (2008) 300; Rawlings (1981) 68–70 discuss how this unique phrase connects the two contexts in which it is used. Corcyra in book one and Egesta here want Athenian help in a war of their own making which was not really Athens' business. In order to get Athenian help, each "freely" offers money and assistance for a war which will supposedly come to Athens whether the city agrees to assist them or not. It is, as it were, the Athenian "code" to accept such appeals, whether idealistically (tragedy and the *epitaphioi*) or for more self-interested aims (Thucydides).
164 Thucydides' focus on colonization in his Sicilian history may indicate that he thought of Athens' expedition to Sicily as an essentially colonial adventure: Avery (1973) 8–13; cf. Kallet (2001) 25–7.
165 Westlake (1973) 105–8 argues convincingly that Thucydides' account of these speeches represents quite closely what was actually said on this occasion, though, as ever, in condensed form which may add some slight distortion: see later on 6.18.2.
166 νομίζων δὲ τὴν πόλιν οὐκ ὀρθῶς βεβουλεῦσθαι, ἀλλὰ προφάσει βραχείᾳ καὶ εὐπρεπεῖ τῆς Σικελίας ἁπάσης, μεγάλου ἔργου, ἐφίεσθαι.
167 The powerful frequently complain of the ingratitude of those with less power: earlier, p. 24.
168 The power of Athenian ideology to influence real-life political decisions may be seen here, if Lewis (1992) 391 n.64 is right to agree with Nicias that Athens did indeed tend to accept more alliances than was feasible: see also Hornblower (2011b) 77–8.
169 Though a Syracusan, he is portrayed as very Athenian, even Thucydidean in his ideas of human nature (Orwin (1994) 163), and his speech doubtless contains purely Thucydidean material: Hornblower (1996) 223.
170 Using loyalty to allies as a cover for less-noble motives is not confined to Athens: compare Corinth at 5.30.2.
171 Though the word ἀγαθά is very general, one is reminded of Pericles' more sanitizing claim that the size of the city brings it all the ἀγαθά of others, at 2.38.2.

172 Hornblower (2008) 322.
173 His opening claim at 6.16.1 that he is worthier than others for command strongly resembles Athenian claims for the unique worth of the city in Greeks: καὶ προσήκει μοι μᾶλλον ἑτέρων, ὦ Ἀθηναῖοι, ἄρχειν . . . καὶ ἄξιος ἅμα νομίζω εἶναι. Similarly, his assertion (16.5) that those who show distinction in life are often hated by contemporaries but their brilliance is posthumously recognized resembles Pericles' final words about Athens at 2.64.5: Macleod (1983d) 75. For Alcibiades as representative of Athenian national character, see Luginbill (1999) 85; Orwin (1994) 123; Debnar (2001) 212. The virtues of intelligence and boldness, traditionally joined in Athenian mythological figures such as Theseus and considered quintessentially Athenian in mainstream ideology, appear in their corrupt version in Alcibiades: Macleod (1983e) 128. Or perhaps corruption is the reality, and the ideal a myth.
174 For example, at 6.17.6: Kagan (1981) 182–3; Hornblower (2008) 349; cf. 411, discussing 6.38.3.
175 Macleod (1983d) 78. At 6.68.2, Nicias contrasts the quality of the Sicilian troops with their own and notes that their daring and knowledge (τόλμα and ἐπιστήμη) are not equal, with an implied contrast between these and the Athenians in whom both (at this time) are supreme.
176 Some specific examples of Athenian response to appeals for help in Thucydides include 1.104.1–2; 3.34.2, 63.2, 63.4 and 82.1: on Alcibiades' claims at 6.18.2, cf. Rengakos (1984) 108–11.
177 Cf. Hornblower (2008) 323. Even allowing for Thucydides' probable abbreviations, these speeches may represent relatively closely what was actually said on this occasion: Westlake (1973) 105–8.
178 Macleod (1983d) 82–3; Rood (1999) 200–1; Kirby (1983) 196–9: compare 2.36.4, 40.1, 61.4, 64.2, 62.1–3. Macleod (1983b) 149–51 connects the themes of Pericles' funeral speech and Alcibiades' words here with those of Euripides' *Suppliants*, exploring the contrasts between the ideal and the reality inherent in all three, noting that Alcibiades' conception of expansion as key to Athens' survival (Thuc. 6.18.7) ominously echoes Herodotus' Xerxes (Hdt.7.8α.1).
179 Alcibiades later claims that Sicily was a mere stepping stone to Carthage and the whole of the Greek world: Thuc. 6.90.2–3; cf. 34.2; Plut. *Nic.* 12.2.
180 De Romilly (1963) 50–7 (cf. 313–21) discusses the element of compulsion that imperialism brings upon imperialists: Thuc. 1.75.3, 76.1, 76.2; 2.63.2; 3.40.4; 5.105.2; 6.18.3, 87.2.
181 Ἔρως and tyranny are connected: Cornford (1907) 201–9; Rogkotis (2006) 82–5; Kallet (2001) 79–82; Ludwig (2002) 141–70. On ἔρως directed to the power of the city, compare 2.43.1; 6.13.1, 24.3 (cf. ἐπιθυμία at 6.33.2). Ἔρως and Athenian imperialism are also connected: Forde (1989) 30–43; Ludwig (2002) 348–76; cf. Dougherty (1993) 61–80, who discusses a general connection between colonization and erotic imagery, especially domination in the service of civilization.
182 Hornblower (2008) 23–31 (cf. 568) suggests that Thucydides suppresses the role of the council in the decision, to emphasize the rashness of the people.
183 In Thucydides' description of the embarkation of the Sicilian expedition, non-aristocratic elements of Athens are prominent, not the ideal aristocratic *demos*, and they are motivated by public pay, not the free service to the state that the funeral speeches emphasize, as Thucydides once more reveals the reality under the rhetoric: cf. Steiner (2005). Sagan (1991) 201 observes the unification of society by imperialistic activity: "Rich and poor together can sail off to Sicily, flags flying, hearts throbbing to the melody of one united, conquering *polis*."
184 Thuc. 7.12.3, 62.1–4, 77.3–4; Connor (1987) 194–8; Rogkotis (2006) 59–6; Taylor (2010) 180–4; Fornara (1971) 79–91. Though it is especially strong in book seven, the Athens-Persia comparison may be found elsewhere in Thucydides: Scanlon (1987) 286–8.

On comparisons between Athens and Persia, see also Rood (1999); Harrison (2000a); Kallet (2001) 85–95.
185 Connor (1987) 171–2.
186 Cornford (1907) 201; cf. Harrison (2000b) 48; Rood (1999) 163. Rosenbloom (1995), esp. 91–5, traces comparable patterns in historiography and tragedy.
187 Connor (1987) 172; Farber (2001) 41–8; cf. Kirby (1983) 186–90.
188 The Thebans' accusations of "Atticism" against Plataea (3.62.2) already signal Athens' gradual metamorphosis. Herodotus' polarization of Greek toughness and Persian luxury is reworked by Thucydides as Spartan austerity versus Athenian glamour: Hornblower (1996) 127.
189 The demagogue Athenagoras shows that at least internally, they already resemble Athens: Connor (1987) 171; Dover (1970) 301. At 6.78.2 the acknowledgement that Syracuse's power can cause envy or fear echoes Pericles' claims about Athenian power at 2.64.4–5: Hornblower (1996) 22 and (2008) 648–9. Edmunds (1975) 122–3 (cf. 90, 109–20) shows how the original antithesis between Athens and Sparta – vital in idealizing texts promoting Athenian exceptionalism – is blurred in the Sicilian expedition as the Periclean Alcibiades promotes the expedition whose chief strategist is the Spartan Nicias, while Syracuse is becoming a "new Athens . . . in Dorian dress." Hermocrates is even made to state (7.21.3) that Athens' naval skill was not (as idealizing accounts claimed) ancestral or eternal but merely forced by the Persians: Harrison (2000a) 88. On a more generally disintegrating polarity between Ionian and Dorian, see Connor (1991).
190 Avery (1973) 1–8; Hornblower (2008) 403; Rood (1998) 7–8, 197–8. At 7.56.2–3, the Syracusans savour the glory of liberating Greece and their eternal remembrance for standing with the Peloponnesians, bravely sacrificing their city and playing a pre-eminent role in Sicily's naval triumph. Perhaps Thucydides was attributing to them some of the psychology familiar from Athens' construction of the Persian war: see Hornblower (1996) 145. The verb προκινδυνεῦσαι (7.56.3) significantly appears only here and in the Athenians' account of Athens' role in the Persian Wars (1.73.4): Rawlings (1981) 173.
191 Thuc. 7.55.2, 8.96.2; cf. 6.20.3: Hornblower (2008) 648–53.
192 Tzifopoulos (1995) 112–3. For Hermocrates' career, see Westlake (1969a). Everything fits together so nicely – the beginnings of the fall of Athens and its assimilation to Persia, the rise of Syracuse with a new, vigorous leader, the close verbal connections between Hermocrates' and Euphemus' speeches (de Romilly (1956) 193–4; Rawlings (1981) 120–1) and with the Corinthian and Athenian speeches in book one – that Hermocrates' speeches seem suspiciously appropriate (thus invented) for the occasion, but Farber (2001) 39–41 makes a good case that Hermocrates himself was one of Thucydides' sources.
193 Another way in which Syracuse is for Athens what Athens was for the Persians: Harrison (2000a) 85–6.
194 A "Spartan" concept, the opposite of Athenian hyperactivity, cf. 1.69.4, 70.8, 71.3.
195 On thematic connections between Euphemus' speech and that of the Athenians in book one, see Rengakos (1984) 113–8; Strasburger (2009) 208–11, Heath (1990) 386–7. Raubitschek (1973) 36–8 argues that they represent two different stages in the Athenians' claim that they are entitled to rule, moving from a claim based on virtue to one based on power, but the seeds of the later speech are embedded in the earlier one, in my view: cf. Taylor (2010), who argues that little or no difference exists between Periclean imperialism and its later incarnations.
196 Euphemus' claim hints at the way Athens promoted its role as supposed mother city of the Ionians as propaganda for imperial cohesion, for example by requiring allies to send a cow and panoply to the greater Panathenaea "like colonists": *ML* 46:41–2, 69:56–8, 49:11–13; cf. *ML* 40:3–5 and cf. earlier, pp. 93–5. Barron (1964), (1983) and

(1986) 92–4 discusses evidence that the Athenians tried to propagate Athenian cults in the empire as a uniting device: see, however, Smarczyk (1990) 58–153; Parker (1996) 141–6. On the general importance of the Dorian and Ionian distinction, see Alty (1982).

197 For Hornblower (2008) 504, there is "a certain diabolical Athenian logic" in their invocation of Spartan liberation propaganda (cf. 2.8.4).
198 Compare the slackness of the allies condemned at Thuc. 1.99.3; cf. 6.77.1.
199 Forde (1989) 62–5; for Cogan (1981) 110–11 Euphemus' claims are quite simply "a lie."
200 ἀνθ' ὧν ἄξιοί τε ὄντες ἅμα ἄρχομεν, ὅτι τε ναυτικὸν πλεῖστόν τε καὶ προθυμίαν ἀπροφάσιστον παρεσχόμεθα ἐς τοὺς Ἕλληνας: cf. Hdt. 8.61, 48; Thuc. 1.74.1.
201 ἅμα δὲ τῆς πρὸς Πελοποννησίους ἰσχύος ὀρεγόμενοι.
202 Note too, the use of this and related words with the φθον- root in Nicias' last speech, 7.77.2, 3, 4.
203 Compare 1.122.3, 124.3; 2.63.2 and 3.37.2, but the Corinthians speak as enemies about an enemy, while Pericles and Cleon used the comparison at home. Euphemus now drops all pretence and proclaims it outside Athens. Sagan (1991) 154–5, writing from a broadly psychoanalytical perspective, comments that no tyrant can really believe that his tyranny will be permanent and always has "the overwhelming necessity to prove that one has absolutely no need of anyone else." This fiction can only be maintained if those on whom the tyrant is in fact dependent give what is needed without any resistance. Hence the need for control and torture; see also Wohl (2002) 184–8.
204 The "agony of inheritance" (Thuc. 1.140.5, 144.3–4; 6.17–18) places a terrible burden placed on people like the Athenians and ultimately causes the paradoxical diminution of their power over time: Rood (1998) 224 (cf. (1999) 158).
205 ἐν παντὶ γὰρ πᾶς χωρίῳ, καὶ ᾧ μὴ ὑπάρχομεν, ὅ τε οἰόμενος ἀδικήσεσθαι καὶ ὁ ἐπιβουλεύων διὰ τὸ ἑτοίμην ὑπεῖναι ἐλπίδα τῷ μὲν ἀντιτυχεῖν ἐπικουρίας ἀφ' ἡμῶν, τῷ δὲ εἰ ἥξομεν, μὴ ἀδεεῖ εἶναι κινδυνεύειν, ἀμφότεροι ἀναγκάζονται ὁ μὲν ἄκων σωφρονεῖν, ὁ δ'ἀπραγμόνως σῴζεσθαι. The translation is by Smith (1913).
206 Although Thucydides knew Nicias well, so he would have had a good idea of what he might have said: Kallet (2001) 161 n.38.
207 Compare Thuc. 6.30.2 with 7.75.7; the word λαμπρότης is used at 6.31.6 and 7.69.2. Now the Athenians must fight a sea battle as a land battle (7.62.2, 4) in a narrow space disadvantageous to them (Thuc. 7.36.4, 70.6). Compare Hdt. 8.60 and Thuc. 2.89.8, where Phormio specifically avoids fighting in this manner, because it will be disastrous: Macleod (1983b).
208 Macleod (1983b) 144–5.
209 κοινωνοὶ μόνοι ἐλευθέρως ἡμῖν τῆς ἀρχῆς . . .
210 On a possible echo of Herodotus' account of Salamis (8.94.3) in the κατα- prefix of καταπροδίδοτε, see Hornblower (2008) 679.
211 The emotional hold of Athens, largely set aside since Pericles' funeral speech, is now given full focus just as the city's power is about to suffer a devastating blow. "By having the foreigners in the fleet share in this Periklean conception [of Athens], Nikias tries to make the whole force homogeneous – an image of Athens": Rood (1998) 193.
212 That they were πρῶτοι resembles the Athenians' claims to be the first to resist the sight of Median dress at Marathon (Hdt. 6.112.3): Harrison (2000a) 86.
213 Compare Hermocrates' assessment of Athens' rise to naval competence, 7.21.3, and his prediction that those who meet them with daring (ἀντιτολμῶντας) will most intimidate them.
214 Gylippos combines λόγος, an articulate and intelligent confidence, with the ἔργον of military preparedness and skill, a combination claimed by Athens (and other imperial powers) in multiple ways.

215 ἐπὶ ναῦς ἀναβάντες (7.67.2) may echo ἐσβάντες ἐς τὰς ναῦς (1.73.4, 74.2), in another link between Syracuse and Salamis to set beside the familiar image of a mass of ships forced to fight a land battle on sea (7.62.2, 4). A confusion of land and sea was fundamental to Greek understanding of the *hybris* of Xerxes which caused his failure and their victory: Taylor (2010) 139–40.
216 It consists of one huge sentence whose "uncharacteristically paratactic style" (Rawlings (1981) 155) captures Nicias' desperation.
217 On this term, see Lateiner (1985), esp. 204–8; Hornblower (2008) 690.
218 Hornblower (2008) 689 states here that Thucydides gives us far fewer of such appeals than were actually offered in real life, an interesting admission in the light of the argument of this book.
219 Hornblower (2008) 692–3; Scardino (2007) 635–6, n.625; Wohl (2002) 200–1. Compare 7.69.2 especially with 2.36.1, 37.2: also the end of 1.143.5 with the famous claim (7.77.7) that men, not walls, make a city.
220 "[M]ore properly a funeral oration in the traditional sense than is Pericles'": Rawlings (1981) 157.

Bibliography

Abbreviations

DK. Diels, H. and W. Kranz (1964) *Die Fragmente der Vorsokratiker*, 11th ed. Zurich and Berlin: Weidmann.
FGrH. Jacoby, F. (1923–54) *Die Fragmente der griechischen Historiker* (FGrHist). Berlin: Weidmann.
KA. Kassel, R. and C. Austin (1984) *Poetae Comici Graeci*, vol. 3.2: *Aristophanes: testimonia et fragmenta*. Berlin and New York: de Gruyter.
KA. Kassel, R. and C. Austin (1986) *Poetae Comici Graeci*, vol. 5: *Damoxenus to Magnes*. Berlin and New York: de Gruyter.
LIMC. *Lexicon Iconographicum Mythologiae Classicae* (1981–99) Zürich, Munich and Düsseldorf: Artemis & Winkler.
LSJ. Liddell, H. and R. Scott (1968) *Greek-English Lexicon*, 9th ed., rev. H. Stuart Jones; suppl. by E.A. Barber and others. Oxford: Oxford University Press.
ML. Meiggs, R. and D. Lewis (1969) *Greek Historical Inscriptions to the End of the Fifth Century BC*. Oxford: Clarendon Press.
PW. Parke, H.W. and D.E.W. Wormell (eds.) (1956) *The Delphic Oracle*, 2 vols. Oxford: Blackwell.
RE. Pauly, A., G. Wissowa and W. Kroll (1894–1980) *Real-Encyclopädie der klassischen Altertumswissenschaft*. Stuttgart: J. B. Metzler.
TGrF. Snell, B., S. Radt and R. Kannicht (1981–2004) *Tragicorum Graecorum Fragmenta*, vols. 1–5. Göttingen: Vandenhoeck & Ruprecht.
Tod. Tod, M. (1948) *A Selection of Greek Historical Inscriptions Vol. II from 403 to 323 BC*. Oxford: Clarendon Press.

Abernethy, D. (2000) *The Dynamics of Global Dominance: European Overseas Empires, 1415–1980*. New Haven, CT: Yale University Press.
Adkins, A.W.H. (1976) "*Polypragmosyne* and 'Minding One's Own Business': A Study in Greek Social and Political Values", *CPh* 71: 301–27.
Adler, E. (2011) *Valorizing the Barbarians: Enemy Speeches in Roman Historiography*. Austin, TX: University of Texas Press.
Adler, E. (2012) "Speeches of Enemies and Criticism of Empire in Early Imperial Historiography", in Hoyos (2012): 291–304.
Albini, U. (1967) "Lettura dei *Persai* di Eschilo", *PdP* 22: 252–63.
Alcock, S., T. D'Altroy, K. Morrison and S. Sinopoli (2001) *Empires: Perspectives from Archaeology and History*. Cambridge: Cambridge University Press.
Allan, W. (2001) *The Children of Heracles*. Warminster: Aris and Phillips.

Allan, W. (2003) *The Andromache and Euripidean Tragedy*. Oxford: Oxford University Press.

Allan, W. (2012) "Turning Remorse to Good Effect?: Arginusae, Theramenes and Aristophanes' *Frogs*", in Marshall, C. and G. Kovacs (eds.) *No Laughing Matter, Studies in Athenian Comedy*. London: Bristol Classical Press: 101–4.

Allan, W. and A. Kelly (2013) "Listening to Many Voices: Athenian Tragedy as Popular Art", in Marmodoro, A. and J. Hill (eds.) *The Author's Voice in Classical and Late Antiquity*. Oxford: Oxford University Press: 77–122.

Allison, J. (1979) "Thucydides and Polypragmosyne", *AJAH* 4: 10–22.

Aloni, A. (2001) "The Proem of Simonides' Plataea Elegy and the Circumstances of Its Performance", in Boedeker and Sider (2001): 86–105.

Alty, J. (1982) "Dorians and Ionians", *JHS* 102: 1–14.

Anderson, C. (2003) "The Gossiping Triremes in Aristophanes' *Knights*, 1300–1315", *CJ* 99: 1–9.

Ando, C. (2000) *Imperial Ideology and Provincial Loyalty in the Roman Empire*. Berkeley, CA: University of California Press.

Andrewes, A. (1960) "The Melian Dialogue and Pericles' Last Speech", *PCPS* 6: 1–10.

Andrewes, A. (1961) "Thucydides and the Persians", *Historia* 10: 1–18.

Andrewes, A. (1962) "The Mytilene Debate: Thucydides 3.36–49", *Phoenix* 16: 64–85.

Andrewes, A. (1970) *A Historical Commentary in Thucydides*, eds. A.W. Gomme, A. Andrewes and K.J. Dover, vol. 4, Books V.25–7. Oxford: Clarendon Press.

Andrewes, A. (1978) "The Opposition to Pericles", *JHS* 98: 1–8.

Andrews, J. (1994) "Cleon's Ethopoetics", *CQ* 44: 26–39.

Anti, C. (1954) "Il Vaso di Dario e I Persiani di Frinico", *Arch. Class.* 4: 23–43.

Apte, M.L. (1985) *Humor and Laughter: An Anthropological Approach*. Ithaca, NY: Cornell University Press.

Arrowsmith, W. (1964) "A Greek Theatre of Ideas", *Arion* 2: 32–56.

Arrowsmith, W. (1973) "Aristophanes' *Birds*: The Fantasy Politics of Eros", *Arion* 1: 119–67.

Asheri, D. (2007) "General Introduction to *A Commentary on Herodotus Books I-IV*", eds. A. Asheri, A. Lloyd, A. Corcella, O. Murray and A. Moreno with a contribution by M. Brosius, trans. B. Graziosi, M. Rossetti, C. Dus and V. Cazzato. Oxford: Oxford University Press.

Avery, H. (1964) "Dramatic Devices in Aeschylus' *Persians*", *AJP* 85: 173–84.

Avery, H. (1973) "Themes in Thucydides' Account of the Sicilian Expedition", *Hermes* 101: 1–13.

Badian, E. (1968) *Roman Imperialism in the Late Republic*. Oxford: Blackwell.

Badian, E. (1992) "Thucydides on Rendering Speeches", *Athenaeum* 80: 187–90.

Badian, E. (1993) *From Plataea to Potidaea: Studies in the History and Historiography of the Pentekontaetia*. Baltimore, MD: Johns Hopkins University Press.

Bakker, E. (2006) "Contract and Design: Thucydides' Writing", in Rengakos and Tsakmakis (2006): 109–29.

Bakker, E., I. de Jong and H. van Wees (2002) *Brill's Companion to Herodotus*. Leiden, Boston and Cologne: Brill.

Balandier, G. (1970) *The Sociology of Black Africa: Social Dynamics in Central Africa*, trans. D. Garman. New York, NY: Praeger. Originally published 1955.

Balcer, J. (1977) "Imperial Magistrates in the Athenian Empire", *Historia* 25: 257–87.

Balot, R. (2001) *Greed and Injustice in Classical Athens*. Princeton, NJ: Princeton University Press.

Bang, P. (2009) "Commanding and Consuming the World: Empire, Tribute, and Trade in Roman and Chinese History", in Scheidel, W. (ed.) *Rome and China: Comparative Perspectives on Ancient World Empires*. Oxford: Oxford University Press: 100–20.
Bang, P. and D. Kolodziejczyk (2012) *Universal Empire: A Comparative Approach to Imperial Culture and Representation in Eurasian History*. Cambridge: Cambridge University Press.
Bang, P. and D. Kolodziejczyk (2012a) "'Elephant of India': Universal Empire through Time and Across Cultures", in Bang and Kolodziejczyk (2012): 1–40.
Baragwanath, E. (2008) *Motivation and Narrative in Herodotus*. Oxford: Oxford University Press.
Barjamovic, G. (2012) "Propaganda and practice in Assyrian and Persian imperial culture" in Bang and Kolodziejczyk (2012): 43–59.
Barfield, T. (2001) "The Shadow Empires: Imperial State Formation along the Chinese-National Border", in Alcock, Altroy, Morrison and Sinopoli (2001): 10–41.
Barnes, B. (1988) *The Nature of Power*. Urbana and Chicago: University of Illinois Press.
Barrett, W.S. (1964) *Euripides: Hippolytus*. Oxford: Clarendon Press.
Barron, J. (1964) "Propaganda of the Delian League", *JHS* 84: 35–48.
Barron, J. (1983) "The Fifth-Century Horoi of Aigina", *JHS* 103: 1–12.
Barron, J. (1986) "Chios in the Athenian Empire", in Boardman, J. and C. Vaphopoulou-Richardson (eds.) *Chios: A Conference at the Homereion in Chios 1984*. Oxford: Clarendon Press: 89–103.
Bedford, P. (2009) "The Neo-Assyrian Empire", in Morris, I. and W. Scheidel (eds.) *Oxford Studies in Early Empires: Dynamics of Ancient Empires: State Power from Assyria to Byzantium*. Oxford: Oxford University Press: 30–65.
Behr, C. (1986) *P. Aelius Aristides the Complete Works*, vol. 1, Orations 1–16. Leiden: Brill.
Belich, J. (1986) *The Victorian Interpretation of Racial Conflict*. Montreal: McGill University Press.
Bell, D. (2006) "From Ancient to Modern in Victorian Imperial Thought", *Historical Journal* 49: 735–59.
Bernek, R. (2004) *Dramaturgie und Ideologie: Der politische Mythos in den Hikesiedramen des Aischylos, Sophokles und Euripides*. Munich and Leipzig: Saur.
Blundell, M. (1989) *Helping Friends and Harming Enemies: A Study in Sophocles and Greek Ethics*: Cambridge: Cambridge University Press.
Blundell, M. (1993) "The Ideal of Athens in *Oedipus at Colonus*", in Sommerstein, Halliwell, Henderson and Zimmermann (1993): 287–306.
Bodin, L. (1940) "Diodote contre Cleon", *REA* 42: 36–52.
Boedeker, D. (1998) "Presenting the Past in Fifth-Century Athens", in Boedeker and Raaflaub (1998): 185–202.
Boedeker, D. (2001) "Heroic Historiography: Simonides and Herodotus on Plataea", in Boedeker and Sider (2001): 120–34.
Boedeker, D. and K. Raaflaub (1998) *Democracy, Empire and the Arts in Fifth-Century Athens*. Cambridge, MA: Harvard University Press.
Boedeker, D. and D. Sider (1996) "The New Simonides", *Arethusa* 29: 167–92.
Boedeker, D. and D. Sider (2001) *The New Simonides: Contexts of Praise and Desire*. Oxford: Oxford University Press.
Boegehold, A. (1982) "A Dissent at Athens ca. 424–421 BC", *GRBS* 23: 147–56.
Boegehold, A. and A. Scafuro (1994) *Athenian Identity and Civic Ideology*. Baltimore, MD: Johns Hopkins University Press.
Bond, G. (1981) *Euripides: Heracles with Introduction and Commentary*. Oxford: Oxford University Press.

Bosworth, A. (1993) "The Humanitarian Aspect of the Melian Dialogue", *JHS* 113: 30–44.
Bosworth, A. (2000) "The Historical Context of Thucydides' Funeral Oration", *JHS* 120: 1–16.
Bowersock, G.W. (1968) "Constitution of the Athenians: Pseudo-Xenophon", in Marchant, E.C. (ed.) *Xenophon Scripta Minora*. Cambridge, MA: Harvard University Press.
Bowie, A. (1993) "Religion and Politics in Aeschylus' *Oresteia*", *CQ* 43: 10–31.
Bowie, A. (1993a) *Aristophanes: Myth, Ritual, Comedy*. Cambridge: Cambridge University Press.
Bowie, A. (1997) "Tragic Filters for History: Euripides' Supplices and Sophocles' *Philoctetes*", in Pelling (1997): 39–62.
Bradeen, D. (1960) "The Popularity of the Athenian Empire", *Historia* 9: 257–69.
Bradford, A. (1994) "The Duplicitous Spartan", in Powell and Hodkinson (1994): 59–85.
Bradley, M. (2010) *Classics and Imperialism in the British Empire*. Oxford: Oxford University Press.
Bradley, M. (2010a) "Tacitus' Agricola and the Conquest of Britain: Representations of Empire in Victorian and Edwardian England", in Bradley (2010): 123–57.
Brantlinger, P. (1990) *Rule of Darkness: British Literature and Imperialism*. Ithaca, NY: Cornell University Press.
Braund, D. (1994) "The Luxuries of Athenian Democracy", *G&R* 41: 41–8.
Bremer, J. (1991) "Poets and Their Patrons", in Harder, A. and H. Hofmann (eds.) *Fragmenta Dramatica: Beiträge zur Interpretation der griechischen Tragikerfragmente und ihrer Wirkungsgeschichte*. Göttingen: Vandenhoeck & Ruprecht: 139–60.
Bremmer, J. (1997) "Myth as Propaganda: Athens and Sparta", *ZPE* 117: 9–17.
Bridges, E. (2015) *Imagining Xerxes: Ancient Perspectives on a Persian King*. London: Bloomsbury.
Bridges, E., E. Hall and P. Rhodes (2007) *Cultural Responses to the Persian Wars: Antiquity to the Third Millennium*. Oxford: Oxford University Press.
Broadhead, H. (1960) *The Persae of Aeschylus*. Edited with Introduction, Critical Notes and Commentary. Cambridge: Cambridge University Press.
Brock, R. (1998) "Mythical Polypragmosyne in Athenian Drama and Rhetoric", in Austin, M., J. Harries and C. Smith (eds.) *Modus Operandi: Essays in Honour of Geoffrey Rickman*. London: Institute of Classical Studies: 227–38.
Brunt, P. (1978) "Laus Imperii", in Garnsey and Whitaker (1978): 159–91.
Bryce, J. (1914) *The Ancient Roman Empire and the British Empire in India: The Diffusion of Roman and English law Throughout the World: Two Historical Studies*. London: Humphrey Milford.
Büchmann, G. (1895) *Geflügelte Worte: Der Citatenschatz des deutschen Volkes*. Berlin: Haude und Spener (F. Weidling).
Buck, R. (1962) "The Minoan Thalassocracy Re-Examined", *Historia* 11: 129–37.
Burian, P. (1974) "Oedipus as Suppliant and Saviour", *Phoenix* 28: 408–29.
Burian, P. (1977) "Euripides' *Heraclidae*: An Interpretation", *CPhil.* 72: 1–21.
Burian, P. (1985) "Logos and Pathos: The Politics of the Suppliant Women", in Burian, P. (ed.) *Directions in Euripidean Criticism*. Durham, NC: Duke University Press: 129–55.
Burkert, W. (1983) *Homo Necans: The Anthropology of Ancient Greek Sacrificial Ritual and Myth*, trans. P. Bing. Berkeley and Los Angeles: University of California Press.
Burkert, W. (1985) *Greek Religion*, trans. J. Raffan. Cambridge, MA: Harvard University Press.
Burnett, A. (1976) "Tribe and City, Custom and Decree in *Children of Heracles*", *CPhil.* 71: 4–26.

Burton, P. (2011) *Friendship and Empire: Roman Diplomacy and Imperialism in the Middle Republic (353–146 BC)*. Cambridge and New York: Cambridge University Press.
Cain, P. and A. Hopkins (2002) *British Imperialism 1688–2000*. London: Longman.
Cairns, H. (1965) *Prelude to Imperialism: British Reactions to Central African Society 1840–1890*. London: Routledge and Kegan Paul.
Calame, C. (2011) "Myth and Performance on the Athenian Stage: Praxithea, Erechtheus, Their Daughters, and the Etiology of Autochthony", *CPhil*. 106: 1–19.
Campbell, B. (2012) "Imperialism and Its Failures, 60 BC-AD14", in Hoyos (2012): 169–80.
Calhoun, C., F. Cooper and K. Moore (2006) *Lessons of Empire: Imperial Histories and American Power*. New York, NY: The New Press.
Canfora, L. (1992) *Tucidide e l'impero*. Rome: Laterza.
Cannadine, D. (2001) *Ornamentalism: How the British Saw Their Empire*. Oxford: Oxford University Press.
Carter, D. (2011) *Why Athens: A Reappraisal of Tragic Politics*. Oxford: Oxford University Press.
Carter, D. (2011a) "Plato, Drama, and Rhetoric", in Carter (2011): 45–67.
Carter, L. (1986) *The Quiet Athenian*. Oxford: Oxford University Press.
Cartledge, P. (1997) "'Deep Plays': Theatre as Process in Greek Civic Life", in Easterling (1997): 3–35.
Castriota, D. (1992) *Myth, Ethos and Actuality*. Madison, WI: University of Wisconsin Press.
Castriota, D. (1998) "Democracy and Art in Late Sixth- and Fifth-Century Athens", in Morris, I. and K. Raaflaub (eds.) *Democracy 2500? Questions and Challenges: AIA Colloquia and Conference Papers No. 2*. Dubuque, IA: Kendall and Hunt Publishing.
Champion, C. (2004) *Roman Imperialism: Readings and Sources*. Oxford: Blackwell.
Chapman, G. (1978) "Aristophanes and History", *AC* 21: 59–70.
Chiasson, C. (1999) "Σωφρονοῦντες ἐν χρόνωι: The Athenians and Time in Aeschylus' 'Eumenides'", *CJ* 95: 139–61.
Christ, M. (2006) *The Bad Citizen in Classical Athens*. Cambridge: Cambridge University Press.
Christ, M. (2012) *The Limits of Altruism in Democratic Athens*. Cambridge: Cambridge University Press.
Clarke, K. (2001) "An Island Nation: Re-Reading Tacitus' Agricola", *JRS* 91: 94–112.
Clarke, K. (2008) "Text and Image: Mapping the Roman World", in Mutschler and Mittag (2008): 195–214.
Cline, E. and M. Graham (2011) *Ancient Empires from Mesopotamia to the Rise of Islam*. Cambridge: Cambridge University Press.
Cogan, M. (1981) *The Human Thing: The Speeches and Principles of Thucydides' History*. Chicago and London: University of Chicago Press.
Cogan, M. (1981a) "Mytilene, Plataea, and Corcyra: Ideology and Policy in Thucydides, Book Three", *Phoenix* 35: 1–21.
Colås, A. (2007) *Empire*. Cambridge: Polity.
Cole, T. (1997) "The Ion of Euripides and Its Audience(s)", in Edmunds, L. and R. Wallace (eds.) *Poet, Public, and Performance in Ancient Greece*. Baltimore and London: Johns Hopkins University Press: 87–96.
Collard, C. (1972) "The Funeral Oration in Euripides' Supplices", *BICS* 19: 39–53.
Collard, C. (2008) *Persians and Other Plays*. Oxford: Oxford University Press.
Collard, C. and M. Cropp (2008) *Euripides Vol. VII: Euripides Fragments: Aegeus to Meleager*. Edited and Translated. Cambridge, MA and London: Harvard University Press.

Collard, C. and M. Cropp (2008a) *Euripides Vol. VIII: Oedipus-Chrysippus and Other Fragments*. Edited and Translated. Cambridge, MA and London: Harvard University Press.
Collingwood, R.G. (1946) *The Idea of History*. Oxford: Oxford University Press.
Conacher, D. (1959) "The Paradox of Euripides' Ion", *TAPA* 90: 20–39.
Conacher, D. (1987) *Aeschylus' Oresteia: A Literary Commentary*. Toronto, Buffalo and London: University of Toronto Press.
Connerton, P. (1989) *How Societies Remember*. Cambridge: Cambridge University Press.
Connor, W.R. (1971) *The New Politicians of Fifth-Century Athens*. Princeton, NJ: Princeton University Press.
Connor, W.R. (1977) "Tyrannis Polis", in D'Arms, J. and J. Eadie (eds.) *Ancient and Modern: Essays in Honor of Gerald F Else: Center for Coordination of Ancient and Modern Studies*. Ann Arbor, MI: University of Michigan Press: 95–109.
Connor, W.R. (1987) *Thucydides*. Princeton, NJ: Princeton University Press. First published in 1984.
Connor, W.R. (1991) "Polarization in Thucydides", in Lebow and Strauss (1991): 53–69.
Connor, W.R. (2009) "A Post-Modernist Thucydides", in Rusten (2009): 29–43. First published in *CJ* 72 (1977): 29–43.
Constantokopoulou, C. (2007) *Dance of the Islands: Insularity, Networks, the Athenian Empire, and the Aegean World*. Oxford: Oxford University Press.
Cooper, E. and H. Dinerman (2003) "Analysis of the Film Don't Be a Sucker", in Brooker and Jermyn (2003) *The Audience Studies Reader*. London: Routledge: 27–36.
Cornford, F. (1907) *Thucydides Mythistoricus*. London: Routledge and Kegan Paul.
Cox, M. (2004) "Empire, Imperialism and the Bush Doctrine", *Review of International Studies* 30: 585–608.
Cox, M. (2005) "Empire by Denial", *International Affairs* 81: 15–30.
Craig, J. (1924) "The Interpretation of Aeschylus' Persae", *CR* 38: 98–101.
Crane, G. (1998) *Thucydides and the Ancient Simplicity*. Berkeley and Los Angeles: University of California Press.
Croally, N. (1994) *Euripidean Polemic: The Trojan Women and the Function of Tragedy*. Cambridge: Cambridge University Press.
Cromer, E. (1910) *Ancient and Modern Imperialism*. New York: Longman.
Cropp, M. (1995) "Erechtheus" in Collard, C., M. Cropp and J. Gibert (eds.) *Euripides: Selected Fragmentary Plays Volume 1*. Warminster: Aris and Phillips: 148–94.
Csapo, E. (2012) "'Parade Abuse', 'From the Wagons'", in Kovacs, G. and C. Marshall (eds.) *No Laughing Matter: Studies in Athenian Comedy*. London: Bristol Classical Press: 19–33.
Csapo, E. and M. Miller (1998) "Democracy, Empire, and Art: Towards a Politics of Time and Narrative", in Boedeker and Raaflaub (1998): 87–125.
Davidson, J., F. Muecke and P. Wilson (2006) *Greek Drama III: Essays in Honour of Kevin Lee*. London: Institute of Classical Studies.
Davies, J.K. (1984) *Wealth and the Power of Wealth in Classical Athens*. Salem, NH: Ayer.
Debnar, P. (2001) *Speaking the Same Language: Speech and Audience in Thucydides' Spartan Debates*. Ann Arbor, MI: University of Michigan Press.
De Romilly, J. (1956) *Histoire et Raison chez Thucydide*. Paris: Les Belles Lettres.
De Romilly, J. (1963) *Thucydides and Athenian Imperialism*, trans. P. Thody. Oxford: Blackwell.
De Romilly, J. (1966) "Thucydides and the Cities of the Athenian Empire", *BICS* 13: 1–12. Also in Low (2008): 277–93.
De Romilly, J. (1974) *Eschyle: Les Perses*. Edition, introduction et commentaire. Paris: Presses Universitaires de France.

De Romilly, J. (1979) *La Douceur dans la Pensée Grecque*. Paris: Les Belles Lettres.
De Ste Croix, G. (1954) "The Character of the Athenian Empire", *Historia* 3: 1–41.
De Ste Croix, G. (1972) *Origins of the Peloponnesian War*. London: Duckworth.
De Ste Croix, G. (1996) "The Political Outlook of Aristophanes", in Segal (1996): 42–64. First published in de Ste. Croix (1972): 355–76.
Detienne, M. (1970) "L'olivier: un mythe politico-religieux", *RHR* 178: 2–23.
Detienne, M. (1996) *Masters of Truth in Archaic Greece with a Foreword by P Vidal-Naquet*, trans. J. Lloyd. New York, NY: Zone.
Dewald, C. (2005) *Thucydides' War Narrative: A Structural Study*. Berkeley, Los Angeles and London: University of California Press.
Dewald, C. (2009) "The Figured Stage: Focalizing the Initial Narratives of Herodotus and Thucydides", in Rusten (2009): 114–47.
Dhuga, U.S. (2005) "Choral Identity in Sophocles' 'Oedipus Coloneus'", *AJP* 126: 333–62.
Di Benedetto, V. (1978) *L'ideologia del potere e la tragedia Greca: Ricerche su Eschilo*. Einaudi: Turin.
Dilke, C.W. (1868) *Greater Britain*. London: Macmillan.
Dillon, M. (1997) *Pilgrims and Pilgrimage in Ancient Greece*. London and New York: Routledge.
Dirks, N. (2006) *The Scandal of Empire*. Cambridge, MA: Harvard University Press.
Dobrov, G. (1997) *The City as Comedy: Society and Representation in Athenian Drama*. Chapel Hill, NC: University of North Carolina Press.
Dobrov, G. (2010) *Brill's Companion to the Study of Greek Comedy*. Leiden and Boston: Brill.
Dodds, E.R. (1973) "Morals and Politics in the *Oresteia*", in *The Ancient Concept of Progress and Other Essays*. Oxford: Clarendon Press: 45–63.
Dorfman, A. (1983) *The Empire's Old Clothes: What the Lone Ranger, Barbar, and Other Innocent Heroes Do to Our Minds*. New York: Pantheon.
Dougherty, C. (1993) *The Poetics of Colonization: From City to Text in Archaic Greece*. Oxford: Oxford University Press.
Dover, K. (1957) "The Political Aspect of Aeschylus's Eumenides", *JHS* 77: 230–7.
Dover, K. (1970) in Gomme, A.W., A. Andrewes and K. Dover (eds.) *A Historical Commentary on Thucydides*, vol. 4: V(25)-VII. Oxford: Clarendon Press.
Dover, K. (1972) *Aristophanic Comedy*. Berkeley and Los Angeles: University of California Press.
Dover, K. (1974) *Greek Popular Morality in the Time of Plato and Aristotle*. Oxford: Blackwell.
Dover, K. (1975) "The Freedom of the Intellectual in Greek Society", *Talanta* 7: 24–54.
Dover, K. (1981) "Appendix 1: Indications of Incompleteness", in Gomme, A.W., A. Andrewes and K. Dover (1981) *A Historical Commentary on Thucydides*, vol. 5, Book 8. Oxford: Clarendon Press: 361–83.
Doyle, M. (1986) *Empires*. Ithaca, NY: Cornell University Press.
Drake, S. (1993) "Theater Review: Peter Sellars' Persians'", http://articles.latimes.com/1993-10-02/entertainment/ca-41199_1_director-peter-sellars
Dray, W. (1999) *History as Re-Enactment: R. G. Collingwood's Idea of History*. Oxford: Oxford University Press.
Drexler, H. (1959) "Iustum Bellum", *Rh. Mus.* 102: 97–140.
Dubois, T. (2005) "Imperialism, Hegemony and the Construction of Religion in East and Southeast Asia", *History and Theory, Theme Issue* 44: 113–31.

Dué, C. (2006) *The Captive Woman's Lament in Greek Tragedy*. Austin, TX: University of Texas Press.
Dunbar, N. (1995) *Aristophanes' Birds Edited with Introduction and Commentary*. Oxford: Clarendon Press.
Dunn, F. (2000) "Euripidean Aetiologies", *CB* 76: 3–28.
Easterling, P. *The Cambridge Companion to Greek Tragedy*. Cambridge: Cambridge University Press: 3–35.
Ebbott, M. (2000) "The List of the War Dead in Aeschylus' 'Persians'", *HSCP* 100: 83–96.
Eckstein, A. (2009) *Mediterranean Anarchy, Interstate War, and the Rise of Rome*. Berkeley and Los Angeles: University of California Press.
Edmunds, L. (1975) *Chance and Intelligence in Thucydides*. Cambridge, MA: Harvard University Press.
Edmunds, L. (1980) "Aristophanes' *Acharnians*", *YCS* 26: 1–42.
Edmunds, L. (1981) "The Cults and Legends of Oedipus", *HSCP* 85: 221–38.
Edmunds, L. (1987) "The Aristophanic Cleon's 'Disturbance' of Athens", *AJP* 108: 233–63.
Edmunds, L. (2009) "Thucydides in the Act of Writing", in Rusten (2009): 91–113. Originally in Pretagostini, R. (1993) *Traditizione e innovazione nella cultura greca da Omero a l'età ellenistica*. Rome: Gruppo Editoriale Internazionale: 831–51.
Ehrenberg, V. (1947) "*Polypragmosyne*: A Study in Greek Politics", *JHS* 67: 46–67.
Engel, M. (2001) "Iraqmania Grips the US", *The Guardian*, May 12.
Erskine, A. (2010) *Roman Imperialism*. Edinburgh: Edinburgh University Press.
Euben, P. (1986) *Greek Tragedy and Political Theory*. Berkeley and London: University of California Press.
Falkner, T. (2005) "Engendering the Tragic Theates: Pity, Power, and Spectacle in Sophocles' Trachiniae", in Sternberg (2005): 165–92.
Farber, C. (2001) "Hermocrates and Thucydides: Rhetoric, Policy, and the Speeches in Thucydides' History", *ICS* 26: 37–51.
Felson, N. (2011) "Children of Zeus in the Homeric Hymns: Generational Succession", in Faulkner, A. (ed.) *The Homeric Hymns: Interpretative Essays*. Oxford: Oxford University Press: 254–79.
Ferris, I. (2000) *Enemies of Rome: Barbarians through Roman Eyes*. Stroud: Sutton Publishing.
Festinger, L. (1957) *A Theory of Cognitive Dissonance*. Palo Alto, CA: Stanford University Press.
Fincham, G. (2001) "Writing Colonial Conflict, Acknowledging Colonial Weakness", in Davies, G., A Gardner and K. Lockyear (eds.) *TRAC 2000: Proceedings of the Tenth Annual Theoretical Roman Archaeology Conference*. Oxford: Oxbow: 25–34.
Finley, J. (1938) "Euripides and Thucydides", *HSCP* 49: 23–68.
Finley, J. (1967) *Three Essays on Thucydides*. Cambridge, MA: Harvard University Press.
Finley, M.I. (1987) "The Fifth-Century Athenian Empire: A Balance Sheet", in Garnsey and Whittaker (1978): 103–26.
Fitton, J. (1961) "The *Suppliant Women* and the *Herakleidai* of Euripides", *Hermes* 89: 430–61.
Flashar, H. (1969) *Der Epitaphios des Perikles: Seine Funktion im Geschichtswerk des Thukydides*, SB der Heidelberger Akademie der Wissenschaften Philosophisch-Historiche Klasse. Jahrg. 1969, Abh. 1.
Flory, S. (1990) "The Meaning of τὸ μὴ μυθῶδες (1.22.4) and the Usefulness of Thucydides' History", *CJ* 85: 193–208.

Flower, M. and J. Marincola (2002) *Herodotus: Histories Book IX*. Cambridge: Cambridge University Press.
Forde, S. (1986) "Thucydides on the Causes of Athenian Imperialism", *APSR* 80.2: 433–48.
Forde, S. (1989) *The Ambition to Rule: Alcibiades and the Politics of Imperialism in Thucydides*. Ithaca, NY: Cornell University Press.
Fornara, C. (1971) *Herodotus: An Interpretative Essay*. Oxford: Clarendon Press.
Fornara, C. and L. Samons (1991) *Athens from Cleisthenes to Pericles*. Berkeley, Los Angeles and Oxford: University of California Press.
Forrest, W.G. (1963) "Aristophanes' 'Acharnians'", *Phoenix* 17: 1–12.
Forrest, W.G. (1975) "Aristophanes and the Athenian Empire", in Levick, B. (ed.) *The Ancient Historian and His Materials: Essays in Honour of C.E. Stevens on His Seventieth Birthday*. Farnborough: Gregg: 17–29.
Foster, E. (2010) *Thucydides, Pericles, and Periclean Imperialism*. Cambridge: Cambridge University Press.
Frangeskou, V. (1999) "Tradition and Originality in Some Attic Funeral Orations", *CW* 92: 315–36.
Frank, T. (1912) "The Import of the Fetial Institution", *CPhil.* 7: 335–42.
Friedrichs, J. (2000) *Aufschlussreiche Rhetorik: ein Versuch über die Redekultur und ihren Verfall bei Thukydides*. Würzburg: Ergon.
Furley, D. (2006) "Thucydides and Religion", in Rengakos and Tzakmakis (2006): 415–38.
Gagarin, M. (1975) "The Vote of Athena", *AJP* 96: 121–7.
Galinsky, K. (1996) *Augustan Culture: An Interpretive Introduction*. Princeton, NJ: Princeton University Press.
Gamble, R. (1970) "Euripides' 'Suppliant Women': Decision and Ambivalence", *Hermes* 98: 385–405.
Garland, R. (2017) *Athens Burning: The Persian Invasion of Greece and the Evacuation of Attica*. Baltimore, MD: Johns Hopkins University Press.
Garnsey, P. and C. Whittaker (1978) *Imperialism in the Ancient World*. Cambridge: Cambridge University Press.
Garofoli, J. (2006) "Film Touches Deep Nerve for Families of Flight 93 Victims", www.sfgate.com/politics/joegarofoli/article/Film-touches-deep-nerve-for-families-of-Flight-93-2499479.php
Garrity, T. (1998) "Thucydides 1.22.1: Content and Form in the Speeches", *AJP* 119: 361–84.
Garvie, A.F. (2009) *Aeschylus: Persae with Introduction and Commentary*. Oxford: Oxford University Press.
Georges, P. (1994) *Barbarian Asia and the Greek Experience from the Archaic Period to the Age of Xenophon*. Baltimore, MD: Johns Hopkins University Press.
Gervasi, R. (1981) "The Concept of ELPIS in Thucydides", Dissertation, Ohio State University, Columbus, OH.
Gibert, J. (1997) "Euripides' Hippolytus Plays: Which Came First?", *CQ* 47: 85–97.
Gill, C., N. Postlethwaite and R. Seaford (1998) *Reciprocity in Ancient Greece*. Oxford: Oxford University Press.
Gillis, D. (1971) "The Revolt at Mytilene", *AJP* 92: 38–47.
Giovannini, A. (1990) "Le Parthenon, le Trésor d'Athéna et le Tribut des Alliés", *Historia* 39: 129–48. Also in Low (2008): 164–84 as "The Parthenon, the Treasury of Athena and the Tribute of the Allies", trans. G. Glasman.
Godley, A.D. (1922) *Herodotus with an English Translation*, vol. 3. London and New York: W. Heinemann and G.P. Putnam's Sons.

Goff, B. (1995) "Aithra at Eleusis", *Helios* 22: 65–78.
Goff, B. (2005) *Classics and Colonialism*. London: Duckworth.
Goldhill, S. (1987) "The Great Dionysia and Civic Ideology", *JHS* 107: 58–76.
Goldhill, S. (1988) "Battle Narrative and Politics in Aeschylus' Persae", *JHS* 108: 189–93.
Goldhill, S. (1990) "The Great Dionysia and Civic Ideology", in Winkler and Zeitlin (1990): 97–129.
Goldhill, S. (1997) "The Audience of Athenian Tragedy", in Easterling (1997): 54–68.
Goldhill, S. (2000) "Civic Ideology and the Problem of Difference: The Politics of Aeschylean Tragedy, Once Again", *JHS* 120: 34–56.
Goldhill, S. (2002) *The Invention of Prose*. Cambridge: Cambridge University Press.
Gordon, R. (1990) "Religion in the Roman Empire: The Civic Compromise and Its Limits", in North, J. and M. Beard (eds.) *Pagan Priests: Religion and Power in the Ancient World*. London: Duckworth: 238–55.
Gomme, A.W. (1937) "The Speeches in Thucydides", in *Essays in Greek History and Literature*. Oxford: Blackwell: 156–9.
Gomme, A.W. (1954) *The Greek Attitude to Poetry and History*. Berkeley and Los Angeles: University of California Press.
Gomme, A.W. (1956) *A Historical Commentary on Thucydides*, vol. 2. Oxford: Clarendon Press.
Gomme, A.W. (1959) *A Historical Commentary on Thucydides*, vol. 1. Oxford: Clarendon Press.
Gomme, A.W (1996) "Aristophanes and Politics", in Segal (1996): 29–41. Originally published in *CR* 52 (1938): 97–109.
Goossens, R. (1962) *Euripide et Athènes*. Brussels: Palais des Académies.
Gotteland, S. (2001) *Mythe et Rhétorique: Les Examples Mythiques dans le Discours Politique de l'Athènes Classique*. Paris: Les Belles Lettres.
Gould, T. (1965) "The Philosophers on Oedipus the King", *Arion* 4: 363–86.
Grant, J.R. (1965) "A Note on the Tone of Greek Diplomacy", *CQ* 15: 261–6.
Green, P. (1999) "War and Morality in Fifth Century Athens", *AHB* 13: 97–110.
Green, P. (2008) *The Shadow of the Parthenon: Studies in Ancient History and Literature*. Berkeley and Los Angeles: University of California Press. Originally published in 1972.
Greenwood, E. (2005) *Thucydides and the Shaping of History*. London: Duckworth.
Gregory, J. (1991) *Euripides and the Instruction of the Athenians*. Ann Arbor, MI: University of Michigan Press.
Gregory, D. (2004) *The Colonial Present*. Oxford: Blackwell.
Grethlein, J. (2003) *Athen und Asyl: die Konstruktion kollektiver Identität in der griechischen Tragödie*. Stuttgart: Metzler.
Grethlein, J. (2007) "The Hermeneutics and Poetics of Memory in Aeschylus's 'Persae'", *Arethusa* 40: 363–96.
Grethlein, J. (2013) *The Greeks and Their Past: Poetry, Oratory and History in the Fifth Century BCE*. Cambridge: Cambridge University Press.
Griffin, J. (1998) "The Social Function of Attic Tragedy", *CQ* 48: 39–61.
Griffin, M. (2008) "Iure Plectimur: The Roman Critique of Roman Imperialism", in Brennan, T. and H. Flower (eds.) *East and West: Papers in Ancient History Presented to Glen W. Bowersock*. Cambridge, MA: Harvard University Press: 85–111.
Griffith, G. (1978) "Athens in the Fourth Century", in Garnsey and Whittaker (1978): 127–44.
Griffith, M. (1995) "Brilliant Dynasts: Power and Politics in the *Oresteia*", *CA* 14: 62–129.

Griffith, M. (2007) "The King and Eye: The Rule of the Father in Aischylos' Persians", in Lloyd, M. (ed.) *Oxford Readings in Classical Studies: Aeschylus*. Oxford: Oxford University Press: 93–140.
Grube, G. (1941) *The Drama of Euripides*. London: Methuen.
Gustafson, L. (2000) *Thucydides' Theory of International Relations: A Lasting Possession*. Baton Rouge, LA: Louisiana State University Press.
Hall, C. and S. Rose (2006) *At Home with the Empire: Metropolitan Culture and the Imperial World*. Cambridge: Cambridge University Press.
Hall, E. (1989) *Inventing the Barbarian: Greek Self-Definition through Tragedy*. Oxford: Oxford University Press.
Hall, E. (1993) "Asia Unmanned: Images of Victory in Classical Athens", in Rich and Shipley (1993a): 108–33.
Hall, E. (2004) "Aeschylus, Race, Class, and War", in Hall, E., F. Macintosh and A. Wrigley (eds.) *Dionysus since 69: Tragedy at the Dawn of the Third Millennium*. Oxford: Oxford University Press: 169–97.
Hall, E. (2007) *Aeschylus: Persians*, 2nd ed. Warminster: Aris and Phillips.
Halliwell, S. (1991) "Comic Satire and Freedom of Speech in Classical Athens", *JHS* 111: 48–70.
Halliwell, S. (1993) "Comedy and Publicity in the Society of the Polis", in Sommerstein, Halliwell, Henderson and Zimmermann (1993): 321–40.
Halliwell, S. (2002) *The Aesthetics of Mimesis: Ancient Texts and Modern Problems*. Princeton, NJ: Princeton University Press.
Halliwell, S. (2008) *Greek Laughter: A Study of Cultural Psychology from Homer to Early Christianity*. Cambridge: Cambridge University Press.
Hammond, M. (1948) "Ancient Imperialism: Contemporary Justifications", *HSCP* 58–59: 105–61.
Hammond, N. (1973) "The Particular and the Universal with Special Reference to That of Hermocrates at Gela", in Stadter (1973): 49–59.
Handley, E. (1985) "Comedy", in Easterling, P. and B. Knox (eds.) *The Cambridge History of Classical Literature*. Cambridge: Cambridge University Press: 355–425.
Handley, E. (1993) "Aristophanes and the Generation Gap", in Sommerstein, Halliwell, Henderson and Zimmerman (1993): 417–30.
Hanink, J. (2013) "*Epitaphioi Mythoi* and Tragedy as Encomium of Athens", *TC* 5: 289–317.
Hansen, M. (1993) "The Battle Exhortation in Ancient Historiography: Fact or Fiction", *Historia* 42: 161–80.
Hanson, V. (1991) *Hoplites: The Classical Greek Battle Experience*. New York and London: Routledge.
Hanson, V. (2005) *A War Like No Other: How the Athenians and Spartans Fought the Peloponnesian War*. New York: Random House.
Hardie, P. (1986) *Virgil's Aeneid: Cosmos and Imperium*. Oxford: Clarendon Press.
Hardt, M. and A. Negri (2000) *Empire*. Cambridge, MA and London: Harvard University Press.
Harriott, R. (1986) *Aristophanes Poet and Dramatist*. Baltimore, MD: Johns Hopkins University Press.
Harris, E. (1992) "Pericles' Praise of Athenian Democracy: Thucydides 2.37.1", *HSCP* 94: 157–67.
Harris, W. (1985) *War and Imperialism in Republican Rome*. Oxford: Clarendon Press.
Harrison, T. (1976) *Phaedra Britannica*. Ashford, Bellew.

Harrison, T. (2000a) "Sicily in the Athenian Imagination: Thucydides and the Persian Wars", in Smith, C. and J. Serrati (eds.) *Sicily from Aeneas to Augustus: New Approaches in Archaeology and History*. Edinburgh: Edinburgh University Press: 84–96.
Harrison, T. (2000b) *The Emptiness of Asia: Aeschylus' Persians and the History of the Fifth Century*. London: Duckworth.
Harrison, T. (2005) "Through British Eyes: The Athenian Empire and Modern Historiography", in Goff (2005): 25–37.
Harrison, T. (2008) "Ancient and Modern Imperialism", *G&R* 55: 1–22.
Harrison, T. (2009) "Herodotus on the American Empire", *CW* 102: 383–93.
Haubold, J. (2007) "Xerxes' Homer", in Bridges, Hall and Rhodes (2007): 47–63.
Hawkes, T. (1973) *Shakespeare's Talking Animals: Language and Drama in Society*. London: Routledge.
Headlam, W. (1906) "The Last Scene of the Eumenides", *JHS* 26: 268–77.
Heath, M. (1987) *Political Comedy in Aristophanes*, Hypomnemata, 87. Göttingen: Vandenhoeck & Ruprecht.
Heath, M. (1987a) *The Poetics of Greek Tragedy*. London: Duckworth.
Heath, M. (1990) "Justice in Thucydides' Athenian Speeches", *Historia* 39: 385–400.
Heath, M. (1997) "Aristophanes and the Discourse of Politics", in Dobrov (1997): 230–49.
Hedrick, C. (1993) "The Meaning of Material Culture: Herodotus, Thucydides and Their Sources", in Rosen, R. and J. Farrell, J. (eds.) *Nomodeiktes: Greek Studies in Honor of Martin Ostwald*. Ann Arbor, MI: University of Michigan Press: 17–38.
Henderson, J. (1991) *The Maculate Muse: Obscene Language in Attic Comedy*, 2nd ed. Oxford: Oxford University Press.
Henderson, J. (1996) "The Demos and the Comic Competition", in Segal (1996): 65–97.
Henderson, J. (1997) "Mass versus Elite and the Comic Heroism of Peisetairos", in Dobrov (1997): 135–48.
Henderson, J. (1998) "Attic Old Comedy, Frank Speech, and Democracy", in Boedeker and Raaflaub (1998): 255–73.
Henderson, J. (2007) *Aristophanes' Fragments*. Cambridge, MA: Harvard University Press.
Henderson, M. (1975) "Plato's *Menexenus* and the Distortion of History", *AC* 18: 25–46.
Herrman, J. (2009) *Hyperides: Funeral Oration Edited with Introduction, Translation and Commentary*. Oxford: Oxford University Press.
Heubeck, A. (1980) "*Prophasis* und kein Ende", *Glotta* 58: 222–36.
Hingley, R. (2000) *Roman Officers and English Gentlemen*. London: Routledge.
Hingley, R. (2005) *Globalizing Roman Culture: Unity, Diversity and Empire*. London: Routledge.
Hoffer, S. (1996) "Violence, Culture, and the Workings of Ideology in Euripides' 'Ion'", *Cl. Ant.* 15: 289–318.
Hoffman, M. (2001) "Towards a Comprehensive Empathy-Based Theory of Prosocial Moral Development", in Bohart, A. and D. Stipek (eds.) *Constructive and Destructive Behavior: Implications for Family, School and Society*. Washington, DC: American Psychological Association: 61–86.
Hölscher, T. (1998) "Images and Political Identity: The Case of Athens", in Boedeker and Raaflaub (1998): 153–83.
Hopman, M. (1993) "Layered Stories in Aeschylus' Persians", in Grethlein, J. and A. Rengakos (eds.) *Narratology and Interpretation: The Content of Narrative Form in Ancient Literature*. Berlin and New York: de Gruyter: 357–76.
Hornblower, S. (1987) *Thucydides*. London: Duckworth.

Hornblower, S. (1991) *A Commentary on Thucydides Volume 1: Books I–III*. Oxford: Clarendon Press.
Hornblower, S. (1996) *A Commentary on Thucydides Volume 2: Books IV–V.24*. Oxford: Clarendon Press.
Hornblower, S. (2004) *Thucydides and Pindar: Historical Narrative and the World of Epinikian Poetry*. Oxford: Oxford University Press.
Hornblower, S. (2008) *A Commentary on Thucydides Volume 3: Books 5.25–8.109*. Oxford: Clarendon Press.
Hornblower, S. (2011) *Thucydidean Themes*. Oxford: Oxford University Press.
Hornblower, S. (2011a) "The Religious Dimension to the Peloponnesian War, Or, What Thucydides Does Not Tell Us", in Hornblower (2011): 25–38.
Hornblower, S. (2011b) "Narratology and Narrative Techniques in Thucydides", in Hornblower (2011): 59–99.
Hornblower, S. (2011c) "Thucydides and the Argives", in Hornblower (2011): 139–52.
Hornblower, S. (2011d) "The Fourth-Century and Hellenistic Reception of Thucydides", in Hornblower (2011): 286–322.
Hose, M. (2006) "The Peloponnesian War: Sources Other Than Thucydides", in Rengakos and Tsakmakis (2006): 669–90.
Hoyos, D. (2012) *A Companion to Roman Imperialism*. Leiden and Boston: Brill.
How, W. and J. Wells (1912) *A Commentary on Herodotus*. Oxford: Clarendon Press.
Huart, P. (1968) *Le Vocabulaire de l'Analyse Psychologique dans l'oeuvre de Thucydide*. Paris: Klincksieck.
Hubbard, T. (1991) *The Mask of Comedy: Aristophanes and the Intertextual Parabasis*. Ithaca, NY: Cornell University Press.
Hubbard, T. (1997) "Utopianism and the Sophistic City in Aristophanes", in Dobrov (1997): 23–50.
Hunter, V. (1973) *Thucydides the Artful Reporter*. Toronto: Hakkert.
Hutchins, F. (1967) *The Illusion of Permanence: British Imperialism in India*. Princeton, NJ: Princeton University Press.
Hutchinson, G. (2004) "Euripides' Other Hippolytus", *ZPE* 149: 15–28.
Immerwahr, H. (1973) "Pathology of Power and the Speeches in Thucydides", in Stadter (1973): 16–31.
Irwin, E. (2007) "The Politics of Precedence: First 'Historians' on First 'Thalassocrats'", in Osborne, R. (ed.) *Debating the Athenian Cultural Revolution: Art, Literature, Philosophy, and Politics 430–380 BC*. Cambridge: Cambridge University Press: 188–223.
Irwin, E. (2012) "Bacchylides 17: Theseus, Minos and Delian League Ideology", in Corrêa, P., M. Martinho, J. Macedo and A. Hasegawa (eds.) *Hyperboreans: Essays in Greek and Latin Poetry, Philosophy, Rhetoric and Linguistics*. São Paulo: Humanitas: 51–102.
Isaac, B. (2004) *The Invention of Racism in Classical Antiquity*. Princeton, NJ: Princeton University Press.
Jarvis, C. (2012) "Fiction, Empathy and Lifelong Learning", *International Journal of Lifelong Education* 31: 743–58.
Johnson, C. (2004) *The Sorrows of Empire: Militarism, Secrecy and the End of the Republic*. London: Verso.
Johnson, J. and Clapp, D. (2005) "Athenian Tragedy: An Education in Pity", in Sternberg (2005): 123–64.
Johnston, S. (2015) "The Dangers of Portraying Hitler". www.telegraph.co.uk/culture/film/film-news/11573042/The-dangers-of-portraying-Hitler.html
Jones, A.H.M. (1957) *Athenian Democracy*. Oxford: Blackwell.

Judet de la Combe, P. (2011) "Il mito interpreta la storia. I *Persiani*", in Beltrametti, A. (ed.) *La storia sulla scena: Quello che gli atorici antichi non hanno recontato*. Rome: Carocci editori: 87–103.
Kagan, D. (1969) *The Outbreak of the Peloponnesian War*. Ithaca, NY: Cornell University Press.
Kagan, D. (1974) *The Archidamian War*. Ithaca, NY: Cornell University Press.
Kagan, D. (1975) "The Speeches in Thucydides and the Mytilene Debate", *YCS* 24: 71–94.
Kagan, D. (1981) *The Peace of Nicias and the Sicilian Expedition*. Ithaca, NY: Cornell University Press.
Kagan, R. (1998) "The Benevolent Empire", *Foreign Policy* 111: 24–35.
Kakridis, J. (1961) *Der Thukydideische Epitaphois: Ein Stilisticher Kommentar*. Munich: Beck.
Kallet, L. (1998) "Accounting for Culture in Fifth-Century Athens", in Boedeker and Raaflaub (1998): 43–58.
Kallet, L. (2001) *Money and the Corrosion of Power: The Sicilian Expedition and Its Aftermath*. Berkeley and Los Angeles: University of California Press.
Kallet, L. (2009) "Democracy, Empire and Epigraphy in the Twentieth Century", in Ma, Papazarkadas and Parker (2009): 43–66.
Kallet-Marx, L. (1993) *Money, Expense, and Naval Power in Thucydides' History 1–5.24*. Berkeley and Los Angeles: University of California Press.
Kannicht, R. (2004) *Tragicorum Graecorum Fragmenta*, vol. 5. Euripides. Göttingen: Vandenhoeck & Ruprecht.
Kantzios, I. (2004) "The Politics of Fear in Aeschylus' 'Persians'", *CW* 98: 3–19.
Karavites, P. (1980) "'Euergesia' in Herodotus and Thucydides as a Factor in Interstate Relations", *RIDA* 3e ser. 27: 769–79.
Karavites, P. (1982) *Capitulations and Greek Interstate Relations*. Göttingen: Vandenhoeck & Ruprecht.
Katz, B. (1976) "The *Birds* of Aristophanes and Politics", *Athenaeum* 54: 363–81.
Kelley, K. (1979) "Variable Repetition: Word Patterns in the 'Persae'", *CJ* 74: 213–19.
Kelly, A. (2009) *Sophocles: Oedipus at Colonus*. London: Duckworth.
Kelly, D. (2009) *Lineages of Empire: The Historical Roots of British Imperial Thought*. Oxford: Oxford University Press.
Kennedy, D. (1999) "A Sense of Place: Rome, History and Empire Revisited", in Edwards, C. (ed.) *Roman Presences: Receptions of Rome in European Culture 1789–1945*. Cambridge: Cambridge University Press.
Kennedy, R. (2006) "Justice, Geography and Empire in Aeschylus' *Eumenides*", *Cl. Ant.* 25: 35–72.
Kennedy, R. (2013) "A Tale of Two Kings: Competing Aspects of Power in Aeschylus' Persians", *Ramus* 42: 64–88.
Kennedy, R. (2017) "We Condone It by Our Silence: Confronting Classics' Complicity in White Supremacy", *Eidolon*, May 11. https://eidolon.pub/we-condone-it-by-our-silence-bea76fb59b21
Kierdorf, W. (1966) *Erlebnis und Darstellung der Perserkriege*. Göttingen: Vandenhoeck & Ruprecht.
Kirby, J. (1983) "Narrative Structure and Technique in Thucydides VI–VII", *Cl. Ant.* 2: 183–211.
Kirkwood, G. (1986) "From Melos to Colonus: ΤΙΝΑΣ ΧΩΡΟΥΣ ΑΦΙΓΜΕΘ'...", *TAPA* 116: 99–117.

Kleve, K. (1964) "Ἀπραγμοσύνη and Πολυπραγμοσύνη: Two Slogans in Athenian Politics", *SO* 39: 83–8.
Koechly, H. (1857) *Ueber die Vögel des Aristophanes: Gratulationsschrift der Universität Zürich 15 Marz 1857 als dem funfzigjährigen Doctorjubiläum des Herrn Geheimerath und Professor August Boeckh in Berlin*. Zürich: Zürcher und Furrer.
Konstan, D. (1995) *Greek Comedy and Ideology*. New York and Oxford: Oxford University Press.
Konstan, D. (1997) "The Greek Polis and Its Negations: Versions of Utopia in Aristophanes' Birds", in Dobrov (1997): 1–22.
Konstan, D. (2001) *Pity Transformed*. London: Duckworth.
Konstan, D. (2007) "Pity and Politics", in Sternberg (2005): 48–66.
Kowalzig, B. (2006) "The Aetiology of Empire? Hero-Cult and Athenian Tragedy", in Davidson, Muecke, and Wilson (2006): 79–98.
Kowerski, L. (2005) *Simonides on the Persian Wars: A Study of the Elegiac Verses of the "New Simonides"*. New York and London: Routledge.
Krauthammer, C. (2001) "The Bush Doctrine", *Time Magazine*, March 5.
Kriegel, L. (2003) "The Pudding and the Palace: Labor, Print Culture, and Imperial Britain in 1851", in Burton, A. (ed.) *After the Imperial Turn: Thinking With and through the Nation*. Durham and London: Duke University Press: 230–45.
Krummen, E. (1993) "Athens and Attica: *Polis* and Countryside in Tragedy", in Sommerstein, Halliwell, Henderson and Zimmermann (1993): 191–217.
Kubala, L. (2013) "The Distinctive Features and the Main Goals of Athenian Imperialism in the 5th Century BC ('Imperial' Policies and Means of Control in the Mid-5th Century Athenian Empire)", *Graeco-Latina Brunensia* 18: 131–48.
Kunze, E. (1950) *Archaische Schildbänder: ein Beitrag zur frühgriechischen Bildgeschichte und Sagenüberlieferung*. Berlin: de Gruyter.
Lada, I. (1993) "'Empathic Understanding': Emotion and Cognition in Classical Dramatic Audience-Response", *PCPS* 39: 94–140.
Laistner, M. (1927) *Isocrates de Pace and Philippus*. New York and London: Longmans, Green and Co.
Laird, A. (1999) *Powers of Expression, Expressions of Power: Speech Presentation and Latin Literature*. Oxford: Oxford University Press.
Lamb, W. (1930) *Lysias with an English Translation*. Cambridge, MA: Harvard University Press.
Lang, M. (1968) "Thucydides and the Epidamnian Affair", *CW* 61: 173–6.
Langer, W. (1935) "A Critique of Imperialism", *Foreign Affairs* 14: 102–19.
Larson, J. (1995) *Greek Heroine Cults*. Madison and London: University of Wisconsin Press.
Lateiner, D. (1985) "Nicias' Inadequate Encouragement (Thucydides 7.69.2)", *CPhil.* 80: 201–13.
Lateiner, D. (2005) "The Pitiers and the Pitied in Herodotus and Thucydides", in Sternberg (2005): 67–97.
Lattimore, R. (1943) "Aeschylus on the Defeat of Xerxes", in Abbott, K. (ed.) *Classical Studies in Honor of William Abbott Oldfather*. Urbana: University of Illinois Press: 82–93.
Lazenby, J. (1988) "Aischylos and Salamis", *Hermes* 116: 168–85.
Lebow, R. (2003) *The Tragic Vision of Politics: Ethics, Interests and Orders*. Cambridge: Cambridge University Press.
Lebow, R. (2008) *A Cultural Theory of International Relations*. Cambridge: Cambridge University Press.

Lebow, R. and B. Strauss (1991) *Hegemonic Rivalry from Thucydides to the Nuclear Age*. Boulder, CO, San Francisco, CA and Oxford: Westview Press.
Lee, K. (1997) *Euripides Ion: With Introduction, Translation, and Commentary*. Warminster: Aris and Phillips.
Lee, K. (1999) "The Dionysia: Instrument of Control or Platform for Critique?", in Papenfuss, D. and V. Strocker, V. (eds.) *Gab es das Griechische Wunder?: Griechenland zwischen dem Ende des 6. und der Mitte des 5. Jahrhunderts v. Chr.: Tagungsbeiträge des 16. Fachsymposiums der Alexander-von-Humboldt-Stiftung, veranstaltet vom 5. bis 9. April 1999 in Freiburg im Breisgau*. Mainz: Ph. von Sabern.
Lefkowitz, M. (1989) "'Impiety' and 'Atheism' in Euripides' Dramas", *CQ* 39: 70–81.
Legon, R. (1968) "Megara and Mytilene", *Phoenix* 22: 200–25.
Levy, E. (2006) "United 93: Film's Politics". http://emanuellevy.com/comment/the-politics-of-iunited-93i-2/
Lewis, D. (1992) "The Archidamian War: II The war", in Lewis, D., J. Boardman, J.K. Davies and M. Ostwald (eds.) *Cambridge Ancient History*, vol. 5, 2nd ed. Cambridge: Cambridge University Press: 370–432.
Liddel, P. (2009) "European Colonialist Perspectives on Athenian Power: Before and after the Epigraphic Explosion", in Ma, Papazarkadas and Parker: 13–42.
Lincoln, B. (2007) *Religion, Empire and Torture: The Case of Achaemenian Persia, with a Postscript on Abu Graib*. Chicago and London: University of Chicago Press.
Linforth, I. (1951) "Religion and Drama in Oedipus at Colonus", *UCPCP* 14: 75–191.
Loomis, W. (1992) "The Spartan War Fund: IG V I, 1 and a New Fragment", in *Historia Einzelschriften*, vol. 74. Stuttgart: Steiner.
Loraux, N. (1982) "Ponos: sur quelques difficultés de la peine comme nom du travail", *Annali (Napoli) Archeologia e Storia Antica* 4: 170–92.
Loraux, N. (1986) *The Invention of Athens*, trans. A. Sheridan. Cambridge, MA: Harvard University Press.
Loraux, N. (1986a) "Thucydide a écrit la guerre du Peloponnèse", *Métis* 3: 139–61.
Loraux, N. (1993) *The Children of Athena: Athenian Ideas about Citizenship and the Division between the Sexes*, trans. C. Levine. Princeton: Princeton University Press.
Loraux, N. (2002) *The Mourning Voice: An Essay on Greek Tragedy*, trans. E. Rawlinson. Ithaca, NY: Cornell University Press.
Low, P. (2005) "Looking for the Language of Athenian Imperialism", *JHS* 125: 93–111.
Low, P. (2007) *Interstate Relations in Classical Greece*. Cambridge: Cambridge University Press.
Low, P. (2008) *The Athenian Empire*. Edinburgh: Edinburgh University Press.
Ludden, D. (2011) "The Process of Empire: Frontiers and Borderlands", in Bang, P. and C. Bayly (eds.) *Tributary Empires in Global History*. London: Palgrave Macmillan: 132–50.
Ludwig, P. (2002) *Eros and Polis: Desire and Community in Greek Political Theory*. Cambridge: Cambridge University Press.
Lugard, F. (1922) *The Dual Mandate in British Tropical Africa*. Edinburgh and London: Blackwood.
Luginbill, R. (1999) *Thucydides on War and National Character*. Boulder, CO: Westview Press.
Luppe, W. (1994) "Die hypothesis zum ersten 'Hippolytos' (P. Mich. Inv.6222A)", *ZPE* 102: 23–38.
Luppe, W. (2003) "Nochmals sur Hypothesis des ersten Hippolytos", *ZPE* 143: 23–6.
Luschnat, O. (1970) "Thucydides", *RE* Suppl. 12: 1162–83.
Luschnat, O. (1974) "Thucydides", *RE* Suppl. 14: 766–8.

Ma, J. (2009) "Afterword: Whither the Athenian Empire", in Ma, Papazarkadas and Parker (2009): 223–31.
Ma, J., N. Papazarkadas and R. Parker (2009) *Interpreting the Athenian Empire*. London: Duckworth.
MacDonald, P. (2009) "Those Who Forget Historiography Are Doomed to Republish It: Empire, Imperialism and Contemporary Debates about American Power", *Review of International Studies* 35: 45–67.
MacDonald, R. (1994) *The Language of Empire: Myths and Metaphors of Popular Imperialism, 1880–1918*. Manchester: Manchester University Press.
MacDowell, D. (1983) "The Nature of Aristophanes' *Akharnians*", *G&R* 30: 143–62.
MacDowell, D. (1988) *Aristophanes: Wasps Edited with Introduction and Commentary*. Oxford: Clarendon Press.
MacDowell, D. (1995) *Aristophanes and Athens: An Introduction to the Plays*. Oxford: Oxford University Press.
MacKenzie, J. (2005) "Another Little Patch of Red", *History Today* 55.8: 20–6.
MacKenzie, J. (1986) *Propaganda and Empire: The Manipulation of British Public Opinion, 1880–1960*. Manchester: Manchester University Press.
Macleod, C. (1983) "Reason and Necessity: Thucydides III 9–14, 37–48", in Macleod (1983g): 88–102. Originally in *JHS* 98 (1978): 64–78.
Macleod, C. (1983a) "Form and Meaning in the Melian Dialogues", in Macleod (1983g): 52–67. Originally in *Historia* 23 (1974): 385–400.
Macleod, C. (1983b) "Thucydides and Tragedy", in Macleod (1983g): 140–58.
Macleod, C. (1983c) "Thucydides' Plataean Debate", in Macleod (1983g): 103–22. Originally in *GRBS* 18 (1977): 227–46.
Macleod, C. (1983d) "Rhetoric and History (Thucydides 6.16–18)", in Macleod (1983g): 68–87. Originally in *QS* 2 (1975): 39–65.
Macleod, C. (1983e) "Thucydides on Faction (3.82–83)", in Macleod (1983g): 123–39. Originally in *PCPS* 205, n.s. 25 (1979): 52–68.
Macleod, C. (1983f) "Politics and the *Oresteia*", in Macleod (1983g): 20–43. Originally in *Maia* 25 (1973): 267–92 and revised in *JHS* (1982): 124–44.
Macleod, C. (1983g) *Collected Essays*. Oxford: Oxford University Press.
Magnani, M. (2004) "P. Mich. Inv. 6222A 3 P. Pxy LXVIII 4640 c.II; alcune osservazioni sull'argumento (?) del primo 'Ippolito' euripideo", *Eikasmos* 15: 227–40.
Maier, C. (2006) *Among Empires: American Ascendancy and Its Predecessors*. Cambridge, MA: Harvard University Press.
Major, W. (2013) *The Court of Comedy: Aristophanes, Rhetoric and Democracy in Fifth-Century Athens*. Columbus, OH: Ohio State University Press.
Malamud, M. (2010) "Translatio Imperii: America as the New Rome c.1900", in Bradley (2010): 249–83.
Malkin, I. (1994) *Myth and Territory in the Spartan Mediterranean*. Cambridge: Cambridge University Press.
Mann, M. (1986) *Sources of Social Power: A History of Power from the Beginning to AD 1760*. Cambridge: Cambridge University Press.
Mann, M. (2004) "The First Failed Empire of the 21st Century", *Review of International Studies* 30: 631–53.
Mannoni, O. (1964) *Prospero and Caliban: The Psychology of Colonization*, 2nd ed., trans. P. Powesland with a foreword by P. Mason. New York: Praeger.
Mantena, R. (2010) "Imperial Ideology and the Uses of Rome in Discourses on Britain's Indian Empire", in Bradley (2010): 54–73.

Marincola, J. (2007) "The Persian Wars in Fourth-Century Oratory and Historiography", in Bridges, Hall and Rhodes (2007): 105–25.
Markantonatos, A. (2002) *Tragic Narrative: A Narratological Study of Sophocles' Oedipus at Colonus*. Berlin and New York: de Gruyter.
Markantonatos, A. (2007) *Oedipus at Colonus: Sophocles, Athens, and the World*. Berlin and New York: de Gruyter.
Markantonatos, A. (forthcoming) *Brill's Companion to Euripides*.
Mason, P. (1964) *Foreword to O. Mannoni (1964) Prospero and Caliban: The Psychology of Colonization*, 2nd ed., trans. P. Powesland with a foreword by Philip Mason. New York: Praeger.
Mastronarde, D. (1979) *Contact and Discontinuity: Some Conventions of Speech and Action on the Greek Tragic Stage*. Berkeley: University of California Press.
Mattern, S. (2004) "Rome and the Enemy: Imperial Strategy in the Principate" in Champion (2004): 186–200. Excerpted from Mattern, S. (1999) *Rome and the Enemy: Imperial Strategy in the Principate*. Berkeley and Los Angeles: University of California Press.
Mattingly, D. (1997) *Dialogues in Roman Imperialism: Power, Discourse, and Discrepant Experience in the Roman Empire*, JRA Supplementary series 23. Portsmouth, RI: JRA.
Mattingly, D. (2011) *Imperialism, Power, and Identity: Experiencing the Roman Empire*. Princeton, NJ: Princeton University Press.
Mattingly, H. (1996) "The Language of Athenian Imperialism", in Mattingly, H. (ed.) *The Athenian Empire Restored Epigraphic and Historical Studies*. Ann Arbor, MI: University of Michigan Press: 361–85.
McChesney, J. (2007) "Military Hospitals Experiment with Virtual Reality". www.npr.org/templates/story/story.php?storyId=10318758
McClure, L. (2006) "Maternal Authority and Heroic Disgrace in Aeschylus's *Persae*", *TAPA* 136: 71–97.
McCoskey, D. (2012) *Race, Antiquity and Its Legacy*. Oxford: Oxford University Press.
McDevitt, A.M. (1972) "The Nightingale and the Olive", in Lesky, A., H. Schwabl and R. Hanslik (eds.) *Antidosis: Festschrift fur Walther Kraus zum 70. Geburtstag*. Vienna: Wiener Studien: 227–37.
McLeish, K. (1980) *The Theatre of Aristophanes*. New York, NY: Taplinger.
McNeal, R. (1970) "Historical Methods and Thucydides 1.103.1", *Historia* 19: 306–25.
Meier, C. (1993) *The Political Art of Greek Tragedy*. Baltimore, MD: Johns Hopkins University Press.
Meiggs, R. (1943) "The Growth of Athenian Imperialism", *JHS* 63: 21–34.
Meiggs, R. (1972) *The Athenian Empire*. Oxford: Clarendon Press.
Meineck, P. (2012) "Combat Trauma and the Tragic Stage: 'Restoration' by Cultural Catharsis", *Intertexts* 16.1: 7–24.
Meineck, P. (2013) "Under Athena's Gaze: Aeschylus' *Eumenides* and the Topography of Opsis", in Harrison, G. and V. Liapis (2013) *Performance in Greek and Roman Theatre*. Leiden and Boston: Brill: 161–79.
Melchinger, S. (1979) *Die Welt als Tragödie vol.1: Aischylos and Sophokles*. Munich: Beck.
Mendelsohn, D. (2002) *Gender and the City in Euripides' Political Plays*. Oxford: Oxford University Press.
Millender, E. (2001) "Spartan Literacy Revisited", *Cl. Ant* 20: 121–64.
Miller, M. (1997) *Athens and Persia in the Fifth Century BC: A Study in Cultural Receptivity*. Cambridge: Cambridge University Press.

Mills, S. (1997) *Theseus, Tragedy and the Athenian Empire*. Oxford: Oxford University Press.
Mills, S. (2017) "Ektos Sumphoras: Tragic Athens", *Polis* 34: 208–25.
Missiou, A. (1992) *The Subversive Oratory of Andokides*. Cambridge: Cambridge University Press.
Missiou, A. (1998) "Reciprocal Generosity in the Foreign Affairs of Fifth-Century Athens and Sparta", in Gill, Postlethwaite and Seaford (1998): 181–97.
Mitchell-Boyask, R. (2009) *Aeschylus: Eumenides*. London: Duckworth.
Moles, J. (1996) "Herodotus Warns the Athenians", *Papers of the Leeds International Latin Seminar* 9: 259–84.
Monoson, S. and Loriaux, M. (1998) "The Illusion of Power and the Disruption of Moral Norms: Thucydides' Critique of Periclean Policy", *American Political Science Review* 92: 285–97.
Moreno, A. (2009) "'The Attic Neighbour': The Cleruchy in the Athenian Empire", in Ma, Papazarkadas and Parker (2009): 211–21.
Morris, I. (2005) "The Athenian Empire (478–404 BC)", *Princeton/Stanford Working Papers in Classics 2005*. www.princeton.edu/~pswpc/pdfs/morris/120508.pdf
Morris, I. (2009) "The Greater Athenian State", in Morris, I. and W. Scheidel (eds.), *The Dynamics of Ancient Empires: State Power from Assyria to Byzantium*. Oxford and New York: Oxford University Press: 99–177.
Morrison, J. (2006) *Reading Thucydides*. Columbus, OH: Ohio State University Press.
Münkler, H. (2007) *Empires: The Logic of World Domination from Ancient Rome to the United States*. Cambridge: Polity Press.
Munson, R. (2012) "Herodotus and the Heroic Age: The Case of Minos", in Baragwanath, E. and M. de Bakker (eds.) *Myth, Truth, and Narrative in Herodotus*. Oxford: Oxford University Press: 195–212.
Murray, G. (1933) *Aristophanes: A Study*. Oxford: Clarendon Press.
Murray, G. (1972) "The Persae", in McCall, M. (ed.) *Aeschylus: A Collection of Critical Essays*. Upper Saddle River, NJ: Prentice Hall: 29–39. Originally from Murray (1940) Aeschylus, *The Creator of Tragedy*. Oxford: Oxford University Press.
Mutschler, F. and A. Mittag (2008) *Conceiving the Empire: China and Rome Compared*. Oxford: Oxford University Press: 91–114.
Nelis, J. (2000) "Constructing Fascist Identity: Benito Mussolini and the Myth of Romanità", *CW* 100: 391–415.
Newiger, H. (1980) "War and Peace in the Comedy of Aristophanes", *YCS* 26: 219–37.
Nicolai, R. (2009) "*Ktema eis aei*: Aspects of the Reception of Thucydides in the Ancient World", in Rusten (2009): 381–404.
Nicolet, C. (1991) *Space, Geography, and Politics in the Early Roman Empire*. Ann Arbor, MI: University of Michigan Press.
Nisbet, R. and M. Hubbard (1970) *A Commentary on Horace: Odes Book 1*. Oxford: Clarendon Press.
Norlin, G. (1928–29) *Isocrates with an English Translation*. London and New York: William Heinemann and G.P. Putnam's Sons.
Norwood, G. (1930) "The Babylonians of Aristophanes", *CPhil.* 25: 1–10.
Ober, J. (1978) "Views of Sea Power in the Fourth-Century Attic Orators", *Ancient World* 1: 119–30.
Ober, J. (1989) *Mass and Elite in Democratic Athens: Rhetoric, Ideology, and the Power of the People*. Princeton, NJ: Princeton University Press.
Ober, J. (1991) "National Ideology and Strategic Defense of the Population, from Athens to Star Wars", in Lebow and Strauss (1991): 251–67.

Bibliography 197

Ober, J. (1994) "Civic Ideology and Counterhegemonic Discourse: Thucydides in the Sicilian Debate", in Boegehold and Scafuro (1994): 102–26.
Ober J. (1998) *Political Dissent in Democratic Athens: Intellectual Critics of Popular Rule*. Princeton, NJ: Princeton University Press.
O'Connor-Visser, E.M. (1987) *Aspects of Human Sacrifice in the Tragedies of Euripides*. New York, NY: Grüner.
Oliver, J. (1953) *The Ruling Power: A Study of the Roman Empire in the Second Century after Christ through the Roman Oration of Aelius Aristides*. Philadelphia, PA: American Philosophical Society.
Oliver, J. (1968) *The Civilizing Power: A Study of the Panathenaic Discourse of Aelius Aristides against the Background of Literature and Cultural Conflict*. Philadelphia, PA: American Philosophical Society.
Olko, J. (2012) "Aztec Universalism: Ideology and Status Symbols in the Service of Empire-Building", in Bang and Kolodziejczyk (2012): 253–79.
Olson, S.D. (1998) *Aristophanes: Peace*. Oxford: Oxford University Press.
Olson, S.D. (2002) *Aristophanes: Acharnians, Edited with Introduction and Commentary*. Oxford: Oxford University Press.
Olson, S.D. (2010) "Comedy, Politics, and Society", in Dobrov (2010): 35–69.
Orwin, C. (1994) *The Humanity of Thucydides*. Princeton, NJ: Princeton University Press.
Osborne, R. (2000) *The Athenian Empire*. London: London Association of Classical Teachers Occasional Research Series.
Ostwald, M. (1986) *From Popular Sovereignty to the Rule of Law*. Berkeley and London: University of California Press.
Pagden, A. (1995) *Lords of All the World*. New Haven, CT: Yale University Press.
Pagden, A. (2005) "Fellow Citizens and Imperial Subjects: Conquest and Sovereignty in Europe's Overseas Empires", History and Theory 44.4, *Theme Issue* 44: Theorizing Empire: 28–46.
Papadimitropoulos, L. (2008) "Xerxes' Hybris and Darius in Aeschylus' *Persae*", *Mnemosyne* 61: 451–8.
Parker, R. (1987) "Myths of Early Athens", in Bremmer, J. (ed.) *Interpretations of Greek Mythology*. London: Routledge: 187–214.
Parker, R. (1996) *Athenian Religion: A History*. Oxford: Clarendon Press.
Parker, R. (2009) "Aeschylus' Gods: Drama, Cult, Theology", in Jouanna, J. and F. Montanari (eds.) *Eschyle a l'Aube du Théâtre Occidental: Neuf Exposés Suivis par Discussion*. Vandoevres-Geneva: Fondation Hardt: 127–54.
Parker, V. (2007) "Herodotus' Use of Aeschylus' *Persae* as a Source for the Battle of Salamis", *SO* 82: 2–29.
Parry, A. (1981) *Logos and Ergon in Thucydides*. Salem, NH: Ayer.
Pearson, L. (1952) "*Prophasis* and *Aitia*", *TAPA* 83: 205–23.
Pelling, C. (1997) *Greek Tragedy and the Historian*. Oxford: Clarendon Press.
Pelling, C. (1997a) "Aeschylus' *Persae* and History", in Pelling (1997): 1–19.
Pelling, C. (1997b) "Conclusion", in Pelling (1997): 213–35.
Pelling, C. (1999) *Literary Texts and the Greek Historian*. London: Routledge.
Pelling, C. (2009, originally 2000) "Thucydides' Speeches", in Rusten (2009): 176–87.
Perlman, S. (1968) "Athenian Democracy and the Revival of Imperialistic Expansion at the Beginning of the Fourth Century B.C.", *CPhil*. 63: 257–67.
Perlman, S. (1991) "Hegemony and *Arkhe* in Greece: Fourth Century BC Views", in Lebow and Strauss (1991): 269–86.
Piccirilli, L. (2001) "La Diplomazia nella Grecia Antica", *MH* 58: 1–31.

Pillar, P. (2013) "Ingratitude in Afghanistan and Elsewhere". http://nationalinterest.org/blog/paul-pillar/ingratitude-afghanistan-elsewhere-8757

Plant, I. (1999) "The Influence of Forensic Rhetoric on Thucydides' Method", *CQ* 49: 62–73.

Podlecki, A. (1966) *The Political Background of Aeschylean Tragedy*. Ann Arbor, MI: University of Michigan Press.

Podlecki, A. (1970) *The Persians: A Translation with Commentary*. Englewood Cliffs, NJ: Prentice-Hall.

Pohlenz, M. (1919) *Thukydidesstudien* reprinted in Dörrie, H. (1965) *Kleine Schriften*. Hildesheim: Olms: 210–80.

Pomper, P. (2005) "The History and Theory of Empires", *History and Theory* 44.4, Theme Issue 44: Theorizing Empire: 1–27.

Poole, W. (1994) "Euripides and Sparta", in Powell and Hodkinson (1994): 1–33.

Porter, B. (2004) *The Absent-Minded Imperialists*. Oxford: Oxford University Press.

Porter, B. (2005) "We Don't Do Empire", *History Today* 55.3: 31–3.

Pouncey, P. (1980) *The Necessities of War: A Study of Thucydides' Pessimism*. New York: Columbia University Press.

Powell, A. and S. Hodkinson (1994) *The Shadow of Sparta*. London and New York: Routledge: 59–85.

Pratt, M.L. (1992) *Imperial Eyes: Travel Writing and Transculturation*. London and New York: Routledge.

Prickard, A.O. (1879) *The Persae of Aeschylus: Edited with Introduction, Notes, and a Map*. London: Macmillan.

Pritchard, D. (2000) "The Fractured Imaginary: Popular Thinking on Citizen Soldiers and Warfare in Fifth Century Athens", Doctoral Thesis, Macquarie University, Sydney.

Pritchard, D. (2012) "Aristophanes and Ste Croix: The Value of Old Comedy as Evidence for Athenian Popular Culture", *Antichthon* 46: 14–44.

Quincey, J. (1964) "Orestes and the Argive Alliance", *CQ* 14: 190–206.

Quinn, T. (1981) *Athens and Samos, Lesbos and Chios, 478-404 BC*. Manchester: Manchester University Press.

Quint, D. (1993) *Epic and Empire: Politics and Generic Form from Virgil to Milton*. Princeton, NJ: Princeton University Press.

Raaflaub, K. (1987) "Herodotus, Political Thought, and the Meaning of History", *Arethusa* 20.1: 221–48.

Raaflaub, K. (1994) "Democracy, Power, and Imperialism in Fifth-Century Athens", in Euben, P., J. Wallach and J. Ober (eds.) *Athenian Political Thought and the Reconstruction of American Democracy*. Ithaca, NY: Cornell University Press: 103–46.

Raaflaub, K. (1998) "The Transformation of Athens in the Fifth Century", in Boedeker and Raaflaub (1998): 15–41.

Raaflaub, K. (2001) 'Father of All, Destroyer of All: War in Late Fifth-Century Athenian Discourse and Ideology', in McCann, D. and B. Strauss (eds.) *War and Democracy: A Comparative Study of the Korean War and the Peloponnesian War*. London and New York: Routledge: 307–56.

Raaflaub, K. (2002) "Philosophy, Science, Politics: Herodotus and the Intellectual Trends of His Time", in Bakker, de Jong and van Wees (2002): 149–86.

Raaflaub, K. (2004) *The Discovery of Freedom in Ancient Greece*, trans. R. Franciscono. Chicago and London: University of Chicago Press.

Raaflaub, K. (2006) "Thucydides on Democracy and Oligarchy", in Rengakos and Tsakmakis (2006): 189–222.

Raaflaub, K. (2007) "Searching for Peace in the Ancient World", in Raaflaub, K. (ed.) *War and Peace in the Ancient World*. Malden, MA: Wiley-Blackwell: 1–33.
Raaflaub, K. and Boedeker, D. (1998) "Reflections and Conclusions", in Boedeker and Raaflaub (1998): 319–44.
Rabinowitz, N. (1981) "From Force to Persuasion: Aeschylus; *Oresteia* as Cosmogonic Myth", *Ramus* 10: 156–91.
Rabinowitz, N. (1993) *Anxiety Veiled: Euripides and the Traffic in Women*. Ithaca and London: Cornell University Press.
Raleigh, T. (1906) *Lord Curzon in India: Being a Selection from His Speeches as Viceroy and Governor-General of India 1898–1905*. New York: Macmillan.
Ramamurthy, A. (2003) *Imperial Persuaders: Images of Africa and Asia in British Advertising*. Manchester: Manchester University Press.
Raubitschek, A. (1973) "The Speech of the Athenians at Sparta", in Stadter (1973): 32–48.
Rawlings, H. (1975) *A Semantic Study of Prophasis to 400 BC*. Wiesbaden: Steiner.
Rawlings, H. (1977) "Thucydides on the Delian League", *Phoenix* 31: 1–8.
Rawlings, H. (1981) *The Structure of Thucydides' History*. Princeton, NJ: Princeton University Press.
Reckford, K. (1987) *Aristophanes' Old-and-New Comedy: Six Essays in Perspective*. Chapel Hill, NC and London: University of North Carolina Press.
Reinhold, M. (1985) "Human Nature as Cause in Ancient Historiography", in Eadie, J. and J. Ober (eds.) *The Craft of the Ancient Historian: Essays in Honor of Chester G. Starr*. Lanham, MD and London: University Press of America: 21–40.
Reisz, E. (2010) "Classics, Race, and Edwardian Anxieties about Empire", in Bradley (2010): 210–28.
Rengakos, A. (1984) *Form und Wandel des Machtdenkens der Athener bei Thukydides*. Steiner: Wiesbaden.
Rengakos, A. and Tskamakis, A. (2006) *Brill's Companion to Thucydides*. Leiden and Boston: Brill.
Revermann, M. (2006a) *Comic Business: Theatricality, Dramatic Technique, and Performance Contexts of Aristophanic Comedy*. Oxford: Oxford University Press.
Revermann, M. (2006b) "The Competence of Theatre Audiences in Fifth- and Fourth-Century Athens", *JHS* 126: 99–124.
Revermann, M. (2008) "Aeschylus' Eumenides, Chronotopes, and the 'Aetiological Mode'", in Revermann, M. and P. Wilson (eds.) *Performance, Iconography, Reception: Studies in Honour of Oliver Taplin*. Oxford: Oxford University Press: 237–61.
Rhodes, P. (1985) *The Athenian Empire*. Oxford: Clarendon Press.
Rhodes, P. (1987) "Thucydides on the Causes of the Peloponnesian War", *Hermes* 115: 154–65.
Rhodes, P. (1988) *Thucydides History II Edited with Translation and Commentary*. Warminster: Aris and Phillips.
Rhodes, P. (1992) "The Delian League to 449 BC", in Lewis. D., J. Boardman, J.K. Davies and M. Ostwald (eds.) *Cambridge Ancient History*, vol. 5, 2nd ed. Cambridge: Cambridge University Press: 34–61.
Rhodes, P. (1993) *A Commentary on the Aristotelian Athenaion Politeia*. Oxford: Clarendon Press.
Rhodes, P. (1994) "In Defence of the Greek Historians", *G&R* 41: 156–71.
Rhodes, P. (2003) "Nothing to Do with Democracy: Athenian Drama and the Polis", *JHS* 123: 104–19.

Rhodes, P. (2006) "Thucydides and Athenian History", in Rengakos and Tsakmakis (2006): 523–46.
Rhodes, P. (2007) "The Impact of the Persian Wars on Classical Greece", in Bridges, Hall and Rhodes (2007): 31–45.
Rich, J. (1993) "Fear, Greed, and Glory: The Causes of Roman War Making in the Middle Republic", in Rich, J. and G. Shipley (eds.) *War and Society in the Roman World*. London and New York: Routledge: 38–68.
Rich, J. and G. Shipley (1993a) *War and Society in the Greek World*. London and New York: Routledge.
Richardson, J. (1990) "Thucydides 1.23.6 and the Debate about the Peloponnesian War", in Craik, E. (ed.) *Owls to Athens: Essays on Classical Subjects Presented to Sir Kenneth Dover*. Oxford: Oxford University Press: 155–61.
Richardson, J. (2008) *The Language of Empire: Rome and the Idea of Empire from the Third Century BC to the Second Century AD*. Cambridge: Cambridge University Press.
Robinson, R. (1972) "Non-European Foundations of European Imperialism: Sketch for a Theory of Collaboration", in Owen, R. and R. Sutcliffe (eds.) *Studies in the Theory of Imperialism*. London: Longman: 117–40.
Robinson, E. (2014) "The 'Ungrateful Volcano' of Iraq", *Washington Post*, June 23. www.washingtonpost.com/opinions/eugene-robinson-iraqs-calamity-stirs-a-reminder-of-the-ungrateful-volcano/2014/06/23/23f05090-fb07-11e3-8176-f2c941cf35f1_story.html?utm_term=.b86a4268fba0
Rogkotis, Z. (2006) "Thucydides and Herodotus: Aspects of Their Intertextual Relationship", in Rengakos and Tsakmakis (2006): 57–86.
Roisman, J. (1987) "Contemporary Allusions in Euripides' *Trojan Women*", *SIFC* 15: 38–47.
Roisman, J. (1988) "On Phrynichos' *Sack of Miletos* and *Phoinissai*", *Eranos* 86: 15–23.
Rokeah, D. (1982) "*Ta deonta peri ton aiai paronton*: Speeches in Thucydides: Factual Reporting or Creative Thinking?", *Athenaeum* 60: 386–401.
Rood, T. (1998) *Thucydides: Narrative and Explanation*. Oxford: Oxford University Press.
Rood, T. (1999) "'Thucydides' Persian Wars", in Kraus. C. (ed.) *The Limits of Historiography: Genre and Narrative in Ancient Historical Texts*. Leiden, Boston and Cologne: Brill: 141–68. Also in Rusten (2009): 148–75.
Rood, T. (2006) "Objectivity and Authority: Thucydides' Historical Method", in Rengakos and Tsakmakis (2006): 225–49.
Root, M.C. (1985) "The Parthenon Frieze and the Apadana Reliefs at Persepolis: Reassessing a Programmatic Relationship", *AJA* 89: 103–20.
Roselli, D. (2007) "Gender, Class and Ideology: The Social Function of Virgin Sacrifice in Euripides' *Children of Herakles*", *Cl. Ant.* 26: 81–169.
Roselli, D. (2011) *Theater of the People: Spectators and Society in Ancient Athens*. Austin, TX: University of Texas Press.
Rosen, R. (1988) *Old Comedy and the Iambographic Tradition*. Atlanta, GA: Scholars Press.
Rosen, R. (1997) "The Gendered Polis in Eupolis' *Cities*", in Dobrov (1997): 149–76.
Rosen, R. (2010) "Aristophanes", in Dobrov (2010): 227–68.
Rosenbloom, D. (1993) "Shouting 'Fire' in a Crowded Theater: Phrynichos's *Capture of Miletos* and the Politics of Fear in Early Attic Tragedy", *Philologus* 137: 159–96.
Rosenbloom, D. (1995) "Myth, History and Hegemony in Aeschylus", in Goff, B. (ed.) *History, Tragedy, Theory*. Austin, TX: University of Texas Press: 91–130.
Rosenbloom, D. (2006a) *Aeschylus: Persians*. London: Duckworth.

Rosenbloom, D. (2006b) "Empire and Its Discontents: *Trojan Women, Birds*, and the Symbolic Economy of Athenian Imperialism", in Davidson, Muecke and Wilson (2006): 245–71.
Rosenbloom, D. (2011) "The Panhellenism of Athenian Tragedy", in Carter (2011): 353–81.
Rosenbloom, D. (2014a) "Athens", in Roisman, H. (ed.) *The Encyclopedia of Greek Tragedy*. Malden, MA: Wiley-Blackwell: 164–7.
Rosenbloom, D. (2014b) "Thebes", in Roisman, H. (ed.) *The Encyclopedia of Greek Tragedy*. Malden, MA: Wiley-Blackwell: 1390–2.
Rosenfeld, G. (2014) *Hi Hitler! How the Nazi Past Is Being Normalized in Contemporary Culture*. Cambridge: Cambridge University Press.
Rosenmeyer, T. (1952) "The Wrath of Oedipus", *Phoenix* 6: 92–112.
Rosivach, V. (1987) "Autochthony and the Athenians", *CQ* 37: 294–306.
Rowe, C. (2007) "Plato and the Persian Wars", in Bridges, Hall and Rhodes (2007): 85–104.
Rubincam, C. (1991) "Casualty Figures in the Battle Descriptions of Thucydides", *TAPA* 121: 181–98.
Ruffell, I. (2000) "The World Turned Upside Down: Utopia and Utopians in the Fragments of Old Comedy", in Harvey, F.D. and J. Wilkins (eds.) *The Rivals of Aristophanes: Studies in Athenian Old Comedy*. London: Duckworth and the Classical Press of Wales: 473–506.
Ruffell, I. (2011) *Politics and Anti-Realism in Athenian Old Comedy: The Art of the Impossible*. Oxford: Oxford University Press.
Russo, C.F. (1994) *Aristophanes: An Author for the Stage*, trans. K. Wren. London and New York: Routledge.
Rusten, J. (2006) "Thucydides and Comedy", in Rengakos and Tsakmakis (2006): 547–58.
Rusten, J. (2009) *Thucydides: Oxford Readings in Classical Studies*. Oxford: Oxford University Press.
Rusten, J. (2009a) "Thucydides and His Readers", in Rusten (2009): 1–28.
Rutledge, S. (2000) "Tacitus in Tartan", *Helios* 27: 75–95.
Rynearson, N. (2013) "Courting the Erinyes: Persuasion, Sacrifice, and Seduction in Aeschylus' *Eumenides*", *TAPA* 143: 1–22.
Sagan, E. (1991) *The Honey and the Hemlock: Democracy and Paranoia in Ancient Athens and Modern America*. New York: Basic Books.
Said, E. (1978) *Orientalism*. New York: Pantheon.
Said, E. (1993) *Culture and Imperialism*. New York: Vintage.
Said, S. (1988) "Tragédie et renversement. L'exemple des Perses", *Métis* 3: 321–41.
Said, S. (1998) "Tragedy and Politics", in Raaflaub and Boedeker (1998): 275–95.
Said, S. (2002) "Herodotus and Tragedy", in Bakker, de Jong and van Wees (2002): 117–47.
Samons, L. (2000) *Empire of the Owl: Athenian Imperial Finance*. Stuttgart: Steiner.
Sampson, C.M. (2015) "Aeschylus on Darius and Persian Memory", *Phoenix* 69: 24–42.
Samuel, R. (1998) *Island Stories: Unravelling Britain*. London: Verso.
Scanlon, T. (1987) "Thucydides and Tyranny", *Cl. Ant.* 6: 286–301.
Scanlon, T. (1994) "Echoes of Herodotus in Thucydides: Self-Sufficiency, Admiration, and Law", *Historia* 43: 143–76.
Scardino, C. (2007) *Gestaltung und Funktion der Reden bei Herodot und Thukydides*. Berlin and New York: de Gruyter.
Scheidel, W. (2006) "Republics between Hegemony and Empire: How Ancient City-States Built Empires and the USA Doesn't (Anymore)", Stanford Working Papers in Classics, Princeton.

Schumpeter, J. (1955) "The Sociology of Imperialism", in *Imperialism and Social Classes*. New York: Meridian: 3–98.
Segal, E. (1996) *Oxford Readings in Aristophanes*. Oxford: Oxford University Press.
Shapiro, H. (1989) *Art and Cult Under the Peisistratids*. Mainz: von Zabern.
Shapiro, H. (1998) "Authochthony and the Visual Arts in Fifth-Century Athens", in Boedeker and Raaflaub (1998): 127–51.
Sidgwick, A. (1903) *Aeschylus' Persae with Introduction and Notes*. Oxford: Clarendon Press.
Siewert, P. (1977) "The Ephebic Oath in Fifth-Century Athens", *JHS* 97: 102–11.
Silk, M. (2000) *Aristophanes and the Definition of Comedy*. Oxford: Oxford University Press.
Smarczyk, B. (1990) *Untersuchungen zur Religionspolitik und politischen Propaganda Athens im Delisch-Attischen Seebund*. Munich: Tuduv.
Smarczyk, B. (1999) "Einige Bemerkungen zur Datierung der Beiträge zu Spartas Kriegskasse in IG V, 1, 1", *Klio* 81: 45–67.
Smith, C. F. (1913) *Thucydides, with an English Translation*, vol. IV. Cambridge MA and London: Harvard University Press.
Smith, D. (2004) "Thucydides' Ignorant Athenians and the Drama of the Sicilian Expedition", *Syll. Class.* 15: 33–70.
Smith, W. (1967) "Expressive Form in Euripides' *Suppliants*", *HSCP* 71: 151–70.
Snell, B. (1986) *Tragicorum Graecorum Fragmenta*, vol. 1. Göttingen: Vandenhoeck & Ruprecht.
Snyder, J. (1991/2003) *Myths of Empire: Domestic Politics and International Ambition*. Ithaca, NY: Cornell University Press.
Sommerstein, A. (1980) *Aristophanes: Acharnians*. Warminster, Aris and Phillips.
Sommerstein, A. (1981) *Aristophanes: Knights*. Warminster, Aris and Phillips.
Sommerstein, A. (1985) *Aristophanes: Peace*. Warminster, Aris and Phillips.
Sommerstein, A. (1986) "The Decree of Syrakosios", *CQ* 36:101–8.
Sommerstein, A. (1987) *Aristophanes: Birds*. Warminster, Aris and Phillips.
Sommerstein, A. (1989) *Aeschylus: Eumenides*. Cambridge: Cambridge University Press.
Sommerstein, A. (2010) *Aeschylean Tragedy*, 2nd ed. London: Duckworth.
Sommerstein, A., S. Halliwell, J. Henderson and B. Zimmermann (1993) *Tragedy, Comedy and the Polis: Papers from the Greek Drama Conference, Nottingham, 18–20 July 1990*. Bari: Levanti Editori.
Sonnino, M. (2010) *Euripides Erechthei Quae Extant*. Florence: Felice Le Monnier.
Sourvinou-Inwood, C. (1989) "Assumptions and the Creation of Meaning: Reading Sophocles' *Antigone*", *JHS* 109: 134–48.
Sourvinou-Inwood, C. (2003) *Tragedy and Athenian Religion*. Lanham, MD: Lexington Books.
Spurr, D. (1993) *The Rhetoric of Empire: Colonial Discourse in Journalism, Travel Writing, and Imperial Administration*. Durham, NC: Duke University Press.
Stadter, P. (1973) *The Speeches in Thucydides: A Collection of Original Studies with a Bibliography*. Chapel Hill, NC: University of North Carolina Press.
Stadter, P. (1973a) "Thucydidean Orators in Plutarch", in Stadter (1973): 109–23.
Stadter, P. (1992) "Herodotus and the Athenian *Arche*", *ASNP* 22.3, series III: 781–809.
Stahl, H.-P. (1973) "Speeches and Course of Events in Books Six and Seven of Thucydides", in Stadter (1973): 60–77.
Stahl, H.-P. (2003) *Thucydides: Man's Place in History*. Swansea: Classical Press of Wales. Originally published in German in 1966.
Starr, C. (1955) "The Myth of the Minoan Thalassocracy", *Historia* 3: 282–91.

Starr, C. (1987) "Athens and Its Empire", *CJ* 83: 114–23.
Steinbock, B. (2013) *Social Memory and Athenian Public Discourse: Use and Meanings of the Past*. Ann Arbor, MI: University of Michigan Press.
Steiner, D. (2005) "For Want of a Horse: Thucydides 6.30–2 and Reversals in the Athenian Civic Ideal", *CQ* 55: 407–22.
Steiner, G. (1996) "Tragedy Pure and Simple", in Silk, M.S. (ed.) *Tragedy and the Tragic*. Oxford: Oxford University Press: 534–46.
Sternberg, R. (2005a) *Pity and Power in Ancient Athens*. Cambridge: Cambridge University Press.
Sternberg, R. (2005b) "The Nature of Pity", in Sternberg (2005): 15–47.
Stevens, E.B. (1944) "Some Attic Commonplaces of Pity", *AJP* 65: 1–25.
Stoneman, R. (2015) *Xerxes: A Persian Life*. New Haven, CT: Yale University Press.
Storey, I. (2003) *Eupolis, Poet of Old Comedy*. Oxford and New York: Oxford University Press.
Storey, I. (2008) *Euripides: Suppliant Women*. London: Duckworth.
Storey, I. (2010) "Origins and Fifth-Century Comedy", in Dobrov (2010): 179–225.
Strasburger, H. (2009) "Thucydides and the Political Self-Portrait of the Athenians", trans. Rusten, in Rusten (2009): 191–219. Originally published as "Thukydides und die Politische Selbstdarstellung der Athener", *Hermes* 86 (1958): 17–40.
Strauss, B. (1986) *Athens after the Peloponnesian War: Class, Faction and Policy, 403-386 BC*. London and Sydney: Croom Helm.
Stroud, R. (1994) "Thucydides and Corinth", *Cheiron* 24: 267–304.
Süvern, J. (1827) "Über Aristophanes Vögel", *Abhandlungen der Akademie der Wissenschaften. Berlin. historisch-philologisch Kl.*: 1–109.
Swain, S. (1993) "Thucydides 1.22.1 and 3.83.4", *Mnemosyne* 46: 33–45.
Swift, L. (2008) *Euripides: Ion*. London: Duckworth.
Syme, R. (1958) *Tacitus*, vol. 2. Oxford: Clarendon Press.
Takacs, S. (2009) *The Construction of Authority in Ancient Rome and Byzantium*. Cambridge: Cambridge University Press.
Taplin, O. (1977) *The Stagecraft of Aeschylus: The Dramatic Use of Exits and Entrances in Greek Tragedy*. Oxford: Clarendon Press.
Taplin, O. (1996) "Fifth-Century Tragedy and Comedy", in Segal (1996): 9–28.
Taplin, O. (2006) "Aeschylus' *Persai*: The Entry of Tragedy into the Celebration Culture of the 470s?", in Cairns, D. and V. Liapis (eds.) *Dionysalexandros: Essays on Aeschylus and His Fellow Tragedians in Honour of Alexander F. Garvie*. Swansea: Classical Press of Wales: 1–10.
Taylor, M. (2010) *Thucydides, Pericles, and the Idea of Athens in the Peloponnesian War*. Cambridge: Cambridge University Press.
Taylor, P. (1993) *War of the Worlds: Peter Sellars' Adaptation of Aeschylus' The Persians*. www.independent.co.uk/arts-entertainment/theatre-edinburgh-festival-war-of-the-worlds-paul-taylor-on-peter-sellars-adaptation-of-aeschylus-1461817.html
Tharoor, S. (2017) *Inglorious Empire: What the British Did to India*. London: Penguin.
Thomas, R. (1989) *Oral Tradition and Written Record in Classical Athens*. Cambridge: Cambridge University Press.
Thomas, R. (2006) "Thucydides' Intellectual Milieu and the Plague", in Rengakos and Tsakmakis (2006): 87–108.
Thornton, A.P. (1965) *Doctrines of Imperialism*. New York: John Wiley and Sons.
Timmons, H. (2006) "Four Years on, a Cabin's-Eye View of 9/11". www.nytimes.com/2006/01/01/movies/four-years-on-a-cabinseye-view-of-911.html

Todd, S. (2007) *A Commentary on Lysias Speeches 1–11*. Oxford: Oxford University Press.

Tompkins, D. (1972) "Stylistic Characterization in Thucydides: Nicias and Alcibiades", *YCS* 22: 181–214.

Too, Y.L. (1995) *The Rhetoric of Identity in Isocrates: Text, Power, Pedagogy*. Cambridge: Cambridge University Press.

Trendall, A. and T. Webster (1971) *Illustrations of Greek Drama*. London: Phaidon.

Tritle, L. (2006) "From Melos to My Lai", in Rengakos and Tsakmakis (2006): 128–36.

Tully, J. (2009) "Lineages of Contemporary Imperialism", in Kelly (2009): 3–29.

Tuplin, C.J. (1985) "Imperial Tyranny: Some Reflections on a Classical Greek Political Metaphor", in Cartledge, P. and F.D. Harvey (eds.) *Crux: Essays in Greek History Presented to G.E.M. de Ste. Croix on his 75th Birthday*. London: Duckworth: 348–75.

Tyrell, W.M. and F.S. Brown (1991) *Athenian Myths and Institutions: Words in Action*. New York and Oxford: Oxford University Press.

Tzanetou, A. (2005) "A Generous City: Pity in Athenian Oratory and Tragedy", in Sternberg (2005): 98–122.

Tzanetou, A. (2011) "Supplication and Empire in Athenian Tragedy", in Carter (2011): 305–24.

Tzanetou, A. (2012) *City of Suppliants: Tragedy and the Athenian Empire*. Austin, TX: University of Texas Press.

Tzifopoulos, Y. (1995) "Thucydidean Rhetoric and the Propaganda of the Persian Wars Topos", *PdP* 50: 91–115.

Van Erp Taalman Kip, A. (1987) "Euripides and Melos", *Mnemosyne* 40: 414–1.

Van Rossum-Steenbeek, M. (2003) "POxy 4640 Hypothesis to a Theseus and Hippolytus?", in Gonis, N., D. Obbink and P. Parsons (eds.) *The Oxyrhynchus Papyri*, vol. 68. London: British Academy: 7–22.

Van Wees, H. (1998) "The Law of Gratitude: Reciprocity in Anthropological Theory", in Gill, Postlethwaite and Seaford (1998): 13–49.

Vasaly, A. (1993) *Representations: Images of the World in Ciceronian Oratory*. Berkeley and Los Angeles: University of California Press.

Vasunia, P. (2003) "Hellenism and Empire: Reading Edward Said", *Parallax* 9.4: 88–97.

Vasunia, P. (2005) "Greater Rome and Greater Britain", in Goff (2005): 38–64.

Vasunia, P. (2009) "Virgil and the British Empire 1760–1880", in Kelly (2009): 83–115.

Vasunia, P. (2011) "The Comparative Study of Empires", *JRS* 101: 222–237.

Vasunia, P. (2013) *The Classics and Colonial India*. Oxford: Oxford University Press.

Vaughn, P. (1991) "The Identification and Retrieval of the Hoplite Battle Dead", in Hanson (1991): 38–62.

Vellacott, P. (1975) *Ironic Drama: A Study of Euripides' Method and Meaning*. Cambridge: Cambridge University Press.

Vernant, J.P. (2006) *Myth and Thought among the Greeks*, trans. Janet Lloyd and Jeff Fort. New York: Zone Books.

Vidal-Naquet, P. (1986) *The Black Hunter: Forms of Thought and Forms of Society in the Greek World*, trans. A. Szegedy-Maszak with a foreword by B. Knox. Baltimore, MD: Johns Hopkins University Press.

Vidal-Naquet, P. (1988) "Oedipus between Two Cities: An Essay on *Oedipus at Colonus*", in Vernant, J.P. and P. Vidal-Naquet (eds.) *Myth and Tragedy in Ancient Greece*. New York: Zone: 329–59.

Visvardi, E. (2011) "Pity and Panhellenic Politics: Choral Emotion in Euripides' Hecuba and Trojan Women", in Carter (2011): 269–91.

Vlassopoulos, K. (2010) "Imperial Encounters", in Bradley (2010): 29–53.

Vogt, J. (2009) "The Portrait of Pericles in Thucydides", trans. J. Rusten, in Rusten (2009): 220–37. Originally published as "Das Bild des Perikles bei Thukydides", *Historische Zeitschrift* 182 (1956): 249–66.
Von Reden, S. (1998) "The Well-Ordered Polis: Topographies of Civic Space", in Cartledge, P., P. Millett and S. von Reden (1998) *Kosmos: Essays in Order, Conflict and Community in Classical Athens*. Cambridge: Cambridge University Press: 170–90.
Wade-Gery, H.T. (1958) *Essays in Greek History*. Oxford: Blackwell.
Walbank, F. (1951) "The Problem of Greek Nationality", *Phoenix* 5: 41–60.
Walbank, F. (2008) "Proxeny and Proxenos in Fifth-Century Athens", in Low (2008). Originally in Walbank (1978) *Athenian Proxenies of the Fifth Century BC*. Toronto and London: 2–9.
Walker, H. (1995) *Theseus and Athens*. Oxford and New York: Oxford University Press.
Wallace, R. (1994) "Private Lives and Public Enemies: Freedom of Thought in Classical Athens", in Boegehold and Scafuro (1994): 127–55.
Wallace, W. (1964) "Thucydides", *Phoenix* 18: 251–61.
Wallace-Hadrill, A. (1986) "Image and Authority in the Coinage of Augustus", *JRS* 76: 66–87.
Walsh, G. (1978) "The Rhetoric of Birthright and Race in Euripides' Ion", *Hermes* 106: 301–15.
Wander, P. (1997) "The Rhetoric of American Foreign Policy", in Medhurst, M. (eds.) *Cold War Rhetoric: Strategy, Metaphor, and Ideology*. East Lansing, MI: Michigan State University Press: 152–84.
Walters, K. (1980) "Rhetoric as Ritual: The Semiotics of the Athenian Funeral Oration", *Florilegium* 2: 1–27.
Walters, K. (1981) "We Alone Fought at Marathon: Historical Falsification in the Attic Funeral Speech", *Rh. Mus.* 124: 204–11.
Walters, K. (1981a) "Four Hundred Athenian Ships at Salamis?", *Rh. Mus.* 124: 199–203.
Wassermann, F. (1940) "Divine Violence and Providence in Euripides' *Ion*", *TAPA* 71: 587–604.
Wassermann, F. (1956) "Post-Periclean Democracy in Action", *TAPA* 87: 27–42.
Weaver, B. (1996) "A Further Allusion in the Eumenides to the Panathenaia", *CQ* 46: 559–61.
Webster, J. (1996) "Roman Imperialism and the 'Post Imperial Age'", in Webster, J. and N.J. Cooper (eds.) *Roman Imperialism: Post-Colonial Perspectives*. Leicester: University of Leicester School of Archaeological Studies: 1–17.
Webster, J. (1996a) "Ethnographic Barbarity: Colonial Discourse and 'Celtic Warrior Societies'", in Webster and Cooper (1996): 111–23.
Welsh, D. (1983) "The Chorus of Aristophanes' *Babylonians*", *GRBS* 24: 137–50.
West, M.L. (1992) *Iambi et Elegi Graeci ante Alexandrum cantati*, vol. 2, 2nd ed. Oxford: Clarendon Press.
West, W. (1970) "Saviors of Greece", *GRBS* 11: 271–82.
West, W. (1973) "The Speeches in Thucydides: A Description and Listing", in Stadter (1973): 3–15.
Westlake, H.D. (1953) "Euripides 'Troades' 205–229", *Mnemosyne* 6: 181–91.
Westlake, H.D. (1960) "Athenian Aims in Sicily 427-424 B.C.", *Historia* 9: 385–402.
Westlake, H.D. (1969) *Essays on the Greek Historians and Greek History*. Manchester and New York: Manchester University Press.
Westlake, H.D. (1969a) "Hermocrates the Syracusan", in Westlake (1969): 174–202.

Westlake, H.D. (1969b) "Thucydides and the Fall of Amphipolis", in Westlake (1969): 123–37.
Westlake, H.D. (1973) "The Settings of Thucydidean Speeches", in Stadter (1973): 90–108.
Whitman, C. (1964) *Aristophanes and the Comic Hero*. Cambridge, MA: Harvard University Press.
Wickersham, J. (1994) *Hegemony and the Greek Historians*. Lanham, MD: Rowman and Littlefield.
Wiles, D. (1977) *Tragedy in Athens: Performance and Theatrical Meaning*. Cambridge: Cambridge University Press.
Wilkins, J. (1990) "The State and the Individual: Euripides' Plays of Voluntary Self-Sacrifice", in Powell, A. (ed.) *Euripides, Women and Sexuality*. London: Routledge: 177–94.
Wilkins, J. (1993) *Heraclidae with Introduction and Commentary*. Oxford: Clarendon Press.
Wilkins, J. (1997) "Comic Cuisine: Food and Eating in the Comic Polis", in Dobrov (1997): 250–68.
Williams, R. (2012) *Savage Anxieties: The Invention of Western Civilization*. London: Palgrave.
Williams, W.A. (1980) *Empire as a Way of Life: An Essay on the Causes and Character of America's Present Predicament Along with a Few Thoughts about an Alternative*. Oxford and New York: Oxford University Press.
Willis, I. (2007) "The Empire Never Ended", in Hardwick, L. and C. Gillespie (eds.) *Classics in Post-Colonial Worlds*. Oxford: Oxford University Press: 329–48.
Wilsdon, C. (2000) *Mural Painting in Britain 1840–1940: Image and Meaning*. Oxford: Oxford University Press.
Wilson, C. (1966) "Thucydides, Isocrates, and the Athenian Empire", *G&R* 13: 54–63.
Wilson, J. (1982) "What Does Thucydides Claim for His Speeches?", *Phoenix* 36: 95–103.
Winkler, J. and F. Zeitlin (1990) *Nothing to Do with Dionysos? Athenian Drama in Its Social Context*. Princeton, NJ: Princeton University Press.
Winnington Ingram, R. (1965) "Τὰ Δέοντα Εἰπεῖν: Cleon and Diodotus", *BICS* 12: 70–82.
Wohl, V. (2002) *Love among the Ruins: The Erotics of Democracy in Classical Athens*. Princeton and Oxford: Princeton University Press.
Wolff, C. (1965) "The Design and Myth in Euripides' *Ion*", *HSCP* 69: 169–94.
Woodhead, A. (1960) "Thucydides' Portrait of Cleon", *Mnenomsyne* 13: 89–317.
Woodhead, C. (2005) "Murad III and the Historians: Representations of Ottoman Imperial Authority in Late 16th-Century Historiography", in Karateke, H. and M. Reinkowski (eds.) *Legitimizing the Order: The Ottoman Thetoric of State Power*. Leiden: Brill: 85–98.
Woodman, A. (1988) *Rhetoric in Classical Historiography*. London and Sydney: Croom Helm.
Woolf, G. (1997) "Beyond Romans and Natives", *World Archaeology* 28(3): 339–50.
Woolf, G. (2001) "Inventing Empire in Ancient Rome", in Alcock, D'Altroy, Morrison and Sinopoli (2001): 311–22.
Yang, H. and Mutschler, F. (2008) "The Emergence of Empire: Rome and the Surrounding World in Historical Narratives from the Late Third Century BC to the Early First Century AD", in Mutschler and Mittag (2008): 91–114.
Yates, R. (2001) "Cosmos, Central Authority, and Communities in the Early Chinese Empire", in Alcock, D'Altroy, Morrison and Sinopoli (2001): 351–68.
Yoshitake, S. (2010) "*Arete* and Achievements of the War Dead: The Logic of Praise in the Athenian Funeral Oration", in Pritchard, D. (ed.) *War, Culture and Democracy in Classical Athens*. Cambridge: Cambridge University Press: 359–77.

Zacharia, K. (2003) *Converging Truths: Euripides' Ion and the Athenian Quest for Self-Definition, Mnemosyne, Supp. 242*. Leiden and Boston: Brill.

Zanker, P. (1988) *The Power of Images in the Age of Augustus*. Ann Arbor, MI: University of Michigan Press.

Zeitlin, F. (1990) "Thebes: Theater of Self and Society", in Winkler and Zeitlin (1990): 130–67.

Zeitlin, F. (1996) "The Dynamics of Misogyny: Myth and Mythmaking in the *Oresteia*", in Zeitlin, F. (ed.) *Playing the Other: Gender and Society in Classical Greek Literature*. Chicago and London: University of Chicago Press: 87–119.

Zimmermann, B. (2006) "Poetry and Politics in the Comedies of Aristophanes", in Kozak, L. and J. Rich (eds.) *Playing around Aristophanes: Essays in Celebration of the Completion of the Edition of the Comedies of Aristophanes by Alan Sommerstein*. Oxford: Aris and Phillips: 1–19.

Ziolkowski, J. (1981) *Thucydides and the Tradition of Funeral Speeches at Athens*. New York: Arno Press.

Ziolkowski, J. (1993) "National and Other Contrasts in the Athenian Funeral Orations", in Khan, H. (ed.) *The Birth of the European Identity: The Europe-Asia Contrast in Greek Thought 490-322 BC*. Nottingham: University of Nottingham: 1–35.

Zuckerberg, D. (2019) "Racism, Responses, Responsibilities", *Eidolon*, January 28. https://eidolon.pub/racism-responses-responsibilities-a3d96b414f19

Zuntz, G. (1963) *The Political Plays of Euripides*, 2nd ed. Manchester: Manchester University Press.

Index

Aelius Aristides 9, 18
Aeneas as representative of the Roman empire 15
Aeschylus 14, 18, 47, 48, 50–1; *Eleusinioi* 18, 51; *Eumenides* 48, 50, 59–64, 76n152, 77n173, 78n187, 85; *Oresteia* 47; *Persians* 47, 50, 52–9, 73n105; use of distance by 48
Agamemnon, Thucydides' treatment of 138–9
agriculture, Athenian 18–19
Alcibiades 7, 20, 160–61
Alexander the Great 13
Amazons 8, 18, 21, 61–2
anti-intellectualism 50
archē, rather than "empire" as term for Athens' power 2, 5–6, 10
Aristophanes 11, 46, 100; anti-intellectualism used by 50; *see also* comedy, Aristophanic
Athenian empire: abuses of power in 22–3; agriculture in 18–19; compared to other nations 1–2, 5–6; confidence of 4–5; drive for temporal and spatial expansion in rhetoric of 6–7, 9–12, 13, 21, 28n48, 29n50, 60–1, 63, 84, 148, 150, 161; idealized virtues of 9–10, 23–4, 110–11; incorporating heroes from other cities into Athens 61–3, 68, 91–2, 94; introduction to 1–6; justification for war-making in 20–4, 27n25, 27n30, 32n99, 173n163; mental wallpaper of 3, 6; military force and power of 15–20, 170n85, 173n157; popularity of 25–6, 151–2, 155, 161; profit of 22–3, 61, 65, 85, 87, 91, 112; "racism" and 16; seductions and self-deception of 24–6, 42n287, 155, 159; source problems and imperial rhetoric of 7–9; speaking for its subjects 14–15, 55, 164; symbols of imperialism and 13; Thucydides' Book five on 157–9; Thucydides' Book one on 147–52; Thucydides' Book seven on 163–4; Thucydides' Book six on 159–63; Thucydides' Book three on 155–7; Thucydides' Book two on 152–5; *see also* imperialism, *ponos* and *polypragmosynē*
Athens, image in Athenian rhetoric: assimilated to Greece 17, 18, 56–7, 58–9, 63; city containing everything in harmony, even contradicting elements 11–12, 13, 14–15, 16–17, 18, 55–6, 66, 83, 90, 94, 114–5, 152–4; *see also* middle way; as first or only city in admirable achievements 12, 17–18, 25, 57, 59, 63, 65, 67–8, 82, 85, 88, 119, 149, 152–3, 161, 163; idealized combination of power, mercy and wisdom 23, 90, 148, 152, 157; love of hearing its own praise 46, 111; city outside the disaster 14, 20, 54, 65, 82, 86, 99–100; pitying city 53, 65, 67, 83–4, 92, 152, 156–7; self-sufficient helper city 19–20, 23–4, 51, 65, 68, 83–5, 90–1, 91–2, 153–4, 159–61, 163; as tyrant city 23, 116, 121, 130, 155–7, 158, 161–2; *see also* rewards for imperialists' efforts for others, *ponos* and *polypragmosynē*
autochthony 17, 93–4 and "racism" 82, 120, 140, 161

Babylonian Empire 13
Balandier, G. 2
Bang, P. 10
British Empire 9, 13, 15, 18; cult of amateurism in 24; racism of 17; self-deception of 25, 38n220

Caesar, J. 14
catalogues in imperial discourse 11–12, 114–5
Cicero 12, 20
Cleon 25, 50, 176n203; comedic portrayals of 108–10, 112, 115–18; Thucydides' portrayals of 155–7
Clive, R. 16
Colås, A. 2
comedy, Aristophanic 122n7; *Acharnians* 109, 111, 113–15; attitudes to empire 11, 110, 111–12, 113–4, 115–117, 118–22; *Babylonians* 109; *Birds* 100, 109, 118–22; free speech and 123n17; heroes of 122n6; *Clouds* 24, 50, 108, 120 *Holkades* 11, 126n80; *Horae* 11; *Knights* 50, 108, 109, 111, 115–17, 119, 120; *Lysistrata* 118; *Peace* 109, 117–18; remnants of the ideal Athens in 110–11, 112, 113–4, 116–7; and truth in portraying Athens 107–10; *Wasps* 109, 111–12, 114, 119, 120

Delian League 4, 14, 32n101, 55, 57, 149
Demosthenes 18
Dionysia 46–7, 109–10

Eleusinian mysteries 19, 60, 88, 91, 96
empire and imperialism, definitions of 1–6, 10
epitaphios logos 7–9, 13–14, 18–19, 24, 33n138, 36n191, 46, 130, 152–3, 159, 163, 164; comedy and 110, 112, 116, 117; relationship to 5th century imperial politics 7–9; time in 9, 13; tragedy and 46, 56, 62, 88, 99
euphemia 122n7
Euripides 13, 19, 24, 50; distance used by 49; *Andromache* 98; *Erechtheus* 50–1, 83, 95–6; *Heracles* 7, 14, 50, 60, 82, 85, 91–2; *Heraclidae* 7, 24, 50–1, 81, 82, 83–8, 96; *Hippolytus* 83, 97–8; introduction to 81–3; Ion 82, 93–5; *Medea* 14; *Peirithous* 50, 82, 85, 92–3; *Suppliants/Suppliant Women* 13, 19, 49, 50–1, 82, 88–91, 148; *Telephus* 113; *Theseus* 14, 92–3; *Trojan Women* 82, 98–100

free speech 123n17

Goldhill S. 45, 46, 73n105
Gorgias 7, 18, 19

Hall, E. 57
Hanson, V. D. 2
Heath, M. 45
hegemony 12, 26n8
Heracles, children of helped by Athens 19, 22, 51, 60, 81, 82; *see also* Euripides *Heraclidae*
Hermippus 11
Herodotus 7–8, 9–10, 58–9; in *Persians* 53, 54, 56–7; on uniqueness of Athens 17, 19
Homer 11, 24; *Iliad* 12, 24; *Odyssey* 54
Horace 14, 55
Hyperides 17

idealized Athenian virtue 9–10, 23–4, 110–11
imperialism, drive for expansion and transcendence of time and space 6–7, 9–10, 12, 13, 21, 60–1, 63, 84, 148, 150, 161; importance of concealing violence 15–16, 20–1, 23, 25; importance of naturalizing 7, 9–10, 12, 13, 15–16, 17, 24, 163; justification by appeal to generosity of imperialists 18–20, 23–4, 83, 149, 151, 154–7; by appeal to gods' support for empire 4–5, 15, 24, 54, 58, 92, 86, 159; by appeal to superior civilization of imperialists 7, 11, 12, 13, 15–16, 17, 18–19, 21, 57, 60–1, 62, 149, 152, 156; psychology of 3–4, 6, 9; subjects' "ingratitude" to imperialists 24, 85, 152, 160; symbolism 13
Ionians 56, 93–4, 162
Isocrates 8–9, 12, 21, 22–3

Kipling, R. 21
Kolodziejczyk, D. 10

Lang, M. 130–1
Lee, K. 47
Lenaea 109–10
Low, P. 25
Lugard, F. 15
Lysias 8, 21

Ma, J. 2
Marathon 113–4, 116–7, 149–50
Meineck, P. 47
Melos 9, 22, 98–100, 109, 118, 151, 157–9, 163
middle way, importance in imperial rhetoric 16–17, 62–3, 99, 162–3; *see also* moderation

military power and force 15–20; abuses of 22–3
Minos 139–40
moderation, importance in imperial rhetoric 68, 152, 156, 158–9, 163; see also middle way
Murray, Gilbert 58
mythology and Thucydides 138–40

Nebuchadnezzar, King 13
Nicias 26, 159–64

olives 19, 66, 99, 107–10
Orestes in *Eumenides* 19, 59–63, 85
Ottoman Empire 13

past, importance of in imperial rhetoric 13, 114
Pelling, C. 45
Pericles 7–8, 11–12, 14, 80n231, 176n203; in Book three of Thucydides 155–7; in Book two of Thucydides 153–5; "racism" and 17; on uniqueness of Athens 17–18
Persian Wars 4, 8, 18, 19, 111, 150; Athenian justifications of their power based on 8–9, 19, 21, 25, 55–7, 112, 139, 148, 149–50, 152, 158, 162; mythology of 139; Thucydides' account of Sicilian expedition containing echoes of motifs of Persian Wars 161–2, 164; see also Persians
Phrynichus 47, 52
Pindar 4, 59
Plato 8, 45–6; *Menexenus* 8, 46; *Minos* 139
polypragmosynē 22–4, 61, 67, 81, 83–5, 88–90, 119–21, 148, 154–5, 163
ponos 21–2, 83, 86, 88–90, 114, 148, 155, 158; see also *polypragmosynē* and Athens as self-sufficient helper city
profit of imperialism as justified 22–3, 61, 65, 85, 87, 91, 112
punishing the wicked 5, 19, 23, 58, 67, 81, 86, 88–9, 119

racism, analogues of in Athenian rhetoric 16, 21
rewards for imperialists' efforts for others 22–3, 61, 65, 85, 87, 91, 112
rhetoric, imperial: connection with imperialism 5–7; desire for expansion in 6–7, 28n48, 29n50; idealized Athenian virtue in 9–10, 23–4, 110–11; justification of 15–16, 20–4, 27n20, 32n99; source problems and 7–9
Rhodes, P. J. 46
Roman Empire 13, 14, 18; justification for war-making in 20–1, 27n20; as paradigm of empire 15; "racism" of 16

Salamis 56, 64, 99
Seeley, J. R. 25
self-deception of empire 24–6
Serrault, A. 15
seven against Thebes story 7–8, 18, 19, 49–50, 51, 60, 81, 82, 88–91
Sicily 159–62
Simonides 58
Socrates 8, 45–6, 50; on Minos 139–40
Sophocles 19, 50; distance used by 49; *Antigone* 49, 95; *Oedipus at Colonus* 19, 50, 64–8, 85, 102–3n68; *Oedipus Tyrannus* 49
Sourvinou-Inwood, C. 48
Sparta 8–9, 21, 22, 59–60, 89, 98–9, 117–8, 137–8; Thucydides' Book one on 147–52
Spurr, D. 20
Stoa Poikile 58
Suppliants, reception of 19–20, 60–2, 64–5, 83–4, 88–9, 153–4, 156–7

Thebes 49, 64–8, 88–93; see also seven against Thebes story
Theseus at Athens 18, 50–1, 58–9, 60, 63, 88–91, 97–8, 138–9, 152
Thucydides 3, 4, 5, 6, 14, 110–11; on Athens' power 15; Book five on Athens by 157–9; Book one on Athens by 147–52; Book seven on Athens by 163–4; Book six on Athens by 159–63; Book three on Athens by 155–7; Book two on Athens by 152–5; criticisms of poets by 134–5; on innovatory quality of his history 135–6; methods of 130–8, 156, 161; mythology and 138–40; narratives moulded by 131–4; oddities in portrayal of Epidamnus affair by 130–1; relation of his speeches to reality 132–7, 143n30; reliability of 134–8, 140–1, 144–5n67, 146n88; on self-deception 24; skepticism of mainstream Athenian imperial rhetoric 25; and in general 135–7, 140; sophistic thought and 45–6; under-representation of topics

by 136–7; on uniqueness of Athens 17–18
tragedy 81–3; Aeschylus' *Eumenides* 48, 50, 59–64, 76n152, 77n173, 78n187; Aeschylus' *Persians* 47, 50, 52–9, 73n105; as affirmative 46–7, 49–50, 51–2, 81–2, 87–8, 90–91, 95, 98–100; anti-intellectualism in 50; Athens' experiences with 45–52; comfort zones created in 49–50; at the Dionysia 46–7; and democracy 45–7 distance and closeness between audience and circumstances in 47–9, 70n38, 81–2, 84; Euripides' *Erechtheus* 50–1, 83, 95–6; Euripides' *Hippolytus* 83, 97–8; Euripides' *Ion* 93–5; Euripides' *Peirithous* 50, 82, 85, 92–3; Euripides' *Theseus* 14, 92–3; Euripides' *Trojan Women* 82, 98–100; Euripides' *Heracles* 7, 14, 50, 82, 85, 91–2; Euripides' *Heraclidae* 24, 50–1, 81, 82, 83–8, 96; Euripides' *Suppliants* 13, 19, 49, 50–1, 82, 88–91; intellectualized portraits of 45–6; as political 46; Sophocles' *Oedipus at Colonus* 19, 50, 64–8, 85, 102–3n68
Trojan War 9, 12, 18, 58–9

United States, the 1–2, 6

Victoria, Queen 13
Virgil 9, 14, 16, 19

Xerxes 4, 9–10, 55–7